Alec Guinness : The Films

Also by Kenneth Von Gunden

Twenty All-Time Great Science Fiction Films
(with Stuart H. Stock, 1982)

Alec Guinness: The Films

by
Kenneth Von Gunden

McFarland & Company, Inc., Publishers
Jefferson, North Carolina, and London

Library of Congress Cataloguing-in-Publication Data

Von Gunden, Kenneth.
   Alec Guinness : the films.

   Filmography: p. 275
   Bibliography: p. 335
   Includes index.
   1. Guinness, Alec, 1914–   . 2. Actors —
Great Britain — Biography. I. Title.
PN2598.G8V65   1987   791.43'028'0924 [B]   85-43596

ISBN 0-89950-205-9 (acid-free natural paper) ∞

Printed in the United States of America

McFarland & Company, Inc., Publishers
   Box 611, Jefferson, North Carolina 28640

This book is for Donna:
supporter, first reader, advisor, critic, helpmate, cheerleader,
and the one person who guided me through it all.

Acknowledgments

I would like to extend my appreciation to the following people, who helped make this book possible: Linda Brevelle; Linda Bushyeager; Bob Casto; Joseph Francavilla; Linda Friend; Steve and Nancy Gould; Bill Harding; Alex Hay; Virginia Kidd; Philip Klass; Carolyn Meredith; Karl Olson; Fred Ramsey; Harry Shadle; Kathy Shields; Stanley Weintraub.

I would also like to thank Patrick Beaver, my research associate in London.

And very special thanks to Charles Mann, curator of the Penn State Rare Books Room, who freely allowed me access to his private collection of British film magazines.

Contents

Introduction
Sir Alec Guinness:
A Biographical Sketch

Alec Guinness de Cuffe was born out of wedlock on April 2, 1914, in Marylebone, a lower-middle-class section of West London, the son of Miss Agnes Cuffe. His mother married a Scots army captain named David Stiven when Alec was five years old. Until young Alex left preparatory school, he was known as Alec Stiven, a name he rather liked despite the loathing he held for his stepfather (who, according to Guinness in *Blessings in Disguise*, "once held me upside down from a bridge, threatening to drop me in the river below; and another time he held a loaded revolver to my head").

Alec, once he was aware that he was illegitimate, began to suspect that a certain elderly gentleman friend of his mother's named Andrew Geddes was his real father. Geddes was a managing director of the Anglo-South American Bank and fifty-four years old when Alec was born. Later, digging through the circumstances of his mysterious birth, Guinness was told by in-law Michel Salaman that an Edwardian gentleman's best friend—presumably in this case a man named Guinness—would often allow his name to be given to the real father's child.

Guinness remembers little of his natural father. "He was a handsome old man, white-haired. A Scotsman," Guinness recalled in *Time* magazine. "I saw him only four or five times. I was taught to call him uncle, but I suppose I always knew he was my father." In *Blessings*, Guinness adds, "The last time I saw him was when I was eight years old, prior to going to my preparatory school in Southborne. He died when I was sixteen."

Guinness is not remotely related to the famous Guinness brewing family—a misconception that darkened Guinness' early stage career because many people assumed he was heir to great wealth and bought his way onto the stage. "Nothing could be further from the truth!" Guinness bristles. "I have no connection with the family and no inherited wealth. My father was able to put aside a small educational fund for me, but I've had to support myself ever since leaving school."

1

Sir Alec Guinness, in a publicity still taken about the time of *The Bridge on the River Kwai.*

Although Andrew Geddes was wealthy, little of that wealth went to Guinness' mother, Agnes. With her little boy in tow, she moved from boarding house to boarding house, up and down the channel coast. At the age of six, Guinness was sent packing to a middle-class English boarding school called Pembroke Lodge Preparatory School, the expenses paid for out of the educational fund his father had established for him. His school days were not happy ones; Guinness was poor at team sports and did not make friends easily. "One was a most unprepossessing child," is all Guinness says, his shyness revealed in his reluctance to use the personal pronoun "I." Feeling himself a failure, Guinness developed an intense hatred for his own face and personality. It takes no great leap of imagination to see the import of this in his desire to become an actor — to escape behind makeup and the personalities of others.

He passed the lonely hours by building model theaters and pretending to be an actor, playing all the parts in his imaginary productions. "One tried to escape from oneself in any way possible," he says. Working up his nerve, he tried for a school production and was turned down. Looking at his scrawny frame, the headmaster just shook his head sadly. "You'll never make an actor, Guinness," was his assessment.

When he was twelve, Guinness transferred to another school, Roborough. It was at this time that Guinness first seriously considered becoming an actor, joining the dramatic society. But since that society specialized in Gilbert and Sullivan, Guinness was relegated to working behind the scenes, moving scenery. When he confessed to one of the masters his secret desire to be an actor, the teacher just shook his head, repeating the words of the old headmaster: "You'll never be an actor." Guinness would not be talked out of his ambitions for a life upon the stage and finally landed the parts of the Messenger and Third Murderer in the school's production of *Macbeth*.

In this, his first known appearance upon the stage, young Guinness employed his own version of "method" acting. Timing himself perfectly, he first ran around the rugby field several times, then rushed through the side door of the school auditorium and onstage at the moment his cue was given. Out of breath, he staggered up to the startled young Macbeth and gasped out his few lines. The audience at first stared in amazement, then broke out in cheers and wild applause.

Guinness left school at the age of seventeen, hoping and planning to be an actor but without the slightest idea of how to go about it. He knew no one in show business and had absolutely no connections. The money from the educational fund his father had established was almost gone, so he had to find a job. Since he'd always been a good writer, Guinness was told by a friend of an opening in a London advertising agency — Arks Publicity in Lincolns Inn Fields. He applied for the minor post and was hired.

Starting as a junior copywriter and "visualizer," Guinness began his apprenticeship in the advertising business earning a pound a week — about five dollars at that time. Even though England was in the depths of the depression and prices were extraordinarily low, the money did not go far. But when added to the dribble that remained from his educational fund, it was a living wage.

Even on his tight budget, Guinness was able to put aside sixpence a week for weekly pilgrimages to the London stage. "I saw every show in London," he later recalled. "I saw everything [Sir John] Gielgud ever did. It was during that period that I saw the greatest single performance of my life—Ernest Milton as Hamlet." (It was about this time that he took acting lessons from Marita Hunt: See the *Great Expectations* chapter.)

Despite a strong dislike for his advertising job, Guinness stuck it out for a year and a half, writing and designing ads for radio tubes, electric light bulbs, and bottled lime juice. "I am singularly knowledgeable about lime juice," Guinness later said proudly. "Used to put together booklets for housewives, giving them all the medical facts about the stuff."

Unhappy but employed—his salary even climbed to two pounds, ten shillings a week—Guinness might have continued indefinitely at the advertising agency had he not made a major mistake. Told to get a four-inch-square printing block, he accidently sent for an electrotype measuring four feet by four feet instead of four inches by four inches. Guinness realized his error when it took two burly, sweating laborers to deliver the heavy block. Since it was 144 times the size he'd contracted for, the client declined to pay for Guinness' folly. Although his employers did not fire him, Guinness knew it was time for him to get out of the advertising business. "They were so nice about it," Guinness ruefully recalls, "that I knew I could never hold my head in their office—so I left."

Out of work and living on a pound a week, Guinness was reduced to taking his daily walks in his bare feet, saving his only pair of shoes for more important occasions.

In 1964, reminiscing with Robert Redford in Sardi's West during the New York run of *Dylan*, Guinness told the young actor, "I remember *my* early days in this strange business, back in 1933, before you were even born, I suppose. I was in acting school in London and I suspect I was even broker than you were at Malibu Beach. I lived in an attic room and existed on apples, buns, and milk. I remember that I used to walk four miles each evening from my lodgings to sit up in the gallery of the Old Vic. I ached to be an actor in those days. Now I really don't care that much for it anymore."

Hearing that the Fay Compton School of Acting offered scholarships to worthy young would-be actors, he showed up at an audition. One of the judges at the school, who requested anonymity, recalls Guinness' audition. "It was a very hot day and I was tired and irritated. I had seen a long procession of candidates of the sort Noel Coward had in mind when he wrote 'Don't Put Your Daughter on the Stage, Mrs. Worthington.' Then this boy came in and I sat up. He was nervous, yet somehow assured. He was terribly thin and angular, all ears, I remember. And not much hair even then. Although he was obviously talented I tried to discourage him — told him to stick to a steady job in business."

Guinness won an eighteen-month scholarship. Soon he and several fellow students landed walk-ons in Edward Wooll's courtroom drama *Libel!* On April 2, 1934, his twentieth birthday, Alec Guinness appeared on stage as a professional actor for the first time, earning the magnificent sum of twelve shillings a week for his efforts.

When Robert Redford asked, "What was your first play?" Guinness replied, "A dreadful little turkey called *Libel!* — I sat at a courtroom table in a junior counselor's wig and didn't have a single line."

Shortly before *Libel!*, Guinness had landed work as an extra in the film *Evensong* (1933). He resented being treated like a nobody, and the experience was so frustrating and so far from what he knew acting to be all about that he vowed he'd starve before he took another job like it.

Guinness made the rounds unsuccessfully. Auditioning at the Old Vic, he walked onstage, opened his mouth to speak, and was quickly told by the producer, "You're not an actor! Buzz off!"

Soon after his stage debut, Guinness performed in a competition at the Studio's Public Show, an annual matinee to showcase the most promising of the students. Among the judges who awarded Guinness first prize was his idol, John Gielgud. "This boy with the gaunt face and figure came on in a pantomime part," Gielgud recalled. "He did not have a line to speak, but there was never a question in our minds as to the winner." Unfortunately, the last of Guinness' education fund had dried up, and he was forced to drop out of school the next day.

Forcing himself to ask Gielgud for help in landing acting roles, Guinness was told by the great actor: "You're far too thin." Gielgud recalls the incident this way: "A bit later, he came to me for help, but he refused my money. Unusual, wasn't it? Well, Alec is an unusual person. . . ." Impressed by Guinness' spirit as well as his talent, Gielgud resolved to keep the "far too thin" Guinness in mind for parts in his productions.

Guinness was down to his last few pennies when, in August 1934, he walked into a rehearsal for Noel Langley's *Queer Cargo* and was hired to play several minor parts, once again for twelve shillings a week. "I must have been mad," Guinness remembers, "but I said, 'Isn't the Equity minimum three pounds a week?' The stage manager said, 'We don't want any of that stuff!' so I accepted. But afterward I telephoned Equity and they sent an officer 'round, so I got my three pounds."

Of his second play, Guinness said to Redford: "I went into something called *Queer Cargo*, in which I played three roles, a Chinese cook, a French pirate, and a British sailor, and got my reputation for being allegedly versatile. But *Queer Cargo* was another awful play."

Still, Guinness *was* acting; and when he saw Gielgud in the audience at another play he was attending, he resolved to "bump" into him at intermission. "I hero-worshiped him anyhow," Guinness said, "but I wanted to see if he remembered me and to tell him I had a job. Instead, he said, 'Where have you been? I've been trying to get hold of you for a week. I want you to play Osric in my *Hamlet*. Would seven pounds a week be all right?' I practically fainted clean away."

Gielgud's *Hamlet* ran for 155 performances and Guinness earned his seven pounds by doubling as the Third Player. In 1935, while Gielgud was playing the title role in a play called *Noah*, he hired Guinness to play the part of one of the animals aboard the ark, a wolf. Playing a tigress was an attractive, petite redhead named Merula Salaman. The two shy but strong-willed individualists hit it off right away but didn't see each other again for two years. In 1938, Guinness and Merula were married, and she retired from the stage.

Also in 1935, with Gielgud directing himself as Romeo, Guinness was cast in *Romeo and Juliet* as Samson and the Apothecary. At a luncheon party during *Dylan's* run on Broadway, Guinness treated his director, Peter Glenville, to an anecdote from the play: "I was watching from the wings. John went bounding into the tomb carrying a great flaming torch. Just as he said, 'Thou detestable maw, thou womb of death,' he made this grand circling gesture. Well, all the wadding flew out of the torch and started to set the stage afire. John gallantly leapt on it with both feet, quite forgetting his boots were made of velvet and soon he was performing a swift little dance in which he managed to step on both his burning feet at once. He got quite a nice round of applause from the audience. None of us backstage was any help at all; you see, we were all quite helpless with laughter. It was glorious!"

Guinness stayed with Gielgud's company until 1936, learning his craft from one of the greatest actors of the English stage. But after spending one year at the Old Vic, he returned to Gielgud and the Queen's Theater. Then, in 1938, he rejoined the Old Vic to tour Europe.

In 1938, Alec Guinness, under the direction of Tyrone Guthrie, attempted his first *Hamlet*. His low-key performance in a modern-dress version of the play was well received in some quarters, but it lacked power and conviction. James Agate noted that Guinness' Hamlet failed "because it deliberately refuses to succeed." Guinness was rejecting the grand gestures, the rhetorical flourishes of "classic" Shakespearean acting, but with his own soon-to-be-honed powers of underplaying not yet fully developed and in in place, he had nothing to replace what he discarded. His failure weighed heavily on him, and he essentially gave up after opening night. Sir John Gielgud put it into perspective when he said, "Of course no one is ever satisfied with his own Hamlet, and Alec will worry. He worries dreadfully! Success has been a great burden to him. I wish he could be as sure as I am that, whatever he does, he'll do it well."

By the time of the Second World War, Guinness had played thirty-four parts in twenty-three plays by Shakespeare, Sheridan, Pinero, Chekhov,

Shaw, and others, and was beginning to attract a following among discerning theatergoers. As director Tyrone Guthrie noted some years later, "It was obvious that he was going to be tremendously talented; it was not so obvious that he was going to be popular."

But duty beckoned, and Guinness joined the Royal Navy as an ordinary seaman, serving on a coastal tanker. "It was very dull," Guinness remembers. "I suppose I had a lot of miseries, but looking back I don't remember them. It now seems to me to have been a quiet, pleasant time, with some very fine friendships." It was about this time that he and his wife had their only child, a son they named Matthew.

After being chosen for officer's training, Guinness was sent to Boston to take command of a brand new ship, a landing craft. When he got there, he discovered that his first command was only half finished. The Royal Navy then sent him to New Jersey on an unusual assignment: "I was in charge of transforming the Berkeley-Carteret Hotel, in Asbury Park, into barracks for British personnel — hardly an outstanding contribution to the war effort," Guinness says.

Fortunately for Guinness, a play by Terence Rattigan about the R.A.F. called *Flare Path*, which was a huge success in England, was looking for an English actor to play the part of Flight Lieutenant Graham. Realizing the pro–British production could only help the English war effort, the Admiralty readily gave the young officer permission to appear in *Flare Path*.

Flare Path opened at the Henry Miller Theater the day before Christmas Eve, 1942. Twentieth Century–Fox then deemed Guinness worthy of a Hollywood screen test; he declined the offer. The play ran only a few weeks, and Guinness was soon back at sea. As Guinness was to put it later, ". . . I knocked about the Mediterranean for quite a spell."

Guinness was not a born sailor. Once, while on convoy duty, he couldn't keep his ship in its proper position, threatening not only his own craft but also those around him. After several days of mediocre maneuvering, Guinness received a puzzling message from the flagship: "Hebrews 13:8." Looking it up in his ship's Bible, he found it said, "Jesus Christ, the same yesterday, and today, and forever."

Guinness filled the empty hours on board ship by writing. One of his letters, entitled "I Took My Landing Craft to the Sicily Beaches," was edited for publication in the *Daily Telegraph* of August 20, 1943. Guinness had made history of a sort when, through a typical military mix-up in orders, his was the first landing craft to reach shore in Sicily. "We came in so hard that it took three weeks to refloat us," he recalled. "There were a few Italians lurking about in pill boxes, brandishing rifles. But they looked the other way and we landed quite unopposed." Thus, Guinness was the first Allied fighting man to step ashore on the Sicily beachhead. When the admiral in charge finally arrived on the scene, Guinness blithely told him such an ill-timed entrance would be frowned upon in the theater.

After that, Guinness and his crew transported supplies to Yugoslav partisans. On one such mission, his supply ship was destroyed when a powerful gale blew it onto the rocks of Termoli. He escaped censure because the storm was so violent that Guinness' ship was far from the only one to suffer such an ignoble fate.

After the war, Guinness soon regained his momentum. During the 1946–47 season, he played a well-received Fool to Laurence Olivier's King Lear. *Time & Tide* found his very original interpretation near "perfection." And the *Daily Telegraph* trumpeted his performance as De Guiche in Tyrone Guthrie's *Cyrano de Bergerac* as "a remarkable feat."

It was about this time that he began to reconsider his vow to eschew films. As he was later to say, "On the stage I never seemed to have a chance to wear trousers." (For more about his capitulation, see the *Great Expectations* chapter.)

In 1953, his film career well in hand, Guinness traveled to Canada to inaugurate Stratford, Ontario's Festival Theater, appearing as the King of France in *All's Well That Ends Well* and Richard in *Richard III.*

Awarded the CBE [Commander of the Order of the British Empire] in 1955, Guinness was knighted in 1959 — becoming Sir Alec Guinness.

Before the war, Guinness briefly entertained the idea of becoming a Buddhist, reading all he could on the subject. However, after some consideration, he decided Buddhism was not what he was looking for and continued to cast about for a spiritual center for his life.

After meeting Pope Pius XII in Italy in 1945, Guinness wrote to a friend, "I was deeply impressed by the Pope's personality. I felt for the first time I had seen a saint." Beginning in 1955, Guinness was instructed in the rituals and obligations of the Roman Catholic Church. Before he himself was accepted into the church, his son Matthew, then fifteen, was taken in.

Guinness' wife Merula did not immediately join her husband and son in this most private and agonizing of decisions. But when Guinness was in the jungles of Ceylon, filming *The Bridge on the River Kwai*, he received a letter from her telling him that she, too, had converted to Roman Catholicism.

For Guinness, an unforgettable incident had helped light his way to his new faith. Filming *Father Brown*, and still in his priest's garb, he was mistaken for a real priest by a young French boy: "Suddenly I felt my hand taken by a seven-year-old boy, who walked with me all the way back to the village swinging my hand and chattering. I remained absolutely silent, and eventually he squeezed my hand and disappeared, and I thought it was simply marvelous that a child in . . . a dark lane will run up to a man because he's dressed as a priest. And it totally changed my attitude. . . . I don't base my religion on that. But . . . I've always looked back on it as a magic moment. . . ."

Sir Alex Guinness will continue to burrow beneath the placid surfaces of the characters he plays to reveal the man inside as long as good parts come his way. But with advancing age, he will surely limit the number and intensity of his appearances upon the stage and screen.

"I get exhausted whatever I do," Guinness admitted on the set of *Return of the Jedi*. "I'm not as passionate about it any more. A long stage run is the most exhausting of all. The shorter the contract the better these days. As T.S. Eliot once said about writing, 'Every sentence is a struggle. You know you're not going to get it quite right, but you have to go ahead and try.' That applies just as much to acting." He later said, "Every day provides some little scene — even if it is only a minute or so — in which you have the opportunity for a little moment of genuinely creative work. That helps to make it all worthwhile."

In 1979, the Academy of Motion Picture Arts and Sciences awarded Sir Alec Guinness an honorary Oscar "For advancing the art of screen acting through a host of memorable and distinguished performances."

Dick Cavett's anagram, made from rearranging the letters in Alec Guinness' name, is marvelously appropriate: "Genuine Class."

From the pleasant-faced Herbert Pocket in Lean's *Great Expectations* to the Brahman Professor Godbole in Lean's *A Passage to India*, from Sidney Stratton in *The Man in the White Suit* to Ben (Obi-Wan) Kenobi in the *Star Wars* trilogy, from genocidal mass murderer to gentle pope, Alec Guinness has defined screen acting. We will not soon see his like again. Giants pass through but once... but, if we're lucky, once is enough.

I. Guinness Ascending: The First Golden Age

"You may permit yourself great expectations."
— Mr. Jaggers to Pip in *Great Expectations*, by Charles Dickens

"Photography is truth. And cinema is truth twenty-four times a second."
—Jean-Luc Godard

Great Expectations (1946)
to
Tunes of Glory (1960)

1. *Great Expectations* (1946)

"The casting was perfect, and there were some memorable
performances, particularly from an actor who was
making his first appearance on the screen —
Alec Guinness, whose Herbert Pocket was a delight...."
— John Mills, in his autobiography

In the early 1930s, while he worked in advertising as a reluctant trainee, Alec Guinness resolved to break into acting and the theater. An old headmaster and several others (see the biographical sketch of Guinness) had already told the young man he had no aptitude for acting, but he saw in the rehearsed public appearances of people upon the stage a way to overcome his inherent shyness. Seated in the gallery at the Old Vic, where he often went to escape the dull routines of his life, Guinness mustered up enough courage to contact John Gielgud to ask his help in getting into the theater not as a paying customer but as an actor.

Gielgud was apparently so impressed by his determination to become an actor that he met with Guinness, pressed some money into his hand, and recommended him as a student to actress-teacher Marita Hunt.

Miss Hunt was dressing when Guinness arrived and she asked him to make some cocktails while she finished. Guinness had never mixed a cocktail before in his life, but he gamely went ahead, taking a little from every bottle on the table. Miss Hunt's reaction is lost to posterity, but wrongly assuming he was a member of the Guinness brewing family (here, perhaps, is one instance in which that misconception *did* help him), she accepted him as a student.

Miss Hunt could see little promise in this drab young man, and after a dozen lessons, dismissed him, saying as others had before her, "You'll never make an actor, Mr. Guinness."

In December 1939, Guinness' own adaptation of Charles Dickens' *Great Expectations* opened in Rudolf Steiner Hall, just off London's West End. Guinness took the part of Herbert Pocket, Pip's fun-loving and warm-hearted roommate. Playing Miss Havisham was Marita Hunt — the same Marita Hunt who'd told Guinness he was wasting his time trying to become an actor. If doing well is the best revenge, then Guinness clearly scored a personal

13

triumph—one that would be repeated when both Hunt and Guinness reprised their roles for the film version.

David Lean was preparing to adapt Dickens' novel to the screen for his Cineguild producing company when he recalled Guinness' highly acclaimed performance as Herbert Pocket. Knowing that Guinness was wary of film acting, Lean convinced him that the small but important role of Herbert Pocket would be an appropriate initiation into movie acting.

As Guinness said in an interview in *Films and Filming*, "I had no interest in films at all when I was a young actor. The theatre was my love and I didn't care whether I was asked to do films or not. The only time I'd done anything in a film studio was a *crowd artist* [emphasis added—Guinness was an *extra* in *Evensong*, 1933] one day when we were treated like idiots. It was such misery that I swore I'd never have anything to do with fiilms. It was David Lean who kind of persuaded me."

Certainly, *Great Expectations* and *Oliver Twist* demonstrated Guinness' versatility and talent. Never was he to be as buoyant and effervescent on screen as he was as Herbert Pocket in the former, nor as comically nasty and submerged beneath makeup and voice as Fagin in the latter. These two wildly diverse performances in his first two films established Alec Guinness as a cinema artist of the first rank. Films would do for Guinness what the English stage could not: They would make him rich and famous.

Movies on TV, edited by Steven H. Scheur, called *Great Expectations* (hereafter just *Expectations*) "a film great," and noted that it was "faithfully transcribed, painstakingly produced, superlatively directed, acted, photographed."

British critic Richard Winnington called *Expectations* "the first big British film to have been made, a film that sweeps our cloistered virtues out into the open."

In 1969, one critic called the film, "the best Dickens adaptation, and arguably David Lean's best film."

American film critic and screenplay writer James Agee wrote that *Expectations* is "almost never less than graceful, tasteful, and intelligent, and some of it better than that."

Leslie Halliwell also gives *Expectations* his highest rating, calling the film "a superbly pictorial rendering of a much-loved novel, with all the famous characters in safe hands and masterly judgment in every department."

After an opening narration by the adult Pip, we follow him as a boy into a graveyard as he visits the grave of his mother. Pip is confronted by an escaped convict named Magwitch (Findley Currie), who asks for the boy's help. Pip returns to the home of his sister and her blacksmith husband, Joe Gargery (Bernard Miles). Later, Pip sneaks out to the graveyard with a stolen file and some food. Magwitch takes the food, but he's aroused when he learns his enemy, a scar-faced escapee, is nearby.

Before his sister discovers the thefts, Pip is saved by the appearance of police who are pursuing the escaped convicts. After the two convicts are recaptured, a fearful Pip shakes his head at Magwitch to indicate he didn't turn him in. In return, Magwitch "confesses" to taking the file and food himself.

A year passes, and Pip learns he is to be allowed to play at Satis House, the home of a mysterious recluse, Miss Havisham (Marita Hunt). There he meets the beautiful but haughty Estella (Jean Simmons), Miss Havisham's adopted daughter. Miss Havisham sits all day in a boarded-up room, wearing a soiled white wedding dress. She tells Estella in front of Pip her desire that the girl "break his heart."

After seeing Miss Havisham's moldering wedding cake, Pip meets in the garden a "pale young gentleman," who challenges him to a fistfight. Pip easily eludes the boy's clumsy punches and knocks him down twice. Seeing his "victory," Estella permits Pip to kiss her. Pip continues his visits to Miss Havisham's, and the more Estella insults and demeans him, the more he loves her.

At the age of fourteen, Pip begins his blacksmith apprenticeship with Joe Gargery. At twenty, Pip is still an apprentice, but he is a young man (and now played by John Mills). Mr. Jaggers (Francis L. Sullivan), a London lawyer, arrives to inform Pip that he may permit himself "great expectations." On the condition that he forever retain the name Pip, he is to be heir to property and will receive an education in manners and in life. Jaggers will act as Pip's guardian. Pip strongly suspects his benefactor to be Miss Havisham.

In London, Pip goes to Jaggers' office and learns he will share rooms with Mr. Herbert Pocket. Young Mr. Pocket, his blond hair falling over his forehead, turns out to be the pale young gentleman Pip fought in Miss Havisham's garden. Pocket tells Pip that Miss Havisham raised Estella to wreak havoc on the male population, presumably in retaliation for the jilting she received on her wedding day.

Pip learns to appreciate the good life all too well. The money goes fast, and Pip finds his debts piling up. Fortunately, when he turns twenty-one, his allowance is increased.

When his old friend and surrogate father Joe Gargery comes to visit him, Pip is embarrassed by this well-meaning hayseed: "In trying to become a gentleman, I had succeeded in becoming a snob." Realizing that Pip has grown apart from him, Joe tells him that Miss Havisham has sent for him and then leaves.

At Satis House once again, Pip learns that Miss Havisham has called him back to meet the now-grown-up Estella (Valerie Hobson), a heartless, empty woman. Presented to London society, Estella soon wins the heart of Bentley Drummle, a dashing cad.

Wearing an eyepatch, Magwitch pays a late-night visit to Pip's rooms. Pip only gradually realizes who he is—but still has no idea why Magwitch has come to see him. Now a sheepfarmer in Australia, Magwitch tells Pip that his good fortune has enabled him to endow someone with great expectations. Pip is utterly astonished to learn that Magwitch is his benefactor.

Later, Pip confronts Jaggers, who denies leading him on about the source of his good fortune. Jaggers also points out that Magwitch could be hanged for returning to England. Pip returns to Satis House, angry at Miss Havisham for allowing him to believe her his benefactor. While there, Pip tells Estella he loves her; she coldly informs him she is to marry Drummle and leaves. A log from the fireplace catches Miss Havisham's dress on fire. Pip rushes to put it out — burning his hands — but it is too late; Miss Havisham is dead.

In London, Jaggers' clerk, Wemmick, warns Pip not to return home because an old enemy of Magwitch's knows he's back in England and is having Pip watched. Planning a river escape for Magwitch, Pip and Herbert work out a scheme to transfer the old convict to a packet boat. The police arrive in a boat with a scar-faced convict — Compeyson, Magwitch's old enemy. Magwitch and his adversary struggle and the two fall into the water. Compeyson is struck and killed by the approaching paddle boat.

With Magwitch condemned to hang, the state, rather than Pip, will inherit his property. A blood heir, however, can still inherit the money and land. From Jaggers, Pip learns that Estella is really Magwitch's daughter — born to a murderess working for Jaggers. After telling a dying Magwitch that his daughter is alive and beautiful and that he loves her, Pip watches the old man die in peace.

Falling ill, Pip is nursed back to health by Joe Gargery and Joe's new wife. Pip returns to the ruins of Satis House to find Estella sitting in Miss Havisham's old chair. Rejected by Drummle once he learned of her heritage, Estella plans to become another Miss Havisham. Pip defies Miss Havisham's memory and tears down the room's curtains, letting in the sun. Estella finally believes she has a future... with Pip.

It is somehow appropriate that David Lean should have been Alec Guinness' first director. Guinness did five more films with Lean (counting the recent *A Passage to India*), and it was his performance in Lean's *Bridge on the River Kwai* that won Guinness the Academy Award for best actor in 1958. Theirs has been a tempetuous relationship, an off-again, on-again partnership that has seen the two men arise from relative obscurity to worldwide fame.

David Lean was born on March 25, 1908, at Croydon, England. In 1927, the nineteen-year-old Lean began working for Gaumont studios as a tea boy. Within a year of this humble beginning, he was clapper-boy and a messenger for various Gaumont productions. Working his way up through the studio ranks, Lean became a cutting room assistant, then an assistant cameraman, and finally an assistant director.

By 1930, Lean was chief editor for Gaumont-British News. In 1931, the fast-moving Lean became an editor for British Movietonews and later served in the same capacity for Paramount-British News.

In 1935, Lean began editing major British productions such as *Escape Me Never* and went on to edit, among others, *Pygmalion* (1938), *Major Barbara* (1941), and *49th Parallel* (1941).

In 1942, Lean, by then known as an outstanding film technician, was chosen by Noel Coward to help the neophyte director with his first film, *In Which We Serve*. Not only did Coward find his codirector's work satisfactory, but also he was so pleased that he chose Lean to direct three more films he'd written: *This Happy Breed* (1944), *Blithe Spirit* (1945), and *Brief Encounter* (1945).

At the same time he was working with Coward, Lean, along with Ronald Neame (*Expectations'* producer) and Anthony Havelock-Allan, founded Cineguild, which produced many of the best British features of the postwar years.

Finally, it was the Cineguild production of *Expectations*, released in 1946, which propelled Lean into the front ranks of British directors and made him a force to be reckoned with in the British film industry.

David Lean was not the first filmmaker to adapt Dickens' sprawling and beloved novel for the screen. There were at least three other versions. A 1916 adaptation starred Jack Pickford and Louise Huff. Hollywood's 1934 version was directed by Walter Armitage and starred Jane Wyatt, Phillips Holmes, Henry Hull, and Francis L. Sullivan (playing Jaggers, a role he would reprise for Lean). A 1974 musical version was planned, but the music was removed. Directed by Joseph Hardy, this filming starred Michael York, Sarah Miles, James Mason, Margaret Leighton, Robert Morley, and Anthony Quayle. This version aired on American TV.

David Lean's *Expectations*, however, is one of the truest filmings of any novel ever accomplished. It retains the essence of Dickens while, of necessity, trimming his plot and colorful characters.

Lean wrote the script with Neame and Havelock-Allan and with actress Kay Walsh (then married to Havelock-Allan and later to Lean himself) and Cecil McGivern. The book's skeleton is at the core of the script, but most of the minor and secondary characters have been removed.

The film veers most sharply away from Dickens' novel at the end, when Pip goes to Satis House one last time. Dickens had originally written an unhappy ending, which has Pip, his inheritance lost to the Crown after Magwitch's death, sailing off to New South Wales, never to see Estella again. Fortunately, Dickens' friend and fellow novelist, Edward Bulwer-Lytton (a splendidly bad writer; it was he who penned the immortal lines, "It was a dark and stormy night. . . .") convinced him to write a final scene which has Pip visiting the ruins of Satis House and finding the now-widowed Estella. It is implied, though not made clear, that Pip and Estella were soon to marry after this bittersweet meeting.

The film's ending has Pip defying Miss Havisham's anti-life philosophy and waking Estella from her living nightmare. Aware that she can choose life over death, Estella goes off with Pip; presumably, they live happily ever after. Lean and company's ending might be considered an improvement over both of Dickens' endings in that it leaves the viewer satisfied and enriched.

Great Britain is a terribly class-conscious country, of course, and both novel and film reflect this obsession with class and status. In A Critical History of British Cinema, Roy Armes discusses Joe Gargery's "common man" and "typical Englishman" social standing with the "snobbish contempts and aspirations" of Miss Havisham and Estella, typical of the upper-middle classes.

Armes says that Magwitch is the " 'father' of both young people's fortunes" and thus, although "Pip thinks that all [that] is best in his life comes from the upper-middle classes...it [in fact] comes from the proletarian underworld."

David Lean is a great handler of actors. He seems able to extract fine performances from everyone he works with. John Mills, as the adult Pip, is no exception—although his performance in Expectations veers off in several directions at times.

In his autobiography, John Mills writes, "I had always felt that Charles Dickens' novel Great Expectations would, if properly handed, make a magnificent film. I was therefore more than delighted when David Lean rang me with the news that he had chosen it for his next picture; and, he added, he couldn't see any other actor playing Pip (incidently, neither could I!)." (For more on John Mills, see the chapter on Tunes of Glory and the notes on that film in the Appendix.)

Guinness' performance in his first movie role is a breath of fresh air—rarely if ever again would he be so boyish and charming, so full of open-faced innocence and guileless optimism. From the moment he appears on screen, bringing home fresh fruit from the market as a greeting for his new roommate Pip, he wins over the audience. He undertakes Pip's education in the social graces with a smiling offhandedness. When Pip attempts to use his knife like a fork, Guinness as Pocket remarks, "Let me introduce the topic by pointing out that in London it's not the custom to put the knife in the mouth—for fear of accidents..." and adding "It's not usually considered necessary to fill the mouth to its utmost capacity."

Guinness is appealing in his top hat and long scarf, and his sense of timing adds immeasurably to the comic scene in which an ill-at-ease Joe Gargery fumbles his top hat into Pip and Herbert's pot of tea. Later, when Magwitch swears him to secrecy, Guinness' Herbert is appropriately wide-eyed and speechless.

Enough. One cannot make Guinness' small part into the lynchpin of the film; nevertheless, it is a fine performance and an impressive film debut.

In an article entitled "Alec's Way," Time magazine said, "Alec's first screen role...decided him that here was the life. He promptly hired an agent to rustle him up some more movie jobs, preferably 'a Hollywood picture for the good it does one—not financial especially, but for one's reputation.' His agent's impression: 'There's no bloody nonsense about Alec.' "

These are two interesting quotes, but I'm not sure I believe either of them, knowing what I do about Alec Guinness' approach to his acting and to his career. His next picture, certainly, was no Hollywood-produced piece of fluff. Guinness' next role was Fagin in David Lean's second Dickens adaptation, *Oliver Twist*. And it was two years in coming — five years, actually, if you count its American release after much controversy over Guinness' portrayal of one of the most famous Jews in literature and film.

One thing is certain: After avoiding films for so long, Guinness had taken the plunge and found he liked the experience.

The film career of one of the world's great actors had begun.

2. *Oliver Twist* (1948)

> "Oliver cried lustily. If he could have known that he was an
> orphan, left to the tender mercies of the church-wardens
> and overseers, perhaps he would have cried the louder."
> — *Oliver Twist* by Charles Dickens

Oliver Twist was released in England in June, 1948. Its United States release, however, was delayed more than three years, until July, 1951. The reason for the hold in the film's American release was simple: both *Oliver Twist* and Guinness' portrayal of Fagin were seen as being anti-Semitic. Alec Guinness' second film would be the most controversial of his long career.

Oliver Twist is a film remarkably faithful to its source, the 1837 novel by Charles Dickens. It is the story of an orphan who suffers a life under harsh and inhumane conditions. Raised in the workhouse, Oliver is later sold as a servant to an undertaker for daring to ask for more of the watery gruel that is his main sustenance. In the undertaker's house, Oliver (John Howard Davies) defends his dead mother's honor and is whipped for it.* He then escapes from the undertaker's and makes his way to the teeming city of London — a cesspool of poverty, crime, and degradation for those born without money or hope. Immediately spotted by the "Artful Dodger" (Anthony Newley), a proficient young criminal, Oliver is taken in by the Dodger's mentor — Fagin (Guinness), a wizened old man who oversees a gang of young thieves and cutpurses.

Oliver laughs at Fagin's seemingly comic lessons in thievery, but is sobered by the old man's threats after accidentally seeing where Fagin keeps his "treasures." Later, Oliver, innocently watching as Dodger lifts a gentleman's purse, is mistakenly identified as the thief.

Oliver's frenzied dash through the crowded streets is cut short by a blow from a man's fist to his chin. After Oliver regains consciousness, the gentleman whose wallet was taken, Mr. Brownlow, identifies Oliver and the boy is taken to court.

With Nancy (Kay Walsh), an adult graduate of Fagin's gang, in attendance, Oliver's trial begins. Woozy from the blow he received and reeling

---

*This scene, with Oliver spread-eagled over a barrel and whipped, is duplicated almost exactly in Lean's later filming of *Lawrence of Arabia*, when Lawrence is tortured by the Turks.

from an infection, Oliver passes out. Fortunately, an eyewitness testifies it was another boy and not Oliver who stole the wallet. Brownlow (Henry Stevenson), his sympathies aroused, carries the unconscious Oliver to his carriage and takes him home to recuperate.

For the first time in his young life Oliver knows love. The nanny, Mrs. Bedwin, and Mr. Brownlow nurse Oliver back to health. He enjoys his first taste of decent food. A friend of Brownlow's chides the old gentleman about the boy's natural inclination toward crime; in response, Brownlow sends Oliver out to return several books and gives him a five-pound note to pay his bill. His friend insists that it's the last they'll see of the boy.

Spotted by Fagin's gang, Oliver is kidnapped by Bill Sikes and Nancy. Sikes (Robert Newton) and Nancy perceive Oliver differently; Sikes sees a small boy who can climb in windows and unlock doors for him; Nancy sees an innocent, an unspoiled soul much as she was before Fagin's lessons turned her hard.

Nancy, stricken with guilt over what she's done, arranges to hand Oliver over to Brownlow—he's discovered he's the boy's grandfather—but she'll not "peach" on her friends. Dodger, given the task of tailing Nancy, reports what she said to Fagin, who then tells Bill. Furious, Sikes beats Nancy to death.

Nancy's body is discovered and both Sikes and Fagin are sought by the police. Led to Fagin's hideout by Sikes' dog, the police capture Fagin. Sikes, however, escapes to the roof, with Oliver as hostage. After Sikes slips a rope around his body, the police fire a single shot. Sikes is hit and falls from the roof only to be brought up short by the rope—now around his neck. Oliver is restored to Mr. Brownlow's house and to Mrs. Bedwin's loving care.

In *Films in Review*, Henry Hart wrote that "this splendid film...gives us a glimpse of some of the social and economic evils of nineteenth century England. In short, it does for movie-goers what Dickens' writing did for several generations of book readers."

British film critic Richard Winnington called the film "a thoroughly expert piece of movie entertainment."

Roy Armes wrote that Lean "uses his technical command to make us identify with the young...Oliver...."

Lean's film starkly sets forth the evils of nineteenth-century England as well as presenting many of the film's characters as devoid of redeeming, or even human, traits. Many of these characters, notably the chief warden of the boys' workhouse, are Christian, one of them is Jewish—Fagin. But Fagin's Jewishness is *never mentioned* in the film. Yet when *Oliver Twist* was released in Britain in 1948, Zionists objected that Fagin was shown in the same way that Jews were vilified by Julius Streicher in *Der Stermer*, a slanderous Nazi film.

When Eagle-Lion Classics, Inc., the American distributor of *Oliver Twist*, realized a covert boycott against the film was likely, it proposed to the

Anti-Defamation League that together they defray the costs of a test to determine if *Oliver Twist* did indeed incite anti–Semitism.

The league finally said no to Eagle-Lion's test, suggesting instead that the offer be made to the National Community Relations Advisory Council, representing twenty-six Jewish agencies. The NCRAC also refused Eagle-Lion's proposed test.

In the fall of 1950, Eagle-Lion decided to try to get bookings for *Oliver Twist* and asked the Production Code Administration (PCA) of the Motion Picture Association of America for its seal. As required, the J. Arthur Rank Organization had submitted the script to the PCA. Joseph I. Breen, the code administrator, had passed the script, but asked for eight small changes — none involving Fagin's character.

In his own handwriting, however, Breen had added, "We assume, of course, that you will bear in mind the advisibility of omitting from the portrayal of Fagin any elements or inference that would be offensive to any specific racial group or religion. Otherwise, of course, your picture might meet with very definite audience resistance in this country."

The PCA finally refused to grant a seal to *Oliver Twist*, citing a clause in the code prohibiting films that "unfairly represent" a race or nationality. The failure of the film to get the PCA seal was given as the reason a Texas theater circuit cancelled its bookings. However, Eagle-Lion discovered that a Jewish circuit owner in New York City had telephoned the Texas exhibitor and persuaded him to drop the film.

Bowing to the pressure, Eagle-Lion deleted several shots involving Fagin and was finally issued a seal by the PCA. But the damage had been done: as Murray Schumach noted in his study of censorship, *The Face on the Cutting Room Floor*, "Jewish pressure was probably the main reason that the picture...was never shown widely in this country."

Why did Guinness' portrayal of Fagin spark such controversy? Guinness' performance is certainly a bravura one, brimming with touches rarely seen in the playing of such a comic villain. When Henry Hart's review said Fagin was "curiously and mincingly played by Alec Guinness," it was clear he didn't know what to make of Guinness' interpretation. Lean's own production notes for *Oliver Twist* make clear that he wanted Fagin to be seen by Oliver "as an amusing old gentleman; gradually this guise falls away and we see him in all his villainy."

It is difficult to fully assess Guinness' performance today since so much of it is missing from the film, lost to suppression and "good taste." Among the scenes which fell victim to the censor's scissors is the one in which he threatens Oliver when the boy accidentally sees him gloating over his store of loot. Other "comic" sequences involving Fagin were also cut.

Certainly one can argue that Guinness' Fagin is grim but not entirely unlikeable. Moira Walsh's review in *America* notes that "the movie projects Fagin simply as an individual — sinister and grotesque perhaps, but understandable and even somewhat sympathetic within the framework of the social abuses which Dickens was exposing."

The large, beaked nose Guinness wore as Fagin was probably the single most important reason Jews felt the character was a caricature. Guinness' makeup and costumes were entirely based on classic Cruikshank engravings, which were themselves based on Dickens' own description of Fagin: "A very old shrivelled Jew, whose villainous-looking and repulsive face was obscured by a quantity of red hair. He was dressed in a greasy flannel gown, with his throat bare."

Guinness is not noted for being a "physical" actor. And yet, as Fagin, Guinness' gestures and movements are fluid, graceful, and athletic—he throws himself about the sets. Fagin's pickpocketing demonstration for young Oliver's benefit is also quite physical: Guinness prances, hops, and spins with an easy grace he's rarely exhibited elsewhere.*

Ironically, Guiness' voice, today so well known and recognizable, is well disguised in *Oliver Twist*, when he was hardly known at all. Guinness gives Fagin's voice a raspy, lispy quality. While some viewers were puzzled by Guinness' voice, others knew he was adhering to how an English Jew of the time might have spoken.

Guinness put it all together: His Fagin is a marvelous blend of makeup and voice, gesture and costuming, direction and acting.

Finally, I don't think it's reaching for a point to say that Guinness' Fagin sees that his boys are sheltered and fed well. The workhouse, its walls bearing carvings proclaiming emptily that "God is Love," is filled with half-starved orphans, "voracious and wild with hunger" in Dickens' words, whose deaths would induce no pity in the wardens. Fagin serves a purpose.

Lean's 1948 version was not the first filming of Dickens' classic novel. Silent versions were filmed in 1909 and 1910, by Pathé and Vitagraph respectively. Nat C. Goodwin starred as Fagin in a 1912 version, and in 1916 Tully Marshall played Fagin to Marie Doro's Oliver. Lon Chaney and Jackie Coogan were Fagin and Oliver in a 1922 film, and in 1933 the roles were played by Irving Pichel and Dickie Moore. Sir Carol Reed's 1968 musical version starred Ron Moody and Mark Lester and won six Oscars. But Lean's melodramatic version, expertly photographed by Guy Green and designed by John Bryan, is considered the definitive *Oliver Twist*.

The similarities of the musical version, *Oliver!*, to *Oliver Twist* are enormous and striking. Carol Reed, a longtime friend of Lean, apparently decided that Lean and coscripter Stanley Haynes had done such a good job of compressing and adapting Dickens' novel that he and his writer, Vernon Harris, duplicated the earlier screenplay's dialogue virtually word for word. Reed's version also closely followed original production designer John Bryan's sets and narrow, twisted London streets to recreate the period atmosphere.

---

*Guinness *did* learn to mambo quite well for his role in *The Captain's Paradise*.

Ron Moody's whirling-dervish characterization of Fagin in *Oliver!* owes much to Guinness' inspired physical and vocal portrayal. However, Moody's Fagin, minus the enormous hooked nose Guinness was forced to wear, is more lovable and less a villain. And, while Guinness' Fagin is collared by the police at the end of *Oliver Twist*, Moody's soft-hearted villain literally dances off into the sunrise. What is striking, if one recalls the furor the 1948 film caused, is that Moody's Fagin aroused no charges of anti–Semitism — even though those scenes cut in the earlier version are intact in *Oliver!* Perhaps the lack of furor can be attributed to the softening of Fagin's character.

Leslie Halliwell, in *The Filmgoer's Companion*, called Robert Newton (1905–1956), who played the role of Bill Sikes in Lean's production, a "British star character actor with a rolling eye and a voice to match; a ham, but a succulent one."

Newton's Sikes, unlike his later comic villain characterizations, is totally evil, totally unsympathetic. After he has cruelly beaten Nancy to death, Sikes inspires a quivering terror even in his battle-scarred and mangy dog. His death at the end of a rope is a catharsis for the audience; if only all the evils of the Dickens novel could be so easily vanquished. (For Newton's other films, see notes on *Oliver Twist* in the Appendix.)

Kay Walsh, born in 1914, and the wife of David Lean when she made *Oliver Twist*, played the ill-fated Nancy. Her films include four others with Guinness: *Last Holiday* (1950), *The Horse's Mouth* (1958), *Tunes of Glory* (1960), and *Scrooge* (1970). She also appeared in husband Lean's *In Which We Serve* (1942) and *This Happy Breed* (1944).

John Howard Davies, the boy who played Oliver, was born in 1939. Looking for a nine-year-old boy who was healthy, yet thin and wan-looking enough to pass for an emaciated and underfed orphan, director Lean was having no luck in his search. Then, almost convinced he'd never find the right child, Lean went to a dinner party at the Davies' house. When their son came down to say goodnight, Lean realized he'd found his Oliver.

Young Davies' father and mother had both come from theatrical families, so they quickly agreed to let him play the part. As it turned out, the boy only spent an hour a day on the set once he'd learned his part. Davies went on to make *The Rocking Horse Winner* (1949), *Tom Brown's Schooldays* (1951, featuring Robert Newton as Dr. Arnold), and others. In later life he became a television director for the BBC.

While some saw anti-Semitism in Alec Guinness' playing of Fagin, others saw brilliance. Moviegoers weren't quite sure what the man hidden under the makeup and wig looked like, but they *were* sure of one thing: he was an actor to be reckoned with.

3. *Kind Hearts and Coronets* (1949)

"Kind hearts are more than coronets
And simple faith than Norman blood."
— Tennyson

Nineteen hundred forty-nine marks the beginning of Alec Guinness' golden decade — the years between 1949 and 1959 — the period in which the still-young actor made his most important films and gave his best performances. The fifties were the high-water mark of Guinness' fame with the moviegoing public and his popularity with movie studios and theater owners. It was not until *Star Wars* in 1977, followed by his first playing of George Smiley in the long-form television miniseries, *Tinker, Tailor* that Sir Alec was to regain the luster and renown that came his way in those golden years.

Kind Hearts and Coronets was Alec Guinness' first of six films for the legendary Ealing Studios. British film, perhaps at its peak of popularity and influence between the years 1940 and 1960, was all but synonymous with Ealing Studios. For two decades, the Ealing films sought to show what was best and indigenous in British life and society to a receptive outside world. And for much of the world, British comedy meant Ealing comedy — a curious blend of manners, morals, class distinctions, and boundless good cheer and optimism in the face of any adversity.

If comedy was synonymous with Ealing Studios, Ealing was synonymous with Michael Balcon. Balcon became head of production at Ealing in 1938. Balcon immediately set to work to realize his dream: "the building up of a native industry with its roots firmly planted in the soil of this country...making British film production...a significant part of our national life." Toward achieving this goal, Balcon ran Ealing, as Harry Watt recalled, as "a small, compact, self-contained unit run on paternalistic communal lines.... Under him there were half a dozen directors and associate producers, who formed interchangeable teams to make specific pictures, and who, once they got the go-ahead, worked pretty much on their own...." Hence, for fifteen years, nearly all of Balcon's films were written by a handful of men like T.E.B. Clarke and John Dighton and directed by men who'd graduated from editing to directing under his stewardship.

And yet *Kind Hearts*, perhaps the most British of British films, made for

Louis Mazzini (Dennis Price, *right*) looks on as the doctor tends to Lord Ascoyne D'Ascoyne (Alec Guinness).

the most British of British studios, was essentially the creation of one man — writer/director Robert Hamer.

Hamer, who was born in 1911 and died in 1963, brought his own style of filmmaking to his work for Balcon and Ealing. His films, much more than other Ealing productions, pay close attention to small details of atmosphere and locale and reach levels of sophistication few rival directors can match — at least not so effortlessly. His films abound with nuances of wit and social maneuvering (*Noblesse Oblige*, rather aptly, was *Kind Hearts'* title in France).

After receiving a classic public school education (note that the English "public" school is the equivalent of the American "private" school), Hamer studied economics at Cambridge in preparation for a career in the Treasury before taking a job as a clapper-boy at the Gaumont-British studios in 1934. Hamer joined London Films as a cutting-room assistant and worked closely with Erich Pommer, who produced Hitchcock's 1938 film, *Jamaica Inn*, on which Hamer worked as an editor. Before joining Ealing in 1941, Hamer briefly worked for the G.P.O. Film Unit.

Beginning as an editor for Balcon at Ealing, Hamer was following the path of many other Balcon protégés who also began as editors before moving up to more important positions. At Ealing he soon made the leap from editor to associate producer in 1944, and in 1945 he wrote and directed the "Haunted Mirror" episode of *Dead of Night*.

Like so many of Ealing's core of editors, producers, writers, and directors, Hamer often spoke of the studio as "we," indicating that he, too, believed Ealing was less a traditional film studio than a tightly knit group of talented people who happened to make movies. But although studio head Balcon admired his obvious talents, Hamer's bent toward self-destruction caused tension between them. Hamer found solace in the bottle, and it ended his brilliant career and, ultimately, led to his death at age fifty-two.

Hamer believed his most consistent directorial trait was the taking of a preposterous story or situation and then treating the characters as realistically as possible under the circumstances. (For Hamer's other films, see notes on *Kind Hearts and Coronets* in the Appendix.)

Kind Hearts and Coronets, considered Hamer's masterpiece and one of the best British films ever made, was lightly based on *Israel Rank*, a novel of the Edwardian era written by Roy Horniman. If *Kind Hearts* stands apart from the classic Ealing films—concerned with community and a sense of duty to the nation—it does so partly because the film reflects the style and sophistication of Robert Hamer.

Hamer was clear from the first on what he wanted to accomplish. He wanted to produce a film "not noticeably similar to any previously made in the English language," and to use that language in varied and interesting ways. He had only scorn for what he called the pedantic objection to dialogue "because it didn't exist at the time of Caligari." He also wanted *Kind Hearts* to ignore the established, but not practiced, moral conventions, not to shock, but "from an impulse to escape the somewhat inflexible and unshaded characterization which convention tends to enforce in scripts."

Kind Hearts' script, by Hamer and John Dighton, contained neither cutting nor camera instructions. Hamer believed in walking onto the set and beginning by rehearsing the scenes with the actors. As the actors "walked through" the script, Hamer made mental notes about camera placement and how the scene should be cut in the editing. He also left details of character and motivation deliberately vague, trusting his own skill and that of the actors to bring dimension to the characters and the story. For an actor like Alec Guinness, a man who slowly builds his characters through a hundred minor details, this freedom gave him a heady independence to mold his interpretations of the characters to his own dimensions.

The funeral scene, justly noted for the six roles played by Guinness, is *Kind Hearts'* most famous and reveals a paucity of secondary detail of the sort normally found in most scripts:

LOUIS *takes a seat in one of the side pews, facing the nave.*

LOUIS' VOICE: The occasion was interesting in that it provided me with my first view of the D'Ascoynes en masse. Interesting and somewhat depressing, for it emphasized how far I had yet to travel.

The Camera takes in the members of the family as he enumerates them.

LOUIS' VOICE: There was the Duke. There was my employer, Lord Ascoyne D'Ascoyne, there was General Lord Rufus D'Ascoyne, there was Admiral Lord Horatio D'Ascoyne, there was Lady Agatha D'Ascoyne, and in the pulpit talking interminable nonsense, the Reverend Lord Henry D'Ascoyne.

LOUIS *yawns discreetly behind his hand.*

LOUIS' VOICE: The D'Ascoynes certainly appeared to have accorded with the tradition of the landed gentry and sent the fool of the family into the church.

Kind Hearts and Coronets is told in flashback by Louis Mazzini, Tenth Duke of Chalfont, awaiting execution in prison for a murder. The alleged murder was actually a suicide, and Louis is innocent. However, to avenge the humble circumstances of his mother's life and death — a member of the D'Ascoyne family who married for love, she was disowned for her rash act — Louis *has* killed seven of the eight D'Ascoynes who stood between him and the coronet. Thus, *Kind Hearts* is a black comedy of class distinction and of placid surfaces hiding boiling cauldrons of desire and emotion. It is this calm exterior that has unfairly given *Kind Hearts* the reputation of being a cold and distancing film. As brilliantly played by Dennis Price, Louis is the most proper of Edwardian gentlemen. His cool, ironic style masking the barely restrained resentment he feels, Louis throws off the shackles of convention only in bed and in the liberating act of murder.

Freed from prison with the complicity of his lover, Sibella, Louis is presumably found out, to face murder charges again, by his memoirs, unthinkingly left behind in his jail cell. That all he has to do to remove this danger is go back to his cell and retrieve the revealing memoirs is left to the viewer to work out. (The United States censor, aware of this plot twist, demanded that a scene showing the memoirs being handed over to the authorities be inserted in prints playing in America.)

In casting *Kind Hearts*, Hamer wanted the same actor to play the three D'Ascoyne family members the script originally called for. He wanted the characters to bear enough resemblance to one another to indicate they were members of the same family. Guinness, however, convinced Hamer to increase the number of D'Ascoynes from three to eight.

Guinness is actually seen as ten D'Ascoynes, not eight. In addition to the flesh-and-blood D'Ascoynes he portrays on screen, his likeness is seen as the first duke of Chalfont (in an oil painting in Louis' mother's home) and as the first duke and his wife in effigies carved on the family vault. (Often overlooked is Dennis Price's dual role as both Louis *and* his briefly seen Italian father.)

Still, it is Guinness' bravura playing of eight similar yet distinct characters in *Kind Hearts* that captured the imagination of the moviegoing public and the film critics of the time.

The *Saturday Review* said, "As a direct descendent of Proteus, Mr. Guinness thinks nothing of raising the ante. He takes on the eight obstructing D'Ascoynes ill-fated enough not to have died natural deaths.... One thing is certain. Whatever Mr. Guinness does in *Kind Hearts and Coronets* he does well, incredibly well. He is an all-star cast in his own person."

The first D'Ascoyne Guinness gives us is Ascoyne D'Ascoyne, son of the banker who will become Louis' benefactor. Young Ascoyne is an arrogant snob, a Monty-Pythonish upperclass twit and playboy given to abusing sales clerks. After Ascoyne D'Ascoyne's rudeness leads to the young fop having Louis fired, the chain of events begins which will see the D'Ascoynes dead and Louis elevated to the rank of duke of Chalfont.

After young Ascoyne's death, Guinness rematerializes as the elder Ascoyne D'Ascoyne, a banker dignified to the point of catatonia. Guinness effects his impersonation of the banker by wearing a pince-nez underneath a shock of white hair. Everything about Guinness' performance bespeaks of advanced age and an equally advanced social position—from his slow movements and tired and pinched voice to his bearing as a gray eminence of the financial world.

Henry D'Ascoyne, the photography enthusiast, required Guinness to shift gears. As the (apparently) youngest of the D'Ascoynes, Henry is played with puppy-dog enthusiasm by Guinness. Young and dark-haired (did ever an actor receive so much assistance from his wig-maker?), Henry is a pleasant and mild aristocrat. Idly rich, he wants little from life beyond his passions for all things photographic and for well-aged spirits. This open-faced young man was a challenging assignment even for Guinness because the actor had to suggest Henry's basic niceness while implying a hollow center that meant a life devoid of any real meaning. For all his mildness, Henry is just another rich dilettante.

General Lord Rufus D'Ascoyne is almost a caricature of a military man, from his bullet-shaped head to the bristling mustache that quivers beneath his hawk-beaked nose. Seen today, the general resembles nothing so much as a Herblock drawing of a bomb with beetling eyebrows and a nasty sneer.

Playing an elderly suffragette might seem his greatest challenge, but Guinness pulls it off flawlessly. He is helped, it must be conceded, by the fact that Lady Agatha D'Ascoyne says nothing beyond telling one of her male counterparts to "Sh-h-h-h!" at young Henry's funeral. And while Guinness' impersonation of a woman might have been novel in 1949, today—after Benny Hill, the Monty Python gang, and Peter Sellers all slipping into women's clothing without anyone blinking an eye—it's difficult to recall the stir it caused then.

Given her severe hairstyle, Lady Agatha, the erstwhile suffragette, resembles no one so much as Norman Bates' mummified mother in *Psycho*.

Still, it would have been great fun to hear Guinness tackle this *grande dame*'s voice.

Louis is saved the bother of dispatching Admiral Lord Horatio D'Ascoyne by the naval officer's streak of stubbornness—he refuses to change a wrongly given order and goes down with his ship after it collides with another warship on maneuvers. In *The Bridge on the River Kwai*, Guinness was to refine this example of British bulldog tenacity and mix in equal doses of heroism and stupidity for his Academy Award–winning performance as Colonel Nicholson. (Prior to the admiral's self-induced demise, Louis is seen poring intently over a diagram of a "whitehead torpedo" in one of the film's funniest sight gags. Fortunately for Louis, the admiral's own bullheadedness makes such an extreme measure unnecessary.)

Perhaps Guinness' most well-rounded characterization in *Kind Hearts* is that of the Reverend Lord Henry D'Ascoyne—the "fool of the family" sent into the church. A stooped old man, the Reverend D'Ascoyne speaks in a tremulous voice and walks with the slow shuffle of the aged. Sporting a great thatch of white hair abetted by full sideburns, the reverend is an inspired creation. Guinness twists his mouth to suggest the old man is no more a stranger to false teeth than he is to his daily ration of port.

As the reverend, Guinness gets a chance to say one of Hamer and Dighton's choicest lines. Showing Louis (disguised as a visiting bishop) around his church, the Reverend D'Ascoyne says, "I always say that my west window has all the exuberance of Chaucer, without, happily, any of the concomitant crudities of his period." It is a marvelous line—pure Hamer—and Guinness delivers it flawlessly.

Guinness' last D'Ascoyne is Ethelred, eighth duke of Chalfont. As created by Hamer and played by Guinness, the old duke is a tough and no nonsense member of the aristocracy. Brusque and balding with a brush mustache, the duke has been a blue-blood far too long to have any feelings for the average man or woman. Out shooting birds, he has his manservant thoroughly thrash a poacher caught in one of his outlawed "man traps." (Louis is along, but he declines to participate in the bird shooting because his principles will not allow him to engage in blood sports!)

Hamer told an interviewer that the scene in which Louis traps the duke in one of his own man traps, then explains his motive for killing off the D'Ascoynes one by one, was intended to generate more sympathy for Dennis Price's character. Unfortunately, audiences found Louis' coldblooded shooting of the trapped duke too brutal and instead felt sorry for the old monster. It is a tribute to Guinness' acting skills that, after seeing him portray seven other D'Ascoynes, the audience accepts his duke as a real person facing death and not just old Alec done up again.

Guinness had this to say about his eight performances: "Quick transformation from one character to another has a disturbing effect. I had to ask myself from time to time: 'Which one am I now?' I had fearful visions of looking like one of the characters and thinking and speaking like one of the others. It would have been quite disastrous to have faced the cameras in the make-up of the suffragette and spoken like the admiral."

Although Guinness' *tour de force* acting dominated *Kind Hearts*, Dennis Price gave the best performance of his career in the difficult central role of Louis Mazzini, the ever-so-proper killer. His delicious underplaying gives the film its sense of malicious mischief—Louis sitting with Edith, discussing young Henry's future, when the smoke behind Edith has revealed that Henry has no future at all. Price's Mazzini is a natural aristocrat wrongly relegated to a life beneath his social station, and he constantly proves the error of his displacement by being far more gracious and cultured than those who have denied him his birthright. (See notes on *Kind Hearts* in the Appendix for Price's other films.)

Of Joan Greenwood, who plays the dangerous and rapacious Sibella—a perfect match for Louis in deviousness and hidden passions—we shall hear more in the chapter devoted to *The Man in the White Suit*. Suffice it to say that her Sibella is a finely etched portrait of a woman willing to use all her charms to attain her goals. Her whiskey-voiced appeal proves far more compelling than poor Edith's stately good looks and proper demeanor.

Kind Hearts and Coronets was Alec Guinness' third film, and it turned him into Britain's number-one star and character actor virtually overnight. Unfortunately, moviegoers in the United States had to wait for its release here until 1950, when the National Board of Review declared Guinness the best actor of the year.

Guinness, Hamer, and Ealing Studios were to make more films together, but none could quite attain the level of this masterpiece of acting, writing, and direction. Still, Alec Guinness was off and running. A decade of great films and performances lay ahead for the actor one publication called "a one-man repertory company."

4. A Run for Your Money (1949)

"Slight, bright, British chase comedy with characterizations
as excellent as they are expected."
— Halliwell's Film Guide

Following Ealing's three other comedies of 1949—Passport to Pimlico, Whiskey Galore/Tight Little Island, and the sublime Kind Hearts and Coronets—A Run for Your Money (hereafter just Money) could hardly help being lost in the shadow of these giants. Not that Money is a bad film; it's actually quite amusing. It's just not up to its predecessors.

Money was Charles Frend's first comedy, and he was the coauthor of the screenplay with associate producer Leslie Norman and Welsh novelist Richard Hughes—the same Richard Hughes who went on to write the highly-acclaimed novel A High Wind in Jamaica.

Guinness played the role of Whimple, a mild-mannered horticultural columnist for a newspaper. While not the challenge that Kind Hearts was, Money gave the thirty-five year-old Guinness another chance to take on a new character's appearance and mannerisms. With the aid of a small mustache and an old fishing hat, Alec Guinness disappeared, and Whimple was born.

Sir Michael Balcon, the head of Ealing Studios, had long believed that the way to crack the American market was not even to try to aim for American tastes. In other words, Balcon believed that English films should first please English audiences; if success in America followed, so much the better. The wisdom of this early policy can be seen in the great Canadian film debacle of the 1970s. Canadian producers, assuming Americans wouldn't be interested in films recognizably Canadian in content, tried to copy the American product by using fading American stars in films of dubious quality. Almost without exception, these bland, "generic" productions, half-Canadian and half-American, pleased no one and lost their backers enormous sums of money— much of it provided by the Canadian government itself.

In contrast, during the same period, Australian filmmakers una-pologetically produced movies which relied heavily on Australian actors and actresses and used the striking landscapes and wonders of Australia itself. By remaining true to their own heritage, they made films that people wanted to see because they were good, not because they mimicked American films.

Correspondingly—but long beforehand—the Ealing Studio comedies, overwhelmingly English in character and tone, gained a tremendous following in the United States, and they helped make Guinness an international star. As Guinness himself told Gene Phillips in *Focus on Film* ("Talent has many Faces"): "...I still maintain that we should aim at making films that will be truly British in character. After all, we go to French and Italian films because they *are* French and Italian. A country's films should reflect that country's history and temperament." In *Money*, Guinness got his wish, for it is as British a film as one is ever likely to see.

Variety's reviewer, "Clem.," said, "This is a light-hearted comedy from the same stable that bred *Passport to Pimlico*, *Another Shore*, and *Whiskey Galore*. Should provide good local entertainment, but, like its predecessors, its specialized dialogue and atmosphere may limit its appeal abroad. Direction is on the same competent scale that characterized the earlier comedies and will be largely responsible for this one's undoubted success."

Philip T. Hartung's review in *The Commonweal* noted, "The English have sent over another of those unpretentious little items that put audiences in a good humor without seeming to make any effort. *Money* isn't up to *I Know Where I'm Going* or *Tight Little Island* [*Whiskey Galore*], but it has a sparkle and so much vivid imagination that your interest never lags. Most fun in this amusing film comes from Alec Guinness, who portrays the gardening correspondent of the newspaper giving the prize."

The New Yorker's review of the film began by stating, "The English comedy *A Run for Your Money* has in its favor the presence of Alec Guinness, the actor who has been creating such a stir as the mystical psychiatrist in [T.S. Eliot's] *The Cocktail Party*. It is hardly likely that Mr. Guinness' role in this film will excite any speculation about what he is supposed to represent, but it should prove that he has a talent for slapstick rather rare in those who move on the tony intellectual tundras of T.S. Eliot." (The reviewer's focus on Guinness' "serious" roles before *Money* are a result of *Kind Hearts*' delayed release in America, where it was not seen until 1950.)

"A.W.," writing for the *New York Times*, said, "...This amiable and decidedly brisk antic treating of a junket to London by a couple of prize-winning Welsh coal miners, is, despite its regional dialogue, contagiously funny. Its laughs may not be abdominal but its light-hearted gaiety is genuine and universal. This combination of deft delineations and daft situations should, in short, give the customers a run for their money."

In Hafoduwchbenceubwllymarchogcoch, a Welsh mining town, two brothers, Dai and Twm (Donald Houston and Meredith Edwards), mine more coal than any other team in the pits, winning 200 pounds and the best seats at the football (rugby) match between England and Wales at Twickenham. The newspaper which sponsored the contest, the *Weekly Echo*, assigns its tweedy gardening editor Whimple (Guinness)—a man who much prefers plants to people — to chaperon the two lucky rustics around London and see that they get to the big match. Whimple resists the assignment and is blackmailed into accepting it by the threat that "Mr. Whimple's Garden Beautiful can always be dug over."

Whimple misses the two lads at the train station and the three are immediately separated, not to see each other again until day's end on the homeward-bound train. Dai, the younger of the two brothers, meets a blonde "pro and con"(a professional confidence girl) hustler named Jo (Moira Lister), who immediately develops designs on his impressive bankroll. She gets him to buy her a diamond ring and whirls him about the city, taking him to see the Tower of London and momentarily separating him from his wallet.

Meanwhile, Twm runs into an acquaintance from back home, a harp-playing exile named Huw (Hugh Griffith), who's hocked his harp to raise enough cash to stay permanently sodden. Becoming pub-crawling buddies, they, too, manage to see a lot of the city in their few hours together.

Once Twm retrieves Huw's harp from the pawnshop, the two attempt to board a subway with it and are rebuffed by the crowds leaving the rugby stadium. The subway passengers attempt to give the strangers directions but can't agree on how to get from here to there.

Whimple's adventures include a fight in a pub and his arrest when the police mistake him for a bag-snatching thief. He's led away to "a nice quiet cell where I can write my story in peace."

Exhausted by their adventure-filled escapades, the two Welsh brothers are reunited on the train to home — where they'll have a lot to tell their friends about the big city.

Director Charles Frend (1909–1977), who was born in Pulborough, joined British International Pictures, Elstree, in 1931, working in the cutting rooms. He became a first-rate editor, like many of Balcon's directors, and later edited Alfred Hitchcock's *Secret Agent* and *Sabotage* at Gaumont British.

After moving over to MGM–British Studios in 1937, he worked on *The Citadel* (1938), *A Yank at Oxford* (1938), *Goodbye, Mr. Chips* (1939), and *Major Barbara* (1941). In 1941, he went to work for Balcon at Ealing and directed his first feature, *The Big Blockade*, in 1942.

A Run for Your Money was Frend's first comedy, and it followed such stirring dramatic films as *Scott of the Antarctic* (1948).

Guinness, playing a character older than himself, has several fine moments in *Money*, especially when he cannot help leaping into the air at the rugby match and shouting, "England!" As is his wont, Guinness underplays his role so much you really believe he *is* a bulb-caressing, timorous writer.

Joyce Grenfell caricatures the sort of snobby clerks one finds in too-too posh establishments — the sort where one is likely to hear someone describe a dress as "quel perfect."

All in all, Guinness' fourth film is a cheerful romp.

5. *Last Holiday* (1950)

"Fate does not jest and events are not a matter of chance —
there is no existence out of nothing."
— Gamal Abdel Nasser

"There are no accidents whatsoever in the universe."
— Baba Ram Dass

"Everybody dies."
— John Garfield

In 1949, at the Edinburg Festival, Guinness played the role of Sir Henry
Harcourt Reilly in T.S. Eliot's *The Cocktail Party*. His performance was
typically Guinness: he was masterly as the smoothly-austere Reilly, first a
mystery man and then, ostensibly, a world-weary psychiatrist who turns out
to be a Greek god in disguise among the mortals.

Although the role went to Rex Harrison on the London stage, Guinness
reprised the character for the play's successful transplantation to Broadway,
where it opened in January 1950. *The Cocktail Party* was an instant success,
and Guinness' reputation as a serious stage actor was indelibly etched in the
minds of those who saw his otherworldly Reilly. With this one play, Guinness
established himself in the minds of the influential New York stage and film
critics and the public so firmly that his films were eagerly awaited in the
United States. Although the play ran over 400 times, Guinness returned to
England to appear in two films: *Last Holiday* and *The Mudlark*.

Unlike *The Mudlark*, which had Irene Dunne, *Last Holiday* had no
American stars to entice American filmgoers into the theaters. Yet, somehow,
the word-of-mouth on the film and on Guinness' performance were such that
the film did even more business in this country than in England. The "Alec
Guinness phenomenon" was underway, to be reinforced with the release of
The Mudlark, *The Lavender Hill Mob*, and the delayed openings of *Oliver
Twist* and *Kind Hearts and Coronets*.

An empty shell of a man, farm implements salesman George Bird is told
by his physician that he is infected with an incurable and fatal malady called
Lampington's disease. Given only a few weeks to live, Bird decides to take his

35

life savings from the bank and live it up at an expensive and exclusive luxury hotel at the resort of Pinebourne.

With nothing to lose, Bird hopes to do all the things he has been afraid to do: make friends, gamble, and generally just enjoy what little time he has left.

When he arrives at his destination, Bird is viewed as a man of mystery and substance because he refuses to divulge who or what he is. The others at the hotel think him a rich eccentric, since he wears a first-rate wardrobe he picked out at a secondhand shop before arriving at the hotel.

At first meek and mousy around the socially imposing hotel guests, Bird soon becomes a welcome sight around the hotel, giving an inventor solid advice on how to improve the subsoil digger he's perfecting and advising a cabinet minister on the problems of modernizing and mechanizing farms. As Bird works his way through the hotel's guest list, the film introduces us to the guest and their problems à la *Grand Hotel*.

Mrs. Poole (Kay Walsh), the embittered housekeeper of the Torquay Hotel, knows his secret and is sympathetic to his unfortunate state of affairs. Sheila Rockingham (Beatrice Campbell), the attractive wife of a young man who turns out to be a philandering currency smuggler, is consoled by Bird and develops a certain affection for him. Another tourist, as out of place as Bird initially was, is Joe Clarence (Sidney James).

Although Bird never in his life made more than nine pounds a week (roughly twenty-five dollars in United States currency at that time), by shooting his savings and daring to mingle freely with captains of industry, he is showered with offers of important and well-paying positions.

As if to counterbalance his bleak fate, it seems that his luck is limitless. He places a five-pound bet at 8–1 and wins 400 pounds. He makes an impossible 100–1 croquet shot and startles a rich Cockney with his good fortune.

Finally, his time running out, Bird meets Sir Trevor Lampington (Ernest Thesiger), the discoverer of the disease that is allegedly killing him. Lampington tells him his physician's diagnosis is incorrect and he's not going to die after all. Returning to celebrate his reprieve, Bird loses control of his car and is killed in the resulting crash.

Newsweek's review argues that, ". . . Guinness, best known to American audiences as all eight murdered heirs in *Kind Hearts and Coronets*, . . . steals the show as a turned worm, better able to cope with half-hearted acceptance in a strange society than with a final week of his own unquenchable loneliness."

Bosley Crowther's *New York Times* piece begins, "A familiar dramatic situation — the one in which a man has but a short time to live and therefore endeavors to enjoy it to the fullest possible extent — is inflated with tenderness and humor through a J.B. Priestly script and a nice performance by Alec Guinness in the new British film, *Last Holiday*. Simple and modest in structure but delightfully rich in character, this [is an] amusing and poignant little picture...."

Films in Review observed, "Some times the English can take a bedraggled idea and deck it out with pleasant little nosegays of characterization. They have done so here, and the results are 90 entertaining minutes. Mr. Guinness plays the leading role with an impassivity some audiences find enervating."

John McCarten's review in the *New Yorker* concluded with the suggestion that "it is quite likely that *Last Holiday* could not survive the ministrations of an ordinary cast. Happily, its cast is a long way from ordinary: Alec Guinness makes a pleasant and believable salesman, and his companions at the hotel, among them Beatrice Campbell, Kay Walsh, Coco Aslan, and Jean Colin, do their assorted stints with commendable skill."

Finally, "Myro," in *Variety*, writes, "An original J.B. Priestly screenplay with an intriguing situation, directed with a pleasing light touch, plus a capital performance by Alec Guinness are the strong points of *Last Holiday*."

J[ohn] B[oynton] Priestly (1894–1984) was the author of many plays, but he is best known for such popular novels as *The Good Companions* (1929) and *Angel Pavement* (1930), as well as his major critical work, *Literature and Western Man* (1960).

Films have been made from his novels *The Good Companions*, *Benighted* (*The Old Dark House*), *Let the People Sing*, and from several of his plays, including *Dangerous Corner*, *Laburnum Grove*, *When We Are Married*, and *An Inspector Calls* (in which Guinness appeared on the stage).

Priestly's script for *Last Holiday* is an original screenplay and, like his *An Inspector Calls*, a combination allegory and morality play. The script is literate and never dull—if far from lively—and walks a fine line between bathos and slapstick. The ending, typical Priestly, is reminiscent of several of his "time plays" because, as in those philosophical musings about fate, George Bird dies despite his reprieve from the doctor. Given a "last holiday" by fate, Bird cannot alter his destiny.

With a long theater career behind him before he turned to the cinema, Henry Cass has been involved with some interesting scriptwriters—J. Lee Thompson scripted *No Place for Jennifer*, J.B. Priestly wrote *Last Holiday*—and has directed screen versions of several successful stage farces. He has moved into rather more humdrum territory in the last few years, with a series of minor thrillers and comedies.

Henry Cass was born in London in 1902. He first went on the stage in 1923, and later was a producer at Croydon Repertory Theatre. In 1934 he was a producer with the Old Vic. His stage productions included *St. Joan*, *Major Barbara*, *Peer Gynt*, *Desire Under the Elms*. In 1941 he began to direct documentaries for Verity Films (*Danger Area*, *H.M.S. Minelayer*, *Catholics in Britain*, etc.), and in 1945 he produced short adaptations of *Julius Caesar* and *Macbeth* for the British Council; he also directed the documentary *Public Opinion*.

Cass was perhaps too aware of Guinness' burgeoning reputation as a major comic actor. As a result, he somewhat overemphasized the comic side of the film and of Guinness' performance, at the expense of the more serious moments both are entitled to.

Guinness' change from a friendless loner who creeps about the hotel like a "little lost dog" to a self-confident and warmly accepted confidant and advisor is remarkable. His character, a blank slate at the film's beginning, slowly puts out feelers of friendship and human contact.

So often called the "man without a face," Guinness here assumes one right before our eyes, blossoming into a flesh-and-blood character whose death shocks and saddens us.

With *Last Holiday*, Guinness had proven he could assume the central role in a film and carry it off with skill and assurance. His box-office appeal proven, Guinness was about to embark on a series of roles which would establish him as Britain's number-one star attraction for the rest of the world and a film artist of the first magnitude.

6. The Mudlark (1950)

"There is a legend that in the thirty-ninth
year of Her Majesty's reign a small boy
added a footnote to English history."
—From *The Mudlark*'s opening

The Mudlark was Alec Guinness' first production for a major American studio, Twentieth Century–Fox—the studio whose offer of a screen test he'd rejected nearly a decade before when he was appearing in *Flare Path* in New York City.

For Guinness, the chance to play the great Victorian statesman Benjamin Disraeli (1804–1881) was too good an opportunity to pass up. He revered the nineteenth-century prime minister and, in a conversation about the film, was heard to say, "I *adore* Dizzy."

After playing little men, nonentities really, in *A Run for Your Money* and *Last Holiday*, Guinness was anxious to play a mover and a shaker, someone who *didn't* fade into the wallpaper. He brought to the role his extensive knowledge of Disraeli. For instance, rather than submitting to the makeup people's insistence that he wear a black wig, Guinness chose a lighter one instead and dyed it—aware that that was how Disraeli achieved his unique jet-black coiffure in his later years.

When *The Mudlark* was announced by Twentieth Century–Fox, there was a minor wave of indignation and protest in England over the casting of Irene Dunne, a natural-born American from Louisville, Kentucky, as Queen Victoria. Born in 1901, Dunn was one of Hollywood's most popular stars of the thirties and forties. Never a sex symbol, she brought dignity and bearing to her roles and was usually cast as a well-bred woman of means. Viewing *The Mudlark* and the reverential treatment accorded old Vicky, it's hard to see what got so many British traditionalists so hot and bothered. Indeed, Miss Dunne's impersonation is all the more flattering for the fact that she is taller and prettier than Queen Victoria was.

The tempest in a teapot over Dunne's casting blew over; the film was chosen for the Royal Film Command Performance that year; and Guinness won the *Picturegoer* Gold Medal as Britain's most popular actor.

Based on Theodore Bonnet's 1949 best-seller of the same name, *The*

Mudlark is an endearing fantasy, blessed by marvelous performances: Guinness as Disraeli, Andrew Ray as Wheeler, and Finlay Currie as the perpetually tipsy Scot John Brown. The film is just a tad too long—a failing which could have been corrected had the filmmakers jettisoned the secondary plot involving a romance between a lady-in-waiting and a guardsman.

But that objection aside, *The Mudlark* is a classic example of British artistry and American money (such Anglo-American combinations were necessary after World War II because American film companies, not allowed to take the money their pictures had earned during the war out of the country, were forced to invest their profits in joint ventures filmed in England—remember Disney's *Robin Hood* and *Rob Roy* of that era?).

Newsweek's review ended by remarking, "Though this gentle legend lacks the substance that would permit both Miss Dunne and Guinness to distinguish themselves in more meaty versions of the same roles, [producer Nunnally] Johnson and director Jean Negulesco have artfully preserved the fairy-tale quality of the novel."

The Commonweal's reviewer wrote, "[Wheeler's] adventures are fascinating, and although Director Jean Negulesco allows his movie to drag slowly at times and get a bit precious, it will be no means bore you. The sets are the real thing and as beautiful as any I've ever seen. Audiences who like a well-acted, handsomely produced, dignified movie that touches the heart strings are going to like *The Mudlark* and shouldn't miss it."

"Myro," writing in *Variety*, said, "Let there be no illusions about *The Mudlark*. It is not a great picture. But it is a good one, and one that reflects credit on all who were associated with it. Guinness' oratorical display with a seven-minute speech in the House of Commons was a faultless contribution in a distinguished performance. It puts him in the highest category of character actors."

Writing in the *New York Times*, Bosley Crowther begins his review by noting, "Since Christmas is a time for telling stories about children and brotherly love, about the . . . nobility of the poor, it is altogether fitting and proper that Twentieth Century–Fox should bring along its handsome screen version of *The Mudlark* to brighten the holidays. And it is also appropriate to the season that this reviewer should be able to report that this picture . . . is a warm and rewarding show."

Along the banks of the Thames in London, children—mudlarks—grub among the rubble left when the tide recedes. A boy named Wheeler (Andrew Ray) finds the body of a sailor and picks his pockets, finding a medallion bearing Queen Victoria's likeness.

Wheeler takes his treasures to a "fence" but refuses to sell his "picture." The fence sends two boys after Wheeler to steal it. After they take it from him, Wheeler chases the two, who are collared by a night watchman. One of the boys, Sparrow (William Strange), throws the medallion into the river and

Prime Minister Disraeli (Guinness) speaks to Queen Victoria (Irene Dunne). Guinness himself prepared the wig he wore as Disraeli.

Wheeler leaps in after it, though he can't swim. Again the night watchman comes to his rescue.

The old man tells Wheeler the medallion is a likeness of the old queen and calls her the "mother" of England. Wheeler, an orphan, says she looks like a mother. He didn't know she was the queen when he found the medallion; he just likes her face. The night watchman tells Wheeler she's shut herself up in Windsor Castle, twenty miles up the Thames.

Wheeler treks to Windsor and stands wistfully outside the gates, staring at the impassive guards amidst the fog. When the Prime Minister's carriage arrives, the gates are left slightly ajar, and Wheeler sneaks inside.

Inside the castle, Prime Minister Disraeli (Guinness) meets with the queen's loyal manservant John Brown (Finlay Currie). When Disraeli asks Brown if the queen will end her seclusion, the old Scot says she's stubborn as a mule.

Queen Victoria (Irene Dunne) signs the papers Disraeli has brought for her as he flatters her, telling her that the "disturbances" (concerning her refusal to appear in public) are over. But he wants her to end her seclusion and mentions their reform program, saying that only she can win enough support for the program to pass in Parliament. Shrewdly, Disraeli tells her that she *was* England. That's not so today; republicanism is now growing fashionable in her absence.

Disraeli presents the queen with an invitation to appear at a foundling hospital. But she says she's often afraid; she prefers to stay within Windsor's walls, with her comforting memories of Prince Albert.

Meanwhile, Wheeler unceremoniously falls down a coal chute and into the castle. As Wheeler looks in wonder at the many richly furnished rooms, he comes upon a table set for a royal banquet. He hides under the table, but a serving girl named Kate Noonan (Constance Smith) sees him and tells him she'll try to sneak him out. Too late—she's joined by an Irish candle lighter named Slattery (Ronan O'Casey), who speaks of burning the castle down in the name of Ireland. Then Slattery spots Wheeler and realizes the boy's heard every traitorous word. Slattery helps Kate hide him behind a curtain as the banquet guests approach.

As the queen enters, Wheeler settles back and falls asleep. The queen hears someone snoring, and she leaves while Brown and the servants search for the intruder. Brown discovers Wheeler and sends him to be scrubbed and bathed. In reaction to this "plot," Victoria says she'll not go to the hospital celebration. She vows to stay inside Windsor Castle until she dies. When Brown reminds Disraeli that he told him she was "stubborn as a mule," Disraeli replies, "Ah, Mr. Brown, what power of expression there is in a limited vocabulary."

Wheeler is scrubbed and disinfected, hollering like a stuck pig. When the staff confront him, he mentions the "man who wants to burn down Windsor Castle," setting off a flurry of excitement. Brown takes over the questioning and learns that Wheeler walked from London, sneaked in, and fell down "a hole."

Taking Wheeler about the castle grounds, Brown begins to doubt the boy's story—until he himself falls down the coal chute in the fog! Brown, covered in coal dust, looks at Wheeler's "picture," and shows him his own autographed photograph of the queen. Taking a drink, Brown calls the queen a "wee old woman—and a nice one." "C'mon," says Brown, taking Wheeler for a tour of the castle. Brown allows Wheeler to sit upon the throne. "A rare feeling," Brown says. But then the servants discover them and carry Wheeler off; Brown, totally sozzled, is sent to bed.

The next day the papers are full of "The Shocking Occurrence at

Windsor," and the "Mystery of the Dwarf Assassin," as the police grill Wheeler. The queen tells Disraeli these absurd rumors must be stopped; Disraeli is to make no comment, even in the House of Commons, concerning the matter.

The scene shifts to the Tower of London. Outside, carolers sing; inside, Wheeler shivers in a blanket. His friends, brought in to identify him, refuse to admit knowing him. Wheeler speaks to Sparrow, who tells him the queen is dead, murdered by assassins. Alone and friendless, Wheeler sobs to himself.

At 10 Downing Street, Disraeli reads the newspaper headlines and gets an idea. At the House of Commons, the prime minister agrees to answer questions and says there is no Irish conspiracy. Instead, he speaks movingly of Wheeler's harsh life: no parents, no religious training, no schooling, no care of any sort. Yet Wheeler so loves England that he wanted to see the queen — the mother of England. And, since Victoria doesn't appear in public, Wheeler went to Windsor. Disraeli speaks on behalf of all British children like Wheeler and their needs.

Later, Brown tells the queen that such children are "all your brood, Ma'am." The queen, angry at Disraeli's disobedience, sends for him. When he arrives, she rebukes him for his disloyalty. He's unapologetic — the reform program *will* pass. He offers to resign and she all but takes him up on it. Brown intervenes, telling her to serve the living — as Prince Albert did.

A noise: It's Wheeler. The queen wants him taken away. When Disraeli argues for him to stay, Victoria reluctantly agrees. She tells Wheeler he's a very naughty boy. He shows her his picture and she asks him why did it. To see her, Wheeler says. The queen thanks him and Brown takes him away; Disraeli has arranged for Wheeler's care and education.

Disraeli smiles. Chagrined, the queen agrees to go to the foundling hospital and offers Disraeli her hand. The prime minister takes it with affection and loyalty. As she rides in an open carriage, cheering crowds exuberantly applaud the queen, who basks in their love and adoration.

Nunnally Johnson (1897–1977), who produced *The Mudlark* as well as writing the screenplay, was a Hollywood hyphenate — a screenwriter-producer-director. Among his more noteworthy films were *The Grapes of Wrath* (1940, as writer), *The Three Faces of Eve* (1957, writer-producer-director), and *The Dirty Dozen* (1967, writer only).

Johnson's script seems overly reverent concerning the queen and the foibles of the time, but that's typically Hollywood; we may not have royalty in America, but confront us with a real monarch and we all but stand up and salute.

Director Jean Negulesco (1900–) was born in Romania but has been in the United States since 1927. He directed his first American feature, *Kiss and Make Up*, in 1934, scoring his first real success with the 1944 melodrama *The

Mask of Dimitrios. Among his more noteworthy films are *Titanic* (1953), *How to Marry a Millionaire* (1953), and *Three Coins in the Fountain* (1954).

Andrew Sarris, in his book *The American Cinema: Directors and Directions 1929–1968*, has this to say about the director: "Jean Negulesco's career can be divided into two periods labeled B.C. and A.C., or Before Cinemascope and After Cinemascope. *The Mask of Dimitrios*, *Three Strangers*, *Humoresque*, *Deep Valley*, *Road House*, *Johnny Belinda* and *Take Care of My Little Girl* are all Before Cinemascope, and all rather competently and even memorably made. Everything After Cinemascope is completely worthless. Negulesco's is the most dramatic case of directorial maladjustment in the fifties."

If one accepts Sarris' harsh judgment, *The Mudlark* fits rather neatly into the "Before Cinemascope" category. It is a well-directed and memorably made film, and Negulesco gets fine performances from his cast, particularly from eleven-year-old Andrew Ray. In *Films in Review*, Ruth K. Friedlich wrote, "As Wheeler, a London waif, Andrew Ray gives an extraordinarily affecting and unaffected performance in *The Mudlark*. Wise direction has so restrained the natural dramatic gifts of this promising boy actor and subordinated his role, that the picture has far more than this one sentimental appeal."

The two best performances in the film, apart from young master Ray, are turned in by Guinness and Finlay Currie.

Finlay Currie was born Finlay Jefferson in Scotland in 1878. A stage and music hall performer before making his first screen appearance in 1932's *The Case of the Frightened Lady*, Currie went on to appear in many fine films before his death in 1968 at age of ninety. He was in several Guinness films, including *Great Expectations* (as Magwitch) and *The Fall of the Roman Empire*. (See notes on *The Mudlark* in the Appendix for additional films.)

A great character actor, Currie brings all his skills to the fore in his playing of John Brown, the perpetually stiff Scot manservant who was Queen Victoria's loyal companion and friend. The scene in which he teaches young Wheeler how to use a fork is memorable for the warmth and humanity he brings to his character. He also makes a good foil for Guinness' acerbic Disraeli.

Guinness is... well, just wonderful. His superb reading of Disraeli's long, eloquent speech in the House of Commons is one of the highlights of the film and, as *Variety* noted, "puts him in the highest category of character actors."

Variety had Guinness pegged all right—his next three films would all contain great Guinness performances: *The Lavender Hill Mob*, *The Man in the White Suit*, and *The Card/The Promoter*.

7. The Lavender Hill Mob (1951)

"Superbly characterized and inventively detailed comedy,
one of the best ever made at Ealing or in Britain"
—*Halliwell's Film Guide*

The Lavender Hill Mob (hereafter called *Mob*) was Alec Guinness' third Ealing film. Released in 1951, the last really successful year for Ealing Studios, *Mob* was another great hit with the public and the critics alike.

Mob allowed Guinness to develop yet another of his marvelous characterizations. This time he is an apparently mousy and timid little bank clerk who actually harbors a not-so-timid desire: to rob the Bank of England of a shipment of gold bullion. Stanley Holloway, who plays Pendlebury, nearly equals Guinness' achievement by himself turning in a shrewdly realized characterization of a florid, genteelly shabby artist who makes living turning out cast-iron souvenirs that only a tourist could want to buy.

A simple and fast-paced story, *Mob* begins with an apparently wealthy Englishman named Holland enjoying the good life in Rio de Janeiro. Flashily dressed, he begins telling his tale to a man seated next to him. The scene then dissolves to his earlier life and the way he once was—an officious little man in a derby and dark suit, wearing wire-rim glasses and carrying an umbrella. Holland seems the perfect drudge, with no purpose in life beyond his meager and boring routine. Indeed, a superior says of him, "He's no imagination; no initiative." But appearances can be deceiving. Beneath that placid exterior exists the free spirit of a master criminal—or at least a man who wants to be known as "Dutch." Biding his time for years, Holland has been formulating a plan to rob the van that transports the gold bars from the foundry to the bank's vaults.

Living modestly at the Balmoral Private Hotel at Lavender Hill, Holland reads schlocky gangster novels aloud to a fellow resident, an eccentric old lady. A new boarder moves in, a Mr. Pendlebury, who makes hideous cast-iron souvenirs for his firm—Gewgaws, Ltd. Taken on a tour of the plant by Pendlebury, a wide-eyed Holland observes with mounting excitement that the casting process is virtually identical to the way the bank casts its gold bars. Gingerly, he feels out Pendlebury and convinces him they could steal the bank's gold. . .*if* they had a gang.

Guinness as the not-so-mousy bank clerk "Dutch" Holland.

Unfortunately for the plan he's worked out over the years, Holland receives a promotion to another department. Forced to act quickly, he and Pendlebury recruit Lackery and Shorty, two "desperados," who agree to help them pull off the heist. Although there are several hitches in Holland's plan, the gang is successful in robbing the van and making their getaway.

"Our firstborn," Holland says as he admires the first Eiffel Tower cast from the melted-down gold bars. When Holland and Pendlebury travel to Paris to retrieve the sucessfully exported Eiffel Towers, however, they learn that six of them have inadvertently been sold to English schoolgirls on holiday. Following them back to England, Holland and Pendlebury talk five of the girls into giving up their towers for new ones and a 10-shilling note. The sixth girl refuses their offer and gives hers to her "boyfriend" — a policeman working at the Metropolitan Police Training School. When their secret gets out, Holland and Pendlebury elude the police and make their getaway in a police car. Finally, Pendlebury is collared, but Holland gets away by blending in with a crowd of similarly dressed office workers.

Having escaped to Rio with six of the gold statues (worth £25,000), Holland enjoys a year of luxury. But the man he's been relating his adventures to is revealed to be a policeman, who takes him away in handcuffs.

The ending of *Mob*, so similar to that of *Kind Hearts*, really doesn't negate the film's fun. The "gang" in the movie is composed of the mildest criminals possible and theirs is a crime in which no one is hurt and violence is never suggested. The victim of the crime is the rich, imposing, and impersonal Bank of England. The fact that Holland is taken away in handcuffs at the film's conclusion is almost beside the point—they can't take away his year of carefree abandon; in that sense, Holland has gotten away with it.

The Lavender Hill Mob was written by T.E.B. Clarke, an Ealing regular. Born in 1907, Clarke was a journalist and a policeman (accounting for his familiarity with police procedures) before going to Ealing as a contract writer, where his tenure lasted from 1943 to 1957. The newly hired Clarke made a small contribution to Charles Crichton's first directorial effort, an almost documentary-like drama of the air-sea rescue service called *For Those in Peril* (1944). He also joined with Crichton for an episode of 1945's *Dead of Night*, Ealing's celebrated anthology horror film. *Hue and Cry* (1947), also directed by Crichton, was Clarke's first comedy script. His non–Ealing films include *Gideon's Day* (1958), for John Ford, and *Sons and Lovers* (1960).

In his autobiography, *This is Where I Came In*, Clarke recalls how he got the idea for *Mob*. Many of the situations occured to him while he was ostensibly working on the screenplay for a realistic crime drama called *Pool of London* (1951). Pulled from his hard-edged thriller and assigned the script of *Mob*, Clarke used many of his original ideas but now placed special emphasis on the humor inherent in the situations. (See notes on *Mob* in the Appendix for Clarke's other films.)

Clarke's Academy Award–winning screenplay for *Mob* was an original story written in the inimitable Ealing manner of the immediate postwar years— before the warm glow of victory and peace gave way to era of cynicism (of the sort summed up in the Peter Sellers film *I'm All Right, Jack*, 1960).

In his autobiography, Michael Balcon, Ealing's head, writes: ". . . I think our first desire was to get rid of as many wartime restrictions as possible and get going. The country was tired of regulations and regimentation, and there was a mild anarchy in the air. In a sense our comedies were a reflection of this mood . . . a safety valve for our more antisocial impulses."

Alec Guinness' Holland is a vehicle for this chafing under the restraints of order and self-denial. His twenty years of going without things and of making do on a tiny salary can be compared to the hardships and reduced standard of living of the war years all Britons suffered through. Throwing off the shackles of morality and regimentation, Holland does what every Englishman of the time would have liked to do—somehow get hold of a fortune and live the life of a playboy. Seen in this light, *Mob* is a gentle fantasy of wish fulfillment in which no one gets hurt. For a year, Guinness' Everyman lives outside the established social order of work and responsibility. For one glorious year, he's lived the life he deserves to live, not the life fate has handed out, full of rules, bills, and time-clocks to punch.

Director Charles Crichton was born in 1910. He began his career as a film editor and worked on London Films' 1935 production of *Sanders of the River*. After putting in five years as an editor for London Films, he jumped to Ealing to become a producer first, then a director in 1944, working with Clarke on *For Those in Peril*.

While Crichton never attained the fame of so many of the Balcon editor/directors, such as Hamer and Mackendrick, he was a solid craftsman and a very good comedy director. His other popular comedies, however, are not nearly as well done as *Mob*.

The Lavender Hill Mob is a short film, just seventy-eight minutes long, and Crichton's fast-paced direction never allows the viewer to take a breath — or to consider any of the implausibilities of Clarke's script. Perhaps because of all those leisurely, melodramatic "heist" films that become a genre unto themselves, *Mob* has its desperados pulling off their big job in what seems like record time. First, we are introduced to Holland and his job, Pendlebury is also introduced and quickly joins with Holland. Forced to act by Holland's upcoming promotion, the two amateur thieves easily enlist the aid of two professionals; and finally, the robbery is speedily and successfully carried out — as is the exporting of the gold Eiffel Towers.

Whew! In the same amount of time, a picture like *Robbery* (1967) is hardly beyond the putting together of the robbery "team." And *Mob*'s breakneck pace never slackens. There is a fast and giddy descent down the steps of the Eiffel Tower that is as exhilarating for the viewer as it is for Holland and Pendlebury — who, dizzy from rapidly corkscrewing down to the ground, whirl off with their arms flailing, unable to stop rotating.

A marvel of special effects and rear-screen projection, the Eiffel Tower sequence works wonderfully — even though the viewer isn't for a minute fooled into thinking Guinness and Holloway are actually descending the real Eiffel Tower. Holland and Pendlebury's silly and involuntary laughter as their descent makes them dizzier and dizzier invariably makes the viewer laugh as well.

Guinness later described his role in *Mob* as "fubsy" — a word which means "chubby and somewhat squat" and one of Guinness' favorites at the time (a friend dubbed his house in Hammersmith "Fubsy Manor"). Although Guinness liked *Mob*, he made few artistic claims for it and shrugged it off as "a romp." Despite his disclaimers, Guinness clearly appears to be having fun playing Holland in *Mob*. Perhaps Guinness, active on the stage in serious roles since the mid–30s, was beginning to feel the classic stage actor's guilt for commercial success, especially in another medium. Furthermore, the films he was making were mostly comedies. Guinness had nothing against them, but, serious about acting and his own skills, he chafed to make "serious" films which would show his dramatic skills more clearly. Paradoxically, the success of his comedies would initially confine him to comedy roles, but later would give him enough clout to pick the roles and films he believed he should do to grow as an actor. *The Lavender Hill Mob* earned Ealing Studios one million pounds sterling, approximately $2,850,000 at the time, a considerable amount of money for a small picture made on an equally small budget. Guinness found himself in a golden trap—his comedies were proving almost *too* successful.

To prepare for his derby-hatted role in *Mob*, Guinness stalked about the streets of London following unwitting subjects for miles to pick up the mannerisms he was looking for. His face was still unknown to his admirers when he appeared in public, so Guinness was able to walk about as inconspicuously as Holland, who escaped from the police by melting into a crowd of English gentlemen wearing derbies and carrying umbrellas.

Still a young man of thirty-six when *Mob* was made, Guinness again convincingly played a character many years his senior. Outwardly shy and retiring, Guinness' Holland is, like the actor himself, a rather strong and determined personality who goes after what he wants. The innate goodness that exists in so many of the characters Guinness portrays shines through again in his Holland—a would-be criminal mastermind whose most fervent wish is that Pendlebury call him "Dutch." Little is made of it, but Pendlebury is Holland's only real friend, and their affection and concern for each other is evident.

An excellent foil for Guinness' Holland, Stanley Holloway's Pendlebury is a cheery, bluff man who's as decent and big-hearted as he is large of frame. Holloway and Guinness have one marvelous scene together in the foundry at Gewgaws in which Holland is trying gingerly to drop enough hints for Pendlebury to understand that he's being asked to join a criminal conspiracy. Pendlebury, oblivious to Holland's guarded message, finally catches onto what his friend is suggesting. Looking up at Holland with a twinkle in his eye, he says, "By Jove, Holland, it's a good job we're both honest men."

Sidney James (1913–1976), a South African–born character acter with the face of an unmade bed, plays Lackery, the "muscle" of the Lavender Hill mob. Many Americans recognize his face, if not his name, from the seemingly endless "Carry On" movies he made.

Alfie Bass, a character actor who specialized in playing Cockney and Jewish roles, plays Shorty, the diminutive member of the mob more concerned about the "Test Match" than going to Paris with Holland and Pendlebury.

The Lavender Hill Mob has lost none of its charm over the years. It remains an amusing and warmhearted little picture whose contrived plot is merely the foundation for several sharply etched character studies: Guinness' "Dutch" Holland and Stanley Holloway's Pendlebury.

Alec Guinness, frustrated at being considered a "comedy" actor, nonetheless won an Academy Award nomination for his work in *Mob*. Gary Cooper took home the Oscar that year for his performance in *High Noon*, but Hollywood had sent a message to Guinness: We like what you're doing, keep it up.

8. *The Man in the White Suit* (1951)

> *"The Man in the White Suit* emerges as one of the most mature, enjoyable, and intelligent SF films ever made"
> — Stuart H. Stock, *Twenty All-Time Great Science Fiction Films*

As film scholar Stuart H. Stock's comments reveal, *The Man in the White Suit* (hereafter *MWS*) is a science fiction film, Alec Guinness' first, although reviews at the time, including one in the *New York Times*, called it a "satire" and a "fable," unaware of its classic SF underpinnings. Comparing it to *The Lavender Hill Mob*, Hollis Alpert remarked in *Saturday Review* that the film was "so clever in its story and filled with so much whimsical invention . . . I was unable to decide which I liked better."

Variety hailed it as a "new comedy winner." *Time* described it as "top-grade movie material with the quality of good British woolen, the frothiness of fine French lace," and *Newsweek* described it as "a choice piece of movie foolery and effervescent philosophizing." In *Films in Review*, B.G. Marple summed it all up when he said *MWS* "will stand out as one of the most individual experiments in Britain this year."

The Man in the White Suit begins with mill owner Michael Corland trying to get another, larger mill owner, Alan Birnley, to invest in his small mill and to allow him to marry Birnley's daughter, Daphne. This all falls through when it's discovered that someone has set up an unauthorized experiment costing £4000 in Corland's lab. The experimenter, Sidney Stratton (Alec Guinness), slips away and gets a job as a laborer in Birnley's mill. Mistaken for an employee of the microscope company installing a new model, Sid is asked to stay on to work out the bugs. He does, without pay, and takes up his interrupted experiments. Again, he is discovered, and his now-successful experiment's results are unceremoniously poured down the drain. Daphne, Birnley's daughter, convinced Sid is a genius, tries to convince her father at least to hear Sid out. Meanwhile, Sid shows up at Birnley's house unannounced and tries to gain admittance. Finally confronting Birnley, Sid is thrown out without a hearing. Daphne, however, convinces her father to give Sid a chance. Birnley reluctantly hires him and gives Sid control of his laboratory. After many explosive attempts to perfect his formula, Sid finally

Sid (Guinness) displays his miraculous suit to Frank (Patric Doonan) and Bertha (Vida Hope). (Photo courtesy of Nancy and Steve Gould.)

makes it work. The liquid is quickly turned into fibers and woven into cloth — a cloth that will never wear out and never get dirty. The cloth is turned into a weirdly luminous white suit. Daphne says not only does the suit make Sid look like a knight in shining armor, but also the whole world will bless him for his discovery.

A rriving in black limousines, a contingent of mill owners, led by the infamous Sir John Kierlaw, confronts first Birnley and then Sid. The mill owners know that the cloth will mean the end of the textile business. The workers also come to the same conclusion: If Sid's cloth is mass produced, their jobs will disappear forever. Sid is locked in a room in Birnley's house when he refuses to sign over his rights for £250,000. With Daphne's help, Sid escapes while labor and capital agree to join forces to suppress his cloth. Running from everyone, Sid bumps into Mrs. Watson, his landlady, who asks him what's to become of her bit of washing when there's no washing to be done? Only now does Sid realize the havoc his invention may portend. Still running from the workers and the mill owners, Sid is finally cornered. As he's seized by the angry mob, his suit comes apart in their hands — the molecules are unstable. The status quo is preserved...or is it? Sid strides off at the end, determined to try again; he is unbeaten and unbowed.

Director/writer Alexander Mackendrick was born in Boston in 1912 and brought up in Glasgow, Scotland. Mackendrick eventually went to England, where, after a brief stint in advertising, he made documentaries for industry, an experience which brought realism to his depiction of the textile industry in *MWS*. During the Second World War, Mackendrick was in charge of an army unit in Italy which made films for British intelligence. In 1946, Mackendrick joined Ealing as a sketch artist, and eventually he was given a chance to try his hand at scripts. He wrote *Saraband for Dead Lovers* (1948) with John Dighton before being given his first directorial assignment, *Whiskey Galore* (U.S.: *Tight Little Island*, 1949). *MWS* was his second film as director. His other films include *The Ladykillers* (1955), also with Guinness; *The Sweet Smell of Success* (1957); and *A High Wind in Jamaica* (1965).

After making one more film, *Don't Make Waves* (1967), Mackendrick dropped out of movies to accept a teaching position at the California Institute of Arts. (See notes on *MWS* in the Appendix for a full listing of his films.)

Mackendrick's cowriters for the screenplay of *MWS* were John Dighton (who was a cowriter for *Kind Hearts*) and Roger MacDougall. The script was based on an unperformed play of MacDougall's.

Mackendrick saw to it that each scene was meticulously lighted and composed. An artist, Mackendrick used his eye for composition to carefully position the actors. In many of his three-character shots, Mackendrick placed his actors within the frame to show the tension, attraction, or repulsion among them. Many shots are composed of three elements. The most obvious trio is labor, capital, and science—as represented by the workers, the mill owners, and Sid. Nowhere is Mackendrick's eye for the physical dynamics of a scene more apparent than when labor and capital confront each other across a room, warily keeping their distance. When the two normally antagonistic groups agree to work together to suppress Sid's cloth, they merge into a mob and surge out the door as a single group.

In addition to his manipulation of the framing of the characters, Mackendrick used sophisticated camera movement. Mackendrick's visual sense gives us some superb shots: Sid seemingly telling his boss off but really only speaking his mind to a mirror in the men's room; the arrival of the mill owners' long black cars, with the white-suited Sid (glowing, actually) against the black-garbed owners—literally good (white) vs. evil (black).

In a long review of *MWS* in the British film magazine *Sight and Sound,* critic Gavin Lambert said, "While the threat of industrial chaos is wittily analysed, the labour-capital relationship nicely drawn, Stratton as an individual in effect disappears, not to emerge again until the scene of his humiliation..." Perhaps Lambert would have tempered his criticism had he realized that *MWS* is science fiction. Science fiction, especially in literature, emphasizes the idea of the society at the expense of the individual—the reverse of the "mainstream" novel. As true SF, then, *MWS* is less concerned with Sid than it is with the effects of his invention on society.

Although Mackendrick probably did not know, or care, that he was making a science fiction film, he was in many ways a perfect director for *MWS*. As Roy Armes notes in *A Critical History of British Cinema*, Mackendrick's films "explore the gaps between the individual and the community with . . . sense of reality." Mackendrick's eye for the telling detail makes the story work in human terms. Mackendrick sees Sid less as a little man in danger of being devoured by predatory forces he cannot understand than as a self-centered Techno-nerd whose devotion to pure science blinds him to any attempts to reach him on a human level. Sid doesn't mean to be insensitive; he's just oblivious to human needs and desires. Sir John Kierlaw, the dried-up industrialist, senses this immediately. When Sid has accidentally knocked himself out, Kierlaw disinterestedly asks, "Is he all right?" Told Sid is okay, Kierlaw murmurs, "Pity." Grown wise and cynical, Kierlaw sees immediately that Sid's unthinking scientific idealism makes him strangely inhuman — after all, what sensible man would turn down a quarter of a million pounds? Sid is like a man who has constructed his own atomic bomb and won't be satisfied until he can set it off to see if it works — and the consequences be damned!

For the most part a satiric romp, *MWS* has several sequences of pure slapstick. Perhaps the most memorable, certainly the most surrealistic, is the sequence which has Sid trying to get into Birnley's house while a determined butler is trying just as hard to keep him out. At one point, the butler takes Sid's note to Birnley. Birnley, on the phone, is trying to discover who is responsible for spending £8000 on the weird contraption found in his lab. "Send him out here," Birnley says on the phone while ordering the butler to "tell him to go away." It's a neat summation of British industry's plight: blocked, going around in circles, and frustrated because the left hand doesn't know what the right is doing.

B. G. Marple, in *Films in Review*, said that Guinness' role is "a quieter one than he had in *The Lavender Hill Mob*. But he plays it with just as much revelation of character. These character revelations of Guinness' are very appropriate to the kind of comedy the British do so well. For they are without malice. And when truth is without malice it is often amusing."

Alec Guinness, wishing to build his characters on a foundation of reality, is an observer. "The secret, if there is one," Guinness has said, "is to imagine yourself as the character you are portraying. It means studying the character carefully, of course. It's not sufficient to concentrate on his looks. You have got to know his mind — to find out what he thinks, how he feels, his background, his mannerisms."

Just as the mild-mannered bank clerk of *The Lavender Hill Mob* was based on actual clerks whom Guinness followed up an down the streets of London, Sidney Stratton was modeled on a real person, a studio technician. Guinness was on the set of *MWS*, preparing for a scene, when he spotted a cameraman who had exactly the sort of expression he felt he could use for the scientist-inventor perpetually lost in a mental fog of self-absorption. Guinness descended on the poor man and scrutinized him at great length, walking around him and making mental notes. The flustered cameraman could only grin and bear it.

Whatever his inspiration, Guinness brings a marvelous innocence and vulnerability to Sidney Stratton. Sid is a complex, if familiar type: brilliant yet naive, friendly yet oblivious to the outside world. A shy and retiring sort himself, Guinness gives Sid an air of distraction and concentration that must have brought a smile of recognition to the faces of those who worked with him. Perhaps the cameraman who withstood Guinness' close inspection might have said, "Here—what're you staring at me for? You're Sidney Stratton."

Still, no matter how close the similarities on the surface, Alec Guinness is no more Sidney Stratton than he is Fagin, Adolf Hitler, or Ben Kenobi; he's just an excellent actor who knows how to use his instrument—himself—very well.

Mackendrick's direction and Guinness' art create some nice moments. There's Sid arriving at the lab with a fat cigar in his mouth, content to watch Hoskins' anger turn to helpless surprise when Birnley himself turns over the facility to Sid. Sid, however, is not used to cigars and he chokes on the smoke. There's Sid's happy little half-pantomime, half-dance in front of the tailor's mirrors as he models his glowing white suit. It's Sid's supreme moment of self-realization; Guinness makes him more animated and joyful than at any other moment in the film. Finally, there's the look of slow recognition that clouds Sid's face as the meaning of Mrs. Watson's words—concerning her "bit of washing"—sinks in and he realizes the harm his invention may do.

The scriptwriters have left Guinness' scenes with Joan Greenwood as Daphne rather puzzling, to say the least. When they're together, the viewer is often confused by what their relationship is meant to be. At first, it appears Daphne is going to hand him over to her father; then we're led to believe that they might become lovers. But Daphne has bargained with Kierlaw, who has agreed to pay her £5000 if she can seduce Sid. Yet it is Daphne, not Sid, who sees that Sid can escape by using a strand of his unbreakable thread to climb down the side of her father's house. Then, after Sid refuses both the £250,000 the mill owners are offering and Daphne's body, another plot twist reveals that she was only testing Sid's resolve and is relieved that she could not corrupt him. Now he's her "knight in shining armor." When Sid's suit disintegrates and he's humiliated, Daphne is only a face in the crowd, and it's clear she's out of his life for good. It's to Guinness' and Greenwood's credit that their characters' strange behavior doesn't detract from their performances.

Joan Greenwood is known for her unmistakable voice and her portrayals of intelligent, independent women. Born in 1921, she made her debut on the stage when she was only seventeen. Her first film role was in *John Smith Wakes Up* (1940). Her other films include *Whiskey Galore* (1948), also directed by Alexander Mackendrick, and *Kind Hearts and Coronets* (1949), in which she played the ravishing Sibella.

Daphne (Joan Greenwood) prepares to seduce Sid (Guinness). (Photo courtesy of Stuart H. Stock.)

The part of Daphne could not have been an easy one. Miss Greenwood makes the most of this maddeningly ambivalent character, but is forced to rely too much on her obvious sex appeal and whiskey voice.

Cecil Parker (1897–1971, born Cecil Schwabe), who often appeared on screen in snobbish roles such as Alan Birnley, was a perfect choice to play Daphne's father, if for no other reason than his own distinctive voice, a match for that of his "daughter."

In his book *Ealing Studios*, Charles Barr reveals that Mackendrick once told a television interviewer that he advised Cecil Parker to play Birnley by modeling himself "on Mick" — on studio head Sir Michael Balcon. (See notes on *MWS* in the Appendix for more on the actors and their films.)

The Man in the White Suit was Guinness' second film to be released during 1951, following closely on the heels of *The Lavender Hill Mob*. It reaffirmed Guinness' standing as the best comedic actor of his time. Try as he could, Guinness couldn't escape his "comedy actor" label. Thank goodness!

9. The Card/The Promoter (1952)

"I just want to make money. I don't see
anything wrong with that."
Denry Machin to the countess of Chell in *The Card*.

Released in 1952, *The Card*, which was known as *The Promoter* in the
United States, was Alec Guinness' ninth film and first of four for director
Ronald Neame. To his admirers, it seemed the Guinness penchant for picking
outstanding character roles in delicious comedies would continue forever.

The script of *The Card*, written by British novelist Eric Ambler, is based
on one of Arnold Bennett's series of popular novels about the Five Towns
made famous in *The Old Wives' Tale*. It is a charmingly anachronistic work
set in an Edwardian era seemingly devoid of hardship or real poverty.

E.H. "Denry" Machin, the open-faced opportunist Guinness plays so
craftily, uses his wits and good-natured perseverance to rise to the top, financially and socially, of his local town. Denry's journey, seemingly uninter-
rupted by setbacks or reverses of any kind, reminds one of an old sketch on
the original *Saturday Night Live* called "Married in a Minute," in which
several young ladies come to New York City to make their fortunes and
instantly acquire success, fame, and rich husbands. *The Card*, then, is a film
which does not bear close scrutiny; it's simply pure fun.

As Kenneth Tynan noted, Guinness chose the film "partly because... his
role was that of an extrovert opportunist, a new departure for him; and partly
because in it, for the first time since [the play] *Cousin Muriel* in 1940, he got
the girl."

The reviews were mixed, although most favored the film. Robert Kass,
in *Films in Review*, said, "Carefully mounted and tightly directed by Ronald
Neame, *The Promoter* is an enjoyable lark." Bosley Crowther's review in the
New York Times was less enthusiastic: "*The Promoter*, while vastly amusing
in spots, is not a first-rate Guinness show."

However, Arthur Knight, in *Saturday Review*, summed up the reaction
of most critics of the time by observing that *The Card* "represents motion-
picture making on the very highest level, and I very much doubt if there is
going to be a funnier movie around for a long time to come. Even the
renowned Mr. Guinness will find it difficult to top this one."

Young Denry Machin (Matthew Guinness) sneaks into a classroom and changes his grades upward, winning himself a place in an English public school, where he's derided for being the son of a washerwoman.

The adult Denry (Alec Guinness) open-faced and with an unruly forelock of hair, returns the wallet of a Mr. Dunchalf and, for his honesty, is rewarded with a clerkship in his law office. Denry uses his position to invite himself, his dancing teacher, Miss Ruth Earp (Glynis Johns), and others to a ball given by the countess of Chell (Valerie Hobson). At the ball, Denry accepts a bet and asks the countess to dance. They waltz, and the countess' laugh with him is the talk of the ball. Duncalf fires the audacious young man, but Denry offers to collect the rents of Duncalf's dissatisfied clients for less money and becomes a success. Soon, he's "E.H. Machin – Rent Collector."

After Denry first tries to collect Ruth Earp's rent and then ends up paying it, he takes her on a holiday to the shore. Ruth has become his fianceé, and they're chaperoned by young Nellie Cotterill (Petula Clark). Denry buys a salvaged boat and soon has it making sightseeing cruises to the wreck of a Norwegian ship. When an old salt remarks that sixty pounds in three days is a lot of money for "doin' nothin'," Denry replies that he *did* do something— he "thought of it."

After a tiff with Ruth over her extravagant habits, Denry returns home alone, but with enough money to start up an installment-purchase business called the "Universal Thrift Club" whose motto is "Spend as You Save."

Denry continues to be successful: He becomes a town councillor, the savior of the local football (soccer) team, and the husband of a now-grown-up Nellie. The film ends with Denry fortyish and the new mayor of Bursley.

Ronald Neame, the producer of Guinness' Dickens films, *Great Expectations* and *Oliver Twist*, was *The Card*'s director.

Among Neame's successful directorial touches were Denry preparing for the countess' ball, wiping his hands dry on his mother's washing; the young Denry's satisfied smile as he changes his grades upward; the laugh Denry shares with the countess at the ball; Ruth Earp's none-too-subtle offer of herself to Denry when their eyes lock after he's come to collect her rent; and Denry's mother's scream of awe at the sight of all the hard cash he's earned from his tour boat.

Ronald Neame, born in 1911, was the son of show business parents. Elwin Neame, his father, was a director of British silent films, and Ivy Close, his mother, was a British movie star. Only twelve when his father died in an automobile wreck, Neame helped to support himself and his mother by finding a job as a messenger and call-boy at Elstree Studios.

Neame advanced to the position of assistant cameraman and worked on an early Alfred Hitchcock film, *Blackmail*, in 1929. After dropping out of films to begin his own business as a photographer, Neame returned to studio work when he found freelancing less lucrative than he'd imagined.

Guinness' ambitious "card" discovers the charms of the now-grown-up Nellie (Petula Clark).

Eventually, Neame became a cinematographer on *Drake of England* in 1934. Among the other films he worked on as the cinematographer were *Major Barbara* (1940), *In Which We Serve* (1942), and *Blithe Spirit* (1945). After turning producer for Cineguild's *Great Expectations* (Guinness' first film), Neame directed *Take My Life* (1947) and *The Golden Salamander* (1950) before assuming that role for *The Card* in 1952.

Other notable Neame-directed films include three more with Guinness — *The Horse's Mouth* (1958), *Tunes of Glory* (1960), and *Scrooge* (1970) — as well as *The Prime of Miss Jean Brodie* (1968), and *The Poseidon Adventure* (1972).

John Bryan (1911–1969), who won an Academy Award as the production designer on Guinness' first film, the Ronald Neame-produced *Great Expectations*, was *The Card*'s producer. Bryan also served as producer for the Neame and Guinness collaboration, *The Horse's Mouth*.

The acting in *The Card* is superlative — beginning, of course, with Guinness' Denry Machin. Guinness must carry Denry from a callow youth of approximately eighteen to a respectable burgher of forty. Never does Guinness falter in voice or gesture. As Arthur Knight marvelled in *Saturday Review*, "...Guinness can supply...all from details he has seen and remembered, and so completely that it doesn't seem like acting at all, but more like a man's unconscious revelation of his own personality. As one critic [Tynan] has observed, Guinness can act *mind.*"

The sly smile on Guinness' face reveals more than attention to character, however; it reveals that Guinness is thoroughly enjoying himself. A shy man, Guinness was apparently reveling in the chance to play someone he could admire, and yet who was unlike his own personality in that, to use Tynan's phrase, he was an "extrovert opportunist."

Guinness' nuanced performance is full of too many details to enumerate, but a few can be pointed out:

— Denry's look of instant calculation when he sees Duncalf lose his wallet and decides that honesty, in this case, at least, is the best policy;

— Denry's exasperated snapping out of "Rockefeller!" when Ruth's extravagances finally become too much for him to bear;

— Denry's expression — truly a thing to behold! — when Ruth informs him her late husband died because he "over-taxed his strength";

— and, finally, his ear-to-ear grin of self-satisfaction when he proudly presents the top player he's signed for Bursley's football team.

Glynis Johns (1923–), has rarely been better than she is as Ruth Earp, the dancing teacher with expensive tastes and the voice and looks to induce men to indulge them. At one moment seductive, another calculating, yet another helpless and tearful, Miss Johns' Ruth is a marvelous characterization. She is in every way a match for Guinness. When Guinness and Johns are onscreen together, their synergistic talents and acting skills demand the viewer's attention. Johns' voice, no less distinctive than Joan Greenwood's, is a potent instrument capable of producing a remarkable range of vocal gymnastics. (For her other films, see notes on *The Card* in the Appendix.)

Veronica Turleigh, who plays Denry's gruff but tender-hearted mother, is convincing and affecting as she pretends immunity to her son's growing wealth and success. At every new plateau, she refuses to believe that his good fortune is real or that it can last; she's had too hard a life to convince herself that it all won't be taken away somehow — the way life has of cutting down to size those who take things for granted or get too big for their britches.

Valerie Hobson (1917–), who plays the countess of Chell, appeared in *Kind Hearts and Coronets* in a similar role — that of a proper Edwardian noblewoman of impeccable breeding and behavior. Her aristocratic looks and demeanor also graced *The Bride of Frankenstein* (1935) and *Great Expectations* — a film in which practically all of the major participants, on and off screen, of *The Card* seem to have been involved.

The other actors include Edward Chapman, probably best known to

Americans for his role in H.G. Wells' [*The Shape of*] *Things to Come* (1936); Michael Hordern, whose overnight bag of a face has graced such films as *Khartoum* (1966) and *A Funny Thing Happened on the Way to the Forum* (1966); and Petula Clark, who later became a popular singer of the 1960s and 1970s (her hits included "Downtown."). Among Miss Clark's other films was *Here Come the Huggetts* (1948), *Finian's Rainbow* (1968), and *Goodbye Mr. Chips* (1969).

Reluctantly, Guinness agreed to allow his son Matthew to play the part of Denry as a boy. "They wanted someone who could have been me as a boy, and I had to admit that Matthew would do for the part," Guinness said.

The Card is not especially well remembered today. It won few, if any, awards. At the time, however, it was a huge box office success and carried Guinness yet higher in the eyes of most critics. *The Card's* utterly benign view of Edwardian England (no Lean/Dickens realism here) and its glorification of hard work, thrift, and capitalism have led many to incorrectly remember the film as an Ealing Studios production.

Raymond Durgnat, in *A Mirror for England*, noted *The Card's* novel relationship between the aristocracy and the new entrepreneur class while "the burly, jolly workers look happily on; they're happy because, far from striking, all they care about is the success of their local soccer team, through supporting which the lovably crafty card gains their enthusiastic admiration."

While not a classic, *The Card* is an irresistibly warm, human, and funny film that never takes itself too seriously. It's as if everyone involved were in on the joke and taking his cue from Guinness' relaxed and seemingly effortless performance.

Again, Guinness found himself in an increasingly familiar position: *The Card* was another Guinness comedy hit.

By mid–1952, Guinness found himself telling an interviewer, "I hate ruts of any kind. I want a straight part this time. At the beginning, I did the things that came along because it was a matter of bread and butter. But I am now in an economic position to say I don't want to do this or I don't want to do that."

The money, actually, hardly figured in Guinness' thinking when he considered a role. After all, taxes were taking almost two-thirds of his screen and theatrical income of approximately $50,000 a year. Guinness' income was astonishingly low by Hollywood standards, but by British standards he was doing as well as or better than any other British stage or screen star.

Guinness' international screen star recognition was beginning to be felt by the young actor. He could no longer walk the streets of London unobserved, watching other people for gestures he could put to use in his characterizations of everyday men. "*The Card*," Guinness told Joseph Newman, "has given me away rather more than I like being given away."

The Card/The Promoter was the only film Guinness saw released in 1952. He would have two in 1953: *Malta Story* and *The Captain's Paradise*.

10. *Malta Story* (1953)

"This *Malta Story*, unlike the actual one, does not stir the
senses or send the spirit soaring."
— *The New York Times*

Despite the fact that Guinness was well known among theater
afficionados for his marvlous stage work, his film persona was that of a man
who functioned best in heavy, disguising makeup or as a comedian in entertaining but lightweight roles. This typecasting was frustrating to Guinness,
an actor who'd played Hamlet and many other powerful dramatic roles on the
stage.

So it came to pass, after successfully appearing in a string of smash film
comedies, that Guinness wanted to play a straight part — to be a "regular Joe."
Malta Story gave him the opportunity he'd been looking for, but it turned out
to be a trap. The role of flight lieutenant Peter Ross was one that could have
been played by any young juvenile lead under contract — a fact most critics
noted in their reviews. (When *Kind Hearts and Coronets* was released,
Guinness was quoted as saying he longed to play a straight juvenile — "Well,
almost juvenile.")

So, rather than proving Guinness' ability to handle "straight" roles, the
film did just the opposite. The critics and the moviegoing public clamored for
more Guinness — in period makeup, in multiple roles, or in a sparkling
comedy confection. Give us that Guinness, everyone exclaimed, and let wavy-
haired young men play these faceless young airman roles (Guinness has always
been mystified and annoyed by his "faceless man" reputation, but here it not
only fits his Peter Ross character, it is also well deserved!).

"Clem" wrote *Variety*'s 1953 review when the film opened in London.
"Following the successful *The Cruel Sea*, comes this epic story of the courage
and endurance of the people and defenders of the island of Malta. It [is]
handled in grimly realistic but not over dramatic style. With Alec Guinness
as a star name in the U.S., and a strong factual story, pic should have universal
appeal, and do well in the U.S."

However, "Hift" wrote this review for *Variety* when the film opened in
the United States in 1954: "But effective as it may be — and *Malta Story* has
some highly dramatic moments — this type of war story no longer packs the

big punch. It's like watching a slightly aged film with its characters out [of] relation to present times. And not even this kind of cast can make up for the dating of the product."

Nicolas Monjo, in *Films in Review*, said, "...Despite the miscasting of Alec Guinness in a straight part, an adventitious love story (which ends tragically with Guinness' self-sacrifice on an all-important reconnaissance flight), several unnecessary sub-plots, and a very uninspired performance by Jack Hawkins, *Malta Story* has moments in which the reality and power of honor, valor, and faith are made manifest."

Finally, in *The Commonweal*, Philip T. Hartung begins his review by saying, "The long-awaited serious film made by Alec Guinness proves to be something of a disappointment. It's not that Mr. Guinness can't handle sterner stuff; it's just that *Malta Story* is so diffuse and crowded with characters and heroism that amiable Alec gets lost in the shuffle."

Flight Lieutenant Peter Ross (Guinness) is passing through Malta in 1942, on his way to Egypt. After they land to refuel on Malta, the plane is destroyed in a bombing raid, and Ross is stranded there.

Although he's a photographic reconnaissance pilot now, in civilian life Ross is an archaeologist. Following an air raid, he walks about the island, observing the heroism of the civilian population.

Ross reports to the air officer commanding (Jack Hawkins), who tells him Malta is just fifty-eight miles from Sicily and just above Egypt—and German general Rommel's desert army. Malta is strategic to the effort to destroy Rommel's supply ships by cutting the sea lanes.

On his first recon flight, Ross, ordered to budget his fuel, follows and photographs a train. Given hell for wasting gas, Ross later is told his photos reveal crates full of gliders—to be used to invade Malta. Ross spots a girl he's seen earlier, in an air raid shelter. Her name is Maria (Muriel Pavlow) and she works in the operations room. Ross walks her home and later meets her family, including her mother, Melita (Flora Robson).

Malta is heavily bombed and its radar jammed as a prelude to an expected invasion. When forty-seven new Spitfires arrive, twenty of them are destroyed on the ground by bombs.

In the face of increasingly heavy bombing, Malta hangs on. Ross and Maria, visiting ancient temples, speak of their love for each other.

The commandant gets sixty new Spitfires from an American carrier. Ross leads the "Spits" down, and they rearm and refuel just in time to shoot down a wave of enemy bombers—downing sixty-three in twenty-four hours.

Peter and Maria discuss marriage and their life after the war. When she says she wants six children, he says he'd better get a chair (a professorship) in archaeology to support them!

Hard hit by enemy planes, the oil tanker *Ohio* limps into Malta as the populace turns out to watch. With gasoline available now, the commandant says Rommel's supply ships will be sunk by aircraft and submarines from Malta.

The biggest convoy yet is headed for Rommel's troops. But the British lose it in bad weather. The commandant sends Ross up, telling him to find the convoy and radio its position — knowing he'll be giving away his own position to enemy fighters. As Ross flies his route, Maria, in the operations room, tracks him.

Ross spots the convoy and radios its position. Told to break off, Ross is found by enemy planes. Marie hears his last words and realizes he's been shot down.

As Maria looks longingly out to sea, newspaper headlines announce a great British victory over Rommel at El Alamein.

The range of director Brian Desmond Hurst's work has been called almost bewildering. Born in Ireland in 1900, Hurst's films have run the gamut of genres and styles: from a comedy with music, a Mau Mau drama, and a costume romance. Certainly Hurst's work shows a smooth versatility, but this lack of focus has hindered critical and popular recognition of his best work.

An art student in Paris, he later worked as an assistant director for John Ford in Hollywood until he returned to Britain in 1933 to make two short independent features, *The Tell-Tale Heart* and *Riders to the Sea*.

Ironically, Hurst was the director of 1951's *A Christmas Carol,* a superior version of the oft-filmed Dickens tale that was head and shoulders above the limp Ronald Neame version set to forgettable music and starring Guinness and Albert Finney. (See notes on *Malta Story* in the Appendix for Hurst's other films.)

Hurst does okay by his actors, but the film needs a traffic cop more than it does a director. The actors get away with a bit too much stiff-upper-lipping, and Guinness could have used a firmer hand and more guidance. Guinness is an expert at plumbing the hidden depths of the characters he inhabits, but Airman Ross seems to have no hidden depths to explore. Consequently, Guinness is really left to do nothing — Ross' character changes little, if at all, from the film's beginning to its ending.

As the "juvenile" lead, Guinness gets to woo the beautiful — if strangely distant — Muriel Pavlow and even exchange a screen kiss or two. But he clearly looks uncomfortable in the confines of his role and, perhaps, eager to get back into more familiar territory (as he did in the delicious *The Captain's Paradise,* his next movie).

Jack Hawkins, who played the air officer commanding, was making the first of four film appearances with Guinness, the others being in *The Prisoner* (1955), *The Bridge on the River Kwai* (1957), and *Lawrence of Arabia* (1962).

Hawkins (1910–1973) became a major international star — partly on the strength of his domineering personality, and partly due to his magnificent and easily recognizable voice. Unfortunately, after a life saving operation in 1966 which removed his voice box, his lines had to be dubbed, and his film appearances were limited to minor roles until his death in 1973. (For a listing of Hawkins' films, see notes on *The Bridge on the River Kwai* in the Appendix.)

The 122-square-mile Republic of Malta consists of five islands with a combined land area smaller than Philadelphia, and is strategically situated just ninety-seven kilometers (approximately sixty miles) south of the southeastern tip of Sicily. As mentioned several times in the film, Malta has been occupied by the Phoenicians, the Greeks, the Carthaginians, the Romans, the French (under Napoleon), and finally, the British.

British rule was confirmed by the Treaty of Paris in 1814, and the British were still there during World War II. Despite heavy bombing attacks by Italian and German bombers, the island held out and was never invaded. Given its strategic location, Malta served as a fixed-locale aircraft carrier and submarine base from which to attack the Axis forces in the Mediterranean.

During the siege, King George awarded Malta the "George Cross." The bravery on view in the film was real. The filmmakers made skillful use of existing black-and-white battle footage. The battle of Malta, however, was not widely known to American audiences, and the film did not capture the large and attentive audiences that *The Cruel Sea* did. Certainly there was still a market for WWII films in 1953, but *Malta Story* was too British to appeal to large numbers of Americans, even given the marquee appeal of Guinness' name.

Guinness would reappear in uniform — and again in the Mediterranean — in *The Captain's Paradise*, a pleasant farce about a steamer captain with wives in two ports. *This* was the Guinness that American (and many British) audiences wanted to see.

11. *The Captain's Paradise* (1953)

big•a•my: the act of entering into a ceremonial marriage
with one person while still legally married to another
— *Webster's New Collegiate Dictionary*

The Captain's Paradise (hereafter referred to as *Paradise*) is a witty, saucy, and charming film. Whatever risqué value its subject matter had in 1953 is gone, but the film remains a gentle poke at the institution of marriage.

Paradise followed *Malta Story* and was Guinness' fourth hit comedy in a row; at the time, it was one of the highest-grossing foreign films ever to play the United States.

The movie shows Guinness at the top of his form and, again, clearly relishing the chance the film gave him to reveal new talents. Not only did Guinness act in *Paradise*, he also danced — and the mambo, no less!

The critical reaction was quite good. Bosley Crowther's review in the *New York Times* is typical: "*Paradise* . . . is one of the merriest and archest of the mischievous Guinness films. And the performance of Mr. Guinness in it is strictly and flatly nonpareil."

Paradise begins with a disclaimer that the following story is no more than a fairy tale. Then we meet Captain Henry St. James (Guinness), the captain of a steamer plying the Mediterranean waters between Gibralter and Ceuta on the Spanish Moroccan coast, who is before a firing squad and just minutes from execution.

St. James' story and how he came to find himself in such a predicament are related to Lawrence St. James, Henry's uncle, by First Officer Ricco (Charles Goldner) — an admirer of Henry's genius for lifestyle.

In the wild port city of Ceuta, Henry comes ashore in a sporty white suit and a rakish hat. On his way to his modern apartment, Henry stops to buy flowers for Nita (Yvonne De Carlo), his wife. Nita is a torrid Moroccan woman who is not allowed to cook or clean; Henry — or "Jeemy," as Nita knows him — doesn't want his wife's hands made coarse and red by housework. For Nita, he buys silky undergarments and bikinis. They eat out every night and then go nightclub-hopping, drinking and dancing the night away. Nita and "Jimmy" have been married two years.

Halfway across the Mediterranean, Henry flips Nita's picture over to reveal...Maud's picture. Maud (Celia Johnson) is Henry's wife of three years who lives in a cottage in Gibralter. She's a domestic homebody who cooks dumplings for him, darns his socks, and generally takes care of all his housekeeping needs. On shore in Gibralter, a dignified Henry wears his uniform stiffly and enjoys having a "bowl" before his bedtime at ten P.M. sharp. Henry and Maud have separate beds. To underscore the ho-hum nature of their marriage, Henry gives Maud a sewing machine for a gift. And instead of bikinis, he buys Maud aprons.

Slowly, this paradise begins unraveling. Henry inadvertently gives Maud a bikini meant for Nita and Nita an apron. Each gets the wrong message: Maud wants to go to Ceuta and sunbathe; Nita wants to cook and stay home.

"Jeemy" patiently explains to Nita that he wants a soft, feminine woman, not one with housework-induced muscles. Meanwhile, Maud travels to Ceuta without Henry's knowledge and meets Nita while both women are shopping. Chatting, they discover that their two sea captain husbands have much in common. Before they can exchange the name of the ship each commands, the women are surrounded by police, who arrest Maud on a flimsy charge (Henry, hiding nearby, paid the police to get him out of his quandry).

Maud, having tasted the pleasures of Ceuta, is restless and wants more from life. Ever resourceful, Henry quickly sees that Maud is tied down securely again by having to raise several children. But once the children are sent off to school in England, things begin to deteriorate. Maud begins letting her hair down; after all, she's thirty-seven, and life is passing her by. When Henry refuses to change his stick-in-the-mud ways, Maud coldly promises never to ask him to dance again. Instead, she begins to go out with her "cousin," dancing her dissatisfactions away.

Nita, meanwhile, cooks up a surprise for her Jeemy — dumplings, one of Maud's special dishes. Henry is so aghast at this lapse into unwanted domesticity that he flees their apartment in horror. Nita finds him and makes a promise of her own. She'll never cook for him again.

When engine problems force Henry's ship to return to Ceuta, he walks in on Nita and her lover, a local taxi driver for whom she can cook and be a housewife. Though Henry walks out, Nita and her taxi-driver lover quarrel, and she shoots and kills him (off screen).

A gallant Henry takes the blame for the killing and faces the firing squad. When the order is given to fire, the men shoot their officer. Henry gives them money and walks away a free man, ready again to seek a comfortable arrangement or two. Again, the framing message reminds us that what we saw was a fairy tale that couldn't really happen...could it?

As Murray Schumack points out in *The Face on the Cutting Room Floor*, the American censor insisted that the framing device be added to make sure no one in the audience decided to follow Henry's lead and become a bigamist.

Actually, in the American version of the film, Henry is not really married to Nita at all—instead, it's implied that she's his girlfriend. (Apparently, a married man may have a girlfriend, but not a second wife!)

Anthony Kimmins (1901-1963) was the producer/director of *Paradise*. Kimmins, who served in the Second World War as a naval officer, was a playwright who'd worked as an actor and a scriptwriter before he was put in charge (in 1937) of a team which made the immensely popular George Formby films at pre-Balcon Ealing. George Formby, unknown in this country, was a northern England music hall star famous for his wide grin and ukelele playing. Anthony Kimmins wrote two scripts for the Formby series and directed five of the films.

Like that of Fred McLeod Wilcox, the director of *Forbidden Planet*, Kimmins' fine direction is a surprise coming from a man with the reputation of a journeyman director. His solidly crafted films may not have been artistic, but they always were commercial.

Kimmins' direction seemed to agree with Guinness and the other actors. He gets first-rate performances from everyone, not just the ever-reliable Guinness. Celia Johnson as Maud and Charles Goldner as Chief Officer Ricco give especially nuanced performances which add dimension to the film. Johnson, best known for her role as Laura in the Noel Coward/David Lean film *Brief Encounter* (1945), is marvelous as Guinness' frustrated wife in Gibralter. Her transformation from homebody to free spirit is wonderfully done.

Kimmins and cinematographer Ted Scaife effortlessly give the Gibralter and Ceuta scenes distinct atmospheres. They're aided, of course, by Guinness' shrewd performance as the dull and dependable Henry St. James, and then as the suave and debonair Jimmy St. James.

An unexpected bonus in the film is Guinness' rendition of the mambo. Yvonne De Carlo convinced Kimmins to work Guinness into one of her inevitable dance sequences. During a week of dance rehearsals, De Carlo taught the apprehensive Guinness how to mambo with the best of them.

Guinness, much to his own surprise, quickly learned the steps. Practicing constantly, he would go off into a corner during story conferences and continue gyrating his hips to a mambo beat. Guinness happily told reporters, "This opens up vast new horizons which I never even dreamed existed."

Yvonne De Carlo, proud of her fast-learning pupil, said, "Alec may look more like the one-step type, but he has a real flair for this sort of thing." A pleased Guinness responded, "I rather think she's right."

Paradise's script, by Alec Coppel and Nicholas Phipps, has a great many witty lines and situations. It makes the most of its chance to contrast the (alleged) two sides of woman—the happy housewife and the "mate of the tiger." What authors Coppel and Phipps are demonstrating, in a lighthearted manner, is that the same woman who is the mate of the tiger may also be a housewife, or anything else she wants to be; the choice is not necessarily between one or the other.

Guinness' two-sided character, after all, is proof of that. Ever the champion of role playing, Guinness' Henry St. James would be a match for Walter Mitty in the fantasy department. Indeed, had Thurber's short story not provided a star vehicle for Danny Kaye, that frustrated, henpecked mouse of a man who escapes into his vivid daydreams would have been a perfect role for the middle-aged Guinness. As it is, Henry faces a firing squad with bravado, dances a mean mambo with one of the sexiest women in North Africa, and is captain of a ship, albeit a small one, plying the waters of the Mediterranean. Henry St. James has gone Walter Mitty one better: He *lives* his fantasies.

> Then, with that faint, fleeting smile playing around his lips, he faced the firing squad; erect and motionless, proud and disdainful, Walter Mitty the Undefeated, inscrutable to the last.
> — "The Secret Life of Walter Mitty" by James Thurber.

Though he is nominally the same man, Guinness is again playing two characters. Guinness' powers of observation and mimicry enable him to slip effortlessly from the staid and stuffy Henry St. James to the suave and sophisticated Jimmy St. James, bon vivant extraordinaire.

Captain St. James is a genius and hero to his first officer. Ricco wants a passport so he can emulate his captain's lifestyle and have a wife in every port. Finally, his own life (lives?) unraveling, Captain St. James gives in, and Ricco is handed the torch to carry on (he becomes the ship's captain when Henry is arrested).

12. *Father Brown / The Detective* (1954)

"The more you learn about other people, the more you
understand yourself. The more you learn about
yourself, the more you understand other people."
— Father Brown to Flambeau in *Father Brown*.

Father Brown (hereafter *FB*) was Alec Guinness' only film of 1954 and his
second with director Robert Hamer. *FB* was an unusual film, to say the least.
Although set in the present — well, 1954 — it was strangely old-fashioned.
Guinness, as G. K. Chesterton's priest-sleuth, seemed to be in a time warp.
The film, like Chesterton's stories, ignored the changing of social customs and
the annoyances that come with progress. The world in the film is a nicer, saner
place; what little violence there is is very low-key, sex seems not to have reared
its head at all, and people discourse intelligently and wittily.

While Hamer's *Kind Hearts and Coronets* fairly boiled with passions hidden beneath the surface — envy, lust, and violent desires — the world of Father
Brown seems a stranger to such human failings. It is this lack of passion that
gives *FB* such a detached air of complacency. In this nicer world, crooks are
easily convinced to give back what they've taken. It is, presumably, this aspect
of the picture that convinced Guinness to take the role of Father Brown — that
and a chance to work with director Hamer a second time.

As Guinness told an interviewer, "I worked a great deal with the late
Robert Hamer, whom I loved very dearly. . . . I think Hamer also had a very
concentrated ear."

If *FB* is no *Kind Hearts and Coronets,* it is also a better film than Guinness' other two with Hamer — *To Paris With Love* (1955) and *The Scapegoat*
(1959).

Films in Review noted that "Robert Hamer, who directed, allows Guinness to bumble a bit more than is necessary, but he otherwise capably moves
about a capable cast, which includes Joan Greenwood and Ernest Thesiger."

"Myro's" review in *Variety* said, *"Father Brown . . .* is distinguished mainly by the excellent casting of the title role. Alec Guinness is a natural for the
role, and his name on the marquee will help sell many tickets."

Gavin Lambert, in *Sight and Sound,* wrote that Hamer's "talent is the
most civilised one in British films, and this is the first time since *Kind Hearts*

Guinness as the twinkly Father Brown and Joan Greenwood as Lady Warren.

and Coronets that he has been given an opportunity to display its truest qualities."

Bosley Crowther's *New York Times* review stated, "Alec Guinness adds another cordial character to the long list of those he has contrived with his new British film, *The Detective*. . . . He is a quizzical, good-natured old fuddy in a leisurely, good-humored film."

As a petty crook named Bert Parkinson (Sidney James) flees unseen, police see a man in a priest's robes kneeling before an open safe. At the police station, the priest, one Father Ignatius Brown, is not taken seriously when he says he was *returning* the money. A detective searches through his "clergyman impersonator" files, until he learns it's Father Brown and tells the sergeant to call the local monsignor. The monsignor is not pleased by Father Brown's behavior—it's clear this is not the first time something like this has happened—and reprimands him. Bert Parkinson apologizes to Father Brown and agrees to take a job as a chauffeur and go straight.

After his sermon, Father Brown admires a cross in his church once owned by St. Augustus. When Lady Warren (Joan Greenwood) calls it valuable, he says it's priceless, not valuable. When Father Brown walks her to her car, her new chauffeur is an abashed Bert.

The bishop (Cecil Parker) tells Father Brown that his cross of St. Augustus is to be sent to a conference in Rome. Hearing that the master thief Flambeau has pledged to steal it, Father Brown immediately points out three ways Flambeau could steal the cross and offers a plan to protect it. The police turn down his plan and say they will do the safeguarding.

Against the bishop's orders, Father Brown wraps the cross in newspaper to see it safely to the conference himself. Aboard the train he shares his compartment with a number of suspicious-looking characters and a fellow priest (really Flambeau in disguise). Father Brown and Flambeau trade scriptural passages.

On a rough channel crossing, a big, bluff man (Bernard Lee) who was also on the train introduces himself to Father Brown as a "motor car salesman." Father Brown mistrusts him and tells his suspicions to Flambeau.

On the train in France, the car salesman joins Father Brown and Flambeau, who are getting along well by now. In Paris, the car salesman is still shadowing Father Brown. To escape him and another man, Flambeau (Peter Finch) and Father Brown leap on a bus. The car salesman, really Inspector Valentine, and a French cop, Inspector Dubois (Gerard Oury), set out in pursuit.

In the catacombs, Father Brown tells Flambeau he knows who he is; at a cafe, Flambeau ordered a ham sandwich . . . on Friday. Father Brown informs Flambeau that he wants his soul, not his body. They struggle over the package, and Father Brown uses a wrestling hold to secure Flambeau. Seemingly caught, Flambeau tells Father Brown he steals things, not to sell them, but so he can enjoy his art treasures privately. Then Flambeau easily reverses Father Brown's hold and ties him up. Flambeau makes his escape with the cross.

The bishop tells a saddened Father Brown that the archbishop will have to deal with him. Father Brown tells the bishop he gambled with the cross for Flambeau's soul and lost—this time. The bishop gives him two weeks to recover the stolen cross.

Lady Warren shows Father Brown a rare chess set, giving him an idea: He'll set a trap for Flambeau, using the chess set, a "Cellini masterpiece," as bait by auctioning it off.

Inspector Valentine is at the auction to keep his eye on Father Brown and Lady Warren while they in turn look for Flambeau, who's disguised as an elderly auction house employee. After some spirited bidding, an Indian maharajah buys the chess set and immediately gives it back to Lady Warren. Realizing the old employee is Flambeau, Father Brown trips him up, but he escapes with the chess set.

Flambeau appears at Lady Warren's house to repeat the maharajah's generous gesture. But Father Brown wants everything returned, including his cross. Bert appears to warn them that the police are on their way. Father Brown, still after Flambeau's soul, helps him to escape, telling him he spotted him as soon as he noticed that the "old man" had young hands. Father Brown also tells Flambeau that he, a priest, lives more in the "real" world than does

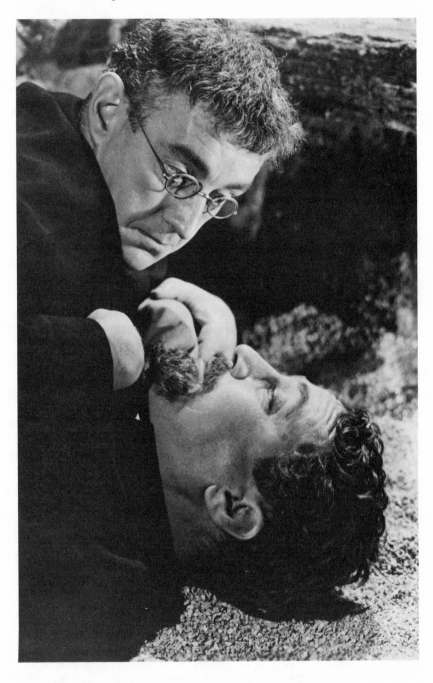

Father Brown (Guinness) gets the upper hand—momentarily—against the devious
Flambeau (Peter Finch).

the gentleman thief. Flambeau, after explaining that he was born into the wrong era and world, bargains with Father Brown: Whatever Father Brown can find, he can have back. Father Brown just nods, having pocketed Flambeau's distinctive cigarette case. Later, the wily priest learns that *flambeau* means torch in French.

Another rough channel crossing finds Father Brown at the National Archives in Paris. The curator, the Vicomte de Verdigris (Ernest Thesiger), is an old man who cannot climb the ladders in the archives. Atop a ladder, Father Brown finds the book he's looking for, but drops his glasses. Coming down the ladder, he steps on the Vicomte's pince-nez glasses.

Now blind as a bat, Father Brown is directed to an optician. The police are waiting for him when he regains his vision. They take him to the river, where he tells them the next man he will speak to will be Flambeau. Father Brown then speaks to an American "Left Bank" painter, who is immediately arrested by Valentine and Dubois. Father Brown mutters "Poor chap," to himself as they lead him away.

When a waiter brings him a bottle of wine at a cafe, it says FLEURENCY on the label, and Father Brown learns there is a grape festival going on there. One step ahead of the pursuing Valentine and Dubois, Father Brown reaches the festival.

After sleeping in a haystack, Father Brown makes his way to the chateau, where he is turned away at the door. Undaunted, he puts on a scarf to look like a peasant woman and rides in on the back of a wagon.

Inside, he finds a hidden passageway in the kitchen just as Flambeau is coming out. Flambeau takes him to his private inner sanctum where his art collection is kept. Father Brown admits stealing the cigarette case and using it to trace Flambeau. Flambeau shows him the Latin family motto: "The best things are always free." Father Brown calls his room a prison, not a paradise, and notes that Flambeau is a rather small sinner after all.

Flambeau offers to give back the cross — to keep his promise — but Father Brown refuses his offer unless he gives back everything. Just then the police arrive and Flambeau makes good his escape.

Father Brown, his cross recovered, is forgiven. The Louvre is showing the art treasures recovered from Flambeau's private collection. Flambeau, walking about the exhibit, sees others enjoying what had been for his eyes alone. He comes to understand Father Brown better when he sees two young boys enjoying one of the paintings he had all to himself.

Father Brown is in his pulpit when Flambeau comes in, crosses himself, and takes a seat beside Lady Warren. Father Brown sees Flambeau in his congregation and smiles — he has won another soul.

Actually, *Father Brown* is somewhat similar to an earlier Robert Hamer film, *The Spider and the Fly* (1949). In that film, set in Paris in 1913, a safecracker matches wits with an inspector of the Sûreté, but finds that World

War I brings things into a new perspective. Hamer admired such "typically French" suave amorality. *The Long Memory* (1952) was another Hamer-directed film that pitted a lone individual against the strictures of the prevailing society around him. All three films present a battle of wits between two evenly matched protagonists. Perhaps the despair beneath the surface humor in these films reflects the despair Hamer must have felt to lose himself in the bottle and then to take his own life. (For more on Hamer, see the chapter on *Kind Hearts and Coronets*.)

The "Father Brown" stories were written between 1911 and 1935, and present a world where nothing ever changes and a rotund little priest is a match for any thief—especially if the man's immortal soul is at stake. Although Guinness is probably the best actor to play Father Brown, there have been several others of note. Walter Connolly played the role in a 1934 Hollywood "programmer" called *Father Brown Detective*. The tubby detective is a favorite in West Germany, where Heinz Ruhmann played the role in two features in the 1960s. Josef Meinrad was Chesterton's sleuthing priest in a 1969 television series. Perhaps the best-known actor, apart from Guinness, to play the part was Kenneth More, who played Father Brown in a 1973 television series widely seen in the United States.

Hamer's script was written by Hamer and Thelma Schnee and is faithful to G. K. Chesterton's original works while still having the flavor of a typical Hamer script: witty and intelligent dialogue between the at-odds protagonists. Hamer and Schnee wisely kept as much of Chesterton's language and phrasing as they could, and the result is a literate and charming combination of English detective story and French Catholic novel.

If the script and resulting film have a major flaw, it's that Flambeau's conversion seems almost too easy, too pat and arbitrary. As Douglas McVey notes in his review in *Films and Filming*, the film never makes plausible "the relation of priestly faith and perseverance to the wrongdoer's spiritual isolation...this moral encounter is never properly realized, and the later sequences decline into merely a series of graceful philosophical asides on conversation...."

Peter Finch, who played Flambeau, was born William Mitchell in 1916. Although British, he gained his early fame in Australia, and only became internationally famous when he returned to England. Until he won a posthumous Academy Award for Best Actor for playing Howard Beal, the slightly nutty newscaster in *Network*, he was probably best known in America for playing the Sheriff of Nottingham in Disney's 1951 filming of *Robin Hood*. He died in 1977. (See notes on *FB* in the Appendix for Finch's other films.)

There is a great deal of humor in *Father Brown*, ranging from subtle wordplay to broad slapstick actions. Much of the humor is of the "appreciative nod" sort, although neither Hamer nor Guinness is afraid to let Father Brown reach for a broader response. For instance, there is Guinness as Father Brown being "attacked" by one of his parishioners, a pickpocket teaching the aging priest how to defend himself (this scene was to be taken to the heights of supreme hilarity when Blake Edwards had Inspector Clousseau, the late Peter Sellers, regularly attacked by his houseboy Kato).

When the bidding on Lady Warren's chess set gets serious, the Texas millionaire, asked if his bid in in pounds, replies, "No, them other things"—meaning guineas. At the end of the auction, a Ming vase is announced, then a crash is heard, and the auctioneer just sighs and goes on to the next item up for bid.

Other touches of humor: Father Brown throws an innocent American Left Bank painter to the police instead of Flambeau. Inspector Valentine, riding in the back of a French police van, is shown a "French postcard" by a prostitute—a postcard of the Eiffel Tower! And in one of the many cafes Father Brown frequents in the movie, a young couple stops cuddling and kissing under the bland stare of the somewhat disapproving and prudish priest.

Guinness does quite well by Father Brown, but it's not one of his best performances. He mugs just a bit too much and seems too conscious of his performance. Still, as Tynan noted, Guinness is quite adept at "iceberg characters, nine-tenths concealed, whose fascination lies not in how they look but in how their minds work; people with secrets to hide from their fellow men, people like poets and killers and saints, Clare and Crippen and Father Brown."

While I find it difficult to disagree with Tynan's analysis, I do wish Guinness hadn't tucked his chin into his chest quite so much; this mannerism, while calculated, grates after a while.

Interviewer Derek Hill told Guinness that some of his "more habitual expressions, such as the sly twinkle first shown by the parson in *Kind Hearts and Coronets*...seemed in danger of becoming mannerisms." Naturally, Guinness was not pleased to hear this: "Had I seen the review, I would have reacted strongly. What do you mean by 'mannerisms'? If you're implying that I deliberately exploit certain tricks of style, I deny it most vigorously. On the other hand, every actor has his own limitations of expression, and as one plays more and more parts a repetition of some of one's mannerisms is bound to occur."

Father Brown/The Detective was not a triumph for either Guinness or Hamer, but it was not a failure either. Certainly it is a better film than *The Malta Story* and was light-years ahead of his next film, the Hamer-directed *To Paris With Love*.

So, for Guinness it was back to Paris again with Hamer—and this time, the result would not be so cheerful or so entertaining.

13. *To Paris with Love* (1955)

Following on the heels of *Father Brown* and preceding *The Prisoner*, *To Paris with Love* would have been overshadowed even had it been a *good* picture. As it is, this short, rather limp and unimaginative film is among Alec Guinness' more forgettable ones. Guinness, like any actor who has appeared in over forty films, has his share of flawed masterpieces (*Kwai*), near misses (*The Ladykillers*), and outright stinkers (*Raise the Titanic*). *To Paris with Love* (hereafter just *Paris*) is no stinker, but it's one of Guinness' lesser efforts.

While the picture has its moments — Guinness delivering some understated but effective "takes"; Guinness with his suspenders embarrassingly caught in his hotel door, and the like — it too often meanders between slapstick, bedroom farce, and bittersweet romance. The performances are as lackluster as the script and direction, with only Guinness making any sort of impression at all.

That *Paris* misses by so much is all the more disappointing for having as its director Robert Hamer, who had just performed that task for Guinness in the subtle and vastly superior *Father Brown*.

The reviews were largely negative. In the *New York Times*, Bosley Crowther, who, noting that he usually has only nice things to say about Guinness' films, writes, ". . . the performance of Mr. Guinness in [*Paris*] is the most pallid and listless he has ever turned in. These are hard words to utter about Mr. Guinness and one of his films, but the lack of his customary vigor is so evident that the words cannot be withheld. Except for occasional moments, when Mr. Guinness takes sudden spurts at farce. . . he walks through his slight romantic pretense as though he were either ill or bored."

Critic Gavin Lambert dismissed *Paris* by saying, "The general impression is somehow too aimless, too muted." In *Halliwell's Film Guide*, Leslie Halliwell, writing from a modern perspective, says *Paris* is "Thin, disappointing taradiddle which is short but seems long."

In his after-the-fact review, Leonard Maltin, in his capsule comment in *TV Movies*, casts a lonely affirmative vote for the film: "Fair comedy of rich father taking son to Paris to learn facts of life. Guinness stands out in average British cast."

A British father and son, Sir Edgar (Guinness) and Jon Fraser (Vernon

Gray), forty-two and twenty respectively, are on their way to Paris in search of romance for each other. The Frasers, quite wealthy, live in a castle in Aberdeen, Scotland, and Sir Edgar breeds racehorses in France. Sir Edgar and Jon go to visit old friends they've not seen for a while—Leon de Colville, his son Victor, and his daughter Suzanne. On their way, they pick up and are introduced to a young girl who falls from the back of a motorscooter operated by her boyfriend, Georges.

Sir Edgar tells Leon that he's worried about Jon's romantic life at the same time that Jon is telling the same thing to Victor. Both Frenchmen vow to help their English guests; Leon is to set up Jon with the girl from the motorscooter, Lisette, (Odile Versois) and Victor will set up Sir Edgar with Sylvia, an "older" woman.

Contrary to the plan(s), not only are Sir Edgar and Lisette thrown together, but also Jon and Sylvia. Sir Edgar and Lisette, after nightclubbing, are sprayed with water by a street cleaner. Drenched, they return to Sir Edgar's hotel suite. (One of the hotel staff remarks, "With his money, you think he could afford a dry girl.") Lisette falls asleep on the couch, where Jon finds her the next morning. Everything was innocent, of course.

Sir Edgar buys Lisette expensive earrings, giving them to her in a nightclub, his face reflecting his tender feelings for her. However, Lisette's boyfriend Georges shows up and naturally thinks she's going out with Jon, not Sir Edgar. As Jon and Georges scuffle, Sir Edgar tries to separate them and gets his suspenders caught in the hotel door ("English!" sniffs one of the hotel staff).

The two odd couples go to Leon's country place for the weekend. Sir Edgar gets himself up a tree retrieving a badminton shuttlecock and has to slump on the porch swing, feeling his age. Jon and Sylvia realize they were both "wrong" about each other; she tells him she loves him. Meanwhile, Lisette tells Sir Edgar that their "romance" was a beautiful dream and kisses him goodbye.

At the end, when Georges picks up Lisette on his motorscooter, father and son, leaving Paris, confess that they tried to set each other up. They're both a little wiser, and Sir Edgar sings a rueful song as they drive away.

Although, at forty-two, Sir Edgar was close to Guinness' age when he made the film, the Scottish horsebreeder sure looks a lot older! Even Jon looks a lot older than his supposed age of twenty. (Given the clothing and hairstyles in 1950s color films, *everyone* by today's standards looks older and swallowed up by the time's voluminous fashions.)

Paris, while slowly paced and poorly executed, is not a bad movie; it is just not a very good one. Its very dated flavor, while detracting from the filmmakers' original intentions, gives the film a satisfyingly quaint air today. In just thirty years, *Paris* has become a relic—amusing, witty at times, and entertaining, but a relic nonetheless.

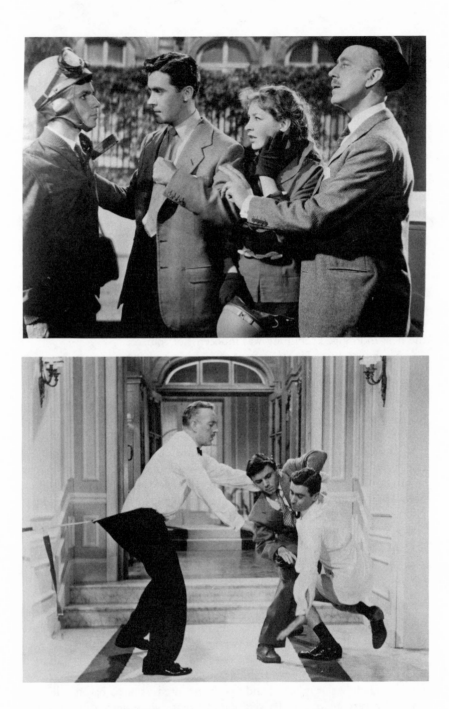

Top: Georges (Claude Romain), Jon (Vernon Gray), Lisette (Odile Versois) and Sir Edgar (Guinness) have an argument concerning a minor traffic incident. *Bottom*: As Jon and Georges scuffle, Sir Edgar gets his suspenders caught in a hotel door trying to separate the two.

Guinness gives a subtle, reasoned performance that stands out all the more for the general lackluster performances of the other actors. A quick glance at the actors' credits reveals no readily recognizable names.

Guinness' performance, then, is the best thing about *Paris*. Even to a lesser film, Guinness brought all the skill and craft he could muster as an actor. But, if nothing else, *Paris* proves that even a great actor has difficulty surmounting an inferior script and lackadaisical direction.

Guinness was now slightly more than halfway through his golden decade of critical and financial successes. Since the so-so *Paris* fell between more typical Guinness hits, it had little negative impact on his reputation—after all, not even Guinness can bat a 1.000 all the time.

14. *The Prisoner* (1955)

> "Any confession I may be said to have made while in prison
> will be a lie...or a sign of human weakness."
> —the cardinal, *The Prisoner*.

Bosley Crowther's review of *The Prisoner* in the *New York Times* said, "The great skill and charm of Alec Guinness in light and comical roles have obstructed somewhat the general knowledge that he is a dramatic actor of rare competence—a fact not too clearly demonstrated in his performance heretofore on the screen. But with the opening of his new film...this range of Mr. Guinness' talent is brilliantly and movingly revealed....This is a film which will make you shiver—and think."

Variety's "Myro" wrote that "The flawless performance by Guinness is matched by a superb portrayal by Jack Hawkins as the public prosecutor. But both of these stars find their equal in Wilfred Lawson's interpretation of the jailer. It is one of the rich performances of the screen."

A *Newsweek* review said, "Guinness gives a magnificent performance, as the bald-headed, ascetic, dedicated man of the church, and Hawkins is not far behind him as the troubled witch doctor of a new regime."

Henry Hart's long piece in *Films in Review* observed that "some Catholics think *The Prisoner* is anti-clerical. Some Protestants think it is Catholic propaganda. Some Jews think it is Christian propaganda."

A strong film, *The Prisoner* was perceived in many, often contradictory, ways. Ireland's Cinema Censorship Board banned the film for being "subtly pro–Communist," while a review committee at the Cannes Film Festival, which included a Soviet delegate, judged the film "anti–Communist," and it was withdrawn. The Venice Film Festival rejected *The Prisoner* for being "politically dangerous."

While the Italian Film Board labeled the picture "anti–Catholic," England's Cardinal Griffin gave permission for Guinness to quote his statement that "this is a film which every devout Roman Catholic should see."

After the stuff and nonsense of *To Paris With Love*, Alec Guinness had found a film role worthy of his subtle talents. The cardinal is a *thinking* man's part; it requires an intelligent actor of the caliber of Guinness to pull it off successfully. The film was not, however, Guinness' first playing of the role;

he had originated the part in Bridget Boland's West End play, and his director there, Peter Glenville, also directed the film version.

The role of the stoic man of the church was perfect for Guinness' technique. As Kenneth Tynan, Guinness' most insightful interpreter, notes, "A big performance from him must concentrate on the interior, not the exterior of the character he is playing. His territory is the man within. Hence, whether he likes it or not (and I suspect he does), his true métier will always be eccentrics—men reserved, blinkered, shut off from the rest of us; and, comically or tragically, obsessed. Within such minority men there is a hidden glee, an inward...glow. Inside their souls, Guinness is at ease."

The Prisoner begins during a Roman Catholic mass in an unnamed eastern European state. As the cardinal (Guinness) says the mass, he is passed a note which reads: POLICE ARE HERE TO ARREST YOU. The cardinal is charged with "treason" to the state. While his faith is slightly mocked by the arraigning officers, they are also somewhat sympathetic to his plight.

The cardinal is turned over to the state's most proficient brainwasher, a man who, with the cardinal himself, had been a hero of the Resistance during the war. Since the war, the cardinal has become a "national monument" and the leaders of the new regime want that monument defaced—by the cardinal himself; he must "confess" to his crimes against the state.

The cardinal wears the slightly smug expression of a man who *knows* he will not break. Still, the interrogator (Jack Hawkins) asks the cardinal to sign the confession, admitting that he intends to use no drugs or torture if he does not. The interrogator reveals that he was once a doctor, then a lawyer, and now a skilled and successful inquisitor. The cardinal is kept in isolation, and constantly fatigued, to break down his physical and mental reserves. He is bombarded by complicated and skillfully worded questions, and when he is returned to his cell, he finds he cannot turn off the overhead light.

The cardinal readily converses with the interrogator, telling him of childhood discontents. These sessions take place in the interrogator's office—a cold room with mirrored walls, tiles in the pattern of a chess board, and circles in circles on the floor. As if to underline the circumstances, the interrogator doodles a man caught in a spider's web while he questions the cardinal.

Since the general is dissatisfied with the interrogator's apparent lack of success, he confronts the cardinal with direct "evidence," which includes a map showing arms depots and viaducts to be seized and defended. The cardinal points out that, as a good resistance fighter, he would blow up the viaducts, not fortify and defend them. A damning record is played, but the cardinal notes that the fluctuating sound levels make it clear his treasonous words are the result of transferring a heavily edited tape onto the record.

After the general's flimsy attempt to frame the cardinal fails, the inquisitor and his prisoner share a laugh over the obviousness of the attempt—and thereby draw closer together.

Outside, in the city, shots are fired at police patrols and fighting breaks

With the help of the jailer (Wilfred Lawson, left) and the warder (Ronald Lewis), the cardinal (Guinness) is checked into the prison where he will undergo his interrogation.

out. A policeman shoots dead a boy found chalking words of resistance on a wall.

Inside, the interrogator confronts the cardinal with the "body" of his mother. Then the shaken prelate discovers that she's drugged, not dead. The interrogator threatens to send her to the "research" ward, the priest still refuses to sign a confession. The interrogator says the priest's lack of humanity disgusts him. The cardinal is left alone to confront his inner turmoil.

The jailer brings a tray of food after the cardinal has been denied meals for several days; then, just five minutes later—or is it?—he brings another tray. The light can now be switched off, but when the prisoner turns it off, he finds he can no longer bear to be without its constant and reassuring glare.

The interrogator finally discovers that the cardinal's weakness is not pride but humility. He is ashamed of his humble origins and of his mother—a whore. The interrogator feeds the broken man's guilt and suggests he confess to betraying his comrades in the resistance to the Nazis.

At the public trial the interrogator, acting as the public prosecutor, circles the cardinal like a hungry cat circling a mouse. The cardinal shocks everyone by freely confessing to his "crimes" against his old comrades and his parishioners. Shattered by his effort, the cardinal collapses, grasping onto the interrogator's robes as the man throws up his arms in victory, as if to say to the people, "There's your hero, your cardinal—guilty, guilty!"

Believing himself "unbreakable," the cardinal (Guinness) readily converses with the interrogator (Jack Hawkins).

Although headlines trumpet the cardinal's guilt and portray the interrogator as a hero, the interrogator is dismayed by what he's wrought.

The jailer brings the cardinal his last breakfast and muses with him about his fate. Suddenly, the interrogator appears with an order — the cardinal is to be set free. There will be no execution, no martyr created by imprisonment. The cardinal is shattered; death was to be his release. The interrogator pulls out a pistol and offers to kill the priest. Grateful, the cardinal considers the offer, then refuses it. It is impossible for him to escape his fate by agreeing to his own murder. "So, the laugh's on me," the interrogator marvels. "You go out of here stronger than when you came in!"

No convert either to the cardinal's faith or to his politics, the interrogator nonetheless turns to the general in exasperation and shame. "I want to be relieved of my duties," he says. "I am too fastidious to be trusted. I cannot half serve a cause."

Told to wait in the outer office, the interrogator paces back and forth while the sun streams through the windows — trapping him in the shadows thrown on the floor by the bars. He's in a prison, too — the whole country is a prison — and he knows it.

The cardinal is released to face a huge and stony-faced crowd. They part for his passing as he slowly strides out to face his destiny.

Bridget Boland adapted the script for the film from her successful London stage version. Both the play and the film are thinly disguised versions of the arrest and imprisonment of Hungary's Cardinal Mindszenty, jailed for six years on vague charges by the Communists. The cardinal was released a broken man after he'd confessed to treason, black-market dealings, and spying.

The stage version, also directed by Peter Glenville and starring Alec Guinness, was an essentially static, two-character production. However, Miss Boland's screenplay makes several modest attempts to take the film out of the prison and into the streets of the capital city. One convention of the 1950s she includes to open the film up is the inevitable "romantic interest," provided by a young couple (the warder and the girl), trying to come to terms with themselves and with what the young man does—he works in the prison. The film's climactic trial scene was also an addition not in the original play.

Like that of many stage adaptations, *The Prisoner's* dialogue is finely tuned and cerebral. The characters discuss, and are motivated by, large philosophical and moral issues. (See notes on *The Prisoner* in the Appendix for Bridget Boland's other films.)

Peter Glenville was born into a theatrical family in Hampstead, England, in 1913. His grandmother had been a member of Dublin's famous Abbey Theatre, and his parents, Shaun Glenville and Dorothy Ward, were both actors. Although he was educated at Oxford, there was never any doubt Glenville was destined for the theater.

Glenville appeared in the Roy William Neil–directed *His Brother's Keeper* in 1939, and his brief film acting career strongly colored his outlook concerning actors and acting in the films he later directed.

Guinness played an ant scientist, among other things, in the April 1952 production of *Under the Sycamore Tree* directed by Peter Glenville at the Aldwych Theatre. The experience was apparently rewarding for both director and actor.

The Prisoner was Glenville's first directing assignment in films. His transition from the stage to cinema was made easier, however, by his having directed Guinness in the well-received West End stage production. In an article, Glenville noted, "*The Prisoner* I did as a play and then a film. I just try to forget what I did with the play because the technique is so different that one has to utilize. Of course, one's fundamental knowledge of the subject and the fact that one has worked with the characters and the subject on the stage helps one in a way of saving time in some circumstances; but in putting it on the screen from the theatre one has to forget what one did in the theatre."

As a former actor, Glenville has little trouble pulling outstanding performances from his talented cast. What *is* remarkable, especially in a first screen effort, is the technical level Glenville's direction achieves. Faced with an essentially stagebound play, Glenville pulls out all the stops to overcome the inherent limitations. He uses a plethora of camera angles and unusual framing devices—shooting over shoulders, into rooms, and past objects in the foreground. Several times, at the climax of a scene, Glenville's camera, mounted on a crane, sweeps from eye level to high overhead, looking down on the protagonists like some all-seeing eye. Glenville makes judicious use of close-ups and extreme close-ups. To counter the confines of the interior sets, Glenville often puts the camera in motion, circling fluidly around the inquisitor and his human fly. All in all, it is an impressive film debut for a novice director. The film's very success would bind Guinness to Glenville in the future for less successful productions. (Notes on *The Prisoner* in the Appendix list some of Glenville's other films.)

Jack Hawkins, Guinness' Communist antagonist in *The Prisoner*, had this to say about working with him: "He's an undercover man — he's unfair to other actors because you know he's doing something really first rate but you can't say what or how."

Kenneth Tynan wrote that he suspected "that Guinness, an actor who specialises in men with obsessions, might be able to emphasise this religious melancholy more tellingly than anyone else. . . ." As Tynan suggests, Guinness' Cardinal, like Colonel Nicholson in *The Bridge on the River Kwai*, is not larger-than-life heroic, but ordinary-man heroic. Just as Colonel Nicholson collapses under the crushing weight of isolation and conditioning, so too does the cardinal collapse.

Much has been made of the fact that Guinness converted to Roman Catholicism within a year and a half of *The Prisoner*'s release. While it is nobody's business but Guinness', it is hard *not* to imagine that his playing of the beleaguered priest profoundly influenced the actor. After all, his art is the art of imitation and of mastering the soul of the man within any character he plays. It would seem odd, then, for Guinness not to be affected by such a long and intimate relationship with the inner life of a man who has found sanctuary within the service of God.

15. *The Ladykillers* (1955)

> *The Ladykillers* "owes its status as a classic to the inspired tightness with which story and imagery are organized to make...an entrancing portrait of a Victorian civilization lingering on, tottering, into the postwar world..."
> —Charles Barr, *Ealing Studios*

The Ladykillers is a late Ealing comedy. The virtues and values stressed in the classic Ealing pictures were being shouldered aside as Britain began to shed its imperialistic burdens and, belatedly, recognized that it was no longer a world power. In this sense, *The Ladykillers*, with its paean to a glorious past that was gone forever, was also a farewell to a style of motion picture-making that was being devalued in the cynical and hectic postwar world. Community was about to give way to individualism, shared values to personal desires, and cooperation to confrontation.

Bosley Crowther, in the *New York Times*, wrote, "Mr. Rose's nimble writing and Alexander Mackendrick's directing skill have managed to assure *The Ladykillers* of a distinct and fetching comic quality...."

Penelope Houston, in *Sight and Sound*, said, "*The Ladykillers* (Rank) emerges as the most consistently ruthless comic fantasy produced by a British studio since *Kind Hearts and Coronets*."

However, Carol Rittgers' review in *Film Culture* did not find the film quite so amusing: "The distinguished comic talents of director Alexander Mackendrick and writer William Rose have misfired in both the conception and execution of *The Ladykillers*."

Screenplay author William Rose, born in 1918, was an American writer who got into British films in 1948 by coauthoring *Once a Jolly Swagman*. After penning *The Gift Horse* in 1951, Rose wrote the much-praised *Genevieve* in 1953. Rose brought an outsider's appreciation of British life and society to his script for *Genevieve*, a lighthearted look at the increasingly frustrating race in which two couples engage in on the way back from the Brighton antique car rally. Seen today, one wonders why the film was such a huge commercial and critical success (I've always found the frustrating predicaments the two couples encounter in the movie to be annoying and off-putting rather than amusing). Still, Gavin Lambert was moved to call *Genevieve* "One of the best things to have happened in British films over the last five years."

Ealing and Rose got together in 1954 when Rose wrote the script for *The Maggie* (also directed by Mackendrick) for the studio. Both partners seemed to profit by the match, and Rose went on to write four more films for the studio: *Touch and Go* (1955), *The Ladykillers* (1955), *Man in the Sky* (1957), and *Davy* (1957).

After his Ealing stint, Rose returned to America to script *It's a Mad, Mad, Mad, Mad World* (1963) and *Guess Who's Coming to Dinner?* (1967) for Stanley Kramer. Rose's other American films include *The Russians are Coming, the Russians are Coming* (1966), *The Flim Flam Man* (1967), and *The Secret of Santa Vittoria* (1969).

The Ladykillers begins by introducing us to Mrs. Louisa Alexandra Wilberforce (Katie Johnson), who starts a baby in its carriage howling and kicking, on her way to tell the police that her "friend's" saucer sighting was all a dream (the friend could be *her*).

This eccentric but apparently harmless old lady is followed by a shadowy figure who turns out to be Professor Marcus (Guinness), a master criminal in search of a few rooms. He rents rooms in Mrs. Wilberforce's off-kilter house and plots a crime, all the while pretending to lead his friends in musical rehearsals. Mrs. Wilberforce is to be part of the gang's plan.

Mrs. Wilberforce offers the men tea and asks for their help in giving her parrot medicine. The bird escapes, causing chaos and slapstick situations. After the professor returns the parrot, the gang pulls the heist. Part of the plan has Mrs. Wilberforce arriving at the train station to receive the "incoming" trunk. On her way home she gets into a scene with a fruit seller, a horse, several bystanders, and the police. Everyone ends up at the police station, and the police wind up bringing her trunk home.

The professor and the others are leaving when the cello case in which they have hidden the loot opens and some of the money falls out. The gang is forced into staying at Mrs. Wilberforce's, and soon her friends come to call. A paper reveals the robbery and she *knows*. After they all gather around the harmonium to sing "Silver Threads Among the Gold," the ladies leave, and Mrs. Wilberforce remonstrates the professor. The gang admits its guilt and pretends to be taking the money back while really plotting how to do in Mrs. Wilberforce. When the major (Cecil Parker) draws the short match, he agrees to the deed, but quickly tries to escape out the upstairs window instead. Louis (Herbert Lom) corners him and, off screen, pushes him off the roof. They dispose of the major's body at the railroad yard.

This time Harry (Peter Sellers) draws the short match. Sent to do in Mrs. Wilberforce, he takes the loot and tries to make off with it. One Round (Danny Green) thinks the sleeping Mrs. Wilberforce is dead. He wanted no one to harm the old lady, so he kills Harry. After Professor Marcus and Louis dispose of Harry's body, an aroused One Round tries to shoot them. Unfortunately for him, he's forgotten to take the safety off; Louis shoots him instead. Now, in the mist and fog, after they've disposed of One Round, the professor and Louis play a cat-and-mouse game, which the professor wins... until a yard signal knocks him into an empty boxcar.

When Mrs. Wilberforce goes to the police, they don't believe her story — just as the professor told her they wouldn't. She leaves the police station, the money hers, vowing to buy a new umbrella. She walks off — an imperturbable, unstoppable force of nature — as the soundtrack plays "The Last Rose of Summer."

William Rose wrote *Ladykillers*' original story after he had dreamed it one night. When Rose showed his story to Mackendrick, the director immediately agreed to make it into a film and showed Guinness the story. Before Rose had finished the script, the actor had agreed to portray Professor Marcus.

Mackendrick, who said of Guinness that he "becomes a much more real person in makeup," also revealed that the actor seized on the role because it offered him yet another opportunity for "making himself invisible."

Rose's script retains an eerie, dreamlike quality that reflects its origins in the subconscious: Mrs. Wilberforce's off-center house (One Round calls her "Mrs. Lopsided"); her penchant for creating chaos and uproar everywhere she goes; the frustration of the gang members as they seek to recapture her elusive parrot; and the way the bodies of the dead gang members are dispatched amid clouds of vapor and steam.

Near the film's end, Professor Marcus' and Louis' increasingly frantic efforts to dispose of the old lady have a nightmarishly stunted feel about them. Both men come to view Mrs. Wilberforce as immortal — a mad joke being played upon them by hostile forces.

It is inevitable, I suppose, that *The Ladykillers* and Mackendrick's direction should be compared to *Kind Hearts* and Hamer's masterful helming of that particular black comedy. In reality, apart from sharing the talents of Alec Guinness and the fact that both films are dark and surreal comedies celebrating the genteel traditions of an England no longer to be found, the two films have little in common. For one thing, Mackendrick's style is not Hamer's; Mackendrick's eye is on the society, not the individual. Mrs. Wilberforce is symbolic of an England that died with its sons in the trenches of World War I, an England where innocence and invincibility go hand in hand, an England whose basic social unit is the neighborhood — safe and secure under the watchful eyes of the local police superintendent.

Mrs. Wilberforce's world, prewar and precynicism, is a well-preserved theme park — "Victorian World," with hot and cold running water and water closets. This nostalgic look back was Alexander Mackendrick's farewell to his adopted country. After *The Ladykillers*, Mackendrick left England for New York and the job of directing *The Sweet Smell of Success* (1956), a blistering black seriocomedy about the previously little-known world of public relations men and how they operate.

As Professor Marcus (Guinness, *left*) looks uneasily on, One Round (Danny Green, *right*) and Harry (Peter Sellers) try to convince Mrs. Wilberforce (Katie Johnson) that they're going to return the stolen money.

As soon as *Success* was completed, Hecht-Hill-Lancaster, the production company, fired Mackendrick. And two years later, a disagreement with producer Harold Hecht led to Mackendrick's removal as director of H-H-L's *The Devil's Disciple*.

Similarly, Mackendrick was to be the director of *The Guns of Navarone* (1960) until he suffered a back injury on location during the first week of shooting, which forced him to retire from the production. Finally, after six years between pictures, Mackendrick directed *Sammy Going South* (United States: *A Boy Ten Feet Tall*) for his old boss from Ealing, Sir Michael Balcon.

While *The Ladykillers* does not hold up as well as the earlier Ealing Studios comedies, its acting is flawless and largely due to its distinguished cast of solid professionals. Guinness, of course, turns in another of his craftily thought-out performances as Professor Marcus, a sinister criminal genius who *may* have spent some time in the booby hatch.

After a rare excursion into serious drama in *The Prisoner*, Guinness was back in the sort of role his audiences expected and all but demanded. His performance as Professor Marcus is a mosaic of considered touches: his little bit of swaying, almost imperceptibly, to the music the first time he plays the phonograph record; the way he smokes his cigarettes by holding them between his middle and ring finger, an affected "continental" posturing; and the way he get his scarf caught beneath Mrs. Wilberforce's feet when he's trying to make a discreet exit with the stolen money. Not everyone found his performance perfect, however. Said Carol Rittgers, "It is a little disturbing to note how much. . . humor. . . is derived from the outrageous maneuvers of his red-lipped, vampire-toothed mobile mouth."

Katie Johnson (1878–1957), who plays the eccentric and unstoppable Mrs. Wilberforce, entered show business in 1896 when she was eighteen. She began by acting in repertory theater and then toured abroad, finally playing on Broadway in *Escape Me Never*. She briefly retired in 1940, but her later career in films and on television made her a star in her old age. She appeared in *Jeannie* (1941) and *How to Murder a Rich Uncle* (1956) as well as many other films. *The Ladykillers*, made just two years before her death, capped her long career and brought her the British Film Academy Award as the best actress of 1955.

Peter Sellers (1925–1980), a graduate of the *Goon Show*, plays Harry, an overstuffed "Teddy Boy" lug of a man. It was a small part, but one with room for a good actor to make it important to the film. At the time he landed the role of Harry, Sellers was a sort of British Mel Blanc and Rich Little rolled into one. He dubbed voices for many films, providing not only uncannily accurate dialects (American, Indian, French) but also vocal special effects. Sellers was so successful with his vocal gymnastics that he despaired of getting flesh-and-blood acting roles.

Originally sent by his agent to read for the more important role of One Round (which he lost to veteran character actor Danny Green), Sellers so impressed director Mackendrick that he was signed, several weeks later, for the smaller part of Harry, a go-fer and aide to Guinness' Professor Marcus.

Sellers made the most of his opportunity, but most of his performance was lopped from the film in the editing.

Sellers, young and decidedly chubby, was somewhat in awe of Guinness' talent and reputation. A prodigious chameleon himself, the young mimic-actor sometimes imitated Guinness after working with him on *The Ladykillers*. Somewhat bemused to have a protégé, Guinness liked Sellers and recommended his work to a London critic. When Guinness was knighted in 1959, Sellers was invited to the gala celebration afterward.

Sellers finally stopped being a second-rate Guinness and became a first-rate Peter Sellers. Still, his first major success, *The Mouse That Roared* (1959), had Sellers playing a very Guinnesslike three roles, including the Duchess of Grand Fenwick.

Playing Chance in *Being There* (1979) got Sellers an Academy Award nomination for Best Actor and finally solidified his reputation as an actor. Sellers died the following year of a massive heart attack. (For more on his films, see notes on *The Ladykillers* in the Appendix.)

The part of Louis was played by Herbert Lom (1917–). Among Lom's other films were *War and Peace* (1956), *Mysterious Island* (1961), *Phantom of the Opera* (1962), *Asylum* (1972), *The Pink Panther Strikes Again* (1977), *The Dead Zone* (1983), and many others. Equally skilled at villainy or softer roles, Lom is a Czech actor whose real name is Herbert Charles Angelo Kuchacevich ze Schluderpacheru (whew!). He's best known as Sellers' foil in the *Pink Panther* films.

The Ladykillers was the penultimate Ealing Studios comedy; it was followed by a Benny Hill vehicle, *Who Done It?*, an unimaginative and somewhat dreary film scripted by T.E.B. Clarke. The Ealing era was ending. Guinness would make one last film for them in 1957, the Charles Frend–directed *Barnacle Bill* (*All at Sea* — United States title), a film made at non–Ealing facilities.

A popular film still run quite often on television, *The Ladykillers* represents the beginning of the end of Guinness' almost-exclusive playing of comedy roles. Those parts would not disappear from his future, but they would begin to alternate with more "serious" straight dramatic roles.

16. *The Swan* (1956)

"A part of every woman is the little girl who dreamt about
the day someone would find her and love her and give
her a ring. A diamond is forever."
—advertisement

"When love is challenged it grows more sure
Uniting two hearts with bonds that endure,
Fulfilling the promise pledged with gold,
To cherish forever...To Have and to Hold."
—To Have and To Hold Romances

The Swan was made immediately prior to Grace Kelly's wedding to
Prince Rainier III of Monaco and released to cash in on the hoopla surrounding
that royal event.

Alec Guinness had made Hollywood films before, but *The Swan* was his
first made-in-America production. Although some cynics insist Guinness
made it for the money, he avers that was not so—unlike a later production,
A Majority of One.

If MGM thought they were grooming Guinness for eventual Hollywood-
type stardom (a farfetched idea, I must admit), then they were not counting
on Guinness' integrity as an actor. His was an actor's performance, not a star's.
Rather than playing to the audience, Guinness' Crown Prince Albert, though
likeable in a gentlemanly way, never condescends to manipulating the
audience's sympathies. Instead, Guinness played him straight: droll, stiff, and
a bit self-preoccupied. In other words, as every bit the "fish" Albert calls
himself in front of his mother, the queen. Guinness has his moments—as
when he goes to bed wearing a mustache binder or attempts to play with the
boys' paddle game.

The film was made twice before, in 1925 and in 1930, when Lillian Gish
made it her first talkie. Guinness' role was played by Adolphe Menjou in 1925
and by Rod La Rocque in 1930.

Not much remembered today except as Grace Kelly's last picture, *The
Swan* was a predictable hit in 1956. Perfectly timed, the film satisfied some
of the curiosity that royalty buffs had about Kelly's real-life marriage to a real
prince—and in Eastman Color and CinemaScope as well!

The reviews were almost unanimously good. *Variety's* "Brog" began his thusly: "Delightful make-believe of Ferenc Molnar's venerable *The Swan* makes for a welcome change of pace from the strong dramatics featured in so many current and upcoming pictures. There's a natural link to international interest in the coming royal wedding of its femme star, Grace Kelly. The entertainment worth indicates its chances would be good in any case."

John McCarten, in *The New Yorker*, wrote, "A good many attractive people have been assembled to enact *The Swan* on film, but despite all their amiable efforts, the thing has no more substance than the collected works of Igor Cassini."

In the *New York Times*, Bosley Crowther called *The Swan* "...A slender and charming fable, as soft as a summer breeze, about a princess in a Ruritanian country that was a myth before World War I...Miss Kelly and her present entourage are entirely enclosed in a vacuum of Old World make-believe, wherein they play out their whisp of regal whimsey with humor and quaint gentility. Far away, both in time and social status, are the world and reality."

According to *Catholic World*'s reviewer, "*The Swan* is so leisurely and well-mannered that it seems at times like a movie made around 1930 or so when Hollywood was indulging madly in all sorts of mythical kingdom pieces about languid princesses, disdainful royal suitors, and romantic poets" and brings to life "ever so briefly, a wonderful, remote, fairyland existence that is gone forever."

Central Europe, 1910. Princess Beatrix (Jessie Royce Landis), receives a telegram which says Crown Prince Albert (Guinness) is coming for a four-day visit. The purpose of his visit, presumably, is to examine Princess Alexandra (Grace Kelly), Beatrix's daughter, as a possible royal bride.

Dr. Nicholas Agi (Louis Jourdan), the tutor to Beatrix's young sons, is briefly seen with his two charges (Van Dyke Parks and Christopher Cook). When Alexandra appears, she's reminded that Albert has turned down practically every eligible princess in Europe. One of the first guests to arrive is Beatrix's brother Karl (Brian Aherne), now a monk called Father Hyacinth.

Prince Albert's train arrives in the middle of the night. In the morning, Beatrix and her pixilated sister Symphorosa (Estelle Winwood) wait in vain for Prince Albert to arise. Breakfast becomes lunch, then dinner—and still no Albert. Just as they decide they *must* eat, Albert is announced. Again they wait—only to learn he's had a huge "breakfast."

Albert, after meeting Dr. Agi and the boys, greets his cousins, including Alexandra. Awkwardly attempting to curtsey, Alexandra bumps Albert under the chin with the top of her head. Beatrix sends everyone to bed so Albert and Alexandra can be alone. Awkwardly, the two attempt small talk and end up exchanging facts. They go out onto the terrace, but still make "Trivial Pursuit" chat. Sensing a losing battle, Albert retires.

A frustrated Alexandra tells her mother of her failure. Beatrix tells her

Guinness as the jaded Prince Albert attempts to woo Grace Kelly as the young princess—a role Miss Kelly would play for real when she married Prince Rainier of Monaco.

not to worry—the prince will be there three more days. To spark Albert's manly instincts, Beatrix has Alexandra invite Dr. Agi to the ball to be held that night.

Albert appears at the ball decked out in his most dashing uniform. Albert asks Beatrix to dance as Alexandra and Dr. Agi speak about the stars. Finally, Alexandra asks Dr. Agi to dance, and the two whirl about in each other's arms, seemingly falling in love as we watch; this is not what Beatrix intended!

Acting as if to cut in on Alexandra and the tutor, Albert goes over to the orchestra and asks to play the bass viol. Alexandra, seeing this, stops dancing and leaves the ball. Getting into a carriage, she's joined by Dr. Agi. He speaks to her about a "mirage": He sees her as a perhaps untouchable vision.

Although the ball continues, the prince must leave. Dr. Agi tells Alexandra something has changed between them and he speaks of his attraction to her. Belatedly, she tells him he was invited merely to help make her the wife of the crown prince. She says she's ashamed of her ploy.

Crushed, the tutor grows distant and formal. She *wants* to be a queen, Alexandra tells him, and she begs his forgiveness; he refuses.

Later, both Dr. Agi and Alexandra gulp down their first glass of wine. Feeling the effects of the alcohol, the tutor takes a sharp tone with Albert. Beatrix gets Albert to take her to her room as Karl stays and speaks to both

Dr. Agi and Alexandra. After Karl's intervention, the two mellow toward each other. Karl leaves them alone, and Alexandra learns that the tutor's name is Nicholas. They speak longingly of love.

When Albert returns to say goodnight, he says Nicholas was insolent and forced unwanted attentions on Alexandra. When Alexandra passionately kisses Nicholas, Albert says, "That's another matter. Quite another matter. In that case, I apologize." He leaves.

The next morning, Albert's mother, Queen Maria Dominika (Agnes Moorehead) arrives—two hours early. Beatrix is certain all is lost. Albert appears and tells his mother he was a "fish" and Alexandra an "icicle" when they met. He mentions the tutor and how Nicholas' love led to romantic complications. Albert adds that he insulted Nicholas because he was. . .jealous.

When the Queen asks to see Alexandra, the two boys say the tutor is leaving. Meanwhile, Alexandra sneaks into Nicholas' room and says she's going with him. To her surprise, she's rejected: Nicholas says she expressed contempt for him in her kiss.

Albert listens to Alexandra's wrath, then tells her to marry her Nicholas—if she loves him. He even gives her his blessing. Alexandra is confused and unsure of what she wants.

As Alexandra watches Nicholas leave, Albert tells her she must be "a swan." On the lake and untouchable, a swan is lovely: silent, white, majestic. On shore, however, a swan becomes a silly goose: waddling, ungainly, and honking. Alexandra, he says, must be a swan and stay on the lake, a cool creature of grace and beauty.

Albert touches her hand and she says, "Take me in, Albert." Alexandra has accepted her station in life. She is, after all, a swan.

John Dighton, born in 1909, who wrote the screenplay, was the coauthor of two of Guinness' most fondly remembered films: *Kind Hearts and Coronets* and *The Man in the White Suit*. His best scripts, it seems, were collaborations with other writers, often writer-directors like Mackendrick.

Oddly enough, *The Swan*, in its central thesis that a princess' dalliance among commoners is to be allowed for as long as she does her duty and the "right thing" in the end, is not that far removed from *Roman Holiday*, a 1953 film that won Oscars for Audrey Hepburn and writers Ian McLellan Hunter and John Dighton.

Director Charles Vidor (no relation to director King Vidor) was born in Budapest on July 27, 1900. After World War I, Vidor started doing odd jobs at Berlin's UFA Studio, moving up the ladder quickly, as first an assistant cutter, then a chief cutter, and finally an assistant director.

Emigrating to New York, Vidor sang in a Wagnerian opera company as a bass-baritone. In Hollywood he worked in pictures in a series of minor jobs until, in 1929, he directed a short drama, *The Bridge*, paid for out of his own savings. Impressed by Vidor's imagination and talent, MGM signed him as a director, and his first Hollywood picture was the 1933 production *The Mask of Fu Manchu*.

Charles Vidor died in 1959. (See notes on *The Swan* in the Appendix for more about Vidor's films.)

If Guinness thought that making a Hollywood picture meant filming it in Hollywood, then he was in for a surprise. Dore Schary, head of production at MGM, was able to secure the fabulous Biltmore estate (built by George W. Vanderbilt in 1895) in Asheville, North Carolina, for all of the exterior and many of the interior scenes. Never before photographed, the estate in the Great Smoky Mountains was invaded for several weeks by a horde of over 100 cast members and technicians. (It was later used as a set for other films, including the 1979 *Being There*, starring Peter Sellers.)

Bronislau Kaper wrote the film's musical score and is responsible for "The Swan Waltz," played when Alexandra and Nicholas waltz into love. Polish-born Kaper arrived in Hollywood in 1936 and immediately began writing songs for MGM. He was not allowed to write a score until four years later, but he then made up for lost time by scoring as many as a dozen films a year.

As Kaper notes in Tony Thomas' *Music For The Movies*, "I love this period. Right at the start of the film you see the legend, '1910 — somewhere in middle Europe.' I get terribly attached to some films and this was one. There were tears in my eyes at the end, and I knew I was going to write good music. The story was delicate and stylish and elegant, with Grace Kelly as the princess, beautiful but cool, Alec Guinness as the prince to whom she is betrothed, and Louis Jourdan as the tutor who falls in love with her. The end scene is one of the most delightful I've ever scored: Guinness is talking to Kelly and telling her why she is like a swan, as Jourdan, still in love with her and knowing she feels something for him, leaves the palace forever. There was a beautiful sadness to it. The Molnar story had a 'once upon a time' quality — almost a swan song for a bygone era."

Grace Kelly was making her last appearance in a film (although *High Society*, filmed earlier, would be released after *The Swan*). Famous for her "iceberg" beauty, she quickly became a major star. She had made only a hand-ful of films, however, when she retired to become Princess Grace of Monaco. She was a particular favorite of Alfred Hitchcock's, and when Hitch made *North By Northwest* and *Marnie*, both with icy blondes at their centers, it was obvious he missed Kelly — his first choice for both roles.

Grace Kelly made only eleven films in all: *Fourteen Hours* (1951), *High Noon* (1952), *Mogambo* (1953), *Dial M for Murder* (1954), *Rear Window* (1954), *The Country Girl* (Academy Award, 1954), *Green Fire* (1954), *The Bridges at Toko-Ri* (1954), *To Catch a Thief* (1955), *The Swan* (1956), and *High Society* (1956). Although there was speculation that she would return to film for the right role, she never did. Princess Grace died in Monaco at the age of fifty-two on September 14, 1982, after suffering a cerebral hemorrhage.

Other notables in the cast included Estelle Winwood, who appeared with

Guinness in *Murder by Death*. Robert Coote, who died of a heart attack in November 1982 at the age of 73, played Guinness' resourceful Captain Wunderlich. A fine character actor, Coote also appeared with Guinness in *The Horse's Mouth*.

Brian Aherne, born in England in 1902, made his first comic screen appearance in *The Swan*, playing Father Hyacinth. When the queen suddenly appears, two hours early, Aherne rushes madly down a corridor, pulling his monkish robes on over his bloomers and yelling at the astonished butler (Leo G. Carroll), "Now you know" (what monks wear under their robes).

If Guinness intended more to come of his quick Hollywood flirtation, he did not let it show. Exiting Hollywood immediately after filming was completed on *The Swan*, Guinness returned to Britain to star in Peter Glenville's stage production of *Hotel Paradiso*.

17. *Barnacle Bill/All at Sea* (1957)

> "I won't be satisfied until everything is piershape and
> Blackpool fashion. I want this to be a happy pier
> because a happy pier is an efficient pier."
> — Captain Ambrose in *Barnacle Bill*.

Barnacle Bill is yet another fine Guinness/Ealing comedy. It is not very much appreciated, however, by most British film scholars, especially those who've written books about Ealing Studios. George Perry, in *Forever Ealing*, calls *Barnacle Bill* a "sad reminder of the former greatness of Ealing."

In *Ealing Studios*, a fine account of this most British of British studios, Charles Barr writes, "This is the weird end to [T.E.B.] Clarke's sequence of comedies: *Barnacle Bill*, made in 1957 at the tail-end of Ealing's existence, and a dismal failure at every level except that of logic."

Writing about *Barnacle Bill* in his book, *Alec Guinness, A Celebration*, John Russell Taylor argues, "...It was already too late in Guinness' career...to produce such lame nonsense."

However, the usually tough Leslie Halliwell had this to say in *Halliwell's Film Guide*: "Quite an amusing comedy which had the misfortune to come at the tag-end of the Ealing classics and so seemed too mild and predictable."

I'll stand beside Halliwell on the merits of *Barnacle Bill*. Because it comes late in the Ealing series of comedies — it's the penultimate Ealing comedy, *Davy* being the last — the film is hammered into a niche it doesn't deserve. Maybe Ealing had lost its way and was stumbling toward oblivion, but *Barnacle Bill* is a genuinely funny film.

Part of the problem, I suspect, is that *Barnacle Bill* echoes too many of the successful Ealing comedies of the past for those critics who find it lacking; several compare the film to *Passport to Pimlico*. They also find Guinness' playing of his six ancestors too close to the eight roles he essayed in that classic of classics, *Kind Hearts and Coronets*, and overlook the fact that the film otherwise bears no resemblance to its exalted ancestor.

Barnacle Bill is pretty much at the end of the Ealing line, that studio's last gasp attempt to recapture its former greatness. But it *does* work and is a fitting tribute to the long line of Ealing comedies that brought — and, through television late shows and film society revivals, continue to bring — so much enjoyment and entertainment to so many.

Captain William Horatio Ambrose (Alec Guinness), an ex-naval officer, is awarded a medal at Lloyd's of London. Afterwards, he meets a reporter at a bar and tells him about his many seafaring ancestors, beginning with a prehistoric man. But Ambrose confesses his secret—while still a cadet he discovered that he suffered from seasickness. He tells the reporter that he was soon being used as a guinea pig in naval seasickness tests and that his malady made a normal naval career impossible.

Both tipsy, Ambrose and the reporter enter Ambrose's bank, where he asks for glasses. As bank personnel realize who he is, they gather round as he begins his tale—the one the reporter's paper paid him £5000 for.

As the tale begins, the film flashes back to show Ambrose approaching an amusement pier in Sandcastle, a seaside resort town, testing the condition of the pier's planking. He tells two employees that he's the new owner and asks to meet the crew. Meanwhile, he wanders into a rude escape artist's act and is singled out to tie the man up. This he does so well the poor man can't escape; the audience laughs at his predicament while Ambrose meets his men and tells them he'll run things navy style.

When First Officer Figg (Victor Maddern) quits, Ambrose gives Tommy (Percy Herbert) his job. Tommy shows Ambrose gambling machines the town council had outlawed and Ambrose orders them returned to operation. Sandcastle's mayor, Mr. Crowley (Maurice Denham), shows up to welcome him.

Ambrose decides to live on the pier (in the fun house) as troubles mount up: Endless rain means no customers, and the police haul away the gambling machines. At the police station, Ambrose convinces the chief the machines represent a game of skill, not chance. Mrs. Arabella Barrington (Irene Browne), who owns a row of bathing huts on the beach and who is on the all-powerful council, shows up to make sure the police acted on her complaint about the machines.

The disgruntled escape artist walks out, and angry teenagers decide to start ripping out the seats in retaliation. Ambrose joins them and tells them he'll turn the room into a dance hall. The kids fix the place up and it reopens with a live band playing. Ambrose jitterbugs with a pony-tailed young lady and is having a marvelous time until the police superintendent shows up to stop the proceedings—Ambrose has no music and dancing license and Mrs. Barrington again reported him. His application for a license is rejected, as is his application to open a bar.

Ambrose has several aquariums full of exotic fish dumped back into the sea and, as he's shaving in the fun house distoring mirror, several excited anglers pull in the just-released specimens.

Although Ambrose paid the mayor £5000 for the pier, the council is planning on seizing it under eminent domain, paying him £2800 for it, and constructing a marine center. Mrs. Barrington's bathing huts will have to go, too. Ambrose spots her crying on the beach and invites her on board the pier to be comforted. She explains about the huts and he offers her space on the pier. As they drink rum-fortified tea, she breaks into tears at his gallant suggestion—and tells him what's planned for his pier.

Slightly drunk, she suggests a "holiday camp" on the pier. This makes Ambrose think of a stationary liner—it would never rock or even move. But there's always the council. Suddenly, he realizes he couldn't "sink his ship" if it *were* a ship—the *Arabella*.

At the Department of Shipping, Ambrose is told he needs plans of the *Arabella* if he's to have his registry accepted. Realizing England won't register his pier as a ship, he goes to the Libermarnian embassy and has his "ship" registered under that country's flag. The pier is converted, and Mrs. Barrington's beach huts become ocean liner cabins, complete with portholes. She christens the pier the *Arabella* and the Libermarnian flag is raised.

The mayor and several council members arrive to tell Ambrose of their purchase; he tells *them* the *Arabella* is now a ship, not a pier, and registered with Lloyd's. Nonplussed, they stalk off.

The pier is now the R.M.S. (Really Motionless Ship) *Arabella* and open for "cruises." Liquor is duty-free since they're at sea, so to speak. The council returns; this time they want Ambrose to pay £247 a day for "port duty." Ambrose simply "casts off" by removing the physical link to the beach and foils the council again.

The mayor plans to have the harbor dredged, removing the pier/ship's safety factor. But the council is split—some members are now making money from the tourists who come to gawk at the *Arabella*. The mayor meets with Figg and asks him to pull the pier down with his dredger.

Mrs. Barrington, informed of Ambrose's seasickness, tells him putting cotton balls in his ears and wearing a tight corset will cure him of his malady. Suddenly, they spot the dredger approaching on radar and see it begin to assault the pier's supporting timbers. Ambrose orders a boarding party but says he can't lead them. The ghosts of his ancestors appear...and turn their backs on him! With new resolve he says, "Gentlemen, I am about to engage the enemy."

Ambrose, Tommy, and several others get into individual paddle boats for their assault. The cotton stuffing works, and Ambrose leads the charge as his ancestors watch approvingly on the radar. Ambrose boards the invader and, after the mayor and the others have been herded into the cabin, uses the dredger's claw-shovel to lift it up and dump it into the sea. The ghostly Ambroses dance a jig as Ambrose's men take his four prisoners on board the *Arabella*.

But the dredger has weakened some supports, and a part of the pier collapses into the sea and begins floating away. Ambrose rides it into the distance, refusing a tow—no salvage on *his* ship. At dawn, Ambrose drifts ashore in France and is proclaimed a hero.

His tale over, Ambrose, the reporter, and the bank employees all stagger drunkenly from the bank as a bemused policeman watches.

The film critics of the time found *Barnacle Bill* much more enjoyable and worthwhile than did the Ealing historians. Bosley Crowther's review in the *New York Times* observed that T.E.B. Clarke's script was not his best. Still, he added, "Even a minor achievement from the team of Guinness and Clarke is worth anyone's time and custom, and this one certainly is. [Guinness] is consistently amusing, in his highly civilized farcical way. This may not be Mr. Guinness' funniest, but it will do until a funnier comes along."

In *Films in Review*, however, Harold Ormesby Clark opined that [Clarke's] "present farce about a British naval officer who gets seasick, leaves the navy, and buys an amusement pier, is far from funny," and called the film's basic situation "unbelievable."

James Morgan's *Sight and Sound* review said, "The beginning is at once charming and comic (the opening, with the—intentionally—nauseating, billowing credit titles and the investiture at Lloyds is rich with promise); the end is a full-scale Will Hay knockabout denouement. The film's strength, though, is Alec Guinness, who plays his own six ancestors with the sense of the picturesque he showed in *Kind Hearts and Coronets*."

In *Variety*, "Rich" wrote, "The combination of Clarke and Alec Guinness in *All at Sea* promised more than has been actually fulfilled. Guinness' name will undoubtedly draw plenty of film patrons. They will be rewarded with amiable light entertainment."

Director Charles Frend, who died in 1977, had worked with Guinness before, on another Ealing comedy called *A Run for Your Money* (1949). Though he directed a few comedies, his special forte was the realistic action sequences in such films as *San Demetrio, London* and *The Cruel Sea*, two of Ealing's distinguished war films. Like those of Lewis Gilbert, Guinness' director in *H.M.S. Defiant*, many of the pictures Frend helmed had something to do with the sea, including, of course, *Barnacle Bill*. (For more about Frend, see the chapter on *A Run for Your Money*.)

Guinness seemed to enjoy his role in *Barnacle Bill* and brought all of his familiar techniques to bear on the character of Captain William Horatio Ambrose, last of a long line of seafaring Ambroses. The six Ambrose ancestors, beginning with a Stone Age sea dog who paddles around in circles and ending with his father, who was gunnery officer aboard H.M.S. *Incompatible*, are all sharply if briefly limned by Guinness. His Elizabethan ancestor is a delight of both physical characterization and makeup artistry.

As the modern-day Ambrose afflicted with permanent *mal de mer*, Guinness is always satisfying and often marvelous. His Captain Ambrose is a model of efficiency and quick thinking, a hard man to discourage or deflect. When the teddy boys begin ripping out his seats, he immediately sees how rotten they are and joins in the destruction, making way for a new floor.

And, as in *The Captain's Paradise* in 1953, Guinness gets a chance to show off his dancing skills as he competently whirls a pony-tailed teenager across the pier's new dance floor.

Guinness, as the seasick-prone Captain Ambrose, may look strangely posed here; he's actually cutting a mean rug on his new dance floor.

Among the other actors in *Barnacle Bill*, Percy Herbert (1925–) as Tommy is noteworthy not only for his acting skills but for the fact that he also appeared with Guinness in *Bridge on the River Kwai* that same year. Herbert also turned in a strong supporting performance in 1960's Guinness/Mills starrer, *Tunes of Glory*.

Irene Browne (1891–1965), who played Arabella Barrington, was mostly active on the British stage. Her few film appearances included *The Letter* (1929), *Cavalcade* (1933), *Berkeley Square* (1933), *The Amateur Gentleman* (1936), *Pygmalion* (1938), *The Prime Minister* (1940), *Quartet* (1948), *Madeleine* (1950), *Rooney* (1958), and others.

Victor Maddern (1926–), who played Figg, the dredger captain, was in another of Guinness' seafaring films, *H.M.S. Defiant*. His is a familiar face to Americans, especially those who can remember his 1962 United States television series, *Fair Exchange*.

Barnacle Bill/All at Sea would be Guinness' last completely comic role for a while. *The Prisoner*, to say nothing of his distinguished stage career, made producers and audiences look at him differently now. Clearly Guinness was succeeding in breaking out of his comedy-role stereotype. His next film, *Bridge on the River Kwai*, would shatter that stereotype forever.

18. *The Bridge on the River Kwai* (1957)

"Two men lost. Some damage done but bridge intact thanks
to British colonel's heroism."
—from the novel *The Bridge Over the River Kwai*
by Pierre Boulle.

Pierre Boulle's novel is about the futility of war and of a certain mentality present in too many career officers — men whose faults would be glaring in civilian life, yet who achieve command rank in the military. Frenchman Pierre Boulle's novel is also notable for its disdain for the British and especially for the British military mind — a strange and uneasy mixture of Blimpism and idealism covered by a veneer of stupidity. Boulle sees the British officer corps as full of men who had served in India and other protectorates and taken to heart Kipling's more jingoistic paeans to king and empire. His novel presents the British as no different from the empire-hungry Japanese who are their cruel captors.

The film is a story of contrasts and of personal confrontations — confrontations of values, cultures, and moral codes. The most obvious of these is the conflict between the Japanese P.O.W. camp commandant, Colonel Saito (Sessue Hayakawa) and a captured British commander, Colonel Nicholson (Guinness). Less obvious is the secondary clash of values between a "looking-out-for-number-one" escaped prisoner, an American enlisted man impersonating an officer named Shears, and a donnish British commando, Major Warden.

Colonel Saito's orders are to build a railroad bridge across the river Kwai in Thailand using British P.O.W.s and their officers as slave labor. The completed railway will make possible the Japanese invasion of the Indian subcontinent. Colonel Nicholson opposes Saito from the beginning — not because of the use to which the bridge will be put, but because Saito wants the British officers to work alongside their men. Nicholson tells Saito that this is against the Geneva convention and refuses to give the order. After a lengthy battle of wills — during which Saito has Nicholson confined to a tin sweat box under the savage sun — Nicholson emerges with a remarkable personal victory over Saito. Colonel Saito uses the celebration of the anniversary of Japan's victory over Czarist Russia as face-saving excuse for releasing Nicholson and his officers. A frustrated Saito sobs over his defeat.

103

Guinness' Colonel Nicholson inspects the completed bridge with Colonel Saito (Sessue Hayakawa).

Free on his own terms, Nicholson says the men have "no order, no discipline," and that their morale and health can best be kept up by building the bridge as solidly as possible—no slacking or sabotage—thus showing their captors, he says, how British men do things.

Meanwhile, Shears, who escaped while Nicholson was in the "oven," is reluctantly returning to the river Kwai as part of "force 316," a commando unit led by a former professor, Major Warden. Their goal is to blow up the bridge and with it the first transport train to pass over it.

Nicholson, blinded by his "memorial" to himself and his men, spots the unit's charges and detonator wires and tries to prevent the bridge from being destroyed. His cries for help alert the Japanese guards, who kill Shears and another of his unit, Joyce, before they can carry out their mission. Realizing what he's done, Nicholson attempts to reach the detonator handle himself, but he's hit by shrapnel from Major Warden's mortar. Dying, he falls on the plunger and in death blows up his beloved creation himself. A doctor watching from a hillside can only mutter, "Madness!...Madness!"

Kwai was Alec Guinness' first big American film. It was his first conscious step toward a greater recognition in Hollywood and America. It was an auspicious first step, since more people saw Guinness in *Kwai* than any other film he'd made up till then, including 60 million Americans who saw the film's network telecast.* Apart from Guinness' other David Lean–directed blockbusters, *Lawrence of Arabia* and *Doctor Zhivago*, only *Star Wars* and its sequels were as commercially and critically accepted as *Kwai*.

In *The Prisoner*, Guinness had shown that he could handle intensely dramatic roles as well as his more customary comedic and seriocomedic ones. Indeed, both films show him doing what he does best: interpreting the sort of character whose greatest conflicts are within himself rather than with a hostile outside world.

For the first time, Guinness' minimalist techniques were seen to their best advantage. His Colonel Nicholson is an enigma wrapped inside a riddle, and yet Guinness makes him almost knowable, at the same time demonstrating that the stubborn military man's character will never be fully revealed to the viewer.

Colonel Nicholson is no hero—and perhaps that is why Guinness' interpretation is so correct. Guinness' technique cannot, or at least does not, encompass the larger-than-life hero. A hero projects superhuman-sized virtues; Guinness' acting suggests all-too-human defects of character. His acting and art are atuned to inner, not outer, space.

A $3,000,000 production, *Kwai* was shot on location in the beautiful but oppressively hot jungles of Ceylon beginning late in 1956. Given Guinness' perfection in the role of Colonel Nicholson, it comes as a shock to many to learn that producer Sam Spiegel and director David Lean first offered the part to Charles Laughton, who turned them down because he thought the difficult role too "chancey."

Guinness himself thought Nicholson "a dreary, unsympathetic man," and had refused the part several times. Guinness told Gene Phillips, in *Focus on Film*, that he turned down the first script "because it was rubbish—filled with elephant charges and that sort of thing. . . . [The part] was offered to me again after the script was revised. I turned it down a second time because I found Col. Nicholson to be a blinkered character. I wondered how we could get the audience to take him seriously. Then Sam Spiegel. . . took me to dinner. He is a very persuasive character. I started out maintaining that I wouldn't play the role and by the end of the evening we were discussing what kind of wig I would wear."

Once on location in Ceylon, Guinness learned from Lean that his old director had really wanted Laughton for the role. After digesting this piece of information, Guinness tried to quit but allowed Lean to talk him out of it. After becoming upset over the leisurely shooting pace Lean effected—one day produced only thirty seconds of film—Guinness again tried to quit and was again mollified by Lean's promises.

Shooting on location took fourteen weeks and wore down cast and crew alike. The only relaxation came from watching movies and sneaking off to

*ABC, Sunday, Sept. 25, 1966. 38.3 Rating; 61 share.

fish in the river ("Never caught a bloody thing," Guinness groused). There was no escape from the flies. "One day I killed 681," Guinness recalled with satisfaction. The minute his last scene had been filmed, Guinness raced to the nearest airport and boarded a plane back to England, his jungle ordeal over.

Just as Guinness was not Lean's first choice for the pivotal role of Nicholson, Lean himself was not producer Sam Spiegel's first choice as director. John Ford later revealed that Spiegel had asked him to direct *Kwai* but that he had told Spiegel, "You'll have to get a director who understands the colonel — I don't." After he saw the film, Ford said he understood the colonel as played by Guinness under Lean's direction. (For more information about Lean's life and career, see the *Great Expectations* chapter.)

The Academy Award for best screenplay went to Pierre Boulle for adapting his own novel. It was an ironic award. Credited alone for the script, Boulle was actually only one of four men to work on the screenplay in addition to Lean's uncredited contributions. The others were Carl Foreman, Calder Willingham, and Michael Wilson. Foreman, blacklisted since the early fifties in the furor over alleged Communist subversion in Hollywood, was first suspected of having a hand in the writing of the screenplay when it was noticed that *Kwai*'s script contained two minor characters named Baker and Weaver. Herbie Baker and John Weaver had served in the army with Foreman, and he subsequently used their names in every screenplay he wrote since *Champion* in 1949. When it became common knowledge in Hollywood that Foreman had worked on *Kwai* — as did other blacklisted writers on other major films — the blacklist lost some of its momentum, and Foreman was able to write and produce his next picture, *The Guns of Navarone* (1961), under his own name. As for the Academy Award, Foreman was ineligible for nomination under Academy bylaws which forbid any professed Communist, or person who refuses to deny he is a Communist, to receive an Academy Award. This bylaw was in effect from February 1957 to January 1959.

In the screenplay's original ending, Nicholson did not betray the commandos, and he consciously blew up the bridge. But Spiegel apparently wanted a more "ironic" and, presumably, antiwar ending in which Nicholson blows up the bridge only when his dead body falls on the plunger. Knowing this, one can more easily understand several puzzling moments in the final film. Early on, it's established that Major Warden was captured, and possibly tortured, by the Japanese. Keeping in mind his suffering, when *his* mortar shells kill Joyce and Shears in the original version, he says, "I had to do it — *they might have been captured.*" Leaving in this line while cutting the original ending makes nonsense of the final ending — Shears and Joyce are obviously killed by the Japanese soldiers — and thoroughly befuddled some reviewers at the time of the film's release.

Certainly, *Kwai* is a very visual film, and director Lean deserves most of the credit for its unquestioned ability to tell much of the story in images. As Nicholson's men approach the Japanese P.O.W. camp, we see the many graves beside the railroad track. Lean's camera reveals a very simple fact: people die here; it is a place of death. Lean introduces us to Colonel Nicholson as he briskly leads his men into camp. We see his pleasure at his men, marching in place and whistling the *Colonel Bogey March*, as the music swells to sweep the viewer into the picture. Lean shows us Colonel Saito in close-up, and Nicholson feels the intensity of Saito's gaze on the back of his neck. With a few swift, visual strokes, Lean has set the tenor of the film and suggested the confrontation to come between two strong-willed and similar men.

Not only has Lean interwoven two separate plot threads in *Kwai* (the Nicholson/Saito conflict and the Shears "adventure" story), but he has also visually framed this duality by placing protagonistic elements on both sides of the Cinemascope screen. Lean arranges Saito and Nicholson on opposite sides of the frame, each man mimicking the other's stance by duplicating it— much as Alexander Mackendrick did with labor and management in *The Man in the White Suit*. Lean also has two brief scenes, virtually back-to-back, where Saito says of Nicholson, "He is mad, your colonel, quite mad," and Nicholson says of Saito, "Actually, I think he's mad."

In another nice touch, the screenplay has Nicholson dismiss Shears' advice on how to stay alive under Saito as the words of someone too long in isolation—Nicholson's later collaboration occurs after he himself spends days in isolation!

Ironically, both Nicholson and Saito think they represent superior cultures. Saito, to Nicholson, "You speak to me of code. What code? The coward's code. What do you know of the soldier's code? Of *bushido*?" Nicholson says to his officers, partly to explain why he wants to build the bridge as best they can, "We can teach...western methods and efficiency which will put them to shame. We'll show them what the British soldier is capable of doing."

The final irony, the final example of Nicholson and Saito's duality, occurs when the deal is struck to build the bridge. Each man has won by losing. Saito will get his bridge, but he has lost face; Nicholson won the war of wills, but his victory includes building a bridge that will open the way to a Japanese invasion of India.

Guinness brings to the difficult and "chancey" role of Colonel Nicholson a quiet authority. He easily slips on the mask of the iron-willed commander who loves his men but will not hesitate to sacrifice them for "what's best"—as when Nicholson convinces the soldiers in the hospital to help complete the bridge on schedule.

Although Guinness plays Nicholson as a man devoid of imagination— and, hence, of humor—there is one very nice moment: Saito tells Nicholson the bridge must be completed on time or he will have to kill himself. When Saito asks what Nicholson would do in his place, Nicholson replies, "I suppose, if *I* were *you*, I'd have to kill myself."

Guinness' Nicholson has blinded himself to the use which the bridge will

Nicholson (Guinness), still blind to his own collaboration with the Japanese, is congratulated as a sign is posted boasting of his men's achievement in designing and building the bridge.

be put and to the fact that he is a collaborator. Told by a fellow officer that there are trees similar to elms in the jungle and "the elm towers of London Bridge lasted six hundred years," Nicholson says, "Six hundred years. That *would* be quite something."

Saito inadvertently taps this wistfulness by looking at the sunset from the completed bridge and saying, "Beautiful." Guinness' Nicholson, thinking Saito means his bridge, agrees, "Yes, beautiful."

Nicholson, leaning over a guard rail, then delivers one of his more revealing speeches:

> ...Still, it's been a good life. I loved India. I wouldn't have it any other way. But there are times when suddenly you realize you're nearer the end than the beginning. And you wonder...you ask yourself...what the sum total of your life represents. What difference your being there at any time made to anything....
>
> *(joyfully)*
>
> But tonight...tonight!

Guinness and Lean have quietly shown that the colonel wants to leave something behind after twenty-eight years in the service—a monument to himself. Guinness, only forty-three at the time *Kwai* was shot, brings a convincing wistfulness to these lines. He's served king and country in India—or so he makes us believe. His Nicholson has lived a life full of only dust and heat and boredom.

Since he was not in Hollywood the night he won the Academy Award for best actor, Guinness picked up his Oscar at a Variety Club luncheon in London's Savoy Hotel. Showing up a half hour late, Guinness made his way unobserved through several hundred people dressed in his costume from *The Horse's Mouth*. Wearing the smeared jacket, soiled green flannel shirt and cracked shoes of the eccentric artist Gulley Jimson, Guinness made his way to the front table, where he shyly accepted the club's award as the best film actor of 1957 and received his Oscar from a Columbia Pictures executive. After the applause died down, Guinness, looking pleased in spite of himself, mumbled a few words of thanks to the "many people in show business who helped me," and sat down. It was a typical "public Guinness" performance.

Is *Kwai* a great film? Perhaps, although I tend to agree with Raymond Durgnat's reassessment in *Films and Filming* in 1963: "A second viewing confirms one's first impression that *Kwai* is a gripping and honourable film, but not a masterpiece. . . . "

Kwai got mixed but generally favorable reviews when it first came out. Colin Young, in *Film Quarterly*, wrote: ". . . technically the film is magnificent—an almost incredible tribute to the director's skill."

Looking at *Kwai* twenty years later, Roy Armes, in *A Critical History of the British Cinema*, says, "In its externalization of all conflicts and drowning of confrontations in epic values, as in its refusal to take any stand outside the consciousness of its characters, *Kwai* typifies the limitations of Lean's later work."

Few elements of the film drew more criticism than the inclusion of an American soldier into the screenplay and getting a major American star, William Holden, to play him. George N. Fenin, in *Film Culture*, called Holden's Shears "the usual cliché of an American gob 'who wants to go home . . . .' " Today, the Shears "adventure" seems less intrusive, less calculated, and less the ploy for box office respectability it transparently was.

More serious attacks were waged on *Kwai*'s claim to be an "antiwar" film. Nearly thirty years later, this debate seems less important than it did in 1957. *Kwai* simply suffers from the schizophrenia common to so many films about war—from *Patton* (1970) to *A Bridge Too Far* (1977), these films show the futility and horror of war while also including a great many rousing action sequences. Only Stanley Kubrick's masterpiece *Paths of Glory* (1958) has avoided the trap of making war glamorous while trying to show its hopelessness and stupidity. During *Kwai*'s final scene, audiences often yell, "Kill him!" when Nicholson is warning the Japanese about the explosives.

The Bridge on the River Kwai's success made Guinness a major star and a respected artist. His Oscar for best actor was Hollywood's seal of approval. It only remained to see what he would do next. What Guinness did was typical . . . of Guinness.

19. The Horse's Mouth (1958)

> "Who lives a million years? A million people every twelve
> months. I'll show you how to look at a picture, Cokey.
> Don't look at it. Feel it with your eye.... You feel all
> the rounds, the smooths, the sharp edges, the flats and
> the hollows, the lights and shades, the cools and warms.
> The colours and textures. There's hundreds of little
> differences all fitting in together."
> — Gulley Jimson, in *The Horse's Mouth*.

Alex Guinness' only film of 1958 and his first after *Kwai* was *The Horse's Mouth* (hereafter simply *Horse's*). *Horse's* is a rare film for attempting to show the drama and comedy of the artist's life. Guinness' Gulley Jimson is often a buffoon, a brilliant man fallen into self-destructive patterns of behavior, who nonetheless sustains an artistic view of life that is indomitable and courageous. His Gulley will gladly play the fool when it suits him, but that is just a disguise—for Gulley cares more for his art than for life itself.

A religious man, Guinness perhaps saw the moral center of Cary's novel as the inspiration for a film concerning creation and the life force itself (there is one brilliant moment in the film when Gulley, wrapped up in a pink blanket, looks every inch a cardinal as he majestically approaches a blank wall and draws his first line). For Guinness (and Cary), the artist seems to be most like God when he is in the act of creation.

Horse's is also the only film for which Guinness ever wrote the screenplay. It was an audacious undertaking, for Joyce Cary's novel, a rambling, witty, stream-of-consciousness *tour de force*, was widely hailed by critics as a masterpiece, a rich brew of language and ideas ill-suited for transfer to the screen. Films are not books and cannot be judged as such, but Guinness needn't apologize to anyone for his faithful and clever screenplay—its strength supports the film and is responsible for its ultimate success.

The reviews were decidedly mixed, but the favorable ones seemed to outnumber the negative ones. In *Film Quarterly*, Henry Goodman wrote, "...Guinness' screenplay and performance amount to a rare comic achievement that speaks of serious things from behind surface flippancies and outrageous hokum."

Paul V. Beckley, in the New York *Herald Tribune*, called *Horse's* "A full expression of the plight of the artist in the modern world... The integrity of every detail of this film is remarkable."

In *Films in Review*, Courtland Phillips found the film *too* outrageous: "A series of unbelievable incidents—amusing, satirical, poignant, farcial, touching, and absurd.... The reason the film misses, I think, is because *it is too faithful to Cary's novel*" Emphasis added. I find this to be a most unusual complaint about a film made from a respected book—namely, that it follows the book too closely!

Variety's "Myro," who wrote his review from the Venice Film Festival, called *Horse's* "An odd and uneasy blending of comedy and farce which doesn't quite come off...."

Time magazine's reviewer essentially said, "Yes, but" when he wrote, "Guinness, of course, is a howl.... He is a highly intelligent actor, but he simply lacks the demonic force to fill out a personality as large as Jimson's."

Finally, Hollis Alpert's *Saturday Review* piece called *Horse's* a "Superbly outrageous movie...Cary's novel might have seemed unfriendly screen material for most screen artists, but not for Mr. Guinness. He has made Gulley Jimson his own."

Modern London. Gulley Jimson (Guinness), fresh from prison, wearing scruffy and tattered clothing, and walking stiffly with hunched shoulders, returns to his houseboat. It's an unholy mess, but he's most concerned with his painting, *The Fall* (*The Garden of Eden*) and the rest of his religious triptych, *The Raising of Lazarus* and *The Last Judgment*.

Gulley phones Mr. Hickson, his sometime patron, and disguises his voice. Hickson (Earnest Thesiger) sees through his charade, and Gulley threatens to burn his house down. Gulley calls back, posing as the "Duchess of Blackpool," his voice quivering by vibrating his throat with his hand. A policeman, sent by Hickson, shows up and warns Gulley to stop the calls.

Gulley goes to see his friend Coker, a barmaid. To get her to lend him money, he reads her a note from A.W. Alabaster, an art critic who wants to do a book on Gulley's life and work. Coker (Kay Walsh) and Gulley go to see Jimson's ex-wife Sara (Renée Houston). Sara signs a paper saying she gave Gulley's paintings to Hickson.

At Hickson's, Gulley shows Coker a nude he did of Sara. Gulley tells her how to "feel" the painting. When Hickson comes in, he explains to Coker that Sara sold him the canvases to settle Gulley's debts. Hickson reveals he's given Gulley over £3000 all told and pocket money of two pounds a week. He'll renew this allowance if Gulley will stop phoning him. Left alone, Coker and Gulley realize Hickson is calling the police. Gulley breaks a window and they escape into a taxi.

Gulley meets Alabaster (Arthur Macrae) at the apartment of two rich art patrons, Sir William and Lady Beeder (Robert Coote and Veronica Turleigh). Gulley sees that they have the perfect wall for *The Raising of Lazarus*.

Gulley Jimson (Guinness, *right*) and Abel (Michael Gough) look through the hole left in the floor of the Beeders' apartment after the sculptor's block of stone falls through to the apartment below.

They get on famously, and Gulley even critiques Lady Beeder's own paintings, using the phrase "straight from the horse's mouth." Gulley gets drunk and larks around the apartment, finally passing out. The Beeders, off to Jamaica for several weeks, leave Gulley in the empty apartment. Getting the key from the maid, Gulley hocks most of the furnishings to pay for his art supplies. He'll create a masterpiece on the Beeders' blank wall.

Gulley uses a black waiter's feet as a model for the feet he wants in the mural, and paints on. A mad sculptor named Abel (Michael Gough) shows up and has a huge block of stone delivered—which immediately falls through the floor into a vacant apartment.

The work continues. After Abel criticizes Gulley's mural, Gulley orders Abel back to the apartment below and covers up the hole in the floor with a rug. However, Gulley reluctantly agrees with Abel's assessment and laments that the finished work is not the vision he had in his mind.

The Beeders and Alabaster return and fall through the rug-covered hole in the floor. Gulley returns to his houseboat and finds Coker living there, having lost her job over the flap at Hickson's. Gulley learns from Coker that Hickson is dead. Close to tears, Gulley grieves for his oldest friend and foe.

Gulley's work now hangs in the Tate Gallery—a gift to the nation from Hickson. Gulley, however, is still after the nude of Sara she's kept for herself. He thinks he's gotten it from her after he's gotten her drunk, but she tricks him and keeps the painting. Furious at being tricked and trying to get his painting back, Gulley accidently knocks Sara out. Flustered, he escapes to a ruined chapel and finds the perfect wall for *The Last Judgment*.

Giving painting lessons, Gulley has his students actually paint the mural, which he hopes will halt the demolition of the ruins. When the mural is finished, there's a confrontation between the workers who are to tear it down and the students who want it left alone. Taking the responsibility for destroying a work of art, Gulley pushes over the wall with a bulldozer.

Casting his houseboat free, Gulley floats down the Thames, surveying the sides of ships—perfect blank walls! Though Gulley can't hear him, Nosey (Mike Morgan) shouts after the retreating artist: "Michelangelo, Rubens, Blake—you're one of them!"

How did Alec Guinness come to write a screenplay based on Cary's novel? As he said to an interviewer, "Once I tried reading the book and just couldn't finish it. My wife insisted that it would make a good film, and when I started reading it from that point of view I got caught up in it. I was making another film at the time and had a lot of free time. So I wrote the script while I was hanging around waiting for my scenes to be shot."

Guinness' script is episodic, like Cary's novel, and really has very little "plot." "You asked me," Guinness told the *New York Times*, "to write you a synopsis of *The Horse's Mouth*, but I'm afraid I find it an impossible task." Much of the script's dialogue comes straight from the horse's mouth—from Cary's novel itself. To a surprising degree, Guinness was able to incorporate into much of Gulley's "incessant mumblings, monologues, and dialogues" the stream-of-consciousness effects that Cary used in his novel. (Stanley Kubrick did much the same thing when he adapted Anthony Burgess' novel *A Clockwork Orange* for the screen.)

Horse's is Guinness' most personal statement on film. He conceived the whole production, talked John Bryan and Ronald Neame into producing and directing it, wrote the script, and played the plum part of Gulley Jimson. For Guinness, there was presumably an ironic parallel to Gulley's belated recognition and success—it is the artist's early work, the work he stopped doing ten years ago because its style no longer seemed important to him, that his reputation rests on and that everyone wants to see more of. Similarly, Guinness found himself ever in demand as a screen comic actor when he ached to do more "serious" work, to stretch himself in straight dramatic parts. It is a question every successful artist faces: whether to repeat oneself—as the public and critics desire—or to set new goals and strike out in new directions.

Author Joyce Lunel Cary was born in 1888 in Ireland, although his parents lived in London. His mother traveled to Londonderry so her son could be born Irish. Following his education in a public (private) school, Cary tried art and the artist's life until he realized he wasn't good enough to make a living as a painter. After attending Oxford University, Cary served in the Balkan War of 1912–1913 and was briefly detained as a spy. After a brief fling in the colonial service in Nigeria, Cary and his wife settled in Oxford. His wife raised their four sons while Cary began a career as a writer. It was at Oxford that he died in 1957.

The Horse's Mouth is the third book in Cary's First Trilogy. The first novel, Herself Surprised, is Sara Monday's account of her life as a wife and mistress. The novel is written from a women's prison where Sara is an inmate because she stole to feed Gulley and his son. To Be A Pilgrim, the second novel, is narrated by Gulley Jimson's enemy, Thomas Wilcher, a man totally opposed to Gulley's values and way of life.

In Horse's, Cary's 1944 novel, Gulley is a balding old man of sixty-seven in prewar London. An irascible genius, Gulley is both kind and cruel, a man resigned to fighting for his art. As he tells Nosey, "How can you be an artist without money? Why look at me. I've been painting for fifty years, and at this moment I don't even possess brushes or paint. No, you can't go in for art without money from somewhere. Art is like roses—it's a rich feeder."

Later, when Alabaster says he couldn't support a wife, Gulley tells him, "Then let her support you. All my wives supported me. It's a very good plan. It gives them a serious interest in life, and it leaves you free to get on with your work." (Cary was obviously being autobiographical in both these passages.)

Gulley's work is of paramount importance to him; it is his reason for existence. Because he believes being a "suffering artist" gives one special insight, Gulley calls himself "the old horse." As scholar Andrew Wright notes in his afterword to Cary's novel, "God, too, is the old horse; and in so far as Gulley is an artist, he is God. 'I had got the feeling,' he says as he repaints Adam, 'straight from the horse.' What comes from the horse's mouth cannot, in Gulley's view, be articulated except with brush and paint on canvas or wall. 'The truth is, THE OLD HORSE DOESN'T SPEAK ONLY HORSE.' "

Cary's novel is chock-full of marvelous and colorful language and images—images in words and sentences on paper rather than in oils and brush strokes on canvas. At one point, Gulley suggests to Alabaster that they put out a "Life and Works of Lady Beeder," saying the directors of the public galleries can "store her with the Turners in the Tate basement until the Thames comes up again and gives her a wash of dead dog and sludge."

With such riches to plumb, it is not hard to see why Guinness kept intact so much of Cary's dialogue. Gulley and Sara's exchange, at one point, is quite similar to that in the novel: " 'It wasn't that one you liked so much,' I said, 'of yourself in the bath?' 'Oh, Gulley, I never liked it, you know. I never liked the way you painted me.' 'Always taking a peep at it,' I said. 'Admiring yourself in your skin.' "

Probably the biggest difference between the novel and Guinness' screenplay is the ending. Cary's novel has Gulley taken off to a hospital by a police ambulance at the end, his fate uncertain. Guinness, looking for a more

Guinness' irascible Gulley Jimson joins his friend Coker (Kay Walsh, *right*) in trying to get one of his paintings back from ex-wife Sara (Renée Houston, *center*).

upbeat ending, has Gulley float off down the Thames, an older version of Sidney Stratton, briefly defeated but ready to take up the fight again.

Certainly, some admirers of Cary's novel were pained by the film; it just didn't do justice to Cary's comic and moral vision. True, but irrelevant, I think. A film is not, cannot be, a book. Novels can take one inside their narrators' minds or leap across the vastness of space; they can play with words and ideas in ways a film cannot hope to equal. But films, communal experiences shared in the dark, can bring a vividness, a directness of experience which books cannot. A panoramic view of the aftermath of a battle can be shown instantly and eloquently in silent images which need no words to convey their message of waste and horror.

Coming on the heels of his Academy Award–winning performance as Colonel Nicholson in *The Bridge on the River Kwai*, Guinness' portrayal of Gulley Jimson is every bit its equal. On the surface, Guinness' Gulley is all bluster and bullying, but underneath there's a sensitive soul who's had a hard life.

Ever the master of disguise, Guinness effortlessly puts on Gulley's persona—his rough stubble of a beard, the harsh razor-blade gargle of a voice, his shuffling gait of a walk as he belligerently holds his arms stiffly to his sides, all combine to quickly sum up Gulley's years of defeats. His spirit is willing, feisty even, but his flesh is oh, so weak.

Though Guinness quickly mastered Gulley's walk, he was most concerned about getting the artist's voice right. While he believed that an educated or upper-class accent would accurately reflect Gulley's intelligence, it would not be true to his eccentric, self-destructive nature. A coarse, lower-class accent would not work either. "So I tried to find a voice in which no one would be able to detect an accent of any sort, a kind of gritty, rough manner of speaking," Guinness said. "When I found it I felt myself free to just relax on that and say the lines as they came."

Guinness is able to make the viewer care for Gulley — despite his attempts to wrest Sara's portrait away from her and his apparent indifference to Coker's and Nosey's feelings. If Guinness' Gulley seems cruel, it's just that he's singlemindedly and ruthlessly self-absorbed; he's an artist before all else and must devote his energies to expressing himself while trying just to live. One gets the idea from Guinness' performance that Gulley would do something else if he didn't *have* to paint. But for Gulley, nothing else will do; it matters more to him than spending time in prison or even continuing to live. *Horse's* is a portrait of the artist as an old man.

The other actors in *Horse's* include Ernest Thesiger, Guinness' old nemesis from *The Man in the White Suit*, as Hickson; Veronica Turleigh, his mother in *The Card/The Promoter*, as Lady Beeder; Michael Gough, also from *MWS*, as Abel, the mad sculptor; and Kay Walsh, who appears in several Guinness/Neame films, as Coker. (See notes on *Horse's* in the Appendix for more on the actors.)

The Horse's Mouth was another triumph for Guinness. With a big assist from Cary's novel, he gave us a sharply etched portrait of the artist, of the agonies and ecstasies of a life lived only to create. It remains a singular accomplishment.

20. *The Scapegoat* (1959)

> "When I made *The Scapegoat* with Alec Guinness, he cut my part into such shreds that my appearance in the final product made no sense at all. This is an actor who plays by himself, and in this particular picture he plays a dual role, so at least he was able to play with himself."
> — Bette Davis.

Whether Alec Guinness was responsible for the obvious and extensive recutting of *The Scapegoat* (regretfully his only film of 1959) is unknown. Despite her protestations, however, Miss Davis comes off rather well in the resulting mess of a film.

When Daphne Du Maurier, a novelist who has written many mysteries and other best-selling works, was visiting northwest France in 1955, she conceived a novel about an unsuspecting teacher who meets and is tricked by his double into stepping into that man's complicated life.

Du Maurier wanted only one man to play the dual role in any film version: Alec Guinness. Guinness agreed, and the two formed a partnership, Du Maurier-Guinness, to film the novel.

While Guinness was pleased that an actress the caliber of Bette Davis had agreed to play his mother, he was unconvinced that Davis, just six years older than he, could convincingly play the role. Miss Davis, aware of his misgivings, told him, "I assure you, Mr. Guinness, that when I am properly made up, I will look old enough to be your mother." (Guinness needn't have worried: *North By Northwest*, made that same year, had Jessie Royce Landis playing Cary Grant's mother—and the two of them were the same age!)

A clear giveaway that *The Scapegoat* missed its intended mark is Guinness' unnecessary voice-over narration. It seems almost a cliché that films which have been extensively cut, so much so that the narrative thread is difficult to follow, resort to this hoary device to keep the audience informed. Unfortunately, as in this case, it almost never works—in fact, it usually makes a confused and confusing film even more so.

The Scapegoat's reviews were mostly negative, although Guinness and Davis, as well as several other cast members, fared well.

Howard Thompson, in the *New York Times*, wrote that *The Scapegoat* was "Pretentious, cold, and slow-moving. Miss Du Maurier's dazzlingly cunning puzzler is now a stately charade—handsome, curious, and untingling.... To put it bluntly, very little happens except conversation (including Mr. Guinness' baffled asides to himself). Only Nicole Maurey, as the lovely mistress, and Geoffrey Keen, as a chauffeur, are truly 'likeable'—the hero's label for the family."

Glen Gleason's review in the *New York Herald Tribune* is one of the few favorable ones: "An enjoyable picture, more remarkable for some of its individual qualities than for its over-all success.... Geoffrey Keen handles a small role with extraordinary finesse."

Films in Review, in Louise Corbin's review, called the film "Facetious and grade-B Du Maurier [with] an ineffective trick ending. *The Scapegoat* is good in every department of filmmaking except the script, which inadequately characterizes the leading parts and insufficiently motivates the major plot-turns. The acting is exceptionally good."

Variety, its eye ever on the box office, printed a review by "Powe," which called the film "Disappointing.... Will be partially satisfying to Guinness fans, although the excellence of its production is subverted by an abrupt and unsatisfactory conclusion and a screenplay that leaves too much unexplained.... Guinness, again, seems unable to give less than a superior performance."

John Barratt (Guinness), an English teacher on holiday in France, is accosted by several people who claim to know him but whom he has never met. A man follows him inside a bar and stands beside him, revealing himself to be Barratt's exact double. The man, an impoverished aristocrat with a chateau, a glass factory, and a family, is Jacques De Gue (also Guinness). He befriends Barratt and, after getting him drunk, takes him to the hotel where he is staying. De Gue puts Barratt to bed and then takes his passport, his clothes, and his car, leaving Barratt to awaken as "Jacques De Gue."

When Barratt protests that he is not really De Gue but an English schoolteacher, no one believes him; De Gue had prepared the way by announcing he was ill and under a delusion he was someone else.

De Gue's driver/butler, Gaston (Geoffrey Keen) takes him "home." A doctor explains to him that he is suffering from a delusion and tries to make him accept that he is De Gue. Barratt, a man without family or friends, is intrigued by the idea and begins to play along. When Marie-Noel (Annabel Bartlett) believes him her father, he does not try to explain. His "daughter" then takes him to see his "mother," the dowager countess (Bette Davis), a morphine addict who De Gue keeps supplied.

Barratt meets Francoise, De Gue's wife, (Irene Worth) and Blanche, his sister (Pamela Brown). They won't believe him when he insists he is not Jacques. Barratt calls the whole thing a nightmare.

In the morning, Barratt begins to enjoy playing his new role. He even combs his hair like De Gue. Gaston brings him his breakfast.

Guinness, as John Barratt, speaks to his "mother," the dowager countess (Bette Davis).

After lunch, Barratt drives Marie-Noel into town for her Wednesday afternoon music lesson, reconciling himself to being Jacques and beginning to enjoy it. He enjoys it even more when he meets Bela (Nicole Maurey), who is De Gue's mistress; Wednesday afternoons are apparently for trysts as well as music lessons.

At the glass factory, things are not well. The glass is hand-blown and expensive to produce. But Barratt tells his mother he is not going to sell the factory. She mentions finances and a certain document—a marriage settlement. In the event of his wife's death, he will inherit a great deal of money to raise Marie-Noel as her legal guardian.

When the next Wednesday comes, Bela tells him she knows he is not Jacques—he cares too much for the feelings of others. She tells him she loves him, however. He tells her his story and how dreamlike it all seems at times.

Learning that De Gue is a crack shot, Barratt, who can't shoot at all, intentionally injures his hand so he cannot shoot a match. Marie-Noel, who is very religious, sees him hurt himself deliberately and assumes it is for atonement.

Gaston takes Barratt to see Bela; supposedly an urgent call from her asked him to come immediately. But when he sees her, she tells him it must be a mistake, she didn't ask him to come. Meanwhile, Blanche overhears the real Jacques arguing with Francoise.

Barratt returns to discover that Francoise fell from a window to her death. Because it was not natural, there is an official hearing into Francoise's death. Even the dowager countess shows up to testify.

Blanche testifies that De Gue was not in town but in his wife's room — she heard his voice. She also mentions the marriage settlement as a reason for murder. However, Gaston testifies that he drove his master (Barratt, of course) to and from town.

Barratt realizes that Jacques has used him as a scapegoat. When Jacques calls and asks to meet Barratt at the factory, he readily agrees. Jacques wants to "relieve" him, but Barratt refuses. De Gue shows him a pistol he has brought, but is caught by surprise when Barratt pulls a gun on *him*.

As they confront each other, Barratt knocks the lamp to the floor. In the darkness, they both fire. The next day, one of them goes to see Bela; when we see his bandaged hand, we know that Barratt has won.

The plot that Miss Du Maurier dreamed up while on vacation in France worked well in her novel, but the film version is so sketchy and undeveloped as to do little more than confuse the viewer. Given the talents involved, one can only wonder what went wrong. Producer Michael Balcon, of Ealing Studios fame, assigned acerbic novelist Gore Vidal to adapt Miss Du Maurier's story for the screen, and director Hamer wrote the screenplay. As Miss Du Maurier said of her original idea, "I wanted to discover, for myself, what happened to a man who was no longer himself. Would he, assuming the identity of another, take on the sins and the burdens and the emotions of the [other] or would his own hidden secret self become released in the other's image and take charge?" Of the novel's blend of mystery, romance, and murder, Miss Du Maurier herself commented, "This time I have gone the whole hog."

Given the extensive cutting the film received before MGM opened it, the fact that there are enormous gaps in the plot, including credibility and character motivation, comes as no surprise. What *is* surprising, however, is how much sympathy and audience identification Guinness is able to impart to Barratt, the weary and emotionally spent university lecturer who becomes the scapegoat of the title. But not even Guinness can do much with the enigmatic Jacques De Gue, a character who writer Douglas McVey calls a "suave, sphinxlike villain," a person who seems to have no depth whatsoever.

The other characters are just that — characters. They rarely come alive as real people; again, this is a fault of the script. Why does the dowager countess take morphine? Why does Blanche hate her brother so much? What has passed between De Gue and his wife that drained the love from their relationship? These people have no dimension, no interior existence.

The split-screen effects are stunning, and Guinness gives his usual marvelous performance. By now, in this his fourth and last film with director Hamer, the two men know each other's rhythms and patterns; it shows. The real shame of *The Scapegoat* is that such a productive partnership ended with such a mess of a film. Still, Guinness' slow awakening to the switch De Gue has perpetrated is convincingly handled, with just the right amount of outrage and curiosity to see where it all will lead. Guinness plays well with Annabel

Bartlett, who plays his daughter Marie-Noel, and with Nicole Maurey, who handles her role as his mistress with charm and conviction.

In a little role as Guinness' chauffeur, Geoffrey Keen is subtle, versatile, and easily the most likeable character in the film, apart from Guinness' love-starved schoolteacher. (Keen also appeared with Guinness in *Dr. Zhivago* [1965].) If Hamer failed with the script, his direction of the actors is as accomplished as usual.

21. *Our Man in Havana* (1960)

"Everything's legal in Havana"
—Jim Wormold in *Our Man in Havana.*

"One never tortures except by mutual agreement"
—Captain Segura.

Alex Guinness' first film of 1960 was a film adaptation of Graham Greene's novel *Our Man in Havana.* The film got mixed reviews and did mixed business. A step up from *The Scapegoat*, it was nonetheless second-rate Greene, Guinness, and Reed.

An interesting failure, *Our Man in Havana* (hereafter called *Havana*) was really a film released before its time. It barely missed, by several years, the spy and spy-spoof boom of the mid-1960s, which began with the James Bond films in England and *Our Man Flint* in the United States.

The film's greatest weakness was its uneasy mixture of dry British humor and standard screen spy melodrama. Several critics panned the film for this reason, calling it two pictures—a light-hearted spy spoof that abruptly turns serious when Dr. Hasselbacher is murdered. (Several reviewers seemed to think Hasselbacher's death was a suicide.)

Havana is set in pre–Castro Havana, and the signs of the coming upheaval are everywhere in the film, an eerie projection of the revolution that would transform Cuba. As Guinness told interviewer Gene Phillips, "Take any of the world's trouble spots, from Cuba to Haiti [the setting for *The Comedians*] and you will find that Greene has been there two or three years beforehand and accurately dealt with the tensions there through the medium of the novel. I have often said jokingly when I hear that Graham is going off to visit some part of the globe that I will avoid that place like the plague because that means that a revolution or some other upheaval is bound to break out soon."

Charles Butler, in *Films in Review*, wrote that *Havana* "purports to be a spoof of British Intelligence, but it isn't very funny, and it often doesn't make sense." He added, "Guinness' heart isn't in this farce, and he doesn't make his part credible or amusing." Similarly, Raymond Durgnat called *Havana* "A lukewarm, yet interesting, film."

Film Quarterly said of *Havana* that "its expected strokes of satire and violence are mostly successful, although the plot gives one the effect of too many *Cuba libres*."

In *Sight and Sound*, Penelope Houston calls *Havana* "An entertainment, certainly, but one which depends on hair-trigger adjustments of mood."

A review by *Variety*'s "Rich" notes that "When tragedy comes in the shape of suicide [sic] by one of the leading characters, murder and the threat of it from unknown sources, *Havana* becomes a different film and not as good a one as promised at the beginning."

An Englishman wearing a bowler and carrying an umbrella strolls through the streets of Havana, his progress observed by Captain Segura (Ernie Kovacs) of the police. After the man goes into a vacuum cleaner shop run by Jim Wormold (Guinness), Wormold's friend Dr. Hasselbacher (Burl Ives) is questioned by Segura. In the store, Jim demonstrates a vacuum to the man, who makes some cryptic remarks and leaves.

Jim tells Hasselbacher of wanting to send his daughter Milly away to school — if only he had enough money. Milly (Jo Morrow) admits to Jim that she knows Captain Segura, "the red vulture."

Hawthorne (Noel Coward) meets Jim in a bar and, taking him into the men's room, admits he is a British agent in charge of the Caribbean and that he needs a "man in Havana." If Jim agrees, he'll make $150 a month and expenses — tax free. As if to convince Jim, Milly wants to join the country club. Reluctantly, Jim meets with Hawthorne, learning about secret inks, using book codes, and recruiting agents.

At Whitehall, in London, Hawthorne meets with "C," the head of British Intelligence. Hawthorne and C (Ralph Richardson) cable Jim to start recruiting agents. While at the country club, Jim fruitlessly tries to recruit agents, innocently sitting beside two men named Montez and Cifentes.

When Jim tells Dr. Hasselbacher he's been hired to get secret information, the doctor tells him to invent secrets and agents — thereby doing no harm. So Jim begins "recruiting" phony agents, who all, of course, require money. He "recruits" Teresa, a popular actress, and is a whirlwind of seemingly intense spying.

Noticing his "atomic pile" vacuum, Jim realizes it looks like a secret installation. He provides drawings of the vacuum and unwittingly uses the name of a real pilot, Montez, to identify his imaginary agent who supposedly spotted the "facility" from his airplane.

Hasselbacher's apartment is ransacked by the police while, in London, Jim's drawings are a sensation. Hawthorne notes there's something strangely familiar about the drawings — they look like a giant vacuum cleaner.

A young woman, Beatrice, (Maureen O'Hara) spots Jim, Milly, and Hasselbacher at a nightclub celebrating Milly's birthday. When Captain Segura joins the party, Beatrice "accidentally" spritzes him with water. Beatrice tells Jim she's his new secretary from C in Whitehall. Jim is stunned

From left: Jo Morrow as Milly, Guinness as Jim Wormwold, and Ernie Kovacs as Captain Segura.

when she adds that she'll be in contact with his agents and that Rudy will be his radio operator. The next day a huge safe arrives at Jim's shop.

The funny papers give Jim an idea—Montez, his fictional pilot, will be "shot down" by enemy agents. Meanwhile, Beatrice tells Jim he's the best agent in the western hemisphere. And a Cuban dispatcher, sending one of Jim's messages to London, notes it is in code. His face unclear, a man is seen buying a copy of Lamb, Jim's code book. Later, Jim finds an identical copy of his code book at Hasselbacher's. Hasselbacher is called to the phone and devastated by news that Montez the pilot was killed in a car crash. Dr. Hasselbacher realizes that the little game he suggested Jim pursue has led to a killing.

Cifentes is tied up and tossed outside the shop. He's taken to police HQ. Beatrice and Jim rush to "rescue" Teresa, and the three of them are taken to see Segura, who's now suspicious of Jim and Hasselbacher. Segura plays Jim a recording of Hasselbacher on the phone, learning that Montez was killed, not "warned" as the doctor requested.

When Jim sees Hasselbacher dressed in an old Prussian uniform, he questions him. Hasselbacher admits giving away Jim's cables, believing them fiction. Hasselbacher now believes the vacuum cleaner drawings are real and that Jim is a real spy.

When Segura questions Jim and Cifentes, Jim remembers that he innocently sat beside Montez at the country club. Segura now asks Jim to pass him the same information he gives the British—for a price, of course.

In Jamaica, Jim meets with Hawthorne, who tells Jim that someone plans to murder him: Jim is to be poisoned at a business lunch.

At the lunch, Hasselbacher also warns Jim he's a target. Jim waves him off, but is suspicious of his Scottish seatmate and trades his food around. Jim accepts a drink from the flask of a man called Carter. When Carter (Paul Rogers) stutters—a giveaway—Jim suspects something funny and spills his drink. A dog licks it up and dies. Carter and Jim look at each other with knowing eyes.

Jim agrees to work for Segura. Hasselbacher is found murdered, but Carter has an alibi. His mind racing, Jim stares hard at Segura's pistol in its holster.

Setting up the miniature liquor bottles he collects on a checkers board, Jim tells Beatrice that Hasselbacher is dead and admits he's a fraud. Segura shows up and he and Jim play "checkers"—taking a piece compels one to drink its contents. As Jim asks Segura questions about Carter, the policeman keeps winning and passes out. Jim takes his gun and goes to meet Carter, telling him, "Everything's legal in Havana." He tricks Carter, shooting him with Segura's pistol. When Segura wakes up, there is Jim seated across from him. Segura goes home, suspecting nothing.

Two funerals: Dr. Hasselbacher's and Carter's. Segura tells Jim he has signed his deportation papers to London. Milly is going to Switzerland to school—without Segura. When Segura says goodbye at the airport, he gives Jim two shell casings and a knowing look.

After Whitehall grills Beatrice, Jim goes in to confront his superiors. C tells Jim his confession was never received and the "apparatus" was dismantled. Instead of a prison term, Jim gets a medal and a job teaching new agents. Outside, in the street, Jim and Beatrice see a vacuum-cleanerlike space toy which says MADE IN JAPAN on its underside.

Havana's confusing script, which lurches from whimsey to tragedy midway through the film with the murder of Dr. Hasselbacher, was written by Graham Greene based on his own novel. Whether the blame for the film's rather limp feel should be directed at Greene's script, Carol Reed's direction, or a combination of the two, is debatable.

Carol Reed's work has been better and more pointed than *Havana* would lead one to believe. Reed's best work, however—films like *Odd Man Out* (1946), and *The Third Man* (1949)—were all made a decade before *Havana*. Reed's keen touch, so evident in films like *The Fallen Idol* (1948), is all too clearly missing here.

Reed and Guinness disagreed over the way the actor should portray Jim Wormold, the film's protagonist. Reed wanted Guinness to act the part of a nonentity, someone invisible in a crowd (certainly no problem for Guinness!).

"Sir Carol and I disagreed there," Guinness later said. "I did not go along completely with the concept of a central character who was a blank surrounded by subordinate characters who were more strongly portrayed than he was. I felt I should play Wormold as more clearly-defined character, an untidy, defeated sort of man."

It's too bad Guinness didn't win that argument; he was right. Wormold is the center of the film and, therefore, his character ought to make more sense to the viewer. There is nothing in the film to suggest he could shoot down Carter, an enemy agent, so cold-bloodedly, even if Carter was responsible for Dr. Hasselbacher's death.

Guinness does his best with the role, however, and his performance is a good one under less-than-ideal conditions.

Burl Ives, the folk singer/actor, is less credible as Doctor Hasselbacher, Wormold's friend, who betrays Jim without really meaning to and gets an innocent man killed. With a German accent that comes and goes with alarming regularity, Ives seems almost to be in an entirely different film by himself. The gravity of his demeanor matches his size—attired in white tropical clothing, Ives resembles a great white whale as he spouts his cryptic dialogue.

Noel Coward is a delight as Hawthorne, the ever-so-proper English gentleman at home in any situation so long as he has a bowler, an umbrella, and regular access to the *Times* of London. Impeccably groomed, as cool and detached as a mandarin, Coward's Hawthorne is a brilliantly etched portrait of the quintessential British civil servant. Mad dogs and Englishmen indeed!

Ernic Kovacs' oily Captain Segura is a smarmy mixture of efficiency and corruption, cruelty and compassion. Kovacs, whose promising career ended abruptly when he was killed in a car crash in 1962, was a fine dramatic actor who usually played comic roles in films like *Operation Mad Ball* (1957), and *Sail a Crooked Ship* (1962). (For more on Kovacs, Coward, and Ives, see notes on *Havana* in the Appendix.)

Maureen O'Hara's Beatrice is spirited yet compliant, and American Jo Morrow, as Guinness' daughter Milly, is blonde and pleasant to look at. Her acting skills are equal to the size of her role.

Ralph Richardson, a favorite of director Reed, is briefly seen as Hawthorne's boss C. He gets off one of the script's better lines when he says that the strange apparatus Wormold has discovered will make the H-bomb a conventional weapon and "nobody worries about conventional weapons."

Guinness' golden decade (actually a shade longer that that) was coming to an end. Although his next film was splendid, Guinness seemed to be fading slightly—with the young Peter Sellers, a Guinness clone, coming up fast on the outside.

The 1960s, it seemed, would be a dangerous time for Alec Guinness.

22. *Tunes of Glory* (1960)

"We'll have all the tunes of glory, to
remember them more clearly..."
—Jock Sinclair, planning Barrow's funeral in
Tunes of Glory.

Tunes of Glory (hereafter just *Tunes*) was Alec Guinness' best role and film since *The Horse's Mouth*, and an interesting companion piece to *The Bridge on the River Kwai*. Guinness, in an unexpected move, played the earthy and abrasive up-from-the-ranks Col. Jock Sinclair. Because the role is so unlike Guinness, it revitalized his screen persona and showed once again his incredible range and versatility.

I seem to be out of step with most critics by preferring John Mills' "Blimpish" Col. Barrow over Guinness' salt-of-the-earth common soldier. Bosley Crowther, for instance, wrote "...there seems to be no alternative for the disposal of our sympathies. The conspicuously egalitarian soldier is to be favored over the snob every time." In *Variety*, "Myro" wrote that Guinness "never misses a trick to win sympathy, even when he behaves foolishly" and that Mills must play "a fundamentally unsympathetic role...."

Perhaps I've been exposed to too many crude, rude, and vulgar Jock Sinclair types in my own life. I find such men to be empty barrels who mask their own inadequacies by demeaning others; they can be loyal and true friends, but also brutishly macho enemies who are completely chauvinistic.

Called a "martinet" by many critics, the Col. Barrow character, in contrast, seems to me rather a reasonable and sensible commander who wants only that his regiment be run efficiently, and that the men behave like soldiers, not little boys playing at war games. Jock is the perfect wartime soldier; Barrow is the perfect peacetime commander, keeping things in readiness for the time a Jock-type leader takes over to lead the men over the top. That the men prefer Jock to Barrow is neither here nor there except in time of war.

Hollis Alpert's *Saturday Review* piece called *Tunes* "An uncommonly well acted and interesting film...." Similarly, in his *New York Times* review, Bosley Crowther wrote, "It is also a film in which tradition itself is magnificently observed in acting that does full justice to the highest standards of an ancient British craft and merits all the honors it has already received."

Going against the adulatory grain, Ellen Fitzpatrick, in *Films in Review*, said that "Guinness should have had the cultured officer-of-the-book role, and Mills should have been the loutish but brave officer-of-the-line. I understand such casting was the original intention. Whoever wacked it around certainly wacked the profit-potential of this film."

A more sympathetic Paul V. Beckley, in the *New York Herald Tribune*, called *Tunes*, "A sternly serious and delightfully penetrating study of men in a man's world...Guinness' performance is brilliant but Mills' is one of the most affecting of his career."

In *Films and Filming*, Richard Whitehall said, "Lacking the analytical brilliance, the sheer virtuousity of Kubrick's *Paths of Glory*, nevertheless [*Tunes*] has much of that film's stern moral probity...."

Finally, *Time*'s anonymous reviewer argued that *"Tunes of Glory* is a thoroughly superior piece of entertainment, thanks to Actor Guinness. It is amazing how this shy, soft man can transform himself—with a hank of hair, a daub of rouge and an almost imperceptible modulation of his India-rubber personality—into a roaring extrovert, all man and a doorway wide."

The film opens on a British army mess in wintry Scotland. As the acting commandant, Lt. Col. Jock Sinclair, struts about his domain, he asks his men, "Am I coarse?" Indeed he is—Jock is a blustery, red-haired and red-faced professional soldier. To his friends and cronies, he is stubbornly loyal and true; but to those he holds in contempt—weaklings and paper-pushers—he can be rude and obnoxious.

Jock tells his men a new colonel is arriving to take command of the regiment. Jock will stay on as second in command. To pass the last night of Jock's command, the officers call in the pipers and start drinking and dancing.

Lt. Col. Basil Barrow (John Mills) arrives in the midst of the party, a day early. Ramrod stiff, he introduces himself and refuses an offer of a whiskey by Jock, preferring instead to have a soft drink. When Barrow reveals his background, Jock snidely remarks, "From Oxford, fancy that."

Barrow makes his first inspection during the morning exercises and proves to be a stickler for detail. After Jock's lax command, the officers naturally grumble about the new regulations and inspections.

Barrow calls a meeting to announce a cocktail party to be thrown for the local civilians. The new colonel angers many of his officers when he tells them they will have to take lessons to learn how to dance correctly—no shouting, no waving the arms above the head. The lessons are to be at 7:15 a.m.

The party and dance are going well. Barrow dances with Jock's daughter Morag (Susannah York) and compliments her on her dancing. A steaming Jock sees a way of getting back at Barrow: He and Capt. Simpson (Allan Cuthbertson) start dancing in their old style—wild and free, with their hands above their heads. Barrow screams at them to stop, his rage astonishing everyone there and ending the evening. After a distraught Barrow storms out,

Guinness (*center*) as the roistering Jock Sinclair, with several of his laddies gathered round to hear his jokes and stories.

Capt. Jimmy Cairns (Gordon Jackson) tells a drunken Jock he had no right to act so badly.

With Jimmy beside him, Barrow takes off in a jeep. He pulls over and tries to explain to Jimmy why he feels he's made a fool of himself: he wants badly to succeed in this new command, but he fears ridicule from the men more than anything else. He senses that he commands by order and tradition, not by respect and loyalty.

Jock, still drunk, heads into town to get more whiskey. Piper Fraser (John Fraser) and Morag are together at the bar. The pipe major (Duncan Macrae) warns Fraser this relationship could mean trouble. Seeing Jock heading toward the bar and a confrontation, his men steer him into another barroom. Unfortunately, Jock sees the two young lovers next door. Jock calls Morag a liar and strikes Fraser. Though Jock was acting as a father, the pipe major tells him, he's done a stupid thing: Fraser was in uniform, and it is a court-martial offense for an officer to strike an enlisted man. When Jock seeks solace in the arms of an old flame named Mary (Kay Walsh), he discovers that his friend Charlie Scott is there "visiting."

Barrow is aware that any punishment will look like revenge after the events of last night. He asks Charlie Scott what to do. Surprisingly, Charlie advises him to file formal charges — for the good of the regiment. Later, Jock learns from Mary that Charlie advised Barrow to send the charges to Regimental Headquarters.

An angry Jock confronts Charlie in the officers' mess, putting on a bluff front. After Barrow comes in, Jock marches off to lunch—getting several of the other officers to join him. Barrow, hearing them laughing together, feels humiliated.

That afternoon, Barrow goes to Jock's room to talk. Saying he's sorry and had no choice, Barrow seems to be pleading for Jock's forgiveness. Jock says he'd give one of *his* men bloody hell but not send the matter to Brigade. Explaining himself, Barrow tells a stone-faced Jock of his long connection with the regiment and his desire to command it one day.

Sensing Barrow's inner turmoil, a cunning Jock asks for a second chance, giving his word to cooperate in the future. "All right," says Barrow in a low, defeated voice. "You won't regret it, Colonel, I promise you that," Jock says, relieved. But, after Barrow leaves, Jock mutters derisively, "Toy soldier!"

Charlie thinks Barrow made a popular if wrong decision. Then Charlie drops a bombshell, telling Barrow that everyone assumed it was *Jock's* decision the matter didn't go to Brigade. When Charlie tells Barrow to go and join the rest of Jock's cronies, Barrow realizes he's totally lost the respect of his men and can never have their loyalty.

Charlie tells Jock that he thinks Jock should have been court-martialed. Suddenly, a shot rings out. Barrow has shot himself. Washing the blood from his hands, Jock whispers, "It's not the body worries me—it's the ghost," and backs fearfully from the room.

Jock calls a meeting of the officers to announce grandiose plans for a funeral with full military honors for Barrow. Guilt pressing on him, Jock begins to "hear" distant drums and ghostly pipes, all the tunes of glory. Jock calls Barrow's death murder—and all of them accomplices.

As Jock begins to rave, the men file out silently—all save Charlie Scott and Jimmy Cairns. When Jock breaks down completely, they rush to support him and escort him home, shielding him to the end.

Like many films, *Tunes* was slow getting backing. After most major British and non-British studios had passed on James Kennaway's script (based on his own novel), producer Colin Lesslie sent a copy to John Mills, who, after a spate of commercially rewarding but artistically unchallenging films like *Swiss Family Robinson* for Disney, wanted to perform in a role he could sink his teeth into.

Mills thought the script was terrific, but saw that the small budget could accommodate only black-and-white, not color. When his wife Mary threatened to divorce him if he didn't try to get the film made, Mills sent his copy of the script along to Sir Alec. When Guinness read the script he agreed to do the film if Mills would commit to it as well.

As Mills notes in his autobiography *Up in the Clouds, Gentlemen Please*, Guinness asked, " 'Which part do you want to play?' 'I don't mind. They're both as good as each other. Let's toss for it.'

Gordon Jackson (*far left*) and John Mills (*left*) listen as Guinness' Jock Sinclair (*center*) plays the sympathetic second-in-command.

"We finally decided that we would do some 'off-beat' casting: I would play the neurotic, nerve-wracked Colonel Barrow, and Alec would play the hard-drinking, tough Scots colonel up from the ranks. With Alec's acceptance the combination and the chemistry looked strong. Colin Lesslie was able to raise the extra money, which meant the film could be made in colour." (Oddly enough, Mills—as did several reviewers at the time of the film's release— baldly states that "Ronnie Neame...made his debut as a director in this film....")

Kennaway's script does a fine job of showing the personality clash between two strong-willed men who have almost nothing in common save their desire to command this particular regiment. Kennaway gives the men all the best lines and—it would be hard to argue otherwise—the film is clearly set in a man's world: the joshing, boys-will-be-boys atmosphere of a remote army outpost. That the women in this film—Susannah York (making her film debut) as Jock's daughter Morag, and Kay Walsh as Jock's sometime lover— are not central to its drama can be seen in the fact that their scenes have been cut drastically in the version seen on television.

Kennaway gives both men strong virtues and faults, seemingly making the point that if you could selectively combine the virtues of both of them you would have one helluva soldier/commander. As it is, Jock is a swaggering braggart given to salty lines like, "Fancy the poor laddie's got tabs instead of tits," and Barrow is a marvelous technician with no feeling for his men.

The biggest weakness of Kennaway's script—and, therefore, of the film itself—is Guinness' breakdown at the end when he realizes his actions have driven Barrow not to resignation but to suicide. That good old Jock would feel personally responsible for Barrow's fate is unconvincing. Everything to that point would argue otherwise. Still, it gives Guinness a great scene to play, and he takes full advantage of the opportunity.

John Mills, in a "heads it's Guinness, tails it's Mills" situation, won the best actor award at the 1960 Venice Film Festival. Guinness, after all, had won the award two years earlier for his Gulley Jimson in *The Horse's Mouth*, so the judges, forced to choose between Mills' Barrow and Guinness' Sinclair, chose the former. It takes nothing away from Mills' intelligently considered performance to assert that Guinness deserved the award just as much as Mills did. (For more on Mills, see notes on *Tunes of Glory* in the Appendix.)

The other actors in *Tunes* are uniformly (no pun intended) good, with the nod going to Dennis Price's subtly shaded performance as Jock's "best friend" Charlie Scott. Appropriately oily while remaining likeable, Price's Scott is clearly recognizable as the opportunist who sees which way the wind blows before committing himself. One wishes Price could have gotten many more such meaty roles.

Gordon Jackson, of "Upstairs, Downstairs" fame, is solid and sympathetic as Captain Jimmy Cairns, Barrow's understanding aide, and Duncan Macrae is outstanding in the small role of Pipe Major MacLean. (See notes on *Tunes of Glory* in the Appendix for more on these actors.)

Still, it is Guinness and Mills who make the film such a feast of good acting. Guinness is even able to disguise the distinctive Guinness voice by layering over it a rough Scottish brogue. Guinness is appropriately hale and hearty, giving Jock the swagger of a man without doubts or indecision. And, despite his character's unlikeability, he invests Jock's breakdown scene with throat-catching intensity.

Mills, again in his autobiography, noted that director Neame's direction was "smooth and unobtrusive; the highly dramatic scenes that Alec and I had to handle were therefore much more effective."

While Ronald Neame has rarely been placed in the front rank of directors, he is more than competent. His compositions for *Tunes* are simple but strong, but it is in his handling of the many fine film actors that he excels. Comparing Neame to Lean, Guinness said, "I think Neame expects more creative invention from his actors."

Speaking of the challenges of acting for the screen, versus the stage, Guinness noted, ". . . On the screen so often you have to mis-time, and it's in the hands of the technicians to put it back into timing. I complained about this to . . . Ronald Neame: 'You force it on the actor when he's performing, who understands why there is this odd timing, and very often it doesn't get put back properly.' And Ronnie started taping scenes as they were rehearsed, which had nothing to do with the set-ups and camera, but as if they were

With Col. Barrow dead, Sinclair begins to crack up in front of Charlie Scott (Dennis Price, *with cane*), Jimmy Cairns (Gordon Jackson, *beside Price*), and the rest of the regiment. Sinclair hears the "tunes of glory."

absolutely played as they were, and that was stuck aside with the idea that when it came to editing, the timing would be adhered to as strictly as possible. This is one of the things that make so much film acting rather subacting." (For more on Neame, see the chapter and notes in the Appendix for *The Card/The Promoter*.)

If the character of Jock Sinclair seemed far removed from Guinness' own true persona, it was nothing compared to the leap he took in his next film, playing a Japanese businessman who falls in love with a Jewish widow in *A Majority of One*.

II. Situation Hopeless But Not Serious:
The Bronze Age

"Think sideways!"

—Edward De Bono

"The main obligation is to amuse yourself."

—S.J. Perelman

A Majority of One (1961)

to

Hotel Paradiso (1966)

23. A Majority of One (1961)

> "Any man more right than his neighbors...
> constitutes a majority of one."
> — Henry David Thoreau

A *Majority of One* (hereafter just *Majority*), Guinness' only film of 1961, is far from being either his best or worst. The reviews were kinder than one might expect, and many filmgoers have fond memories of the movie, relishing its old-fashioned but genuine appeal as a liberal, "right thinking," two-and-a-half hour sudser. You laugh, you cry, you kiss two bucks goodbye.

The script was written by Leonard Spigelgass and based on his play of the same name, which opened on Broadway at the Shubert Theatre on February 16, 1959, and ran for 556 performances.

On Broadway, the leads were played by Gertrude Berg and Englishman Cedric Hardwicke (which might explain why Guinness, another Englishman, was cast in Hardwicke's role). The play was produced by Dore Schary and the Theatre Guild and featured Ina Balin as Alice, Michael Tolan as Jerry, and Mae Questel and Marc Marno, who repeated their roles as Mrs. Rubin and Eddie, respectively, for the film.

When the film was announced by Warner Bros., everyone assumed that Berg would repeat her marvelous characterization. Alas, it was not to be.

Murray Schumach, in his book *The Face on the Cutting Room Floor*, writes: "A different aspect of the fear of anti–Semitism is seen in the reluctance to use Jewish [actors] even when it is mandatory. When A *Majority of One* was made into a movie, Gertrude Berg was obviously perfect for the part of the dumpy middle-aged Jewess she created on Broadway. She wanted the part. It was given to Rosalind Russell." An "inside" Hollywood joke at the time of *Majority* and *Gypsy* ran: "They're going to film *My Fair Lady* and Rosalind Russell will probably play Henry Higgins."

Guinness accepted the role of Koichi Asano mainly for the money, £70,000 (about $200,000), admitting as much himself—but that was what he said *after* the film got terrible notices in England. That he took the part seriously may be seen in the fact that he traveled to Japan to study Japanese customs and behavior. Guinness forsook complex makeup, settling for a set of artificial epicanthic folds one critic likened to "two fat little patties of ravioli hanging from his eyebrows."

The *Harvard Lampoon* awarded *Majority* its 1961 "OK-Doc-Break-the-Arm-Again Award" given annually to the film with the most flagrant examples of miscasting. Edward G. Robinson, in his autobiography, wrote, "My heart bled for [Rosalind Russell]...But even more for Alec Guinness who probably can play any part in the world except that of a Japanese."

Although the reviews were mixed, the reviewers gave the film credit for its theme and warmth. *Variety*'s "Tube" called *Majority* an "Outstanding film...Beautifully mounted and especially notable for the exciting results obtained from some bold, strikingly unconventional casting...Furthermore, this is a choice and unusually substantial family attraction, with a penetrating scrutiny of deeply ingrained passive prejudice."

Time's reviewer called *Majority* "A warm though slightly soggish knish of sentiment...Like the play, [it is] a too-cute intercontinental switch on *Abie's Irish Rose*," lacking "the kindly, take-a-piece-of-fruit intimacy of the play. But Actor Guinness breaks out a sensational Tokyo brogue ('Prease feer free to use my country club')...."

Paul V. Beckley, in the *New York Herald Tribune*, noted "...It is a relatively slight story that cries out for a lightness of touch, a kind of structural legerdemain that would keep us from staring too closely at the interstices. Unfortunately, it has been built on a scale nearly as massive as a spectacle, running [nearly] two-and-a-half hours...."

A.H. Weiler, in the *New York Times*, wrote, "...This comedy blend of specialized, local middle class mores and humor and Nipponese formality becomes a wholly acceptable, truly heartwarming and entertaining affair despite its exotic ingredients."

In *Films and Filming*, Roger Manvell began, "This, from the American point of view, is a good-neighbor film, full of that warm-hearted sentimental simplification of the world's problems that is as much a part of the American way of life as its complement on the screen, the sentimentalizing of violence. And it contains the strange casting of Alec Guinness as a Japanese industrialist."

Finally, Helen Weldon Kuhn, in *Films in Review*, said, "Leonard Spiegelgass, who wrote the play of the same title, also did the adaptation for the screen, and so, I assume, was wholly responsible for the schmaltz, soap-opera sentimentality, and utter untruth, of which this bland and pleasant programmer is composed."

Mrs. Jacoby (Rosalind Russell) is a Jewish widow from Brooklyn whose only son was killed by the Japanese during World War II. Her daughter, Alice (Madlyn Rhue), is a university-educated young woman married to an ambitious young diplomat, Jerry Black (Ray Danton), who is being sent to Japan to help conduct trade negotiations with the Japanese. Jerry and Alice talk Mrs. Jacoby into joining them on the trip.

En route by ship, Mrs. Jacoby meets Mr. Asano (Guinness), a Japanese

Rosalind Russell and Alec Guinness as a most unlikely pair: a Jewish widow and a Japanese businessman.

industrialist who also lost family members during the war. They play cards and, slowly, feel an attraction for each other that Alice and Jerry try to discourage.

Jerry suspects that Mr. Asano, who is also a negotiating member of the trade committee, is using his friendship with his mother-in-law to gain an advantage in the negotiations. Mrs. Jacoby finds this suspicion unlikely but agrees not to see Mr. Asano on their last night of the voyage.

Jerry unintentionally offends Mr. Asano and the negotiations are broken off. Taking things into her own hands, Mrs. Jacoby visits Mr. Asano at his home and the two have a glorious evening — after which Mr. Asano agrees to resume the talks.

With things in order, Mrs. Jacoby and her family are preparing to leave when Mr. Asano startles them all by proposing marriage to Mrs. Jacoby. Angered by Jerry and Alice's racist reaction to Mr. Asano, Mrs. Jacoby nonetheless turns him down, citing the weight of their combined memories as a barrier to a lasting relationship between them.

However, when Mr. Asano arrives in New York City some months later as a delegate to the United Nations, he and Mrs. Jacoby renew their romantic interest in each other. Happily, Mrs. Jacoby is now pleased to accept his honorable intentions.

Apart from the makeup around his eyes, Guinness did little to look Japanese. His studies of Japanese mannerisms and body movements, however, seem to have paid off. Not for one minute do we *really* believe that Guinness is Japanese, yet he does become Mr. Asano through physical suggestion and skillful vocal mimicry.

Rosalind Russell is...well, Rosalind Russell. She's no more a Jewish momma than Guinness is a Japanese industrialist. Still, she brings her patented vigor and energy to the role of Mrs. Jacoby. Sometimes her Jewish matron loses her accent and mannerisms, but for the most part, Miss Russell successfully brings her years of experience to the demands of the role. (For more on Rosalind Russell's films, see notes on *Majority* in the Appendix.)

Producer-director Mervyn Le Roy is the embodiment of Hollywood popular vulgarity. His films give the moviegoing public the splashy, glittering entertainment promised by the words "Made in Hollywood, U.S.A."

Born in 1900, Le Roy began as an actor but quickly found his niche behind the camera, not in front of it. Some of the films he's been involved with loom large in any discussion of Hollywood greats: *Little Caesar* (1930), *I Am a Fugitive from a Chain Gang* (1932), *The Wizard of Oz* (as producer, 1939), *Random Harvest* (1942), *Thirty Seconds Over Tokyo* (1944), *Mr. Roberts* (co-director, 1955), *The Bad Seed* (producer as well as director, 1956), *No Time for Sergeants* (also producer, 1958), and *The FBI Story* (also producer, 1959).

Since the film was released originally at 156 minutes, it's hard to believe *anything* was cut, but the film was "trimmed" before its release to theaters. As Doug McClelland reveals in his book *The Unkindest Cuts*, "The opening scene, in which Russell, working in a dress shop, outfitted bride-to-be Sharon Hugueny, was cut for general release. Miss Hugueny, who had only this one scene but received good billing, remained in the credits of the picture, too. You can't get much better billing than that."

Guinness' so-called Golden Age had ended with *Tunes of Glory*. With *A Majority of One*, Guinness began a new, more modest period—a "Bronze Age." Guinness took his money—and his lumps—and went on.

24. H.M.S. Defiant/Damn the Defiant! (1962)

"A future Drake or Hawkins, with a vicious streak and a
silver spoon—and he has to learn on my quarterdeck!"
—Capt. Crawford of his second-in-command,
Lt. Scott-Paget, in *H.M.S. Defiant*.

Guinness returned to sea in 1962 in *H.M.S. Defiant*. His portrayal of
Captain Crawford in *H.M.S. Defiant* (hereafter just *Defiant*) cannot be
faulted, but as one critic noted at the time, it was a role that could have been
played by any good actor. Though hardly a serious criticism, it is one that
could rarely be leveled at Guinness before. Whether his judgment was
flagging or he simply could not get roles more worthy of his talents is
unknown. Certainly, *Defiant* was a solid if unspectacular commercial success
that gave him an opportunity to play against the sublime Dirk Bogarde, but
it did little to advance or even maintain his reputation.

The film's strength is in its attention to period detail and costuming.
Also, rather than filming the shipboard shots in a studio and intercutting
them with unconvincing model work, director Gilbert had at his command
several full-size reproductions of British and French men-of-war. These
reproductions were constructed by Alan Villiers, who'd built Mayflower the
Second, an accurate duplication of the pilgrims' famous ship. To add to the
authenticity, the scenes at sea were shot off the Spanish coast near Denia.

The battle scenes are convincing and rousing, and the conflict between
Guinness' Capt. Crawford and Bogarde's Lt. Scott-Padget is well developed,
but the film all too often falls flat at other times and is even somewhat boring.
Called *The Mutineers* before production began, and *Battle Aboard the
Defiant* before release, *Defiant* was struck with the rather pathetic title, *Damn
the Defiant!* in the U.S. It did well enough but was clearly overshadowed by
the Marlon Brando/Trevor Howard remake of *Mutiny on the Bounty*.

The critical response to *Defiant* was mixed, with even Guinness' performance drawing fewer raves than usual. *Variety*'s "Rich" called the film a
"Strong naval drama....There is a first-class battle and some scenes of
violence which perhaps are a shade overdone. But mostly it is an intriguing
battle of character between two excellent actors, Guinness and Bogarde...."

"If you're for naval roistering, here is your cup of rum," wrote Bosley Crowther in the *New York Times*. "Let's not say Sir Alec gives a memorable performance. He merely gives a dignified, stiff-lipped portrayal of an English naval gentleman...."

Paul V. Beckley's review in the *New York Herald Tribune* was similarly low-key: "Fails to arouse the excitement that both story and accoutrement promise.... Guinness' performance is meticulous, a little too given to correctness of manner to arouse more than natural sympathy for the man he presents."

Finally, in *Films and Filming*, Robin Bean wrote, "*H.M.S. Defiant* is a skilfully executed, beautiful to watch, period naval drama in the good old British tradition, directed by the expert in wartime one-upmanship, Lewis Gilbert."

Spithead, England, 1797. Press gangs from H.M.S. *Defiant* are roaming the streets, rounding up unwilling conscripts for His Majesty's warships. Meeting with Admiral Jackson (Walter Fitzgerald), Captain Crawford (Guinness) of the *Defiant* argues that discipline, while necessary, is too often overly harsh.

Even the captain's twelve-year-old son is shipping out with his father on this trip. When Captain Crawford returns to the *Defiant*, he gives orders that his son, a midshipman, is to be treated no differently from any other midshipman.

The new crewmen are put through their paces by the ship's second in command, Lieutenant Scott-Paget (Dirk Bogarde). The captain is pleased by Scott-Paget's results but warns him not to press the men too hard. Captain Crawford discusses the effects of harsh discipline with the ship's surgeon (Maurice Denham). Surgeon Goss advises him to beware of Scott-Paget; it seems the ambitious young lieutenant is a strict taskmaster and has friends in high places—friends who've gotten his last two captains sacked.

At gunnery practice, Evans, a common seaman, makes an involuntary gesture as if to strike Scott-Paget. Since he put up his fists, Evans (Tom Bell) is to receive six dozen lashes. Contradicting Scott-Paget's order, Captain Crawford has the punishment reduced to two dozen lashes. The captain is puzzled by a phrase Evans used in his defense, which sounds like a practiced response. Some of the crew say Crawford is a soft captain.

Scott-Paget wants the captain to strike out on his own initiative and ignore his orders. Crawford flares up at this impertinence and at Scott-Paget's threats of using his influence.

Scott-Paget notices the captain's son and gets an idea. Meanwhile, the crew, under the leadership of a seaman named Vizard (Anthony Quayle), plots to join the rest of the fleet in an attempt to seize control.

Scott-Paget shrewdly get Senior Midshipman Kilpatrick (Nigel Stock) on his side by promising him advancement if he'll see that Mr. Crawford is punished at every opportunity. Scott-Paget arranges to have the captain below

Guinness (*right*) as the sympathetic and fair Capt. Crawford, on deck with his cruel and calculating second-in-command, Lt. Scott-Padget (Dirk Bogarde).

decks to "happen upon" the caning of his son for an infraction he didn't commit.

Since Scott-Paget has countermanded several of his sailing orders, the captain uses that as an excuse to have his first officer confined below decks. The captain tells Scott-Paget that only when the lieutenant leaves his son alone will he be returned to duty.

The crew practices its motions for seizing the ship, including a silent shout—which a puzzled Captain Crawford observes. Vizard, who once helped the captain's son down from the rigging, knows the captain saw the rehearsal.

At the rendezvous place, the *Defiant* finds only empty sea. The captain speaks to the crew, telling them they're going to a new meeting place to pick up their wards—ships laden with timber from Italy to build new warships.

Spotting two French ships, one a frigate, the *Defiant* beats to quarters. The battle is furious and bloody as the ships pound away at close range. Scott-Paget is a bastard, but he is nothing if not brave, taking on the French captain saber-to-saber after the frigate is boarded. Vizard, too, proves a fierce fighter.

After the ships are taken as prizes, the captain sends a skeleton crew aboard to sail them back to England; his son is among those sent. The captain has "put right" his mistake; Scott-Paget has no leverage on him now.

When the captain allows a mystery ship to venture too close, it opens fire, severly wounding him; Scott-Paget assumes command and wins the day, capturing a French officer who has plans for the invasion of England.

After Mr. Kilpatrick forces Evans to eat wormy biscuits, the defiant sailor strikes him; the rest of the crew overpowers Kilpatrick and seizes the ship. Meanwhile, the ship's surgeon is amputating the captain's wounded arm.

Vizard visits the captain, who tells him of the planned invasion, stressing that England could be humiliated and overrun by Frenchmen. Vizard agrees to sail back to England with the news. In return, the captain tells him he'll do what he can — but no harm must come to *any* officer. The crew, except for Evans, readily agrees to return to England.

Back with the fleet, the captain greets his son, now serving aboard the admiral's flagship. The captain and Vizard learn that the fleet mutinied and was pardoned by order of the king. The officers, including a nonrepentant Scott-Paget, are set free. Even though the captain orders Scott-Paget put under arrest, it is not enough for Evans, who fatally knifes the lieutenant. A raging Vizard strangles Evans and throws his body overboard. Making for the open sea, the crew spots a French fireship in the fog heading directly for the fleet. Taking on the fireship, *Defiant* grapples it, turns it, and finally sinks it. Hit by a falling piece of rigging, Vizard dies knowing that he has saved England.

The film's script was written by two solid professionals, Nigel Kneale and Edmund H. North. North, a long-time contract writer for Twentieth Century–Fox, wrote, among others, the classic SF film, *The Day the Earth Stood Still.* Nigel Kneale has written many scripts for the BBC, including several concerning Professor Quatermass.

Kneale and North's script, while seemingly documentarylike in sticking to the facts, is actually a distortion, for dramatic effect, of the real events. There *was* a real fleet uprising in 1797 at Spithead and Nore, but it was led by sympathetic officers, not by common seamen fed up with wormy bread and harsh discipline.

Defiant has Guinness' Captain Crawford appeal to the ship's crew's patriotism — do they want Frenchmen in *their* homes, chasing after *their* wives and daughters? In truth, the real mutineers blockaded London so effectively that the admiralty had no choice but to give in to their demands.

The film seems to say that mutiny is okay under the right circumstances, but that once the good officers — i.e., Captain Crawford — reclaim control from the bad officers, the status quo should be returned as soon as possible. To modern viewers, this seems sensible and correct. In actuality, however, the truth is more elusive. The film begins well, showing ruthless press gangs sweeping up and virtually kidnapping any able-bodied man they can find. Captain Crawford bemoans the system of discipline to Admiral Jackson, who, while admitting Crawford has a point, seems to condone almost any activity aboard the ships in his fleet. From this promising beginning, however, the message we're fed is that Scott-Paget is an aberration, that such conduct and routine sadism are rare and hard fought against by sympathetic and kindly officers of the Crawford stripe.

Even given Scott-Paget's outrages against common humanity, Vizard, the decent leader of the ship's mutineers, must die for the sin of mutiny and to pay for Scott-Paget's death.

So, rather than admitting the flaws and built-in dishonesty of the whole rotten system, the film's Spithead and Nore mutinies are reduced to the petty abuses of one ship's sadistic and vengeful officer, Scott-Paget. The film adroitly sidesteps the question of whether or not the British navy is a systematic exploiter, relying on a foreign war to excuse domestic abuses and to maintain the wealth and influence of the few at the expense of the many.

Lewis Gilbert was born in London in 1920. He started in films as a child actor, appearing in numerous movies, including Alexander Korda's *Over the Moon* (1937). Before the Second World War he was an assistant director, and during the war he did work for the United States Air Corp Film Unit.

He made his feature directorial debut in 1947 with *The Little Ballerina*. A "maritime" director, he helmed such seafaring productions as *Albert R.N.* (1953) and *The Sea Shall Not Have Them* (1954). His film about the wartime heroism of R.A.F. flier Douglas Bader, *Reach for the Sky*, was a huge commercial success in America as well as England and made him a "money" director.

He continued his sea picture connection with the taut and almost documentarylike *Sink the Bismarck* in 1960, as well as with *H.M.S. Defiant*. The critically acclaimed social drama *Alfie*, which made an international star of Michael Caine, got Gilbert away from the salt air. In recent years, Gilbert has directed two of the James Bond pictures: *You Only Live Twice*, a 1967 production starring Sean Connery (the first and best Bond), and 1977's *The Spy Who Loved Me*.

Gilbert's direction of Guinness and Bogarde in their many scenes of confrontation is skilled and forthright. But it is in his handling of the action scenes that he sparkles (although one never knows if the director handed over such work to his assistants and the second-unit crew).

Dirk Bogarde, born Derek Van Den Bogaerd in 1920, began his film career in lightweight British comedies, including the hugely successful "Doctor" series. Eventually, he got a chance to tackle more serious roles and became an international star.

Bogarde's suave manner and appearance made him a natural for the role of the social-climbing Scott-Paget. A classically understated actor, Bogarde's style of performing meshed neatly with Guinness' method. The scenes between these two great actors crackle with suppressed emotion and hostility masked by surface correctness. (See notes on *Defiant* in the Appendix for more on Bogarde.)

Guinness, while excellent, is simply coasting. Other than his confrontations with Bogarde, the role of Captain Crawford puts few demands on his honed and polished skills. Perhaps it is a consequence of his subtlety and guile that we swallow whole several of his more trite speeches in which he defends Mother England and appeals to the mutineers' better instincts; coming from the mouth of a less believable and sincere actor, they might have provoked laughs of derision. As it is, we nod agreement and find nothing unusual with the mutineers' decision to return to Spithead and do the "right thing."

Guinness loves heroes, adventurers, and great men. It must have appealed to him to play a character so obviously close to that greatest of British naval heroes, Admiral Nelson. Like Nelson, Guinness' Captain Crawford loses his arm in defense of the nation; like Nelson, Crawford snatches victory from the jaws of defeat by convincing the mutineers that their real enemy is the French; and, presumably, like Nelson, Crawford is a true Englishman — noble, brave, and with an incorruptible conscience.

25. *Lawrence of Arabia* (1962)

"I think you are another of these desert-loving English."
— Faisal to Lawrence in *Lawrence of Arabia*

Lawrence of Arabia (hereafter just *Lawrence*) was Guinness' second film of 1962 and covered the adventures of Thomas Edward Lawrence, a soldier-archeologist who turned mapmaker and agent for British Intelligence (a real-life Indiana Jones). The film begins in Cairo, Egypt, in January 1917, follows Lawrence's famed desert exploits (made famous by Lowell Thomas), and ends with his capture of Damascus from the Turks in October 1918.

In this epic film, Alec Guinness had the rather small, if important, role of Prince Faisal. T.E. Lawrence, the role in which Guinness had shone in Terence Rattigan's 1960 stage play *Ross*, was played by Peter O'Toole.

An admirer of explorers, leaders, heroes, and others who face danger to achieve greatness, Guinness found playing Lawrence (or "Ross") in the Glen Byam–directed stage version a personally fulfilling experience. But, alas, when old friend David Lean approached him for a role in the film, it was to play Faisal, not Lawrence. As Lean said at the time, "Guinness played Lawrence on the stage, but for the film he is too old. The whole point about Lawrence is that he was twenty-eight years old at the time." So the twenty-nine-year-old O'Toole, in just his fourth screen appearance, played Lawrence, while the forty-seven-year-old Guinness put on the robes and beard of the man who would one day rule the Kingdom of Saudi Arabia.

Once, when he was asked how strongly the choice of a director for his films influenced his decision to make the picture, Guinness replied, "Entirely." As he elaborated, "On the whole I've stuck with the same directors over and over again. You become friendly with people, they know your quirks and bad tempers. I like to work with people I know; I would also like to work with a lot of people I don't know because I like their work."

About Lean, directing Guinness for the third time on *Lawrence*, Sir Alec said that "Lean is very keen. He has a very firm picture in his mind of what he wants, and that's it, although he will occasionally break out and give you the stage, so to speak."

Biographer Stanley Weintraub, who wrote *Private Shaw and Public Shaw* and other works about Lawrence, said in his review of *Lawrence* in *Film*

Quarterly, "Whatever the virtues of the film's stunning desert photography, its Lawrence bears much the same relation to Col. Thomas Edward Lawrence that Elizabeth Taylor's Cleopatra does to that famous lady...."

Hollis Alpert's review in the *Saturday Review* called the film "Magnificent.... Here is a motion picture that seems a summing up of the aims and aspirations of the 'big film'...."

Roger Sandall, in *Film Quarterly*, left no doubt as to how he felt about *Lawrence*: "From the director of *Great Expectations*, a galumping camelodrama in *debut de siècle* style. From the producer of *The African Queen*, an Uncrowned King of Arabia suited more for a jester's cap than a coronet. From the writer who gave us a craggily true Sir Thomas More in the play *A Man for All Seasons*, a preposterous golden androgyne."

In *Films and Filming*, Peter Baker praised the film: "*Lawrence of Arabia* makes its first breath-taking impact with the most exciting location photography I have ever seen in the cinema." Baker concluded his longish piece by saying, "...on the level of cinema spectacle, *Lawrence of Arabia* makes the films about Jesus Christ seem as empty as a used can of beer in the desert. And as small."

Variety's "Rich" called *Lawrence* "a kingsize adventure yarn, sweepingly produced, directed and lensed...."

Lawrence begins in Dorset, England. A mysterious motorcycle rider speeds through the countryside. When he tries to avoid some bicyclists, he's thrown from his motorcycle and killed. At St. Paul's Cathedral in London, we learn that the man who was killed was T.E. Lawrence — "Lawrence of Arabia." And his story begins... in Cairo, in 1917.

The young Lawrence gets a mission from Mr. Dryden of the Arab Bureau (played by Claude Rains). He is to find and enlist the aid of Prince Faisal, a Bedouin leader who would be king.

Crossing the desert with his guide, Lawrence briefly meets Sherif Ali Ibn el Kharish (Omar Sharif). Spurning Ali's offer of aid, Lawrence finds Faisal's camp on his own, arriving in the midst of an air raid by Turkish planes. Faisal (Guinness) waves his sword angrily and impotently at the retreating planes. Later, Lawrence tells Faisal and Ali that he supports the Arab cause. "I think you are another of these desert-loving English," Faisal tells him wryly.

Lawrence takes fifty of Faisal's men on a raid against Aqaba across the Nefud Desert. When Gasim, one of Lawrence's Arab serving boys, is lost in the desert, Lawrence goes back for him. When he finds Gasim and brings him back, the Arabs rejoice in his deed.

After burning his British uniform to take up white robes, Lawrence meets Auda Abu Tayi (Anthony Quinn), a fierce Arab sheik. His fighters agree to join Lawrence's march against Aqaba.

Lawrence must shoot Gasim to avenge a wrong — and to insure that a blood feud does not follow the execution. The Arabs then attack the Turks

A behind-the-scenes shot showing Guinness (*left*) in makeup as Faisal. To his right are producer Sam Spiegel, Jack Hawkins in makeup as General Allenby, and director David Lean.

holding Aqaba and defeat them. Lawrence sits atop a camel, moodily listening to the pillage of the city.

Promising to return with guns and gold, Lawrence returns to Cairo to report his victory. General Allenby (Jack Hawkins) grudgingly admits Lawrence's capture of Aqaba was "good work." Lawrence tells Allenby that he enjoyed the killing forced upon him. He accepts a promotion to the rank of major and is sent back to the Arabs.

Lawrence is seen blowing up trains, a golden-haired figure of strange and compelling appeal. All this success goes to Lawrence's head and, while showing off, he is arrested by Turkish police. Lawrence, questioned by the Turkish Bey (Jose Ferrer), plays the fool, but is still stripped and examined. After resisting the Bey's advances, Lawrence is whipped and thrown out into the street, where he is rescued by Ali. His spirit broken, Lawrence returns to Cairo.

After Allenby insists he is extraordinary, Lawrence agrees and returns to his Arab allies once again. On a mission to take Damascus before the British army can, Lawrence's force stops to destroy a Turkish force. A frenzied Lawrence joins in the bloodlust.

The Arabs, a desert people, make a mess of running the public services of a large city like Damascus. Amidst fires, broken water mains, and a lack of working phones, the Arabs leave the city in the hands of the British.

Faisal joins Allenby to make political peace. Lawrence, promoted to

Colonel, is to go back to England. Both Allenby and Faisal admit to being relieved Lawrence is going. When Allenby admiringly calls Faisal a hard man, the Arab leader says, "You are only a general—I must be a king."

Rather than starting out to make a film about Lawrence's Arabian adventures, producer Sam Spiegel and director David Lean, the team who'd made *Kwai*, had wanted to film the life of Indian leader Mahatma Gandhi with Alec Guinness in the role of Gandhi. Lean and Spiegel had even been scouting locations in India before the project fell through. (Gandhi, the role that was almost Guinness', won Ben Kingsley an Oscar for best actor, and Richard Attenborough's *Gandhi* won an impressive seven other Academy Awards, including best picture of 1982.)

Lean and Spiegel then decided to film a version of the life of T.E. Lawrence based on *The Seven Pillars of Wisdom*, Lawrence's own account of his time in the desert. After rejecting Michael Wilson's attempt to capture Lawrence in a workable script, Lean and Spiegel began casting about for someone else to try his hand. According to Lean, it was Sam Spiegel, the producer, who finally gave playwright Robert Bolt (*A Man For All Seasons*) the assignment. As Bolt was later to say of his script: "I tried...for a bold and beautiful verbal architecture."

Lean has called the screenplay "essentially Bolt's own conception of Lawrence," and concedes that Bolt's "treatment for instance shows him to be masochistic."

Noting that many military men passed through Lawrence's campaigns, Lean said, "It would be impossible to include them all...so we have one...who represents them as 'an English military character'...."

Spiegel and Lean's *Lawrence*, which was to end up costing $12,000,000 to produce, was filmed in many of the actual locations where Lawrence's exploits took place. In Jordan, the film's workers found stretches of the Turkish railway line that Lawrence and his army blew up years before. Some camera locations were so hostile and remote not even Bedouins visited them.

As Lean writes in "Out of the Wilderness," published in *Films and Filming*, "We were in Jordan for five months where we did all the big, spectacular desert material. Then we were in Spain where we did a lot of the interiors...interiors of authentic Moorish buildings in and around Seville....Smaller exterior scenes were done among the dunes on the Southern Spanish coast." In Morocco, the *Lawrence* crew found themselves in Ouarzazate, a fiendishly hot desert town. Occupying a building abandoned by the French Foreign Legion, Lean's crew and actors suffered through a July and August shoot that was so hot that Legionaires elsewhere were posted to Ouarzazate for punishment.

David Lean's direction of *Lawrence* is surehanded and confident; he's a man who is sure of what he's doing, a man firmly in charge. Lean's confidence apparently comes from his earlier experiences with films presenting major logistical obstacles. As Lean himself notes, "Perhaps I have become a 'big film' man."

As always, Lean gets the most from his actors, and Guinness, of course, turns in a wonderfully wry and nuanced performance as Prince Faisal, the wily Arab desert fox who knows political victories mean more than military ones— at least, once the heroes have won the day. Guinness looks authoritative as Faisal and he handles the small role well, despite being unable to disguise the distinctive Guinness voice.

Guinness' Faisal, as conceived by Lean and Bolt, is essentially a politician and a patriot. As such, he will gladly use Lawrence's military prowess to push out the Turks. Faisal has no illusions about the British (unlike the naive Lawrence); he's aware they'll step into the vacuum left by the Turks. But he's also aware the British will be less cruel and corrupt masters, and, ultimately, easier for the Arabians to win their independence from. The British, after all, are romantics; worse yet, they're romantics *and* idealists, and Guinness' Faisal is well aware of it.

After telling the American reporter Jackson Bentley (Arthur Kennedy) that the Arabs kill their own wounded rather than let them fall into the hands of the Turks—who would torture them to death—Faisal reacts to the reporter's comments about Lawrence's "mercy": "With Major Lawrence, mercy is a passion; with me it is merely good manners. You may judge which motive is the more reliable. . . ." Lean then cuts to a shot of the "merciful" Lawrence blowing up a train full of Turkish troops.

The role of Faisal, king and politician, amply suits Guinness' particular inner talents. The consummate politician is also a minimalist, just as Guinness is a minimalist actor. Acting, like politics, is about revealing only what is necessary. Emotion and expression must be parceled out sparingly. To give away too much too soon is to overplay one's hand; what is left unsaid is as important as what is spoken aloud.

Under Lean's sure hand, the other actors in *Lawrence* turn in accomplished performances, too. Peter O'Toole, as the neurotic Lawrence, is outstanding in his first major screen role. Though at least half a foot taller than the real Lawrence, O'Toole is perfectly cast. A virtual unknown before *Lawrence,* O'Toole was to emerge a major star for his brilliant acting, and he won an Academy Award nomination for best actor (losing to Gregory Peck in a year of outstanding performances by male actors). (See notes on *Lawrence* in the Appendix for more of O'Toole's films.)

Not far behind Guinness and O'Toole were the performances of Jack Hawkins as General Allenby and Omar Sharif as Ali. Lean said of Hawkins: "It is, I believe, the best performance Hawkins has ever given." *Lawrence* made a leading man out of darkly handsome Egyptian actor Omar Sharif, who would also play the title role in Lean and Guinness' next epic film, *Dr. Zhivago.*

Claude Rains' small role as Mr. Dryden was his last major motion picture appearance. Anthony Quinn was fine as the roughhewn and impetuous Auda Abu Tayi. If his performance seems less impressive today, it's probably because we've seen variations on it for the past twenty-five years.

Sir Donald Wolfit (1902–1968) played General Murray. Wolfit was a famous Shakespearean actor who toured widely in such meaty roles as *King Lear*. His "dresser," Ronald Harwood, wrote a 1971 biography of Wolfit and later wrote a play loosely based on his experiences as confidant and dresser to the great actor. The play, *The Dresser*, was turned into a fine film starring Albert Finney and Tom Courtenay (in 1983).

The editing of *Lawrence* was done by Anne V. Coates, an accomplished editor who'd worked with both Lean and Guinness before. But while Coates was the editor of record, Lean, of course, was heavily involved in the cutting of his film and the assembly of the battle sequences. As Lean says, "I supervise the editing myself, particularly the tricky action sequences. As I was an editor, it is hard to keep my hands off the celluloid. Nobody can prophesy at the script stage how a thing is going to be cut; but I try to get the shots that I know will be wanted, moving the artists from here to there and not repeating the action all over again from another set-up."

Scholar Stanley Weintraub takes the film to task for its more important distortions of fact: "According to Lawrence in *Seven Pillars*. . . the servant-boy Daud dies of exposure at Azrak, when Lawrence was far away to the south. However Daud's companion Farraj is later mortally wounded, and (acting on prearranged agreement among themselves) rather than let him fall into Turkish hands. . . it falls to Lawrence to kill him.

"Neither Farraj nor Daud is Gasim. . . this is apparently Gasim el Shimt, whom Lawrence does rescue from abandonment in the desert" and who is "telescoped with Hamed the Moor," killed by Lawrence.

In London's *The Observer*, Professor A.W. Lawrence, the literary executor of *Seven Pillars of Wisdom*, explained that he refused to allow Lean and Spiegel to use the title of the book as the title of the film because the film's script strayed too far from the truth.

If millions of people have grown to accept the image of Lawrence as presented by the film — tall, blonde, blue-eyed, and a tortured masochist — so be it. The "real" Lawrence is available: through his own *Seven Pillars of Wisdom*, Liddel Hart's biography, and Stanley Weintraub's books about the man.

Whatever its shortcomings, *Lawrence of Arabia* is a stunningly photographed, brilliantly conceived masterpiece of story telling. As Hollis Alpert wrote in his *Saturday Review* piece, Lawrence "required a film made on a grand scale, and it has been accomplished."

26. The Fall of the Roman Empire (1964)

"This was the beginning of the fall of the Roman Empire.
A great empire is not conquered from without, until it has
destroyed itself from within."

The Fall of the Roman Empire (hereafter just *Fall*) was Sir Alec's second of three epic motion pictures in three years, after *Lawrence of Arabia* and before *Dr. Zhivago*. Unlike those two Lean-directed films, *Fall* was neither a commercial nor a critical success. Given its high production costs, it would have needed to gross many times the amount it did for producer Samuel Bronston to recoup his investment. As it was, Bronston lost over $18,000,000.

In 1968, influential film critic and historian Andrew Sarris included *Fall's* director Anthony Mann in his book *The American Cinema: Directors and Directions 1929–1968*. Sarris called Mann an artist who "directed action movies with a kind of tough-guy authority that never found favor among the more cultivated critics of the medium," and who, like Douglas Sirk, "was overlooked by the American critical establishment until it was too late for his career to find a firmer footing than obscure cult interest."

Mann's eventual critical reevaluation and appreciation rests mainly on his westerns, most starring James Stewart, and not on his two epics, *El Cid* and *Fall*. His best films include *Man of the West* (1958), *The Last Frontier* (1956), *Men in War* (1957), *The Naked Spur* (1953), and *Bend of the River* (1952).

On April 29, 1967, while Anthony Mann was completing location work in Germany for *A Dandy in Aspic*, he suffered a fatal heart attack; he was 60 years old.

The reviewers of the time were not kind to *Fall*. Judith Crist, in the *New York Herald Tribune*, wrote, "It's all pomp and poppycock—if you can stand it by the truckload or sit through 188 minutes of it."

Time's reviewer said, "Chopped into five or six half-hour parts, this movie could serve for that all but vanished art form, the Saturday afternoon serial."

Hollis Alpert, in *Saturday Review*, wrote, "It takes about three hours and ten minutes (exclusive of intermission) for Rome to crumble in Samuel Bronston's screen spectacle *The Fall of the Roman Empire*, but even at this accelerated pace the process seems to occur in slow motion...Anyone who wants to learn anything about the fall of Rome had better go back to Gibbon."

On the pro side, *Variety* called the film a "giant-size, three-hour, sweepingly pictorial entertainment carrying (1) a natural box office title, (2) an appeal to universal interest, and (3) a strong cast...the pace is always firm and the film is steadily cinematic in the sense of 'motion' in the pictures...this is a crowded film. Large in theme and concept, colorful in treatment...Sam Bronston's greatest coup de cinema...has a large earning potential."

Joan Horvath's review in *Films in Review* took the opposite position: "For this 'Roman spectacle' Samuel Bronston used the same production staff that turned out *El Cid*, a film which was far from a total success but had some merit. The present picture, however, fails in *every* department—script, direction, acting, spectacle, sets, music, color photography."

In *Films and Filming*, Robin Bean said, "Alec Guinness, as Aurelius with his dreams of a unity of nations, lends quiet wit and resolution to his role....As routine spectacle it is very competent, as anything deeper it falls short of *Spartacus*."

Cinema's reviewer wrote, "*The Fall of the Roman Empire* is not consistent. The fantasy is served with excellent taste. The subtle excellence of both costumes and sets ranks with the finest the screen has had. If Anthony Mann could have decided between soda pop and social welfare, the film might have had a form, but he lost control on the way."

Finally, in *TV Movies*, edited by Leonard Maltin, the reviewer found *Fall* above average, saying, "Intelligent scripting, good direction, and fine acting place this far above the usual empty-headed spectacle. Mason and Guinness are superb; several action sequences are outstanding. A winner all the way."

The film opens along the embattled northern frontier of the Roman Empire of Marcus Aurelius (Guinness) in 180 A.D. The ailing emperor is thinking about his succession. His daughter Lucilla (Sophia Loren) loves his adopted son Livius (Stephen Boyd), who the emperor is thinking of naming his successor in place of his natural son, Commodus (Christopher Plummer).

When Marcus tells Lucilla of his plan to relinquish the throne to Livius, Cleander (Mel Ferrer), a blind prophet sympathetic to Commodus, overhears. When Commodus returns, a distraught Livius tells him his father has asked him, Livius, to be his heir.

After battling the northern barbarians, Commodus and Livius argue and have a furious fight between their two hurtling chariots; their men finally separate the two former friends.

Cleander plots the emperor's death: he'll offer him a poisoned apple. The emperor eats the apple and dies, leaving no will naming Livius his heir. Livius proclaims Commodus the new emperor at Marcus Aurelius' funeral.

Imperial Rome is now ruled by Emperor Commodus. Lucilla, angry at Livius' gesture of support of Commodus, has married the King of Armenia, Sohamus (Omar Sharif). Commodus is tearing down all his father accomplished and is raising taxes to meet his lavish lifestyle.

Flanked by James Mason (*left*) as Timonides and Stephen Boyd (*right*) as Livius, Guinness' Marcus Aurelius addresses a huge gathering of warrior-kings of all nations.

Livius finally defeats the barbarians on the northern frontier. Although they're defeated, their leader Ballomar (John Ireland) says they would rather die than be slaves of Rome. Timonides (James Mason) argues that they will be free men, and undergoes an ordeal by fire to prove his sincerity.

In Rome, Timonides argues for the rights of the nations under Roman rule. Meanwhile, Commodus, angry at Livius for his support of Timonides' ideas, sends him away—away from his love, Lucilla. But, after Commodus' onerous rule causes famine and unrest, he brings back Livius to take charge of his legions and defeat his rebellious enemies in the East.

Fighting in Armenia, Livius discovers that Lucilla is part of the rebellion and wants him to join them. Livius turns from her and continues his destruction of the rebel armies. Sohamus, fatally wounded, tells Livius he left orders for Lucilla to be killed. Livius arrives in time to save Lucilla and takes her back to Rome with him. On the way, he discovers that Commodus had Timonides killed. He enters Rome in anger while his legions await outside.

Commodus, unrepentant, has vast sums of gold distributed to Livius' soldiers, who immediately support Commodus. Livius, Lucilla, and Ballomar are to be burned at the stake, but Commodus offers to fight Livius to the death for their freedom. Commodus, fatally wounded by Livius, shouts, "Burn them!" and the torch is put to the pyres. Though Livius frees Lucilla and himself, Ballomar and others perish in the flames.

Hailed as Caesar, Livius turns down the throne, which is then sold to the highest bidder. It's the beginning of the end for the Roman Empire.

Anthony Mann was born in San Diego, California, on June 30, 1906. At the age of sixteen he started work at the Triangle Theatre in Greenwich Village as a bit player. He gradually progressed to more important roles and went on tour with several repertory companies. He then signed a contract with the Theater Guild, but left after a few seasons to form his own stock company, where he directed such plays as *Thunder on the Left*, *The Big Blow*, and *So Proudly We Hail*. In the late 1930s he went to work for David Selznick as a talent scout. Promoted to casting director, he worked on such films as *Intermezzo* (1939) and *Rebecca* (1940).

In 1939 Mann left Selznick to work at Paramount as an assistant director for three years. MacDonald Carey, a member of Mann's stock company, helped him land his first feature directing assignment in 1942, *Dr. Broadway*. Mann spent the five years, from 1942 to 1947, learning his craft in low-budget potboilers for RKO, Paramount, Republic, and Universal. He devised two main rules for himself when directing: (1) always choose a good story and script, and (2) always make them better. Further, he believed that films were meant to be visual and should not rely on the words of the script alone.

As Mann wrote in an article in *Films and Filming* called "Empire Demolition," "It is the image that really drives home a point. The words are only there to supplement the picture. For us [unlike Shakespeare], the image is always there."

Mann got the idea for *Fall* when he passed Hachards bookshop in Piccadilly and saw a copy of Gibbon's *The Decline and Fall of the Roman Empire* in the window. Having just shot *El Cid*, Mann said to himself, "Now that would make an interesting picture." Fortuitously, Samuel Bronston wanted Mann to direct another epic picture for him.

Mann felt that an exciting storyline might exist in the era of Marcus Aurelius, which is the beginning of the end of the Roman Empire. He hired an Italian writer, Basilio Franchina, to research the era and gave Ben Barzman an assignment to do some initial script work. Once Mann was satisfied with their work, he gave Barzman and Franchina the go-ahead to produce a 350-page script treatment. Philip Yordan, Bronston's script supervisor, joined the two men and helped them work their way through six scripts in a year. Mann wanted one thing from his writers: strong scenes to attract "artists of the calibre of Guinness...."

Mann wrote that he "found on *El Cid* that Spain is great for locations because there are so many different kinds of country. It is ideal for making a spectacle film. But one must be careful not to let the concept of the spectacular run away with you."

Producer Samuel Bronston spent millions to construct the massive and imposing sets, including a Roman fortress. A full-scale reproduction of the Roman Forum as it existed circa 180 A.D. was built on a Spanish plain.

All this attention to detail shows in the film, which has stunning scenes of massed armies, hordes of gaudily dressed warrior-kings, magnificently crumbling fortresses in the snow, and visual delights rarely seen in these epicless days.

The screenwriters, unfortunately, seem torn between a desire to be serious and realistic and a desire to overwhelm the viewer with scenes of slaughter and combat. Shortly after completing filming, Mann confided, "We agreed we would try to avoid all the clichés and try to tell a realistic story of the people of that day. There would not be the usual dancing girls, we'd have no scenes with rose petals falling from the ceiling, no half-clad beauties squeezing grapes into the mouths of corpulent actors with garlands in their hair." Mann succeeded all too well: Most of the reviewers faulted the script, dialogue, and pompous tone of the film. More than a few might have welcomed a few more of the "clichés" that make these historical epics so much fun. Of course, Mann was speaking to the viewers of his day—the early 1960s, a time when, after the assassination of President John F. Kennedy, Americans felt uneasy tremors that produced cracks in their self-image. With an unpopular war in Southeast Asia raging, social and racial unrest at home, and continuing military and technological pressure from the Soviets, Americans were being treated to pop-cult articles in the media that likened the United States to the decadent and crumbling Roman Empire. If one views *Fall* in this light, its strange (for a sword and spear epic) mixture of escapism and civics course makes much more sense. One reviewer even called James Mason's character Timonides a second-century "Peace Corps activist" for his devotion to the oppressed and downtrodden.

The music for *Fall* was written by Russian-born Dimitri Tiomkin. Tiomkin left Russia in 1919, after the Bolsheviks came to power, and became one-half of a duo piano team in Paris. Noticed by an American producer, Tiomkin and his partner landed in New York in 1925 and toured the vaudeville circuit for several years. Tiomkin's wife convinced him to return to Paris, but the Great Depression that followed Wall Street's collapse made a return to the United States necessary.

Since his wife was working for MGM, Tiomkin landed his first film scoring assignments there: writing ballet sequences for several 1930 MGM films, including *Our Blushing Brides*.

In 1931 he wrote his first original film score, for *Resurrection*. His first big break came when he scored Frank Capra's classic fantasy *Lost Horizon* in 1937. He was to do many more Capra films, including *Mr. Smith Goes to Washington* (1939), and *It's a Wonderful Life* (1946).

Tiomkin won an Academy Award in 1955 for his score for *The High and the Mighty*. As well as *Fall*, he also scored Bronston's *55 Days at Peking* (1963) and *Circus World* (1964).

Dimitri Tiomkin's score is one of the film's pluses. It is big, powerful, and underscores the on-screen action beautifully.

The acting of the large cast varied from excellent to tedious. Even Guinness' performance drew mixed reviews. As Marcus Aurelius, Guinness is in only the first third of the three-hour-plus film, dead and buried by the intermission. For many critics, including Bosley Crowther in the *New York Times*, this exit came none too soon: "Alec Guinness is pompous and full of hot air."

But Crowther's comments were benign compared to Judith Crist's barbs in the *New York Herald Tribune*: "Mr. Guinness reaches his apogee when he clutches his side in a spasm of pain amid the roaring and crashing of thunder and says, 'Ah—he has come for me, the silent boatman, to ferry me across the shadowed river.' And I choose to think that his resignation to death is colored by the fact that the silent boatman (thud! crash!) will also ferry him right out of the picture, even before the intermission."

Whew! Despite Miss Crist's broadsides, Guinness gives a restrained and moving performance; indeed, when he dies, a lot of the life and interest of the film dies with him. For that is one of *Fall*'s major problems, an unusual one for director Mann: There is no one central figure or hero that the audience cares for or about. Guinness' Marcus Aurelius is the only likeable character in the film, apart from James Mason's Timonides.

Guinness does as much for his underwritten part as he can—which, as always in Guinness' case, is considerable. He uses his body gestures effectively and, through subtle touches and caresses, shows his affection for his daughter. That he must mouth some banal-sounding lines is not his fault. After all, he didn't write the script.

Sophia Loren, born Sophia Sciocoloni in 1934, began her film career as a bare-breasted extra in films like *Aida* and *The Sign of Venus* (both 1953). Eventually, she was able to land leading roles and became an accomplished actress and international star. She won both the Academy Award for best actress and the British Film Award for best actress for her role in *Two Women* (1961).

Irish leading man Stephen Boyd (1928–1977) was born William Millar. Never a star of the first magnitude, he enjoyed his greatest popularity during the 1960s. He is best remembered for playing Massala in *Ben Hur* (1959), and for his *Fantastic Voyage* inside a living body with newcomer Raquel Welch in 1966. His screen career was cut short by his untimely death at age 49.

Boyd and Loren had the most thankless roles in *Fall*: terribly earnest and, ultimately, boring lovers and characters. Boyd, ostensibly the hero, disappears from the screen for long periods of time, and his acting is stiff if sincere.

James Mason, born in 1909, first became a screen star during the Second World War in his native England. He went to Hollywood and eventually became a major international star and respected actor. In a confusing and at times laughable role, Mason in *Fall* comes off second best to Guinness. He brings dignity and conviction to his role as Timonides, the old emperor's friend and peacemaker. He surmounts some truly impossible lines to win the sympathy of the audience.

Canadian-born (1927–) Christopher Plummer must portray the aptly-named Commodus. A serious stage actor, especially in Shakespearean roles, Plummer did not appear in his first film, *Stage Struck* (1958), until he was 31. In *Fall*, he does what he can with his part, but overacts terribly, chewing the expensive scenery every chance he gets. Fortunately for his career, his next role, as Baron Von Trapp in the hugely successful *The Sound of Music*, overshadowed *Fall* and brought him a measure of fame and stardom. (For more of the films of these actors, see notes on *Fall* in the Appendix.)

Fortunately for Guinness, a stage actor first, he continued to find worthy roles on stage. He won a Tony Award in 1964 for his portrayal of writer Dylan Thomas on Broadway.

So far, for Guinness, the 1960s were but a shadow of his magnificent 1950s. In 1964, the year of *Fall*'s release, he turned 50 years of age — a dangerous turning point in the career of any actor. The future was anything but certain.

27. *Situation Hopeless But Not Serious* (1965)

Situation Hopeless But Not Serious (hereafter just *Situation*), released just weeks before *Zhivago*, was Guinness' return to the sort of comedy film role that had made his fame and reputation. As Guinness himself notes, "I liked the script of *Situation* very much and I have a great respect for Gottfried Reinhardt as a director. It happened to come at a time when I was finishing a play [*Dylan*] in New York. It all fitted rather well, and I was quite keen to do a black and white smallish picture, which I haven't done for some time."

Whether it was the film's odd subject (for a comedy) or other factors, *Situation* did poorly at the box office and was not seen in England until 1969. It was probably released then only to cash in Redford's newfound popularity as a result of the smash hit *Butch Cassidy and the Sundance Kid*.

A postwar film set in wartime Nazi Germany, *Situation* suffered from the inevitable "good German" syndrome, which can be seen in films like *The Enemy Below*, where individual Germans, for the most part, are seen as just folks and certainly not Nazis. Most likely, the film's ambivalence hurt it as much as anything. Was it an all-out comedy or a weird psychological drama with a kinky protagonist? Whatever, audiences stayed away in droves.

Writing in the *New York Times*, A.H. Weiler called *Situation* "a mild, pat comedy that is rarely as funny or as satirical as its title," and noted that the situation in the film "is neither 'hopeless' nor 'serious' but simply pleasantly obvious and occasionally diverting."

Michael Armstrong's review in *Films and Filming* finds *Situation* "A delightfully engaging and entertaining piece of film. Certainly it provides the opportunity of witnessing one of Alec Guinness' best performances— speaking in a soft German accent, [his] is a performance of incredible subtlety and humor and a pure joy to watch. It all adds up to a thoroughly warm and delightful 97 minutes of screen time."

"Robe" begins his review in *Variety* by observing, "Everything is pleasant about [*Situation*] and that may be the trouble with it. With the exception of two really funny scenes, however, there's a shortage of action and an overage of pleasantness. The ending is pat and predictable."

Helen Weldon Kuhn's piece in *Films in Review* was the harshest. "If Alec

Guinness isn't offered better vehicles than this his career has come to a standstill. The script, by Reinhardt's wife Silvia, is devoid of logic. And humor."

American flyers Captain Hank Wilson (Robert Redford) and Sergeant Lucky Finder (Michael Conners) are shot down over Germany in 1944. On the ground, air-raid warden Herr Frick (Guinness) can get no one to use his shelter—or to be his friend. Entering his well-stocked basement, Frick sees shoes behind a curtain. He sneaks out and locks the iron-barred door behind him, trapping the two Americans. Wilson sings German songs, trying to convince Frick his German ancestry makes him a friend.

Hoping to get on Frick's good side, Wilson talks to him and learns how lonely he has been since his domineering mother died seven years ago. Frick lives his life according to his late mother's horoscopes and strictures—the nameplate outside the door still has her name in large print, his in small.

Frick, a milquetoast clerk in a drugstore, enjoys his newfound power over others, and endeavors to keep the news of his two prisoners secret.

A "good German," Frick is nonetheless disheartened by news of the impending German collapse. American troops soon occupy the town.

It's Christmas and Frick is bringing home a scrawny Christmas tree for his prisoners. Wilson and Finder, bickering over life back home, have managed to pick the lock on their door. Coming in, Herr Frick finds Wilson and Finder putting on his clothes and preparing for their break. Finder waves Frick's pistol about. Acting normally, Frick makes them potato soup and sandwiches—and drinks containing a sleeping potion. They wake up back in the cellar, shackled to a pole. Once Frick chains the door, he frees them from their restraints.

Frick hears the news of Germany's surrender on the radio, but still keeps Wilson and Finder prisoners. He's grown attached to them, cooks for them, and plays them music; they're his only companionship. Showing them maps, Fricks convinces them Germany is winning the war, driving the Americans and British back into the sea. They can hear no bombers overhead. Frick tells them Paris has fallen. Finder, however, is skeptical. Frick says London is German—after the V-2s came the V-3s and the V-4s.

Frick asks what Hank and Lucky want for Christmas, and Finder asks for a dame. So, Frick manfully goes to the local brothel looking for a "dame." Unfortunately, when he tells the madame (Mady Rahl) that he's looking for a discreet woman for two men (and, naturally, he'll have to be there), she becomes convinced he's a lunatic and frantically buzzes for her bouncer. Frick is tossed into the street.

Frick suffers a heart attack in 1951 and is taken to a hospital. Breaking out, he's pursued by policemen, who follow him home. Finding their door open, Finder and Wilson hesitantly venture out, only to discover Frick upstairs, hiding from men in uniform. Naturally, Hank and Lucky think they're SS men or worse. They say goodbye to Frick and excape out the

Guinness' crewcut Herr Frick uses a pistol to persuade his "guests" to stay a while longer at his Christmas party.

window, taking with them Frick's pistol. "They'll kill somebody!" Frick laments.

Hiding out, Wilson and Finder see a paper and learn that Truman is president of the United States. They spot jets overhead and believe Germany has won the war with technology. Meanwhile, officials discover evidence of the two flyers' confinement in Frick's basement and call the mild clerk a monster.

Trying to steal a boat, Wilson and Finder encounter the owner's daughter, Wanda (Elisabeth Von Molo), a screwball type who finds them sexy and who knows they're escaped "prisoners" (from the nearby stockade). A boatman named Fritz takes them to a place where they wander onto a World War II movie set. They get into a huge fistfight and have to be rescued by the burly Fritz. Finally, they learn the truth.

They are reunited in San Francisco as Wilson and Finder become hot cocktail party hosts and guests and Hank hires Frick as his butler. Presumably, they all live happily ever after.

During the last week of his eight-month run in *Dylan*, Guinness and his young co-star to be, Robert Redford, sat at a table in Sardi's West and discussed their upcoming film together. When Redford asked Guinness how he decided to make *Situation*, Sir Alec responded, "Oh, I don't know—how does one choose any part? The director, Gottfried Reinhardt, is an old friend—someone I trust and respect. And, since it was being made on location, it meant that I would get to see Germany. I read the script a few months ago, detested it, but then it somehow began to grow on me. I saw possibilities in it. That often happens."

When Guinness told Redford that making a film comedy can often be an ordeal, the young actor said, "Then you're not looking forward to making *Situation*?" "Oh, no, I wouldn't say that," Guinness said. "At the moment, though, I'm looking forward to leaving *Dylan*.... Making *Situation* will probably be a great deal of fun, it's my first comedy in years."

Since Guinness had to be in makeup for an hour to prepare for *Dylan*, the two actors got ready to part. Redford told Guinness that "it's been very pleasant talking with you." Grinning shyly, Guinness replied, "Yes, it's been terribly nice. And I imagine that we'll see a good bit of each other in Germany. We'll have our mornings free, and perhaps we might do a little sightseeing together. There's nothing like sightseeing, is there? Thank you. Good night."

"Thank you, Sir Alec. Until Munich."

"Yes, until Munich."

Gottfried Reinhardt was the film's producer as well as its director, and he scoured the country for war ruins. West Germany's powerful postwar recovery and boom meant that virtually all the cities had been rebuilt, and Reinhardt was forced to construct his scenes of a war-torn country on the

Showing his two prisoners maps, Guinness' Frick convinces them that Germany is winning the war.

backlot at Munich's Geiselgasteig Studios. Some location shooting was done at Lake Starnberg and in Heidelberg.

As Reinhardt looked for ruins, Guinness was perfecting his accent. Guinness spoke no German, yet was able to impart to Frick the sense of a man dealing with English as a language foreign to him.

Discussing whether he liked roles which require accents, Guinness said, "No, I don't, funnily enough. I've never liked that. I've got landed with several. It doesn't attract me, because I like those things to be really good, and they worry me. Occasionally they slip and for me they get in the way of performing very often. For instance, in a tiny little scene in [*Situation*] I have a line which is, 'I think you've always liked my potato soup, sergeant.' With any English or American if there was any emphasis it would go on the word 'soup.' Because of the German language I'm told that the emphasis had to go onto the work 'potato,' which sounds entirely false to me as though it's in contrast to several other soups. But I am persuaded that this is what a German speaking English would do. Gottfried's been very helpful in pointing out things like that to me."

Gottfried Reinhardt, the son of theatrical producer Max Reinhardt, was born in 1911. A producer in his native Austria, Reinhardt followed his father to Hollywood and became an assistant to Walter Wanger. Later, he became a screenwriter, director, and producer. His first script was for *The Great Waltz* in 1937. He then produced *Comrade X* in 1940 and went on to produce such varied fare as *Two-Faced Woman* in 1941 and *The Red Badge of Courage* in 1951. Reinhardt turned director for *Invitation* in 1952.

In an article in *Films and Filming*, Reinhardt discussed the use of narration in films (he used narration extensively in *Situation*). "Writers can, and do, use it as a crutch, as do producers and directors," he admits. "...Good dramaturgy requires that the audience must identify with a character very early if the play or film is to be effective. Sound track narration makes doubly certain that the audience knows who it is rooting for." *Situation's* narration introduces Hank, Lucky, and Herr Frick, telling us that the latter is eager yet friendless. This author believes the narration adds nothing to the film.

Robert Redford (1936–), who is one of America's biggest superstars, had made only one film before *Situation*. Though not a success, *Situation* brought Redford to the attention of producers and critics and his career began to zoom, although it took *Butch Cassidy and the Sundance Kid* in 1969 to propel him into the ranks of box office sure things. (For more on Redford and other *Situation* cast members, see notes in the Appendix.)

Wondering how Guinness planned to approach his role in *Situation*, Redford asked him if he had "certain set theories about comic acting?"

"Theories about comic acting?" Sir Alec responded. "Oh, no—I don't think I have any.... The most important thing is the script—the comic situations have to be there.... In creating a comic character, it's the little touches, the subtle nuances that make the difference. One takes a fairly ordinary character and plays him slightly out of focus.... One has to be careful not to overplay or underplay too much, or one ends up being screamingly unfunny. Film comedy can be particularly difficult and frustrating—one's performance is fragmented into so many little 20- and 30-second bits and pieces.... It's immensely difficult to sustain a properly balanced comic character throughout the three months or so that it takes to make a film."

Well cast, the crewcut Guinness did what he could with the role of Herr Frick. Occasionally looking just a little twinkly—and more than a little like Father Brown—Guinness plays the lonely eccentric with his usual skill. Frick is an oddball, but likeable on his own terms.

Guinness is best in one of the film's funniest scenes: trying to explain to Lissie, the madam, why he needs a discreet "dame" for his friend, who just happens to be chained to another man.

Redford and Conners (best known for his television series, *Mannix*) do justice to Hank Wilson and Lucky Finder, but their characters are not fully supported by the script. Screenplay author Silvia Reinhardt does, however, do a good job capturing the way American flyers of the time might speak.

Redford shows glimpses of the talent and likeability that would propel him to major stardom, while Conners, in a less amiable role, does what he can with his part.

If *Situation* did no serious damage to Guinness' career, the film did nothing to help it, either.

28. *Doctor Zhivago* (1965)

"The private life is dead in Russia"
— General Strelnikov

Dr. Zhivago (hereafter just *Zhivago*) opened two weeks after *Situation Hopeless but not Serious*, in reserved-seat, roadshow engagements at a playing time of 197 minutes — immediately cut to 180 minutes (plus intermission). Filmed on location in Spain, Finland, and Canada, *Zhivago* cost $12,000,000. It was an immediate box office success, earning $15,000,000 in rentals during its primary year of release, 1966 (rentals are what the distributor receives after distribution and exhibition fees are subtracted from the box office gross). It stands in third position among the top-ten moneymaking films of the 1960s, and its total North American rentals (this excludes foreign rentals) to date, according to *Variety*, are $46,550,000 — placing it twenty-sixth on the list of the top 200 moneymaking films of all time.

Alec Guinness received mostly respectful notices for his portrayal of Yuri Zhivago's half-brother, Yevgraf Zhivago, a general in the secret police and the narrator, through flashback, of the story. It was not, however, much of a role.

After *Zhivago*, Guinness would plunge deeper into his own personal recession — his "Lead Age." His Golden Age and his David Lean years were over (though he would be reunited with Lean in 1984's *A Passage to India*). That he would consent to do another film with Lean after *Zhivago* says something about the professional integrity of both men — for, at the start of filming, Lean told Guinness he not only was too old for the part, he looked it as well. After taking a few days off to recover his equilibrium, Guinness returned to the Madrid soundstages where the film was shooting, and things went smoothly.

As Yevgraf Zhivago, Guinness had a meaty challenge: Yevgraf is meant to represent the darker side of the Russian soul, the sometimes benevolent, sometimes cruel (he speaks of dispatching better men than his half-brother with a pistol shot) secret policeman who follows the Party line when it comes to evaluating Yuri Zhivago's poems, but who saves the poems from oblivion after his half-brother's death.

As for director Lean, *Zhivago* represents an interesting blending of the two styles that brought him success in the past: the Dickensian attention to baroque detail (Zhivago's mother's burial), and the spectacular (the massacre of the marchers and the numbing winter train journey from Moscow to the Urals).

While *Zhivago* was a popular and successful film, its reviews were decidedly mixed. *Variety's* "Murf" wrote, "The sweep and scope of the Russian revolution, as reflected in the personalities of those who either adapted or were crushed, has been captured by David Lean in *Dr. Zhivago*, frequently with soaring dramatic intensity. Director [Lean] has accomplished one of the most meticulously designed and executed films—superior in several visual respects to his *Lawrence of Arabia*."

Raymond Durgnat, in *Films and Filming*, found the film less successful: "Though not unintelligent, the film leaves a general impression that Bolt's and Lean's efforts to solve its problems left them exhausted of any further inspiration."

Bosley Crowther's review in the *New York Times* was even more negative: "Mr. Bolt has reduced the vast upheaval of the Russian Revolution to the banalities of a doomed romance. The picture is begun and the story told with the half-brother of the doctor—a Soviet engineer [*sic*], austerely played by Alec Guinness—trying to discover whether a Russian working girl. . . is the lost daughter of Lara and Zhivago. . . . Neither the inquiry nor the device can be reckoned a success."

But *Life* magazine's critic, Richard Schickel, gave the film a glowing review: "At once generous yet austere, huge but never out of human scale, gently unfolded yet full of power, it is a work of serious, genuine art."

Writing in *Film Quarterly*, Judith Shatnoff insisted that "*Dr. Zhivago* is not worth seeing, nor is it worth much discussion except as it shows the selective design and manipulation of political images for a mass audience."

Finally, in *Cinema*, John Cutts wrote, "See it, feel it, treasure it. Don't play games with it. And don't make comparisons. No, I take that back. Make some comparisons with some of the other highly-touted films currently going the rounds. Then go bask in its wonder."

Is it any wonder filmmakers can go crazy from reading the reviews?

An impassive Yevgraf Zhivago is the first image in the film. General Zhivago is looking for the lost daughter of his long-dead half-brother, Yuri. She may be Yuri and Lara's child—the Lara of "the Lara poems."

Yevgraf tells the girl (Rita Tushingham) the story of Doctor Zhivago and his doomed love for the woman Lara. At a funeral in the country, the orphaned Yuri is adopted and raised by the aristocratic Gromeko family (Ralph Richardson and Siobhan McKenna). Yuri (Omar Sharif) grows up to be a young and idealistic medical doctor in Moscow who also writes poetry.

Lara, a young girl, infatuates a powerful and cunning friend of her mother's: Komarovsky. When Lara's mother is ill, he takes Lara instead of her mother to dine at his private club. While they dine, revolutionaries (led by Pasha, Lara's fiancé) marching in the streets for bread and peace are attacked

Guinness' Yevgraf, hoping to convince the girl (Rita Tushingham) that Yuri and Lara were her parents, shows her a copy of the "Lara poems."

by the dragoons. Injured in the massacre, Pasha (Tom Courtney) has Lara hide his revolver.

Lara, having been seduced by Komarovsky (Rod Steiger), confesses to a priest. Suspecting what has happened, Lara's mother attempts suicide. Yuri helps save her and sees Lara with Komarovsky.

Lara takes Pasha's revolver to Komarovsky's Christmas Eve party and shoots and wounds him; Pasha arrives to take her home. Yuri witnesses the shooting and admires both Pasha and Lara. Meanwhile, the Gromekos' daughter, Tonya (Geraldine Chaplin), who loves Yuri, has returned from school; Yuri has asked Tonya to marry him.

Yevgraf is ordered by the Party to enlist when war breaks out in 1914. Pasha, too, enlists; Yuri becomes a doctor at the front. Poorly supplied and poorly led, the Russian army begins deserting. Yuri meets Lara, now a nurse, and tells her of seeing her shoot her seducer and tormentor. They fall in love, but do not consummate their passion for each other.

The war over and the revolution a success, Yuri returns to Moscow to find Bolsheviks living in his family's house: Things have changed for the worse for the Gromeko family. Yevgraf sees Yuri stealing firewood and follows him home. A hard-faced Yevgraf confronts Yuri, and they kiss as brothers. Yevgraf tells him his poetry is disapproved of by the Party and that he should leave for their country home in the Urals.

The train journey is long and harsh. Yuri learns that Pasha is now the hated Strelnikov. Strelnikov meets Yuri and tells him personal life is dead in Russia, and that Lara, who he's not seen in years, is in Yuriatin, near the Gromeko estate.

Yuri and his family learn that their country house has been seized and that the czar and his family were shot. When spring comes, Yuri meets Lara in Yuriatin. This time, they physically consummate their love.

When a guilty Yuri learns that Tonya is pregnant again, he rides to Yuriatin to tell Lara he must never see her again. But on his way home, he's forcibly conscripted by the Partisans, who need a doctor.

After two years of war, Yuri slips away in a snowstorm and makes his way back to Yuriatin. But his family is not there. He goes to Lara's rooms and, ill, falls into a feverish state. He awakens to her concerned but loving face. She tells him his family is in Moscow and that she has a letter from Tonya. Tonya writes that they have a daughter and that they are being deported to France. She has left his mother's balalaika with Lara.

Komarovsky appears, offering help. He tells them that Yuri is a deserter and Lara is Strelnikov's wife — Strelnikov is no longer in favor with the party. They refuse his aid and throw him into the street.

Fearing detection, Lara and Yuri move to the ice-covered summer estate, a magical winter refuge. There, Yuri writes his best poems, dedicated to and inspired by Lara, as the wolves howl outside.

Komarovsky shows up again, this time telling Yuri that Strelnikov fatally shot himself after his arrest and that Lara is in danger since she's no longer bait for his return. Yuri agrees that they will travel to safety with him aboard a train, but at the last minute, he stays behind. Lara tells Komarovsky that she is carrying Yuri's child.

Yevgraf finds work for Yuri in Moscow eight years later, though his half-brother has a bad heart. In Moscow, aboard a trolley, Yuri sees Lara walking in the street. He gets off the trolley, attempts to reach her, and has a fatal heart attack.

The scene returns to Yevgraf and the girl. He tells her of the turnout at Yuri's funeral — hundreds of people who loved his poetry (Yevgraf saved the Lara poems and saw them published), including Lara herself. Lara asked Yevgraf's help in finding Yuri's daughter.

Later Lara vanished, most likely into a prison camp where she perished. All this Yevgraf tells the girl, who refuses to believe she is Yuri Zhivago's daughter. She remembers only Komarovsky, who let go of her hand in a crowd.

As the girl goes off, Yevgraf sees she has a balalaika and asks if she can play it. When her young engineer friend says she's an artist on it, Yevgraf asks who taught her. "No one taught her," the young engineer replies. "Ah, then it's a gift," says Yevgraf, certain at last that he has found Yuri and Lara's daughter, Tonya.

Yuri (Omar Sharif) pours his half-brother, Yevgraf (Guinness), a drink while Tonya (Geraldine Chaplin) and Alexander Gromeko (Ralph Richardson) look on.

Zhivago reunited the scriptwriter-director team of Robert Bolt and David Lean in this the second of their three collaborations (*Ryan's Daughter*, in 1970, would be their third). Soon after Boris Pasternak won the 1958 Nobel Prize for Literature, Carlo Ponti purchased the film rights from an Italian publisher. Bolt immediately began work on adapting the huge, sprawling novel for the screen, a process that was to take him two years.

Bolt wrote about the difficulties of adapting Pasternak's novel: "Time [in the novel] is not covered flowingly but in sudden leaps. At the end of Chapter 14 Lara and Yuri have parted, Strelnikov has shot himself; the main story is over. Chapter 15 commences, 'It remains to tell the brief story of the last eight or ten years of Yuri's life...' and finishes with the reported death of Lara. At the start of Chapter 16 another gulf of years has been jumped; we learn of the existence of Yuri and Lara's daughter, now grown up, and hear from her the story of her childhood.... As if this were not enough, the last section of this chapter begins, 'Five or ten years later....' "

Bolt's script (itself a 224-page book published by Random House) changed the form the novel's narrative took. In the novel, a third-person viewpoint is used to relate the story. In the film, Yuri's half-brother Yevgraf relates the story of Zhivago and Lara to the girl who is probably their daughter, lost since childhood.

Many of the film's jumps and twists are the result of Bolt not daring to move too far away from the novel itself. While admirable, this fidelity to the original novel comes at the expense of the cinematic version. Certainly, it must have been a difficult job to adapt the work of a Nobel-winning author.

While Bolt toiled away on the script, an enormous set representing the streets of Moscow was being constructed in Spain, near Madrid's international airport. The ten-acre site was a detailed reproduction of the Russian city as it looked between 1905 and 1920.

Filming began late in 1964 and continued throughout most of 1965. The necessity of creating the illusion of bitter Russian winters made for some trying filming conditions. As Guinness told interviewer Gene Phillips, "I . . . prefer working in the controlled conditions of the studio to going on location because of weather conditions. When we made *Dr. Zhivago* . . . we were all in Madrid in a temperature of 116 degrees, muffled up to the ears in Russian furs. We just wanted to say our lines and get out of the heat!"

The only scenes for the film not shot in Spain were those involving the arduous train journey Zhivago and his family were forced to endure to return to their summer home in the Urals. For those scenes, producer Ponti arranged for the cooperation of Finnish State Railways and the Canadian Pacific Railway Company.

Until recently, *Zhivago*'s soundtrack album was one of the best-selling movie scores of all time, eclipsed only by the rock-laden tie-ins of the 1980s like *Flashdance*. For his efforts, composer Maurice Jarre won an Oscar for the score.

In his book *Music For the Movies*, Tony Thomas wrote that "in the opinion of most other film composers *Doctor Zhivago* is not a well scored film." Thomas also notes that David Lean asked Jarre to "simplify" his themes, scaling them down to a less-complex level. The "Lara" theme ("Somewhere My Love"), simplified or not, became a popular and hugely successful instrumental, further impressing *Zhivago* upon the mass consciousness of audiences of the time.

The acting for this intimate epic is impressive. Guinness in his small role—the one he was "too old" for—is his usual subtle self. His secret policeman looks and acts like a policeman, always watching and evaluating, his cold eyes betraying few human emotions. Yet he is warm and likeable with the young woman who is almost certainly his niece. In a sense, Guinness seems intuitively to be playing a typical Russian bureaucrat, totally willing to sublimate his wishes to those of the state (however abhorrent they might be to his personal code) and yet, somehow, still human and caring down beneath the cold, harsh exterior he must assume.

Omar Sharif was born Michel Shalhouz in Egypt in 1932. Though he made one film (*Goho*, 1959) before *Lawrence of Arabia* in 1962, it was the latter film that propelled the actor into international stardom in romantic and leading-man roles. (Showing his age more these days, Sharif has become a fine character actor.) Sharif is very good as the sensitive Yuri. Perhaps his large brown eyes do moisten a few times too often, but otherwise his performance in the difficult central role is just fine.

Also good is Julie Christie (who would win the Oscar in 1966 for her performance in *Darling*, not *Zhivago*). Christie is a British leading lady born in 1940. Her Lara has lost a little lustre today because the production is so 1960s—Lara looks just too much like a young Doris Day, hairdo and all. Still, Miss Christie contributed beauty, skill, and restraint to her role in the three-hanky film of the year.

The two outstanding performances in *Zhivago* are turned in by Rod Steiger as Komarovsky and Tom Courtenay as Pasha/Strelnikov. Rod Steiger was born in 1925 and began appearing on the stage and on television after graduating from the Theatre Workshop in New York City. Because of his weight, Steiger played roles much older than his own age early in his career (making him seem like he ought to be older today). Throughout Zhivago, Steiger must be alternately threatening and loathsome, and loyally cunning—it is his self-centered Komarovsky, after all, who manages to save Lara by getting her on the train with him. This was just one outstanding performance for Steiger in a decade of outstanding performances.

Tom Courtenay was born in 1937. He recently returned to the screen as Norman in *The Dresser* (1983), for which he was nominated for an Academy Award. Courtenay, too, is outstanding as the pacifistic intellectual Pasha who later mutates into the chillingly remote General Strelnikov. Courtenay is believable as both Pasha and Strelnikov, his idealism turned into sour nihilism. (For more on the actors, see notes on *Zhivago* in the Appendix.)

Romantic, epic, intimate, combining art with social commentary, and mixing brilliant photography with throbbingly passionate and schmaltzy music, *Zhivago* is at times too much: too long, too "arty," too ambitious for its own good. But, in this era of the "popcorn" movie, *Zhivago* stands out as an intelligently scripted, carefully made film for adults.

29. Hotel Paradiso (1966)

> "Those who run around with women don't walk tight ropes.
> They find it hard enough to crawl on the ground."
> — Isaac Bashevis Singer, *The Magician of Lublin*

Hotel Paradiso (hereafter just *Paradiso*), coming after the spectacle and grandeur of *Doctor Zhivago*, did little to further Guinness' career or reputation. Guinness appears tired and old-looking for *Paradiso*, complete with rather large bags beneath his eyes. Glenville surrounded Guinness with actors his age or older, like Robert Morley, but Sir Alec still looks a bit out of place.

Part of the fault for this can rest with the timing of the film. Glenville and Guinness had planned a film version of their stage hit ever since it opened in the mid-1950s. Unfortunately, they were unable to get together until 1966.

Part of the problem with *Paradiso* lies in its look: It is sumptuously photographed in Paris in Metrocolor and Panavision. The demands of farce, especially bedroom farce, are ill-suited to a wide-screen presentation. The gorgeous color photography is more appropriate to a lushly romantic love story like *Zhivago*, not a fast-moving, logic-defying romp like *Paradiso*.

The critics, if not unkind, were not very enthusiastic, either. *Paradiso* did poorly in the United States and didn't open in England at all until 1971, five years after its American debut. It did no better in English theaters and all but disappeared from view, surfacing mainly on the late, late show on television.

Reviewer Thomas Lask, writing in the *New York Times*, said *Paradiso* "is charming when it should be brisk, amiable when it should be ridiculous." However, he also wrote, "To see Alec Guinness, after declaring his passion for the lady, decorously uncover a square inch of bare arm to imprint a chaste kiss on it is to observe a comic caper at its best."

Variety's "Rino" observed that the "film version of Georges Feydeau's turn-of-the-century *L'Hotel du Libre Echange* is a second generation production of Peter Glenville's recent legit revival of the French farceur in London. Unfortunately, despite its period charm, stylized performances and restful innocence, the dated gentility seems too remote for contemporary audiences."

Peter Buckley, *Films and Filming*: "Peter Glenville's lavish production of Feydeau's classic farce has finally reached England and at last we know what took it so long. Sumptuously dressed, gorgeously photographed, loaded with talent, and five years late, it should have stayed on the shelf. It is a dog, a mangy mongrel of the lowest order, and an insult to all involved. As a film it fails to work on any imaginable level. . . ."

Time's anonymous reviewer noted that ". . . It's the moviegoer who does most of the yawning. The actors work assiduously trying to put new bounce into a comedy written more than half a century ago. . . . Glenville as Glenville hasn't the faintest idea of how to get the fun on film."

William Peper's review in the *New York World Journal Tribune* put it simply and bluntly: "French farce falls flat. . . ."

Films in Review's Wilfred Mifflin wrote one of the few favorable reviews. "As produced and directed by Peter Glenville, and aptly played by an exceptionally able cast, *Hotel Paradiso* is about 100 minutes of comparatively pure entertainment."

Paris, 1900. A writer, Georges Feydeau, silently observes the tangled goings-on of his neighbors. He observes Henri and Marcelle Cot (Robert Morley and Gina Lollobrigida) arguing over Henri's planned excursion to a hotel by himself. An architect, Henri is to determine if the hotel is haunted or just has malfunctioning water pipes. Their next-door neighbor, Benedict Boniface (Guinness), sitting on a swing, overhears their argument and digests what it may mean for his designs on Marcelle. Alone with her, Benedict tells of his deep passion for her, and they plan a hotel rendezvous for that night.

Meanwhile, Henri's nephew, Maxime (Derek Fowldes), also plans a rendezvous with Victoire (Ann Beach), the Bonifaces' maid.

After learning that his wife, Angelique (Peggy Mount), plans to spend the night with her sister, Benedict sees an advertisement for the Hotel Paradiso, which promises discretion in matters of the heart ("It's a miracle!" Guinness/Benedict stage-whispers to the camera).

Mr. Martin (Douglas Byng) and his four daughters arrive, hoping to stay at the Bonifaces' home. Mr. Martin has a strange affliction — he stutters only when it rains. After being told he must stay in a hotel, Mr. Martin overhears Benedict giving Marcelle the address of the Hotel Paradiso.

When Benedict insists on dining out alone that night, Angelique locks him in his room. Benedict escapes through the attic, and Feydeau silently observes his flight. When Angelique's carriage hits a tree in the road and she goes flying through the air, a quick cut introduces us to "la grande Antoinette" (Marie Bell), a rather hefty trapeze artiste who's flying through the air in the cafe where Benedict and Marcelle are dining.

Meanwhile, Henri registers at the hotel — the Paradiso, of course — and immediately begins checking the plumbing for unusual noises.

The innkeeper (Akim Tamiroff) welcomes Benedict and Marcelle. After they are shown to their room, Benedict chases Marcelle around the bed, but soon feels ill. Benedict goes up to the roof for air as Mr. Martin and his daughters arrive and are mistakenly put into Henri's room. Spotting Marcelle,

Martin invites himself and his four daughters in for a visit. Benedict returns, opens the door, is seen by Mr. Martin, and comes in — pretending he was "just in the neighborhood."

When Martin and his girls leave for their room, Benedict goes out with them but tries to sneak back and runs smack into Martin again. Henri returns and goes into his room, unaware of the presence of Martin and his daughters.

Maxime and Victoire arrive and, since Benedict told the bellboy that he and Marcelle were checking out, are put in Benedict and Marcelle's room.

Martin's daughters laughingly put sheets over their heads and dance about, waking Henri — who scares them as much as they scare him. They all run screaming from the room.

When the frightened Henri ducks into Benedict's room, he almost sees Marcelle. To avoid detection, she grabs his hat and pulls it down over her head. Benedict, his face blackened from hiding in the fireplace from Maxime and Victoire, scares off Henri.

The police raid the hotel, and an inspector asks Benedict and Marcelle their names. When she says her last name is Boniface and he says his is Cot, the police arrest everyone in the hotel — while Feydeau, spending the night in his regular suite, looks on in amusement.

Released from jail, Benedict rushes home and climbs back into his room. Henri returns home — he ran from the "ghosts" before he could be arrested — and tells Benedict he had a horrible experience. He didn't see the mystery woman's face, but says he'd recognize the dress that she wore if he saw it again.

Angelique arrives home disheveled after spending the night in a poor family's hovel. She gets a letter requesting her to report to the police station with her identity papers, since "Mrs. Boniface" was arrested at the Hotel Paradiso in the company of a Mr. Cot. Seizing on this stroke of luck, Benedict boldly accuses Angelique of infidelity. Cot readily admits to being at the Hotel Paradiso, but only to inspect the plumbing.

Marcelle gives her dress to Victoire as Mr. Martin shows up and is hustled into the greenhouse by Benedict. The police inspector arrives, sure only of one thing: He can't remember Mrs. Boniface's face, but he can remember the dress she wore. Mr. Martin announces that he was at the Hotel Paradiso and knows who else was there. As he's about to tell all, it starts to rain — and he starts stuttering. As Martin is writing out who was at the hotel, Victoire comes down wearing Marcelle's dress and admits being at the hotel with Maxime. The puzzle "solved," Benedict tears up the list, chastising Victoire.

Much later, both couples attend the premiere of Georges Feydeau's new farce. Though heavily made up, the two actors on stage clearly resemble Benedict and Marcelle, who begin to sink guiltily into their seats as Feydeau's couple plan their illicit rendezvous using the same phrases Benedict used in speaking to Marcelle at the film's beginning.

Georges Feydeau's stage farce *L'Hotel du Libre Echange* opened in Paris

Boniface (Guinness) and Marcelle (Gina Lollobrigida) are caught holding the hot water bottle where they shouldn't be – together in the Hotel Paradiso.

on December 5, 1894, and was an immediate hit. Later, Peter Glenville translated Feydeau's comedy, and it opened at the Winter Garden in London on May 2, 1956. Directed by Glenville, the play starred Alec Guinness as Boniface – the same role he would assume in the film version ten years later.

Produced by Richard Myers and Julius Fleishmann and staged by Glenville, *Paradiso* opened on Broadway at the Henry Miller Theater on April 11, 1957. Bert Lahr played Boniface, Angela Lansbury was Marcelle, and Mr. Martin was played by Douglas Byng, who, at 72 years of age, would repeat his performance for his film debut.

The artifices, plot devices, coincidences, and frantic pace of the play are best suited to the larger-than-life atmosphere of the stage. On film, especially in a widescreen format, the creakiness of the play is underlined. Film is a realistic medium demanding underplaying and subtlety, whereas a stage farce like *Paradiso* demands broad gestures, broad acting, and a willing suspension of disbelief.

The location scenes for *Paradiso* were filmed in Paris, giving the film a look of beauty and reality; stage sets, inherently artificial, are more conducive to slamming doors, scrambling adulterers, and physical slapstick.

Even so, *Paradiso* might have worked as a film had it been more quickly paced and supported by an appropriately frenetic script. Glenville and coscripter Jean-Claude Carriere seem unaware of the difference between stage and screen, and their adaptation of the play never comes to vibrant life.

Glenville's direction lets the action plod along when it should be racing; the audience is given too much time to notice the holes in the bed-hopping action. Finally, the cast, if truly "all-star," is nonetheless ill-suited to the demands of an energetic romp.

Gina Lollobrigida, born in 1927, made her first film, *Pagliacci*, in 1947. Her obvious physical charms paved the way to a long and successful career in film. But although lovely to look at, Lollobrigida is not an accomplished comedienne, and her Italian accent seems out of place in *Paradiso*, a film set in France.

Robert Morley, a fine character actor born in 1908, has been in films since his 1938 debut in *Marie Antoinette*. He is familiar to American audiences from his many character roles in British and American films and his role as a spokesperson for British Airways in American television commercials. In *Paradiso*, Morley seems to have been cast largely to offset Guinness' age and thus indicate that *all* the participants are appropriately middle-aged.

Douglas Byng, as the stuttering Mr. Martin, gives a fine performance, and as Angelique, Benedict's battle-ax wife, Peggy Mount (who also appeared in *Oliver!*) is an excellent argument for adultery. (See notes on *Paradiso* in the Appendix for more on the actors and their films.)

Glenville plays the role of Feydeau, an interesting conceit that, nonetheless, adds nothing to the proceedings.

Guinness seems to be enjoying himself hugely, if somewhat calmly, in a role that demands the demented hysteria of a Cary Grant in *Arsenic and Old Lace*. On stage, Guinness' age would be masked by makeup; on screen, he looks tired and weary. Still, he has his moments: the unbelieving look he registers when the bellboy, drilling a hole into Boniface's hotel room, inadvertantly drills into Boniface's posterior; the looks he directs squarely at the camera in mock exasperation or glee; his attempts to sneak back into his hotel room, only to continually run into Mr. Martin; and his successful blackfaced attempt to scare Henri away before he can discover that Boniface is cuckolding him with Marcelle.

The doldrums that Guinness' career had entered in the 1960s were to continue, declining into a lamentable "leaden age" that would last for several years.

III. Guinness in Decline:
The Leaden Age

"I got a bad feeling about this."

— *Star Wars*

"That's the way it is. . . ."

— Walter Cronkite

"What we cannot speak about we must pass over in silence."

— Ludwig Wittgenstein

The Quiller Memorandum (1966)

to

Hitler: The Last Ten Days (1973)

30. *The Quiller Memorandum* (1966)

> "We got all of them. Well, not all of them, perhaps.
> Most of them."
> — Quiller to Inge in *The Quiller Memorandum*

The Quiller Memorandum (hereafter just *Quiller*) followed *Hotel Paradiso* and preceded *The Comedians*. Unlike those two heavier-than-air films, however, *Quiller* was always interesting if not always good.

In an era of gimmicky Bondlike spy films, *Quiller* is much closer in tone and substance to the classic *The Spy Who Came in From the Cold*. Unlike James Bond, "licensed to kill," Quiller, slightly rumpled looking — a younger Lieutenant Columbo? — doesn't even carry a gun; people who carry guns get hurt or killed.

As Pol, the head of Berlin Control, Guinness, his hair slicked back and his upper lip sporting a thin mustache, was smooth and slightly sinister. Ever the organization man, Guinness' Pol dislikes Quiller's propensity to work alone, without a safety net.

We meet Guinness' Pol in Hitler's grandiose Olympic Stadium, built to house the 1936 games. Quietly self-assured, Guinness hands Quiller his assignment while he eats sandwiches. The scene is both "traditional" and slightly mocking — Pinter's digs at the sort of men who end up running espionage networks.

Many of Guinness' films have been censored or edited for various (and not always convincing) reasons, and *Quiller* is among them. The villains *Quiller* are neo-Nazis, a group that raised its ugly head about the time the film was released. However, before the picture was released in West Germany, all references to neo-Nazism were cut, and it is implied that the terrorists Quiller is pursuing are Communists.

A German film industry spokesman explained the shift in emphasis: "We considered that the presentation of a radical-right secret terrorist group in present-day Berlin was unrealistic. It was also inopportune because of our image toward East Germany and the Communists, who are raising charges of neo-Nazism against us at the moment."

Penelope Houston, in *Sight and Sound*, noted that Pinter had turned out "an engaging script, very mannered and at the same time ingeniously loyal

181

to the genre. It is the script which lifts *The Quiller Memorandum* just—if only just—out of the growing tedium of life among the secret agents. All the same, it is this mixture—the Pinterisation of Bond, as it were—that gives *The Quiller Memorandum* a freakish charm which has perhaps more to do with literary fantasy than with its merits as a film."

In *Films in Review*, Adelaide Connerford saw almost nothing to admire about the film: "From 3000 miles it's difficult to understand why the British film industry is so foolish as to let Harold Pinter write screenplays. Michael Anderson directed this claptrap, much of which was shot in Berlin. As a color-photographed travelogue in and about that divided city *The Quiller Memorandum* has more merit than as a spy-pic, or as propaganda against German nationalism. As the latter, because of Pinter's lurid exaggerations, it's laughable."

In his review for the *New York Times*, Bosley Crowther, too, takes a rather dim view of the proceedings: "If you've got any spying to be done in Berlin, don't send George Segal to do the job. Or rather, don't send the pudding-headed fellow that Mr. Segal plays in *The Quiller Memorandum*. Clearly [the film] is claptrap done up in a style and with a musical score by John Barry that might lead you to think it is Art. But don't let it fool you for one minute—nor Mr. Segal, nor Senta Berger as the girl. The whole thing, including these two actors, is as hollow as a shell."

Finally, Gordon Gow, in *Films and Filming*, wrote, "While stirring up many a deep thought upon life and inhumanity and power and politics, *The Quiller Memorandum* remains essentially a rip-snorting thriller, and often the snorts are quite jolly, to say nothing of the rips. The great thing about this ground-straddling is that the film really evokes the spy-thriller larks of Hitchcock and Lang."

Berlin. A man walks down a deserted street late at night, enters a phone booth, and is shot as he attempts to make a call.

The Olympic stadium in Berlin. Quiller (George Segal) meets Pol, the head of Berlin operations. Pol (Guinness) tells Quiller that neo-Nazis have surfaced in Berlin. New blood, their strength is that they appear to be like everyone else—save for the hardcore. Pol tells Quiller that two previous agents have been killed; his assignment is "not an order but a request."

Quiller spots a "tail," loses him, and then follows him. Introducing himself, Quiller learns that the tail is from Pol. Quiller says he needs no "help."

Going to a school where a teacher with a Nazi past hung himself after his war crimes were discovered, Quiller speaks to the headmistress (Edith Schneider) and then to Inge (Senta Berger), who replaced the dead teacher. Quiller drives her home and begins speaking of people who want a strong Germany, people who will wait ten, twenty, even thirty years or longer to achieve their goals of a unified, rearmed German nation.

Pol (Guinness, right) offers Quiller (George Segal) one of his sandwiches at their first meeting in the Olympic Stadium.

Later, Quiller is bumped into by a man with a suitcase. Followed by a mysterious sedan onto the autobahn, he begins to feel woozy — the man with the suitcase drugged him!

Quiller awakens in the neo-Nazi base and is questioned by their leader, a man called Oktober (Max von Sydow). Injected and questioned about the location of Berlin Control, all Quiller will say is the name "Inge." Finally, Oktober tells one of his followers, "Inject him. When he's unconscious, kill him." Quiller blacks out.

Quiller awakens to find he's been dumped on the banks of a canal. Apparently, Oktober is hoping he'll lead them back to Berlin Control. Instead, Quiller checks into a cheap hotel and calls Inge.

The next day an agent of Pol's asks Quiller what happened. Quiller keeps his own counsel, exasperated by all the passwords and flim-flam of Pol's operatives. The man takes him to see Pol who says that Quiller is in the middle between the Nazis and Berlin Control. He must signal to Pol the whereabouts of the Nazi headquarters without revealing the location of Berlin Control. As Pol puts it, Quiller is "in the gap."

Quiller meets Inge and tells her the truth. In bed, she tells him she's worried about him but knows a man who can help him find the neo-Nazi base. The man takes them to meet Inge's headmistress, who tells him the Nazis' location. Quiller, after giving Inge a phone number to call if he doesn't return in twenty minutes, enters the house.

Quiller is quickly recaptured by the men who held him before. Oktober greets him and takes him down to the basement, telling him they'll be moving to a new base. In the basement, Quiller finds Inge; Oktober says she was sitting in a car nearby. Oktober tells Quiller he'll trade Inge for the location of Berlin Control. He has till dawn — then Oktober will kill Inge and Quiller.

Quiller leaves, but is unable to reach a phone as Oktober's men efficiently shadow him. Finally, at his hotel, he finds a bomb under his car and sets it off, fooling his shadowers into thinking him dead.

He shows up at Berlin Control, rousting Pol from bed. Quiller tells Pol where the neo-Nazi base is and they are all rounded up, including Oktober. But they find no girl.

Quiller finds Inge back at her school ("They let me go," she says) and tells her they got all of them. "Well, not all of them perhaps," he says, looking at her coldly. "Most of them." He tells her he's leaving Berlin.

As she watches him walk away, it's clear he's won the battle but perhaps lost the war: Inge and the headmistress are teaching a new generation of Germans old and dangerous lessons.

Harold Pinter (1930–), a British playwright given to thought-provoking if obscure plays, wrote the screenplay for *Quiller*. His dialogue for the film is less murky than usual and, as always, his work is literate and adult. (See notes on *Quiller* in the Appendix for the films he's written.)

Director Michael Anderson was born in London in 1920 and got a job as office boy at Elstree in 1935. From there he wrangled a small part in *Housemaster*, worked as a crewman on *Pygmalion* and *French Without Tears* and other Elstree films, and finally became the unit manager on *In Which We Serve, School For Secrets, Vice Versa* and others.

Anderson got his start as a director in 1949 when he codirected *Private Angelo* with Peter Ustinov. That was followed by *Waterfront* in 1950 and sundry other features until his first big hit, *The Dam Busters* (1955), arguably one of Britain's finest and most exciting war films. (See notes on *Quiller* in the Appendix for more Anderson films.)

In *Quiller*, Anderson displayed a sure hand. His camera is fluid and well-positioned — many of his shots are more revealing than Pinter's rather sparse and obscure dialogue. Anderson gets a restrained and effective performance from George Segal. For Guinness, all Anderson has to do is train the camera on his face and let Sir Alec handle the rest.

George Segal, who played the enigmatic loner Quiller, was born in 1934 and made his first feature film appearance in 1961's *The Young Doctors* — considered a mildly "daring" film at the time. Segal quickly became a star and was very busy during the 1960s — a confident, loud, and aggressive decade which perfectly suited Segal's onscreen persona.

Expressive and mobile, Segal's face reveals just enough to suggest intelligence and depth as Quiller. His few scenes with Guinness are so well

Guinness as Pol.

acted we forgive their banality and mock seriousness. Not everybody — and this includes Guinness' Pol — takes the film's theses seriously, but Segal does, giving his character credibility.

Max von Sydow is slightly ludicrous in his garish carrot-colored hair; he seems to have stepped in from another film altogether. Austrian-born leading lady Senta Berger (1941–) is beautiful and compelling as the mysterious Inge. Unfortunately, after one apparently glorious time in bed together, Berger's character must tell Quiller: "I love you."

Guinness' performance in *The Quiller Memorandum* was a fine one, and the film itself was good, if not great. Unfortunately, it was a brief bright note amidst the drabness of Guinness' late–1960s doldrums.

31. *The Comedians* (1967)

The Comedians is interesting for many reasons. It was the third teaming of director Glenville and Guinness (after *The Prisoner* and *Hotel Paradiso*), and the second Graham Greene–penned film Guinness starred in (the first was *Our Man in Havana*).

Graham Greene, a British novelist born in 1904, is best known for his "entertainments." Influenced by his strong Roman Catholicism, he wrote his most serious works about the need for salvation and redemption. His faith, his keen eye and ear, and talent made him a favorite of Guinness'.

Producer-director Peter Glenville managed to get a copy of Greene's *The Comedians* while it was still in galley proofs. Glenville was so impressed with the book's filmic possibilities that he immediately purchased the screen rights and persuaded Greene himself to write the screenplay.

The film did okay at the box office and with the critics, although many of them were lying in wait for this reteaming of Richard Burton and Elizabeth Taylor. Also, *The Comedians* was not without controversy over its compelling indictment of modern-day Haiti under strongman and "President for life" Papa Doc Duvalier and his murderous secret police, the dreaded *Tonton Macoute*.

Naturally, the filmmakers were denied permission to shoot in Haiti and made do with Dahomey, West Africa (other locations included Nice and Paris). The cast and crew worked under the shadow of a rumor, never confirmed, that Papa Doc had ordered an assassination squad to attack the film company.

Upon the film's release, the Haitian ambassador protested the picture, calling it "an inflammatory libel against Haiti publicly released to mislead the American people.... It is also an economic assault and a propaganda aimed at disgusting and scaring the American tourist at the beginning of the season. Haiti is one of the...safest countries in the Caribbean."

Graham Greene, his accuracy challenged, responded: "The ruler of Haiti responsible for the murder and exile of thousands of his countrymen is really protesting against his own image in the looking glass. Like the ugly queen in Snow White, he will have to destroy all the mirrors."

Finally, director Glenville, who'd been in Haiti just two years before filming began, said, "I have personally heard the eye-witness accounts of many prominent Haitian citizens now in exile in New York. They confirm that Mr. Greene's description of the Haitian scene is completely accurate and that the situation there has even worsened since he wrote the book."

Guinness' performance as the posturing, comedic "Major" Jones was, for the most part, praised. Some reviewers, however, felt he was poorly utilized in an underwritten role, and the *Harvard Lampoon* went so far as to vote the film an "award" for wasting the talents of Peter Ustinov and Guinness in "roles as dull as they were uninteresting."

Philip Hartung, in the *Commonweal*, wrote, "If ever a movie caught the flavor of a Graham Greene book it is producer-director Peter Glenville's *The Comedians*. And why not, since Graham Greene wrote the screenplay from his own novel and director Glenville is meticulously faithful to it—perhaps too meticulously for an exciting movie melodrama."

Stanley Kauffmann concluded his review in *The New Republic* by saying, "On balance *The Comedians* is not remotely in the same sphere with its author's best films, like *The Third Man*—not even with *The Heart of the Matter*—but it's pleasant to spend two hours again in Greeneland, still well-stocked with bilious minor crucifixions, furtive fornication, cynical politics, and reluctant hope."

Joseph Morgenstern, in *Newsweek*, found the Burtons to be a minus: "Aside from them, as if anything could be aside from them, *The Comedians* might well have been a good film. It has so many things going for it" including "a neat Alec Guinness study in amorality. . . ."

Variety's Murf: "Producer-director Peter Glenville's pic, scripted by Greene, is a plodding, low-key, and eventually tedious melodrama. Production values are good and realistic, but film as whole does not jell."

The film was released in England in 1968, but that was too soon for Michael Armstrong. As he noted in *Films and Filming*: "Several people I have spoken to since [seeing the picture] liked *The Comedians*; many people found it a bore. Alas, I'm sorry, Mr. Glenville, but I must join the latter—which is an insult to your theme and many talented people who expressed it."

Finally, Elaine Rothschild, in *Films in Review*, said, "Graham Greene wrote the screenplay for *The Comedians*, as well as the novel of that title, and therefore is almost wholly responsible for a film that depicts 'black power' as a ghastly amalgam of voodoo and fascism."

A ship arriving at Port-au-Prince in Haiti is carrying only four passengers: Brown (Richard Burton), an aging cynic and politically apathetic lapsed Catholic returning to reopen his deserted hotel; Major Jones (Guinness), a British ex-army officer who all but singlehandedly won the war in Burma (according to him), but who is really just a minor arms merchant always dreaming of big deals; and an American couple, Mr. and Mrs. Smith (Paul Ford and Lillian Gish), who hope to sell the Haitians on the advantages of vegetarian fare like nutburgers and Yeastrol.

Major Jones (Guinness, *center*) has a spot of trouble getting through customs when he arrives in Haiti; he's arrested and thrown into jail.

Major Jones is immediately arrested and thrown into jail when he lands because the minister of defense who provided his credentials has also been arrested and jailed. Soon after Jones' arrest, Brown finds the body of a former government official at the bottom of his empty swimming pool. When the Smiths attend the murdered man's funeral, they witness the Tontons brutally assault his widow (Gloria Foster).

Meanwhile, Brown is carrying on a love affair with Martha Pineda (Elizabeth Taylor), the bored wife of a Latin American ambassador (Peter Ustinov). They meet in her car along a stretch of deserted highway and make passionate love.

The Smiths, after persuading Brown to assist in getting Jones released, are so revolted by the savage conditions (both economic and political) that they beat a hasty retreat to the United States.

Jones, making a bargain with the Tontons to ship them armaments from Miami, finds himself unable to uphold his end of the deal and has to flee. Brown, affected by Smith's commitment to decency, decides to do what he can to help Jones, now hiding in the Pinedas' embassy home. When the police offer Brown $2000 to reveal the whereabouts of Jones, Brown refuses, saying, "Inflation is everywhere. It used to be thirty pieces of silver."

Brown likes Jones—although he doesn't know why—but grows jealous when the arms dealer and Martha develop a warm friendship. Before Jones knows what's happened, Brown has tricked him into volunteering to lead a band of rebels organized by Henry Philipot (Georg Sanford Brown), the nephew of the murdered government minister.

Dr. Magiot (James Earl Jones) has his people smuggle Jones into the nearby hills and asks Brown for help against the corrupt government. In retaliation for his resistance, the Tontons invade Dr. Magiot's operating room in the middle of an operation and cut his throat.

Jones, now disguised as a native woman, is accompanied by Brown as he makes for a rendezvous with the rebel soldiers. Waiting in a graveyard to join the guerrillas, Jones and Brown try to understand the forces that have brought them together.

To pass the long night, Jones begins to tell Brown the truth about himself. His whole military career is a fraud — his flat feet kept him out of the war as the manager of a movie theater — and he has wasted his life in lies and deception. But he sees this mission as his one chance to do something worthwhile. Brown, the lapsed Catholic, listens to Jones' tortured confession and, in an act of kindness, responds with a symbolic absolution.

At dawn, the Tontons discover the two men, and Jones is shot and killed; Brown, however, is saved when the guerrillas arrive and shoot the Tontons before they can kill him as well.

Having undergone a conversion overnight, Brown is talked into taking Jones' place as head of the outgunned and outmanned rebels. As the Pinedas leave Haiti by plane, Martha looks down sadly at the hills where her lover is fighting for a doomed cause.

Richard Burton, born Richard Jenkins in Wales in 1925, died of a stroke in August 1984 at the age of 58. His was a long and tumultuous career, a career based on the need to act and on one of the great voices of theater and film. Elizabeth Taylor was born in England in 1932 but was evacuated to America in World War II; there she became a child star. Burton and Taylor carried on a steamy romance on the set of *Cleopatra* while married to other spouses. Taylor subsequently left husband Eddie Fisher to marry Burton. The marriage was a public affair and the two often acted together, most tellingly in *Who's Afraid of Virginia Woolf?*. (For more on their films, see notes on *Comedians* in the Appendix.)

Burton was signed to play Brown in *The Comedians* for a reported salary of $750,000. Glenville wanted Sophia Loren for the part of Martha Pineda, but readily accepted Elizabeth Taylor instead. To work with husband Burton, Taylor accepted the relatively small part (actually a supporting role) and worked for "only" $500,000 — half her usual asking price.

Burton was made for this sort of tortured, middle-aged wastrel role, and turns in a good performance. However, Taylor's German accent comes and goes without warning, and she is made up so heavily she's almost a caricature of an adultress. She also has to straight-facedly deliver lines like, "My dear, my darling, don't torture yourself." Or, "Sometimes I don't think we can go on as we are." After Burton gets punched in the face by a Tonton, she pouts, "Does it hurt your mouth when we kiss?"

The film was successful, but not overly so. Greene's script deliberately gives the three male leads rather self-consciously anonymous names: Brown, Jones, and Smith. Further, at nearly three hours (without an intermission), the film was too long and could easily have been trimmed to a more judicious length (after its initial release, *The Comedians* was cut to a final running time of 147 minutes), and many of Guinness' scenes were cut.

Glenville gets good performances from Peter Ustinov (for all he's on the screen!), Paul Ford and Lilian Gish, and Burton and Guinness. Guinness, again underplaying his part, is touching and pathetic as the bogus military man who finally admits to living an empty, selfish life.

Glenville, Burton, and Guinness excel in the confession scene in the graveyard. Glenville's camera captures the four-minute dialogue in one long take from a single camera position.

Earlier, Brown had refused to play the part of Judas. Now, with the killing of Jones, this "defrocked priest" (a phrase bandied about with regard to Brown) takes his place on a cross of self-sacrifice. In Greeneland, redemption is possible—but at a terrible price.

32. *Cromwell* (1970)

"The fresh air will do me good."
—King Charles I, on his way to his execution

A product of Guinness' "leaden age," *Cromwell* followed 1967's *The Comedians*. As King Charles I, the grandson of Mary, Queen of Scots, Alec Guinness had a role worthy of his subtle talents—his Charles is alternately strong-willed and determined, then vacillating and weak, certain of his divine right to rule but unable or unwilling to lead. Considered the film's "villain," Charles is actually more sympathetic than Cromwell and gives Guinness many opportunities to show us both the haughty ruler and the devoted family man playing blind man's bluff with his children. It is another outstanding interpretation in a less than outstanding film; unfortunately, poor choice of films is Guinness' Achilles' heel as an actor.

Cromwell was a film that director-writer Ken Hughes had been planning since the early 1960s. As Hughes wrote in "Those Nutty Intellectuals," an article in the January 1963 issue of *Films and Filming*, "I set out to make a film about the poor man's revolution—*Oliver Cromwell*. I've written it. Irving Allen (I think) is going to film it. Money's the problem—1,500,000 pounds. Sometimes I feel very guilty about the amount of money we spend. In *Oliver Cromwell* everytime you turn the page four thousand horses rush across." With the success of the period piece *A Man for All Seasons* in 1966, it seemed that the time was right for Hughes' historical epic.

The film cost a not-unreasonable $9,000,000; unfortunately for Hughes, producer Allen, and Columbia Pictures, *Cromwell* earned only $3,000,000. Like Guinness' earlier historical epic, *Fall of the Roman Empire* (1964), *Cromwell* was a box office bomb.

Hughes' first cut of the film came in at 165 minutes, and included a lengthy sequence, later removed (along with the intermission), in which Cromwell brutally crushed the Irish revolt, storming the towns of Drogheda and Wexford and massacring their garrisons.

The reviews were decidedly mixed. *Newsweek*'s review of the film begins, "*Cromwell* is one of those elaborate, star-studded costume dramas that are long on 'history' but short on human reality. . . . the principals, bearing the brunt of historical exposition, remain pin points on a landscape of events."

191

In the *New Yorker, Cromwell* is called "a dry spectacle, written and directed by Ken Hughes with dedicated stodginess. One doesn't have to know anything about Cromwell to disbelieve the movie. *Cromwell* doesn't make basic sense: this sturdy, honest reformer stalks in and tells the corrupt Parliament what to do, and it proceeds to do it. Why? Just because he's so right? Shakespeare spoiled us for this sort of thing: we wait for great speeches and witty remarks, for rage and poetry, and we get nothing but a relentless academicism. If virtue is as toneless as this Cromwell, who wouldn't prefer vice?"

David Denby's review in *Atlantic* begins by asserting, "*Cromwell* is a classic of hollow prestige, an earnest, rigid, and not very bright exercise in the great-confrontations-of-British-history genre; its conception of history as something heroic, dignified, and unspeakably *important* is exactly what one remembers from dull high school texts."

In *Variety*, "Rich" wrote, "*Cromwell* is streets ahead of most lavish historical epics of recent times and . . . should really woo the legendary family audience if such still exists outside the Disney field. Natch, with so much cash at stake certain niceties have had to play second fiddle to production values, but there is a minimum of pandering to box office. The film represents a triumph in logistics, production and detail. But, despite everything else, such a film stands or falls by its Cromwell and King Charles. Harris and Guinness have done [producer Irving] Allen and [director Ken] Hughes proud and Columbia looks to be on a bold, imaginative, entertaining winner."

Films in Review's Norman Cecil began his piece by stating, "Only a mediocre producer like Irving Allen would have thought Ken Hughes could write and direct an adequate biop about Oliver Cromwell, and only a mediocre writer-director like Hughes would have assented to Richard Harris playing the title role. So few theafilms are worth seeing nowadays I feel guilty about this negative review of *Cromwell*. There *are* ideas in it, after all, and it's certainly more worth seeing than ninety per cent of the dreck so glowingly advertised in this morning's *New York Times*."

In 1640 England, a Puritan member of Parliament and a Cambridge squire, Oliver Cromwell, on the verge of emigrating to the American colonies, is disturbed by the growing injustices of King Charles I's reign, especially when the rights of his friend, John Carter (Frank Finley) are infringed upon. Rather than emigrate, Cromwell (Richard Harris) and his Puritan friends, the Roundheads, ally against the Cavaliers, Charles' supporters in Parliament.

We first see Charles (Guinness) at his prayers, a monarch smugly certain of his divine right to govern England as he pleases. His Catholic wife, Queen Henrietta Maria (Dorothy Tutin), and his staunch supporter, the earl of Strafford (Patrick Wymark), encourage him to recall the Long Parliament (1640–1660) and demand they finance his campaign against the Scots' "Second Bishops' War" being waged against his autocratic rule.

Guinness as King Charles I and Dorothy Tutin as his Catholic queen.

One of several members of Parliament who meet with Charles, Cromwell states his beliefs so firmly that the king includes him among the "Five Members" he unsuccessfully charges with high treason. In return, when Charles accompanies his troops into Parliament to regain control, Cromwell and his allies accuse the king of treason.

Charles raises his standard at Nottingham, and the English Civil War between his royalists and the parliamentarians begins.

After Prince Rupert (Timothy Dalton), who rides into battle with a poodle on his arm, sacks Bristol and routes the Roundheads, Cromwell takes command of the Puritan forces and leads his reformed "New Model" army to victory over Charles' forces at Naseby, Northamptonshire, on June 14, 1645.

In 1646, the Civil War ends with the royalist surrender of Oxford. Cromwell and the king negotiate until, finally, the negotiations collapse over Charles' refusal to accept Presbyterianism as England's national religion and parliamentary control of the militia for a period of twenty years.

Cromwell is forced to hang his friend John Carter for treason. In 1648, after the Second English Civil War, the "rump" parliament calls for Charles' trial. The king is a wily, although ultimately unsuccessful, spokesman for his God-given right to reign, and his arguments shake many of those who hold his fate in their hands.

Found guilty of treason, King Charles is beheaded in 1649. Cromwell, now dictator of England (Lord Protector of the Commonwealth of England,

Guinness (*left*) and Richard Harris as Charles I and Cromwell.

Scotland, and Ireland), himself dissolves Parliament, saying, "You leave me no alternative."

Director Ken Hughes was born in Liverpool in 1922. After winning a national amateur film contest at the age of fourteen, Hughes became a film "rewind boy" a year later, and eventually found employment at the BBC for three years. In 1944, he became a writer and director of documentary films for World Wide Pictures.

In 1952, he directed his first feature film, *Wide Boy*. He followed it up with *Black 13* in 1953 and that same year wrote and directed *Little Red Monkey*. "I only started writing in the first place to protect myself," he added. "No director is better than his script: you can make a mess of a good script but you can't do much with a bad one."

In addition to writing his own film scripts, Hughes has written several novels, including *High Wray* and *The Long Echo*. (For more on Hughes' films, see notes on *Cromwell* in the Appendix.)

Producer Irving Allen (1905–), is a Polish-American producer (not to be confused with Irwin Allen, producer of disaster films like *The Poseidon Adventure* and *The Towering Inferno*). Irving Allen produced the "Matt Helm" series and also was the producer for Hughes' well-received *The Trials of Oscar Wilde*, starring Peter Finch.

Richard Harris, born in 1932, is a hard-drinking, hard-living Irish film star. Gaunt and intense, his roles often find him at odds with the society around him. In the early 1980s, his film career stagnating, Harris took to the stage in a tour of *Camelot*, again playing King Arthur as he did in the 1967 film version (Richard Burton originated the role on Broadway).

Though he settled for Richard Harris as his Cromwell, Hughes originally wanted someone else. As he observed, "Cromwell is a noisy, blustering, vulgar, uncouth farmer — Peter Finch!"

If Peter Finch was Hughes' first choice for Cromwell (in 1963), he had always had someone like Sir Alec Guinness in mind for the role of the complex King Charles I. Certainly Guinness brings to the king all his honed and perfected skills. His Charles has just a hint of Scottish burr in his stammering accent. And, through good makeup, Guinness looks remarkably like Van Dyck's portrait of Charles. Entering the High Court of Parliament, Guinness' Charles, every inch a king, holds his walking stick in front of him as if it were a scepter, and slowly twists it in circles: an arrogant gesture to remind everyone he is their king and they his subjects, even though they are to try him.

Before his execution, Guinness' Charles addresses the crowd in a perfectly delivered speech: "I will not delay you long, but will say only this to you: As God is my witness I have forgiven those who have brought me here and pray that my death be not laid to their charge. For I do endeavor even to the last to maintain the peace — of *my* kingdom. I go now from a corruptible to an incorruptible crown. To everlasting peace."

Sir Alec is in his usual good form, but Richard Harris is not. Reportedly well lubricated during shooting, he batters at his role with bull-like tenacity, but hasn't the dynamic range Cromwell demands. Harris frowns severely, tilts his eyebrows furiously, and generally chews the Spanish scenery for all he's worth. He's no Peter Finch. (See notes on *Cromwell* in the Appendix for more on Harris' films.)

The major problem with *Cromwell* is that, except for moviegoing historians, the film is too deadly dull and repetitious. Certainly, Hughes recognized the pitfalls as early as his 1963 *Films and Filming* article: "After the Civil War it was a period of reasonable progress: they built schools, they laid foundations, they did all sorts of things — education for instance. But dull stuff. Battle, lovely: conflict, cutting the king's head off — marvelous. How do you make a film ending with twenty minutes of building schools?

"I'm pro–Cromwell," Hughes wrote. He also noted, "It's easier to be anti–Cromwell , not so good to be pro–Cromwell because it gets boring. . . ."

33. *Scrooge* (1970)

"A curdled cup of holiday cheer."
—Jay Cocks

Scrooge is based on Charles Dickens' 1847 story *A Christmas Carol*. It was Alec Guinness' third film based on a Dickens work and his least successful. Unlike *Oliver!*, Carol Reed's musical remake of *Oliver Twist*, *Scrooge* is a pallid rendition of Dickens, an unimpressive version of the oft-filmed story of a wretched miser gradually coming to realize the meaning of Christmas. Film and television versions of *A Christmas Carol* are almost too numerous to mention. Among the many: *A Christmas Carol* (1938), filmed by MGM and starring Reginald Owen as Scrooge and Gene Lockhart as Marley; *A Christmas Carol* (1951), a British filming starring Alistair Sim as Scrooge and Michael Hordern as Marley (this is considered by most critics and film buffs as the definitive film version); and a "Mr. Magoo" animated cartoon. Television presented a musical version on *Shower of Stars* in 1954, which starred Fredric March as Scrooge and boasted a libretto by Maxwell Anderson. In 1956, *The Alcoa Hour* offered a ninety-minute musical version starring Basil Rathbone—in his singing debut—called "The Stingiest Man in Town."

In time for Christmas 1983, the Disney studios released a new animated short starring Mickey Mouse as Scrooge and featuring well-known Disney cartoon characters in the other roles. It marked a comeback for Disney's famous mouse star—Mickey had not been animated for years.

Actually, *Scrooge* would be a fine version were it not for its unimaginative, forgettable music and lyrics by Leslie Bricusse. Whereas almost every number in *Oliver!* is memorable, very few are in *Scrooge*. The only song that lingers in one's memory after seeing *Scrooge* is "Thank You Very Much"—and that only because the song is as repetitious and catchy as a commercial jingle ("Thank you very much, thank you very much/That's the nicest thing that anyone's ever done for me/Thank you very much, thank you very much...").

The critical reaction was mixed. Tatiana Balkoff Drowne, in *Films in Review*, wrote,"[Leslie Bricusse's] music and lyrics are in a music hall spirit of Christmas past and present and make this film a cinematic sugar plum."

Less pleased was Jay Cocks in *Time* magazine: "*Scrooge* is a high-budget

196

holiday spectacular, a musical extracted from Dickens' *A Christmas Carol* that turns out to be a curdled cup of holiday cheer.... First frame to last, *Scrooge* is...made with indifference to every quality but the box-office receipts."

It is Christmas Eve, 1860. Ebenezer Scrooge (Albert Finney) counts coins in his office and chases away carolers with a coal shovel. Scrooge's clerk, Bob Cratchit (David Collings), is still at work. Quitting time is 7 P.M., and to Scrooge, it's not 7:00 until the last chime has sounded. Free from work at last, Cratchit and his children go about putting a low-budget Christmas (pigeon instead of turkey) together.

When two men solicit charity funds from Scrooge, he tells them to leave him alone, asking why can't the poor die and "decrease the surplus population." Singing "I Hate People," Scrooge collects loan money due him as the carolers follow and derisively call him "Father Christmas" (song).

Scrooge goes home, but at his door, something strange happens: His doorknocker turns into the face of his dead partner, Jacob Marley. Then he sees a ghostly carriage go by. Inside his drab house, bells ring mysteriously and other odd things happen. Eating his soup, Scrooge hears his name softly called. The door opens and there is the ghost of Marley (Guinness) bound in chains. Angered when Scrooge attempts to dismiss him as a mere stomach disorder, Marley wiggles his hands and rises into the air, smashing the huge locks of his chain together. It is the chain he forged in life; Scrooge is making his own, longer chain to wear when he dies.

Marley takes Scrooge on a voyage to Hell, where the ghost sings "See the Phantoms." Scrooge puts his hands over his eyes and is back in his house. A dream, he thinks—then turns to see Marley back again. After telling Scrooge he'll be visited by three ghosts that night, Marley weirdly backs through the closed door and returns to endlessly roaming the earth as a spirit in agony.

The Ghost of Christmas Past appears and shows Scrooge the young Ebenezer, left all alone at school during the holidays, neglected by his family. Then the Ghost and Scrooge see an older Ebenezer, an apprentice to Mr. Fezziwig, who throws an annual "office party." After everyone sings and dances "December the Twenty-fifth," Ebenezer dances with Isabel, Fezziwig's daughter. Old Scrooge sings a sad lost-love song as he watches his past. Isabel leaves Ebenezer, telling him he loves money more than he does her—and it's true.

The Ghost of Christmas Present is a rollicking giant who allows Scrooge to drink from a cup containing the "milk of human kindness." The ghost takes Scrooge to peer through the windows of the Cratchit home. The Cratchits have nothing, but they're happy. Tiny Tim (Richard Beaumont), dreaming of a brighter future, sings "The Beautiful Day."

After similarly watching a party at his nephew's house, Scrooge begins to realize how much he's shut himself off from life.

The Ghost of Christmas Yet To Come shows him shadows of the future, including a large crowd gathered to express their thanks to Scrooge. Scrooge

Marley's ghost (Guinness) confronts Scrooge (Albert Finney).

is unaware of the source of their joy—he's died and freed them from their debts. His coffin is carried out while the crowd sings, "For He's a Jolly Good Fellow," and Tom Jenkins sings, "Thank You Very Much."

When Scrooge notices the absence of Tiny Tim, the ghost shows him the boy's grave. After showing Scrooge his own grave, the ghost reveals himself as a skeleton, and a terrified Scrooge falls into his open grave and down a fiery tunnel. He awakens at home on Christmas morning.

Was it a dream? No matter; Scrooge will now begin to *live* his life. A new man, Scrooge sees his nephew and his wife and gives them gifts, agreeing to attend their Christmas meal. Dressed as Santa, Scrooge then goes to the Cratchit house and distributes gifts. He also forgives the crowd their debts, and the film ends with a big production number. Scrooge will now honor Christmas and forge a new future for Tiny Tim.

Scrooge's cinematic tricks are first-rate and quite convincing. As Tatiana Drowne noted in her *Films in Review* piece, "Wally Veevers' special effects are worth seeing—not only such things as the locks in Scrooge's stylizedly eerie house and the doorknocker changing into a face, but also the depiction of a red-hot Hades."

Scrooge was the fourth film Guinness made with director Ronald Neame (second only to David Lean's five—though Neame was associated with the early Lean films), a collaboration that began with *The Card* in 1952.

Unfortunately, Neame's direction is sporadically effective at best. His greatest sin, perhaps, is allowing Guinness to play Marley as a mannered fop who, with his bewigged head in a bandage, looks rather like Lady Agatha from *Kind Hearts and Coronets*.

Bashing his huge locks and keys together, angry at being called a digestive ailment, and rising into the air, Guinness' Marley is more silly than anything else. Although many reviewers found Guinness' performance fine, several others definitely did not: Gordon Gow, in *Films and Filming*, wrote, "And soon Marley's ghost walks in, all gray and heavily laden with chains, looking at first sight like poor Buster Keaton but turning out to be Alec Guinness in the throes of a perpetual writhing fit, performed slowly and inexorably and accompanied at one point by a slow floating up towards the ceiling."

Jay Cocks, in *Time*, said, "Sir Alec Guinness materializes from time to time as the ghost of Scrooge's old partner Marley, but he plays the part floating several inches off the floor and flapping his wrists, an interpretation better suited to *The Boys in the Band*."

Guinness actually gets to sing a song, "See the Phantoms," on Scrooge's flight to Hell. In the best Rex Harrison/*My Fair Lady* tradition of nonsinging, Guinness recites the lyrics in a talky, singsong manner.

As a consequence of wearing a flying rig as Marley's ghost, Guinness sustained a double hernia. The injury almost prevented him from playing a role he coveted very much, John Mortimer's blind father in Mortimer's autobiographical play *A Voyage Round My Father*. Guinness' stage performance won him wide acclaim, providing a salve, one imagines, for the hostile notices his Marley won him.

The other actors in *Scrooge* include the film's lead, Albert Finney. Finney, a star who refuses to behave like one, was again stretching himself artistically, playing an old man who is seen as a younger man in flashback scenes. While it is a role a younger Guinness might have convincingly played, it's hard to conceive of Sir Alec doing a better job than Finney as Scrooge. Indeed, Finney and his co-stars—Dame Edith Evans, Kenneth More, Laurence Naismith—are the best thing about *Scrooge*.

Finney, then just thirty-four years old, invests the scenes of the reformed Scrooge with bounce and vigor. It's as if the wonders he's beheld that night have revitalized his body as well as his soul. (See notes on *Scrooge* in the Appendix for more on Finney's films.)

As the Ghosts of Christmas Past and Present, Edith Evans and Kenneth More draw on their own personalities to enrich their characterizations. Evans is prim and proper. Her dignity is amusing and disarming—this starched old Victorian woman is a ghost? Kenneth More, a bearded giant as the Ghost of Christmas Present, gives a wonderfully broad and animated performance as a ghost who "likes life."

In lesser roles, Naismith is infectiously cheerful as Mr. Fezziwig, Anton Rodgers is a delight as Tom Jenkens, David Collings is gaunt but gallant as Bob Cratchit, and Richard Beaumont is refreshingly uncloying as Tiny Tim.

All in all, *Scrooge* is an admirable version of the Dickens classic—if only it weren't for that music!

34. *Brother Sun, Sister Moon* (1973)

Alec Guinness replaced Sir Laurence Olivier in the small but pivotal role of Pope Innocent III in this lush filming of the life of St. Francis of Assisi. Given Guinness' strong Catholic beliefs, it seems easy enough to guess his motives for accepting the role of one of the strongest and most powerful popes of the Middle Ages.

Innocent III (pope from 1198 to 1216) was the head of the Roman Catholic church whose oral sanction in 1210 legitimized Francis of Assisi and his eleven followers as roving preachers, the Franciscans. Under Innocent's rule, the medieval papacy reached the summit of its power and influence. So strong was his temporal power that he forced King John of England to become his vassal, had Emperor Otto disposed of in favor of Frederick II, and initiated the Fourth Crusade (1202). It is hard to imagine Guinness turning down a chance to play such a giant of the Catholic church.

A hooded figure struggles toward the walled city of Assisi and collapses. It is Giovanni Francesco Bernardone (Graham Faulkner), the son of a rich cloth merchant; he is a deserter from the war with Perugia, and ill. As he writhes with fever, we see flashbacks to his earlier, dissolute life as the spoiled son of overprotective and materialistic parents.

When he awakens, he hears a little bird chirping. He follows it out onto the roof and grasps it momentarily. He watches it soar (as Donovan sings "Birds are Singing" on the soundtrack).

Transformed by his illness, he wanders about observing the flowers and the birds, coming upon the ruins of an old cathedral. He meets the beautiful young Clare (Judi Bowker), who tells him that in Assisi, most people think him mad since his transformation; she thought him mad *before*, not now.

His father, Pietro di Bernadone (Lee Montague), shows him the riches he's amassed because of the war. But Francesco wanders into his father's cloth shop and cries at the wretched conditions of the workers, embracing an old man there.

Francesco's father rages that his son took the workers out into the afternoon sun and nothing got done.

At mass, Francesco notices that the incredibly jewel-encrusted rich sit in the front and the poor stand in the back. Looking at the crucifix, he's overcome when Christ's eyes glow, and he screams, "No!" Clare watches him adoringly.

As Donovan sings "Brother Sun, Sister Moon," Francesco romps through the gorgeous Italian fields, again coming upon the ruins. Inspired, he throws his father's goods out of the window to the poor, telling his father, "Our treasures are in heaven."

His father beats him and drags him before the regional governor (Adolfo Celi), who sends them to the bishop of Assisi. The bishop (John Sharp) calls him a threat to society. Saying he wants to be free like the birds, Francesco strips naked and gives away his clothes, walking nude out of the city. Clare watches admiringly from a window as he strides away.

Bernardo (Leigh Lawson), one of Francesco's friends, returns from the Crusades to learn that Francesco is living at the ruined cathedral. He journeys there and, to his own surprise, joins Francesco and the poor in rebuilding the cathedral. Their other friends arrive, and one of them, Giocondo (Nicholas Willatt), also joins Francesco.

When the emperor arrives in Assisi, Silvestro, using Francesco's words, speaks up for the poor and is pushed aside; he joins Francesco now as well.

The small band of friends grows larger. Clare gives them bread. Poor farmers, too, share their meager portions with the band, and both groups feel blessed. Clare joins them, and her beautiful long hair is cut. Soon the cathedral is rebuilt and the peasants gather to celebrate, while the rich stolidly worship in their finery and jewels at Assisi's church.

The bishop sends his soldiers to burn the cathedral, and one of Francesco's followers is killed. Seeking understanding, Francesco wishes to see the pope. Paolo (Kenneth Cranham), an old friend who has not yet joined Francesco, agrees to help.

Rome: pomp and ostentatiousness. There, they confront the majesty and the power of Pope Innocent III (Guinness). "You asked permission to speak to us. Well, speak." Francesco speaks of the birds and the lilies (pretty much from the New Testament, actually), and the courtiers, angry, have them thrown out.

In the ensuing uproar, the pope raises his hand to heaven and calls for Francesco to be brought back. Innocent descends from his throne to Francesco's level, asking the young man what he wants of him and what advice he, as Pope, can possibly give him, saying, "God has given you a most precious gift — the grace to approach him through his beloved creatures. What more can you want?"

When Francesco tells the Pope that he and followers must surely have sinned through presumption, Innocent tells him that he will be forgiven.

Innocent tells Francesco that long before he became Pope, he was an enthusiastic and joyful representative of the church, but that the power and responsibility of his position have taken hold of him and drained him of the freedom to act as humanly as Francesco and his followers.

Guinness as Pope Innocent III.

"And what will happen to those who come after you, have you thought about them?" Innocent asks. "We are encrusted with riches and power. You, in your poverty" — he touches Francesco's rags — "put us to shame." Innocent tells him to go forth and teach the truth to all men. Overcome, he kneels before Francesco and kisses his feet.

Given the pope's blessing, Francesco and his followers leave — prepared, in the pope's words, to "increase a thousandfold and flourish like the palm tree."

Vincent Canby, in the *New York Times*, wrote, "Franco Zeffirelli's *Brother Sun, Sister Moon* is the sort of movie that tries to make poverty look chic, and almost goes broke in the attempt. Zeffirelli makes Francis seem such a bland sort of fellow that we spend most of the time looking at the scenery, the auroral photographic effects, and the costumes, which were also the chief attractions of the director's hugely popular *Romeo and Juliet."*

"Murf," in *Variety*, in one of the few positive reviews, said, *"Brother Sun, Sister Moon* is a delicate, handsome quasi-fictional biography of one of the great saints of the Catholic Church, Francis of Assisi. Franco Zeffirelli, in his first film project since *Romeo and Juliet*, has utilized a style of simple elegance, befitting both the period and the subject."

Jay Cocks' brief review in *Time*, however, was not nearly so appreciative: " 'Brother Sun, Sister Moon, I seldom see you, seldom hear your tune,' warbles Donovan, the unseen balladeer whom Franco Zeffirelli has enlisted to lend a whiff of flower power to this overripe version of the life of St. Francis of Assisi. Zeffirelli's work looks like a Sunday-school coloring book: everything is glowingly photogenic, including poverty, and leprosy."

In *New Republic*, Stanley Kauffmann began his review by saying, "Franco Zeffirelli has made a film about St. Francis of Assisi, and if I were pope, I would burn it."

In *America*, Moira Walsh wrote, "What the film offers, then, is breathtakingly beautiful landscapes and many moving and lovely individual scenes. This may provide a significant experience for kindly disposed audiences who automatically synthesize their prior knowledge of the saint with the on-screen vignettes. But what the average spectator, who cannot be expected to know much about Francis of Assisi, will make of the film is another matter entirely." She added that Donovan's songs "had a jarring and commercial ring."

It's true, as Moira Walsh said, that if one knows little about the life of St. Francis of Assisi (born Giovanni Francesco Bernadone [1181–1226], this film is not the place to learn more. The script was written by director Zeffirelli, Suso Cecchi D'Amico, and Lina Wertmuller (English dialogue by Kenneth Ross) and is a sort of picture-book version of St. Francis' life. The title, incidentally, is taken from St. Francis' "Canticle of Creatures."

Director Franco Zeffirelli, born in 1922, is best known for his two Shakespeare adaptations, *The Taming of the Shrew*, with the Burtons, and *Romeo and Juliet*, a teen-oriented rendering. An Italian stage director, especially of grand opera, Zeffirelli's films are noted for their lavish sets, costumes, use of color, and often youthful performers. His most recent directorial efforts have been filmed operas.

As designed by Corenzo Mongiardino and photographed by Ennio Guarnieri, *Brother Sun* is a feast for the eyes, if not the brain. The costumes, by Danilo Donati, are unbelievably gorgeous and faithful to the time.

Donovan's songs and music, however, are mostly an intrusion into the film. Only occasionally does the music and song mesh comfortably with the visual splendor, despite musical scholar Alfredo Bianchini's research into medieval melodies, which Donovan arranged and lyricized. (Vincent Canby said, "The film is scored to a point that makes your teeth hurt with awful songs. . .by Donovan, sung by him on the soundtrack in a role I assume to be God's.")

The other actors in *Brother Sun* include Lee Montague, Valentina Cortesa, and Adolfo Celi. Montague (1927–) played the role of Francesco's father, Pietro. A vibrant and energetic actor, he's mostly been seen on television and the British stage. Cortesa (1924–), an Italian-born leading lady, played Francesco's mother, Pica. Never a major star, she nonetheless has appeared in many international productions. (See notes on *Brother Sun* in the Appendix for more on Montague and Cortesa.) Celi appeared in *Hitler: The Last Ten Days*, also with Guinness and also released in 1973. (See the *Hitler* chapter and notes for more on Celi.)

Most of the other leads were all young British actors who hadn't appeared in a film before starring in *Brother Sun*, and included Judi Bowker and Leigh Lawson.

Looking incredibly aged and withered, Guinness is excellent as Pope Innocent III. He doesn't appear until the final few minutes of the film, but his presence is immediately felt. As cameos go, this one is both good and well cast. When Innocent rises from Francesco's feet, and his aides reenfold him in the robes of authority, we feel that Guinness' playing of the emotional scene has enfolded him with a very special authority of his own.

Brother Sun, Sister Moon was neither a critical nor a financial success. It came and went without arousing much interest. Guinness' poor luck in picking films continued—but he still gave a fine performance.

35. Hitler: The Last Ten Days (1973)

> "Adolf, you really *are* the most incredible person!"
> — Eva Braun, to Hitler in *The Last Ten Days*

"This film is the result of careful research. The words spoken and the actions presented are all based on authentic historical evidence." — Hugh Trevor Roper, professor of modern history, Oxford University.

Lest we put too much credence in Professor Roper's assurances of accuracy, it is wise to remember that he was the expert who authenticated the "Hitler Diaries" in 1983.

Guinness certainly seems an odd choice to play Adolf Hitler. Guinness is all inner man and Hitler, to all appearances, was all outer man — a powerful, almost elemental, human force capable of towering rages and truly psychotic behavior, hardly the typical Guinness man of doubts and private torments. But according to Maria Pia Fusco, one of the screenwriters, "Sir Alec was our first choice for Hitler. We had him in mind when we wrote our screenplay." Guinness was certainly the right age. He was 58 when the eight weeks of filming began in July 1972 to Hitler's 56 — and the Führer was a much-aged man at his death.

Guinness told one interviewer how he went about getting himself prepared: "I listened to records of his speeches and tried to form my own impersonation of the way he talked. Strangely enough, there are not records available of his normal speaking voice, only the speeches themselves.

"I had no preconception about how to play him during these final days, except the determination that this should not be a caricature. For example, the first shots of the film show me without the familiar lock of hair across the forehead that was almost Hitler's trademark. I didn't want the audience to start out by saying, 'There he is, old Hitler.' "

Guinness certainly looks like the Führer, although his voice, always Guinness' strength or weakness, gives him away. The audience says, "There he is, old Alec."

"Robe," *Variety*'s reviewer, said, "What is good about the film is the treatment of Hitler by Sir Alec Guinness, who gives perhaps the best portrayal yet of that bizarre figure. Guinness' physical creation. . . is exemplary. Nothing suggestive of makeup or exaggeration. Visually, he is Adolf Hitler."

Guinness as Der Führer himself. He looked like Adolf but sounded like Sir Alec.

In the *New York Times*, Vincent Canby wrote, "As a historical re-enactment...*Hitler* is about as exciting as a high-minded, parent-approved comic book about the adventures of James Watt and his steam engine. The film doesn't seem to have been directed, or acted, as much as cast, in the wax-works sense. Guinness looks right as Hitler, and that's about all—but then Hitler may be an impossible role."

In *Commonweal*, Colin L. Westerbeck, Jr., wrote that the film's message is that "all great men of history—whether good or evil, lionized or debunked—are bores. Up close every tyrant, even the most absolute and infamous, is a petty tyrant. This is the disappointment of *Hitler*. Alec Guin-ness wrestles the intractable part of Hitler; but as with history, so with the man, all is lost from the beginning. Guinness adopts a bearish stoop that is startling at first, and his stamping and slapping betray the almost effeminate lack of co-ordination in the supreme *Übermensch*. But the voice Guinness affects is all wrong. It's his Gulley Jimson voice from *The Horse's Mouth*. Nor is there anything Guinness can do about his eyes, which are a basset hound's where Hitler's were a Doberman pinscher's."

The *New Yorker*'s review of *Hitler* says, "Alec Guinness plays the Führer. . . speaking very identifiably in the voice of Alec Guinness and looking exactly like him, too, in spite of heavy work on his hair. . . . It is hard to believe that people who lived through the Second World War could have made a film as flippant as this."

Holiday's reviewer pulled no punches: "It is an understatement to describe this film as stupid. It is even of little importance that all those who lived the last ten days with Hitler are given to us as rather nice, slightly simple, people complacently resigned to impending death, wishing mostly for the cigarettes denied them by their beloved leader's aversion to smoking.

". . .Alec Guinness plays him with such ordinary, self-pitying tedious-ness that one begins to wonder if his Hitler isn't a case of mistaken identity. In all fairness to Mr. Guinness, it should be recognized that an actor playing a ham is confronted with unfair competition, for who's to say where the actor ends and the ham begins? For the time being, I think we will need to be content with Charlie Chaplin's Hitler as the most definitive to date."

Once Hitler determines he will remain in Berlin, a narrator (who sounds suspiciously like Alistair Cooke) gives a brief synopsis of Hitler's rise to power and the Reich's collapse to its current state.

Hauptmann Hoffman (Simon Ward) arrives at the bunker with a message for the Führer. Hitler (Guinness) appears, walking stiffly with his useless left arm clamped to his side. It is April 20, Hitler's fifty-sixth birthday, and his staff and friends give him presents. Later, he receives news of deteriorating military conditions and starts talking about opera — he'd like to see Wagner's works performed by naked singers. A vegetarian, he has pro-hibited smoking in the bunker, to the dismay of most of the others. As explo-sions roar outside, Hitler discusses colonizing Russia and studies the blueprints for his rebuilt Berlin, to be filled with massive monuments.

By April 23, the Russians are just 23 kilometers from the bunker. Refusing to face the inevitable, Hitler dwells on past victories, past glories. He appoints a twenty-seven-year-old officer commander of "Fortress Berlin." Hoffman asks to stay and is welcomed by the bunker's staff. When Hitler learns that one of his generals is not ready to counterattack, he shouts, "Defeatist talk."

Hitler, who speaks scornfully of officers trained in military academies, rages at his staff for betraying him by not executing one of his orders. He threatens them with death by piano-wire strangulation. Calming down, he tells them he will remain in Berlin to the bitter end. Hitler now, for the first

As the Allies close in on his bunker, Guinness' Hitler blithely continues to plan his grandiose Berlin of the future.

time, brings up the idea of killing himself and cries for his lost, beloved, Third Reich.

Outside, his officers, shaken by his threats, refuse to take the initiative in giving orders as Hitler plays with models of his Berlin of the future. He wants photographs of himself saved so all will know what he looked like—he doesn't want to be like Christ, his features open to artists' misinterpretations. Grabbing at straws, he reads a horoscope which offers hope for a German victory still. Further, he is told a rumor about "fighting" between Russian and American troops even as real newsreels reveal otherwise.

At a gathering in his rooms, he speaks of never marrying—to the displeasure of Eva Braun (Doris Kunstmann). As bombs fall outside, Hermann Goering sends a message offering (threatening?) to take over the reins of government. Hitler will hear none of it, even though the Russians have surrounded and cut off Berlin.

The staff gets word that Himmler has initiated peace talks with the Allies. No one dares to be the one to take this news to Hitler, so an enterprising general sends it in on a waiter's tray! Hitler rages at Himmler's perfidy and accuses others of betraying him. As a Hitler Youth arrives for autographed pictures of the Führer, he sees a victim of the Führer's rage being shot by a firing squad. Leaving with the photographs, Berlin crumbling around him, the boy has a look of pure terror on his young face.

Hitler reveals his final plans—to take his own life. They all calmly discuss various methods: poison, gunshot, falling on a bayonet, or leaping from an aircraft over Berlin. The Goebbels will give their children cyanide as well. Eva asks Hitler his plans, and he reveals that he intends to shoot himself and have his body drenched with gasoline and burned.

A nervous Berlin city councilor marries Hitler and Eva, incensing the Führer by asking if he's of pure Aryan blood and free of hereditary disease. Later, Hitler rails against the democracies, insisting people want strong, one-man rule.

On April 30, Hitler learns that Berlin has been cut in two. He had hoped to die on May 5 — like Napoleon — but the Russians are only 300 meters away. Eva, disillusioned, bites on a cyanide capsule and dies. Hitler feels betrayed and, off-screen, shoots himself.

Once they learn of his death, the survivors all light up cigarettes and cigars — they can smoke at last!

The producers were so unsure how the British public might react to Guinness' playing of their country's old nemesis that they had Lloyd's of London insure Sir Alec's life "just in case any fervent anti–Nazi or lunatic got the idea I really was the reincarnation of Hitler and wanted to do away with me," Guinness recalled. The set at Shepperton Studios was closed to all but essential personnel, and security was high.

The security precautions, if understandable, were also laughably unnecessary. As Guinness himself noted, "It astonishes me how few people remember what he looked like. When we photographed uniform tests in Hyde Park, with me fully made up and in uniform, not a soul turned round."

Guinness, with the fascination one might feel when staring into the eyes of a coiled cobra, delved deep into Hitler's private life, unearthing such useful trivia as the fact that the Führer drank mint tea out of a Meissen china cup with a small gold swastika on it. "I became completely immersed in his personality after spending so many months in reading and research and watching endless newsreel films of the period," Guinness said. "It was inevitable, I suppose, that something of this would rub off on to me. But I don't think I took Hitler home with me at night. At least, I hope I didn't!"

To better recreate the man, Guinness, a virtual nonstop smoker, gave up his beloved cigarettes — Hitler was adamant in his refusal to allow anyone around him to smoke tobacco.

The major problem with the film is, no matter how important it is to know all we can about Hitler and the Nazis — the better to avoid another such global conflict — *Hitler* is just plain uninvolving and, ultimately, boring. Is one to like and identify with Hitler? Hardly. And yet there is no other viewpoint to take with regard to this picture, since no one else in the cast, whether as character or actor, is remotely interesting. Hitler (and Guinness' playing of him) commands our attention.

Adolfo Celi, born in 1922, plays General Krebs. He is best known as

James Bond's antagonist in 1965's *Thunderball*. Appearing first on the Brazilian stage, this Italian actor gravitated to semi-stardom by playing villains of every stripe and nationality in the 1970s.

For a while, Diane Cilento (born in Australia in 1933), who plays Hanna Reitsch in *Hitler*, was best known for being Mrs. Sean Connery—"James Bond's wife." Most Americans first noticed her in *Tom Jones* in 1963.

Eric Porter, born in 1928, plays General von Greim. A sturdy and dependable actor, he was in *Fall of the Roman Empire* with Guinness and is internationally famous for playing Soames in TV's *The Forsyte Saga*. (For more on these actors, see notes on *Hitler* in the Appendix.)

Guinness is quite good, but as noted earlier, his voice betrays him. He has Hitler's stiff and awkward movements down pat, but he does not— perhaps *cannot*—convince us he's "old Hitler." We sense, ultimately, that Guinness is. . . well, too *nice* to play the role of this madman.

The film is unintentionally funny at times: Eva's quote which opens this chapter, and Eva's last-minute observation, "Maybe I never knew you," when Adolf admits he doesn't care about the German people, are prime examples. And, finally, it does seem that the people inside the bunker, while millions die in concentration camps or on the battlefield, only care about a chance to smoke a cigarette without the Führer's finding out.

Playing Hitler neither advanced nor hindered Guinness' career. His second film of 1973, *Hitler* saw him go in one year from playing a powerful spiritual leader to playing a psychotic temporal leader—from Pope Innocent III to a human monster. It was a giant step, but he made it well.

IV. Return of Guinness:
The New Golden Age

"Less is more."

— Mies Van Der Rohe

"Where it all ends, there it all begins."

— R.D. Laing

"Things are more like they are now than they ever were before."

— Dwight D. Eisenhower

Murder by Death (1976)

to

A Passage to India (1984) and beyond.

36. Murder by Death (1976)

> "As a man you are barely passable,
> but as a woman you are a *dog!*"
> — Milo Perrier

> "That's *your* opinion, big boy!"
> — Guinness as Aileen Twain in *Murder by Death*

Murder by Death (hereafter just *Murder*) was one of Sir Alec Guinness' infrequent Hollywood films, a Ray Stark production. After appearing in Julian Mitchell's stage adaptation of Ivy Compton Burnett's *A Family and a Fortune* in 1975, Guinness, who'd not made a film since 1973's *Hitler: The Last Ten Days*, decided he'd better find a script before he was forgotten.

Later, when the film was critized, Guinness made no apologies for taking the part of Bensonmum, the blind butler who may or may not have "done it." "It was a very funny film," Guinness said. "The script made me laugh, and not many things in recent times have done that."

Murder marks the beginning of the "return of Guinness" that would see Sir Alec making a comeback of sorts, returning to good parts in some good films.

Charles Champlin, writing in the *Los Angeles Times*, said, "If in the end one feels a certain disappointment (and one did), it may well be the author, the idea, and the cast conjured up impossible dreams. As it is, *Murder by Death* is a literate, sophisticated, impeccably and colorfully acted, well-made diversion that is innocent of either sex or gore...."

In the *New York Post*, Frank Rich wrote: "...Simon's satire becomes...undirected bile that lands equally on the detectives and the movie audience. If you feel any affection for the fictional detectives who are the butts of Simon's practical joke, it's impossible to laugh — and you really can't enjoy the film on any level...."

Dilys Powell, in *The Sunday Times* (of London), singled out Guinness' acting as the best thing in the film: "...Much of the fun, both visual and audible, comes from Alec Guinness as a blind butler (nice to see him bothering to give a good performance)."

Film Information's Bea Rothenbeuchner observed that "the stars obviously relish their roles satirizing some of detective fiction's best-loved sleuths as they appeared both in print and on the screen. No matter that Simon's plot is full of loose ends and crime detection is incidental—it is the flair with which this unsubstantial material is presented that counts...."

In *The Times* (of London), Richard Combs' review concluded with: "...It must be admitted that the cast generally fit their parts like a glove...."

David Sterritt's *Christian Science Monitor* review argues that "...in the end, *Murder by Death* is a mildly amusing diversion, packing more chuckles than guffaws, but generally pleasant and elegant.... Not enough is made of the brilliant Mr. Guinness...."

Finally, in her *Saturday Review* piece, Judith Crist writes, "The beginning and the finale, involving an unlayering of suspects with a neatly unexpected last twist, are worth watching; the director has, mercifully, provided enough tedium between so that you can doze and awake refreshed for the amusing ending."

If the reviews were mixed, the film was a hit with moviegoers, taking in nearly $19 million in rentals that year (placing it eighth on the list for 1976). *Murder* is tied for 103rd place (with *Shampoo* and *The Spy Who Loved Me*) on *Variety*'s list of "Top 200 Moneymaking Films of All Time," with total North American rentals of $22 million. *Somebody* liked the movie.

An unseen figure in a creepy mansion addresses invitations to famous detectives. The blind butler, Bensonmum (Alec Guinness), told to put stamps on the envelopes, licks the stamps...and sticks them to the tabletop.

The detectives are on their way, including Dick and Dora Charleston (David Niven and Maggie Smith), Sidney Wang and his third adopted son (Peter Sellers and Richard Narita), Milo Perrier and his chauffeur Marcel (James Coco and James Cromwell), Sam Diamond and his secretary Tess Skeffington (Peter Falk and Eileen Brennan), and Miss Jessica Marbles and Nurse Withers (Elsa Lanchester and Estelle Winwood).

When the Wangs arrive, someone topples a gargoyle from the roof, just missing them. They ring the bell and discover that it sounds like a woman's scream. Once inside the house, things have been rigged so it looks and sounds as if there's a perpetual thunderstorm going on outside. Bensonmum takes the Wangs to their room. They hear the "cat" barking loudly. Bensonmum says he's built a fire to warm them up; unfortunately, he's built it in the center of the bed. A scream: "Ah, the doorbell," Bensonmum says.

Dick, Dora, and their dog, Myron, are already inside. When Myron growls, Bensonmum says, "Oh, don't mind him, ma'am, it's just the cat." The butler explains that his name is Jamessir Bensonmum, son of "How-ard" Bensonmum. When Dick starts to ask him about all this, Dora says, "Leave it be, Dickie—I've had enough." When Dora screams at a mouse in their room, Bensonmum again says, "Ah, the doorbell."

The new maid (Nancy Walker) arrives and shows Bensonmum a note saying her name is Yetta and that she cannot speak, hear, or read English.

As dinnertime approaches the others arrive, and they all introduce themselves. Bensonmum brings the soup tureen, ladling out nothing until it's brought to his attention. He says he'll speak to the cook and "fires" Yetta — who cannot hear him.

The lights go out and their host, Lionel Twain (Truman Capote), appears. He tells them they'll be locked in for the weekend and one of them must solve a murder mystery, for a reward of a million dollars. The murder will take place at midnight; if they cannot solve it, Twain himself will be the world's number one criminologist.

Yetta enters and screams — soundlessly, of course. She has a note which says the butler's been murdered. Wang, Jessica, and Perrier investigate, finding Bensonmum poisoned. When they return to the dining room, it's empty. Perrier returns to the scene of the crime, only to find Bensonmum's clothes but no body. They reenter the dining room and everyone is back. Eventually, they deduce there are two of everything, including dining rooms.

They join hands as midnight approaches. Yetta is gone. Twain is at the door — dead. He falls into the room with the missing butcher knife in his back. Then Sam discovers Yetta's *parts* in a trunk: She's a robot!

Did Twain murder himself? They find they *all* had a motive to kill him: Twain lent Dick money; Jessica Marbles was jilted by him; Tess is Twain's niece; Wang is Twain's illegitimate adopted son; Twain met Sam in a gay bar and has polaroids of Sam in drag; and Twain killed Perrier's one true love — his poodle.

After all are in bed, Wang and son discover a deadly snake in their room. Dick and Dora are threatened by a poisonous scorpion. Miss Marbles and her nurse are being gassed. Sam and Tess find a bomb in their room. Perrier and Marcel discover that their ceiling is descending on them.

Wang, with the dead snake with him, confronts the villain — Bensonmum, who can see and who planted a plastic body in the kitchen. But then Miss Marbles enters (Nurse Withers inhaled all the poison gas) and calls Bensonmum Irving Goldman, Twain's attorney, who killed him (Twain) five years ago. Dick shows up to say Goldman is really Marvin Metzner, an accountant who killed Goldman six months ago. (Am I going too fast?) Perrier says that's wrong: Metzner is really Miss Aileen Twain, Lionel Twain's daughter. Then Sam says *he's* really J.J. Loomis, an actor who does impersonations, and that Aileen is really Sam Diamond.

Suddenly Bensonmum removes his mask; he's really...Lionel Twain. Tired of all the misleading or vague clues in the detectives' books, he set out to turn the tables on them. A bit downcast, they all leave. After they've gone, Twain pulls off another mask, revealing that he is...Yetta??

Neil Simon, who wrote *Murder*'s script, is perhaps the most successful playwright in America today. Many of his seriocomic plays have been turned into successful films, beginning with *Come Blow Your Horn*, starring Frank

Guinness as Bensonmum, the blind butler.

Sinatra, in 1963. With the film versions of *Barefoot in the Park* (1967) and *The Odd Couple* (1968), Simon reached a level of acceptance rare in filmmaking. Virtually any script he wrote was eagerly sought by producers. Simon had the magic touch.

   In recent years, with *I Ought to Be in Pictures* (1982) and *Max Dugan Returns* (1983), it has seemed as if Simon's magic touch, if not gone, was badly slipping. Simon is now repeating himself: The plots of both those films dealt with long parent-child separations followed by grudging reunions and acceptance. As is the case with many comedy writers, Simon's stretch toward more serious themes is taking him away from what he does best: writing funny plays and films.

The script for *Murder*, the one Guinness found so amusing, *is* amusing; it is also vulgar and ethnically insulting (many "slant-eyed Chinaman" jokes are aimed Wang's way).

Simon throws everything into the stewpot of his script, including puns. Some, like Lionel Twain's name, are moderately amusing; others, like Twain's address — 22 Twain (say it aloud) — are real groaners. A brilliant comic mind, Simon stoops to making sophomoric fart jokes (when Twain tries to poison Miss Marbles and her nurse with gas, the ancient nurse thinks her "gas" is responsible).

The film and script work surprisingly well, however, on a second or third viewing — one has no expectations to be dashed the second time around — and the jokes that *do* work lift the film out of its self-dug lower depths.

One problem with *Murder*, if it is a problem, is that one must be familiar with Sam Spade, Nick and Nora Charles, the Charlie Chan series, and with Agatha Christie's Miss Marple to fully get the jokes and references.

Appearing without a hairpiece, Guinness is at the center of the film's early scenes, showing the detectives to their rooms, giving instructions to the illiterate deaf-mute cook, and functioning as the calm eye of the hurricane of events whirling around him. Patently silly, his "who's on first" verbal juggling act with Dick and Dora Charleston is delivered in the expert Guinness manner.

When Tess faints and says, "Catch me!" Guinness' Bensonmum obligingly holds out his arms as she falls to the floor. Missing from the film's middle section (the nude body of Bensonmum is *clearly* a stand-in's), Guinness returns at the whirlwind conclusion to great effect. In quick succession, he is Irving Goldman, Marvin Metzner, and finally Miss Aileen Twain, daughter of Lionel Twain.

As Aileen, Guinness effeminately puts his hand to the side of his — er...her — face and says, "I prefer to be called Rita." When Perrier calls Aileen/Rita a dog, Guinness sniffs, "That's *your* opinion, big boy."

The others in the film, especially Peter Falk as Sam Diamond and Peter Sellers as Sidney Wang, are all uniformly excellent.

Falk, born in 1927, spent most of his early career on the stage. It was not until the success of two films, *Murder, Inc.* (1960) and *Pocketful of Miracles* (1961), that his film career began to soar. But television provided him with his best-known role: the rumpled, raincoat-garbed homicide detective, Lt. Columbo, in the long-running series *Columbo*.

David Niven (1909–1983) was a wonderfully debonair actor who was comfortable in either dramatic or comic roles. He wrote two well-received autobiographies which revealed, through concise writing, an intelligent and self-effacing man. (For more on the films of Falk and Niven, see notes on *Murder* in the Appendix.)

Nancy Walker has little to do, but her big scene where she silently screams for help is at once obvious and wonderful.

Estelle Winwood, who died in June 1984 at the age of 101, was 92 when she filmed *Murder*. She usually played eccentric types with fluttering hands. She made one other film with Guinness, 1956's *The Swan*.

Writer Truman Capote (*In Cold Blood*), who died in August 1984 at the age of 59, played the cameo part of Lionel Twain.

Murder's director Robert Moore died in May 1984 at the age of 56. An actor before turning to directing, his first directing assignment for the stage was 1968's *The Boys in the Band*, an alternately funny and sad view of the lives of male homosexuals in the sixties. Moore received five Tony nominations for best director.

Moore also directed many of Neil Simon's plays before making his theatrical film debut with *Murder*, including *Last of the Red Hot Lovers* (with James Coco), *The Gingerbread Lady*, and the Neil Simon-Burt Bacharach-Hal David musical, *Promises, Promises*.

Apparently pleased with Moore's work on *Murder*, Simon signed him to direct two more of his film scripts, *The Cheap Detective* (1978, and starring Peter Falk, James Coco, and Eileen Brennan, all from *Murder*), and *Chapter Two*, Simon's 1979 autobiographical comedy-drama starring a miscast James Caan and Simon's then-wife, Marsha Mason.

While Guinness was shooting *Murder*, a strange script came over the transom of his dressing room; he showed it to Robert Moore, *Murder*'s director. Seeing George Lucas' name on the script, Moore pointed to it and said, "Now, there's a real filmmaker. I come from the theater, but Lucas is a *film* man. I'm just putting something on film, but Lucas writes and thinks in the motion-picture idiom. There's a world of difference."

"Well, I thought that very humble, very generous of Robert," Sir Alec said. "Robert, like me, is a man of the theater, although he's made some excellent films. But I knew what he meant about Lucas, so I began to read the script."

What happened next was film history.

37. *Star Wars* (1977)

"It was a darn good story dashingly told, and beyond that
I can't explain it. Failure has a thousand explanations.
Success doesn't need one."
— Alec Guinness, on *Star Wars'* popularity

*"It is a period of civil war. Rebel spaceships, striking from a hidden base,
have won their first victory against the evil Galactic Empire.*

*"During the battle, rebel spies managed to steal secret plans to the Em-
pire's ultimate weapon, the Death Star, an armored space station, with
enough power to destroy an entire planet.*

*"Pursued by the Empire's sinister agents, Princess Leia races home aboard
her starship, custodian of the stolen plans that can save her people and restore
freedom to the Galaxy . . ."*

Star Wars was Sir Alec Guinness' biggest commercial and popular success
in his long and honorable career. It was the film that made it unnecessary for
him to ever work again if he so wished. The role of Ben (Obi-Wan) Kenobi,
a wise and understanding mentor, fit Guinness' personality and screen persona like the proverbial glove. It was that rarest of motion picture occurrences,
the happy merger of performer and role. Neither *Star Wars* (which, because
prequels and sequels were envisioned from the first, is actually titled *Episode
IV: A New Hope*, while *Star Wars* is the series title) nor its two sequels (*The
Empire Strikes Back* and *Return of the Jedi*) would have been quite so successful without Guinness as Luke Skywalker's teacher and moral guardian.

The chapters discussing *Star Wars* and its sequels are long ones, reflecting
the importance they hold in helping to revitalize Guinness' career and
pocketbook.

The argument has been made that, whatever one thinks of Guinness'
performance in the three films, his onscreen participation in the first is limited
and almost nonexistent in the two sequels. I propose a (somewhat) bolder
theory: namely, that Guinness' role as Ben Kenobi is central to the whole *Star
Wars* saga and that Kenobi's importance to the tale ranks second only to Luke
Skywalker himself. For instance:

— The predicament the galaxy faces is largely a result of Ben Kenobi's
hubris and supreme self-confidence. Thinking he could train his pupil Anakin
Skywalker in the ways of the Force just as well as Jedi master Yoda, Ben

Kenobi loses Skywalker to the Dark Side. In this folly, he precipitates the "death" of Anakin Skywalker and the rise of a powerful new evil in the galaxy, Darth Vader.

— Vader joins forces with the evil emperor to hunt down the Jedi and crush the last vestiges of the old republic. Kenobi has unleashed a Frankenstein Monster upon the galaxy and upon his own Jedi knights.

— Having lost Skywalker to the Dark Side and seen the destruction of the Jedi knights, Ben, in shame and repentance, lives a hermitic life in the desert wastes of Tatooine.

— Once Luke Skywalker, Anakin's son, comes to him, Ben sees his chance to undo the evil he's released and introduces Luke to the Force, setting in motion the events which will see his physical death (the better to counsel Luke at all times and to repent for his misdeeds), the proper training of Luke by Yoda, Luke's repudiation of the Dark Side, and Luke's moral restoration of Anakin Skywalker.

— Ben explains and embodies the Force.

— Ben completely deceives Luke about the fate of his father until Luke is a fully trained Jedi knight. In *Empire*, Ben appears to Luke and tells him to travel to the Degobah system, to be instructed by Yoda.

— Finally, in *Jedi*, Ben confesses his "white lie" about Vader killing Luke's father, explaining, "Your father was seduced by the Dark Side of the Force. He ceased to be Anakin Skywalker and became Darth Vader. When that happened, the good man who was your father was destroyed. So, what I told you was true — from a certain point of view." Ben also reveals the saga's last major plot thread — that Leia is Luke's sister and shares his abilities concerning the Force.

So there it is: the central importance of Guinness' role to George Lucas' marvelous trilogy.

A battle occurs in space above the desert planet of Tatooine. An Imperial destroyer engages and captures Princess Leia Organa's blockade runner, but not before she sends a message hidden in her droid, R2–D2, who's accompanied by another robot, C–3PO. Leia (Carrie Fisher) is questioned by a figure in black flowing robes and a black mask — Darth Vader (David Prowse), agent for the dreaded Empire.

On Tatooine, the two droids are captured by Jawas and sold to Owen Lars, Luke Skywalker's uncle, a hard-working farmer. Luke wants to enter the Space Academy and be a pilot like his father before him, rather than stay and be a farmer.

When R2 (or "Artoo," as it's often written) escapes, Luke and C–3PO ("Threepio") follow and are attacked by the Sandpeople. Rescued by Ben Kenobi, Luke learns that he is the "Obi-Wan" Kenobi the little droid is looking for. Artoo delivers Princess Leia's plea for help and Ben asks Luke to join the quest. A frustrated Luke must say no — his uncle's farm comes first.

"That's no moon, it's a space station," Guinness' Ben Kenobi tells Chewbacca (Peter Mayhew, *left*), Luke (Mark Hamill), and Han Solo (Harrison Ford, *right*).

But when Imperial troops, searching for the two escaped droids, kill Uncle Lars and Aunt Beru (Phil Brown and Shelagh Fraser), Luke asks to go with Ben to learn the ways of the Force.

In a cantina in Mos Eisley spaceport, the adventurers hire the spaceship and services of Captain Han Solo (Harrison Ford), a mercenary space jockey and smuggler, and his copilot, a giant Wookiee called Chewbacca (Peter Mayhew). The small band blasts its way off the planet and into hyperspace. When they come out of hyperspace, they discover that their destination, Alderaan, has been blasted to bits by the Empire's Death Star.

Pulled aboard the Death Star by a tractor beam, they hide in small compartments Han uses for his smuggling. They make their way into a control room and, after Ben goes to disable the tractor beam, discover that the princess is being held captive in the cell blocks. Through a series of misadventures, they free Leia and make their way back to Han's ship, the Millennium Falcon.

Ben has succeeded in disabling the tractor beam, but is facing his old pupil, Darth Vader, in a duel to the death with light sabres. Knowing Luke is watching, Ben allows Vader to win the encounter and disappears as Vader's sabre passes through his robes. His disembodied voice counsels Luke to flee.

Luke, Han, and the others make their way to the rebel base, eager to deliver their precious cargo: the plans to the Death Star, hidden in Artoo's memory banks. They have only hours to find a weakness; the Death Star is constantly following them by means of a tracking device hidden in the Falcon.

As a well-rewarded Han Solo prepares to leave, the rebels learn that the Death Star's only weakness is an open port, which leads inside to the reactor core. A torpedo could penetrate to the interior and set off a chain reaction. Wave after wave of single-pilot X-wing fighters take off on an almost hopeless mission: to penetrate the Death Star defenses and blow up the space station before it can destroy their base planet.

The attack goes poorly and, after Vader himself joins the T.I.E. fighters engaging the rebels in ship-to-ship dogfights, it looks like Luke and his friends will all be destroyed before they can even attempt a shot at the vulnerable exhaust port.

It's all up to Luke. At a critical moment, he listens to Ben's voice and turns off his targeting computer in favor of using the Force. But Vader has him in his sights. Suddenly, from nowhere, Han appears behind Vader and his men to blast them before they can get Luke. Trusting his instincts, Luke hits his target and destroys the Death Star. A frustrated Darth Vader spins off into space, defeated but ready to strike back when he gets the chance.

Most reviewers loved the film, sensing its roots deep in our mythology and our popular culture. *Time* called *Star Wars* "a grand and glorious film that may well be the smash hit of 1977, and certainly is the best movie of the year so far. *Star Wars* is a combination of *Flash Gordon, The Wizard of Oz*, the Errol Flynn swashbucklers of the '30s and '40s and almost every western ever screened — not to mention the *Hardy Boys, Sir Gawain and the Green Knight* and *The Faerie Queene*. The result is a remarkable confection: a subliminal history of the movies, wrapped in a riveting tale of suspense and adventure, ornamented with some of the most ingenious special effects ever contrived for film."

Vincent Canby, in the *New York Times*, wrote, "*Star Wars*, which opened yesterday . . . is the most beautiful movie serial ever made. It's both an apotheosis of 'Flash Gordon' serials and a witty critique that makes associations with a variety of literature. . . . The way definitely not to approach *Star Wars*, though, is to expect a film of cosmic implications or to footnote it with so many references that one anticipates it as if it were a literary duty. It's fun and funny."

Critic Ruth L. Hirayama noted that "*Star Wars* is very much like the youngsters for whom it was created: precocious yet naive, charming and full of fun."

"Murf," in *Variety*, called *Star Wars* "a magnificent film. George Lucas set out to make the biggest possible adventure-fantasy out of his memories of serials and older action epics, and he has succeeded brilliantly. Both Guinness and [Peter] Cushing [who played the Grand Moff Tarkin] bring the right amount of majesty to their opposite characters. This is the kind of film in which an audience, first entertained, can later walk out feeling good all over."

In *Films and Filming*, Gordon Gow wrote, "Ben Kenobi is portrayed by Alec Guinness who casually steals the entire show and puts it in his pocket. Articulating smoothly and serenely, he gives the deliberately corny words a dreamy grandeur, and one roots for him eagerly when he crosses laser beams with the black-visored Darth Vader, Dark Lord of the Sith."

Finally, Jack Kroll's *Newsweek* review began, "I loved *Star Wars* and so will you, unless you're...oh well, I hope you're not. Thirty-two-year-old George Lucas, who directed *American Graffiti* has made the rarest kind of movie — it's pure sweet fun all the way. I don't know how Lucas could make so buoyant and exuberant a film, without a smudge of corrupt consciousness, in these smudged times. He says it's a movie for children — what he means is that he wants to touch the child in all of us. Only the hardest of hearts won't let George do it."

George Walton Lucas, Jr., was born Sunday morning, May 14, 1944, in Modesto, California, the son of George Lucas, Sr., the owner of a small stationery business.

A slight child, Lucas escaped often into his own vivid imagination. The world of fantasy claimed him permanently when the Lucas family bought a TV set in 1954. George couldn't get enough of the old serials and adventure films the nearby San Francisco stations showed. Lucas also loved comic books, especially those starring Scrooge McDuck (the billionaire duck providing an early grounding in capitalism for the future movie mogul).

After getting his first car at the age of fifteen, George Lucas eagerly embraced the car culture of California. He became an excellent driver, even dreaming of becoming a race driver.

Then, on Tuesday, June 12, 1962, George's small Fiat was hit broadside by a Chevy Impala, and Lucas was thrown from the car after his seat belt snapped. When George Lucas awoke in the hospital in serious condition, he came face-to-face with his mortality. Then and there, he vowed to do something with his aimless life. Lucas began to *"trust [his] instincts."* He decided to go to film school. Not just any film school, but that of the University of Southern California.

Lucas became a leader at USC and soon got the reputation as someone to look out for — a young man with a future.

At USC, Lucas learned pacing and how to cut his films. His films were all technically superior but often emotionally or dramatically inferior (a charge still leveled at his movies today).

Using a cast and crew supplied by the United States Navy, Lucas wrote and directed *THX 1138:4EB (Electronic Labyrinth)* in 1967 and won first prize at the Third National Student Film Festival. Another of his films, *6–18–67* (Lucas had a thing for numbers), was a documentary of the making of *McKenna's Gold*.

THX 1138 was remade, with a larger budget, and released by Warner

Bros. in 1971. The film did poorly, and little was expected of Lucas' next major motion picture, titled *A Quiet Night in Modesto*. Fortunately, the title was changed to *American Graffiti*, and the film went on to achieve rentals of $55,886,000, returning fifty dollars in profit for every dollar Universal invested and placing it twenty-sixth on the list of all-time box office champs.

When *Apocalypse Now*, the film Lucas had wanted to make for years, got bogged down in negotiations with Lucas' friend and former mentor, Francis Ford Coppola, Lucas turned to another project he had in mind—a space fantasy set in a galaxy far, far away.

After Lucas completed editing *American Graffiti* in early 1972, he began working on *Star Wars*, writing in the morning and using his afternoons to research fairy tales, mythology, and social psychology. By May 1973 he had a thirteen-page plot summary about a world set in the twenty-third century. Among his characters were a General Luke Skywalker and his friend Annikin Starkiller, two Jedi knights who'd survived the evil emperor's destruction of their fellow warrior-guardians. They are joined in their adventures with Princess Leia Aguiae by a band of teenage boys, who eventually learn to fly spaceships and defeat the Imperial fleet.

Just ten days after Universal, which had the first option on Lucas' script, gave him a resounding "no," Alan Ladd, Jr., of Twentieth Century–Fox, signed Lucas, giving him $50,000 to write the script and $100,000 to direct it. *Star Wars* had found its home. Fox and Lucas finalized their deal in December 1975, setting the budget at $8.5 million.

As he began writing the script, Lucas pulled out ideas from everywhere. When his sound editor on *Graffiti*, Walter Murch, asked for "R2, D2" (Reel 2, Dialogue 2), Lucas put the abbreviation in his notebook. One day Lucas was riding in a car with friend Terry McGovern, who said, "I think I just ran over a Wookiee back there." Lucas asked, "What's a Wookiee?" "I don't know," replied McGovern, "I just made it up." "That's great," said Lucas, "I love that word. I'm going to use that."

Lucas threw everything from his readings and his childhood into his *Star Wars* drafts. He got banthas from Burroughs' *John Carter on Mars*, the evil emperor from Emperor Ming of the Flash Gordon books, and Han Solo's character from various "B" western heroes. There are two references to the classic Japanese film *Yojimbo* in Lucas' film. In the cantina, two rough aliens give Luke a hard time, one saying, "You just watch yourself—we're wanted men! I have the death sentence on twelve systems." Toshiro Mifune, the Samurai warrior in *Yojimbo*, faces just such a thug who says virtually the same line of dialogue. The outcome is the same, too: in *Yojimbo* as in *Star Wars*, the man has his arm cut by Mifune's/Guinness' sword/light sabre.

When Luke returns home to find his aunt and uncle's farm burning, it is clearly a fond salute to a film many young directors respect, John Ford's *The Searchers*. *Star Wars* is a "search" film as well: a young man, with a seasoned older man showing him the way, searches for a young girl to rescue her.

Writing in longhand on blue-and-green-lined paper, Lucas made Luke Skywalker a green farmboy rather than a Jedi general, and split off Obi-Wan Kenobi and Darth Vader from one original character, letting them become opposite sides of good and evil.

Lucas' first screenplay, dated May 1974, has many of the ingredients of the final version, including a tall, evil-looking general named Darth Vader. But the hero is called Anakin Starkiller and has an older brother named Biggs, and Lucas' evil emperor was modeled on Richard Nixon.

The second screenplay, titled *Adventures of the Starkiller: Episode One of the Star Wars*, was dated January 28, 1975. Lucas began by slicing away extraneous elements carefully but soon realized a more wholesale reduction was necessary. So he chopped the script in half by focusing on the middle story, the one that began with Luke's adventures. A third script went to Ladd and Fox on August 1, 1975. A fourth script, dated early 1976, is essentially the version we know today. It still included Luke's older brother Biggs, but now as a friend and role model.

Lucas began his search for the actors to play his characters at the old Samuel Goldwyn Studios, seeing as many as 40 actors a day in huge "cattle calls." Mark Hamill was among the 50 or so actors called back to do a reading on videotape. Lucas pared these 50 down to four Luke/Leia/Han trios, mixing and matching the actors in an attempt to find just the right chemistry between them.

Harrison Ford, convinced Lucas would not hire him because he'd appeared in *Graffiti*, grew angry at being asked to read for a part he could not get, and his sullen performances helped him win the role of Han Solo.

One of the final two groups had Christopher Walken as Han, Will Selzer as Luke, and, as Leia, Terri Nunn, a former *Penthouse* pet. (You can probably guess the actors in the other group.) Since Nunn came across as too hard on screen, Lucas decided to hire Carrie Fisher. And, since he'd always preferred Mark Hamill, it remained just to sign a surprised Harrison Ford as Han Solo.

Although George Lucas had briefly considered Japanese star Toshiro Mifune for the role of Ben Kenobi, he really had someone like Alec Guinness in mind for the role.

To Lucas' surprise, Guinness was in Los Angeles in 1975, filming *Murder by Death*. To *his* surprise, Guinness got an unsolicited script "over the transom" one day. It had a drawing of a young man brandishing a sword on its cover. Recognizing Lucas' name, Guinness began reading, even though he thought to himself, "Good God, it's science fiction. Why are they offering me this?"

". . . I began to read the script," Guinness recalled. Although he thought the dialogue "pretty ropey," Guinness found himself caught up in the script's suspense, turning pages to find out what happened next. A meeting with Lucas was arranged.

"We met over lunch," Guinness said, "and I was surprised to find that he was so young. I liked his quiet diffidence. I trusted him. It was the reason why I agreed to play the role. I felt I could safely work with him."

Guinness was cast, but he was not entirely comfortable with the original character of Ben Kenobi. He was especially unsettled by the script's description of Ben as "an old desert rat." Guinness did not wish to play "some wild, eccentric, half-dotty old man appearing out of a hole in the sand dunes." When Lucas explained that the character was meant to resemble Gandalf in the Tolkien trilogy, Guinness responded, "Yes, I can do something like that—a quiet character, not too mystical or strange, but sympathetic."

Signing Sir Alec Guinness, an Academy Award–winning best actor, gave the whole project a new air of respectability. Alan Ladd, Jr., was able to use Guinness' signing to convince Fox's board of directors that *Star Wars* would be a class act. "Guinness didn't sell tickets on his own," Ladd later recalled, "but it was nice that he was in the picture."

For R2–D2, Lucas hired forty-two-year-old, 3'8" Kenny Baker. Anthony Daniels, a thirty-one-year-old former law student who acted with the Young Vic, was chosen to play C–3PO. David Prowse, a 6'7" bodybuilder and weightlifter, was hired to play Darth Vader.

Producer Gary Kurtz scoured European studios, looking for the huge stages the production would need for the duration of the shooting schedule. Thirty minutes from London, he found the decaying Elstree studios, shut down since the mid 1960s. Alfred Hitchcock had made many of his British films there, and MGM's *2001: A Space Odyssey* had been photographed at Elstree.

Lucas recalled the trying shooting conditions in his interview in *Rolling Stone*: "The whole picture was very difficult because it was made on a very short schedule—about 70 days on the sets and locations. In England we couldn't shoot past 5:30 so we worked eight-hour days. It was very short for something that was that complex."

Mark Hamill met Guinness for the first time in Tunisia and was awed at the prospect of meeting a legend. "He was helpful and considerate from the beginning," Hamill remembers. "On that first day he and Lady Guinness sketched the scenery. We moved on to a mosque. She kept sketching, not realizing that it is forbidden to draw or photograph a holy place in Tunisia. Suddenly, an Arab rushed over, grabbed the sketch and tore it up in anger. Sir Alec turned to see and asked what Lady Guinness had done. I replied that the man was probably just the local art critic—at which Sir Alec burst out laughing. We got along famously."

Still wrestling with his script, Lucas could not satisfactorily resolve the fate of Ben Kenobi. For the second half of the film, Ben stood around with little to do, yet he was too important a character to allow to stand around "with his thumb in his ear," as Lucas put it.

Lucas saw that the problem began with Ben and Vader's light sabre fight in the Death Star. "As I originally wrote it . . . Ben hits a door and the door slams closed and they all run away and Vader is left standing there with egg on his face. This was dumb; they run into the Death Star and they sort of take over everything and they run back. It totally diminishes any impact the Death Star had."

When Lucas' wife Marcia suggested that Lucas kill off Ben, Lucas said, "Well, that is an interesting idea, and I [have] been thinking of it."

Predictably, since Lucas had convinced Guinness that he was an integral part of the story, Guinness took the news of his exit from the film halfway through with astonishment and anger. Calling his agent, Guinness raged about walking off the picture. "I'm not going to do this movie," he snapped at Lucas.

Lucas and Kurtz then began wooing Sir Alec back. Soothing his ego, Lucas sat down with Guinness and the two of them enlarged Kenobi's character. As Lucas recalls, "Both Alec Guinness and I came up with the thing about having Ben go forward as part of the Force. There was a thematic idea that was even stronger about the Force in one of the earliest scripts. It was really all about the Force, a Castaneda *Tales of Power* thing."

Not only did Guinness forgive Lucas, he also sent him a gift of Victorian tumblers and a note of appreciation at the end of the filming, saying, "This is just a small token of esteem to say how much I have liked working with you."

Harrison Ford and the other actors killed time by clowning around and amusing themselves. As Ford remembers it, "The only damper on the pure fun of that set was the almost-unanimous attitude of the English crew that we were totally out of our minds, especially George."

Guinness, accepting Kenobi's martyrdom, worked his usual magic on Ben's character, filling it out and giving the old Jedi knight dignity and presence. While the British crew mocked Lucas and the whole cockeyed project, Guinness remained steadfast and true in his support. "At times during *Star Wars* I was perhaps a bit puzzled, but I never lost faith in the project. There were people around who doubted the sanity of the venture and who were critical of George and Gary [Kurtz]. 'Lucas doesn't know what he's doing,' they'd say, or 'Call this filmmaking?' But I had confidence in them."

When Alan Ladd, Jr., visited the set and saw a poorly cut rough assembly of footage—lacking special effects, music, sound effects, and dialogue redubbing (David Prowse originally spoke Vader's lines, his voice muffled by his helmet)—he nearly closed down the film. Lucas convinced him that the forty-minute version he saw was not typical of how the finished film would look, and Ladd kept mum about what he'd seen when he went before Fox's board to give them a progress report.

With Lucas over schedule and over budget, Fox finally said that enough was enough; principal photography was wrapped.

In cutting the film, Lucas eliminated Luke's friend Biggs and a confrontation between Jabba the Hutt and Han Solo. The cantina scene was reshot but never lived up to Lucas' expectations—mainly because of lack of time and money. Lucas got an additional $20,000 for the cantina "monster rally" scene only after Ladd went before Fox's board and called *Star Wars* "possibly the greatest picture ever made. That's my absolute statement."

When George Lucas invited his Hollywood friends to see a rough version of the film, "they all thought it a disaster," he remembers. Fortunately, for Lucas and the rest of us, those most critical of the film had seen it minus John Williams' heroic score. Carroll Ballard, who'd shot the landspeeder footage for the film, saw *Star Wars* before and after the music had been added. "It was a mind-boggling difference," he recalled. "It gave the hokey characters a certain dimension."

Jaws director Steven Spielberg had introduced Lucas to Julliard-educated John Williams in 1975, telling him all about the upcoming science fiction film his friend was planning. Several talks led to Lucas giving Williams a copy of the script to read. Williams agreed to compose the music for the film, and in early 1977 he traveled to Marin County to see Lucas' second cut of the movie. During the next two months, he wrote the score for *Star Wars*.

Williams wrote four themes for the major characters, including the "Princess Theme," "Luke's Theme," "Ben Kenobi's Theme," and "Darth Vader's Theme." Williams also wrote a theme for the Jawas, and composed a short motif for the Death Star, saying, "I think the use of all these themes and the orchestrations give the score a kind of classic operatic quality."

Williams' score helped "sell" *Star Wars* and George Lucas knew it. As Lucas said, "I was very, very pleased with the score. We wanted a very sort of Max Steiner-type, old-fashioned, romantic movie score."

On May 1, 1977, Lucas scheduled a Sunday morning sneak preview of *Star Wars* at the Northpoint Theatre in San Francisco. The theater was filled with Lucas' friends and with an audience abuzz with anticipation; rumors of the film's quality had circulated among hardcore SF fans. When the opening crawl ended and the star destroyer passed overhead on the screen — the Dolby soundtrack rocking the theater — the audience went berserk.

When *Star Wars* opened in 92 theaters on May 25, 1977, there were already lines; the word from the preview had gotten out. *Star Wars* grossed more than $525 million, returning rentals of $193,500,000 to Fox and Lucasfilm. *Star Wars* is second on the all-time film rental champs list in *Variety* (as of January 1984), behind only *E.T. the Extra-Terrestrial*.

For his labors, Guinness received two and one-quarter percent of the net profits, totalling nearly $3,000,000. Guinness admitted his share of *Star Wars'* profits left him "pretty flush."

In *Skywalking*, Dale Pollock quotes Lucas as saying, "Everybody says, 'Oh, the acting in George's films is terrible,' but I don't believe that. I think it's very good, and one of the reasons for my films' success."

Lucas prefers ensemble acting, taking care in the casting to get just the right mix, just the right chemistry. Once his actors are cast, Lucas rarely gives them much specific direction, preferring that they find the core of their characters themselves. Carrie Fisher recalls, "In terms of directing, he'd say, 'Now act more like a princess. Stand up straight'—things like that. Very black and white direction. Faster, more intense. We made fun of 'faster and more intense.' It was very specific. Faster you can do; more intense you can do. That was fine with me. I was glad I wasn't getting directions like, 'There's an amused hysteria about her in this scene, a kind of aggravated lonely.' "

"George directs like John Ford," observes Lucas' friend Francis Ford Coppola. "He doesn't really work a lot with his actors or tell them a lot. But he constructs his scenes so specifically, or narrowly—like a railroad track—that everything comes out more or less the way he sees it."

Guinness, too, was impressed by George Lucas. "Like all the best directors Lucas had very little to say during the actual filming. He simply sensed when you were uncomfortable and just walked across and dropped a brief word in your ear.... He reminded me of a young David Lean. I always had the feeling that, like Lean, deep down he was totally involved in the action."

The actors had rough sledding with George Lucas' deliberately pulpy dialogue. " 'I thought I recognized your foul stench when I was brought on board, Governor Tarkin,' is not every day conversation," laughs Carrie Fisher. "There were times when I issued a threat to tie up George and make him repeat his own dialogue," recalls Harrison Ford. "I told him: 'You can type this shit, George, but you sure can't say it.' But I was wrong; it worked."

Ben Kenobi and Darth Vader get to exchange some of that dialogue in their big confrontation scene: "When I left you I was but the learner. Now *I* am the master," says Vader. "Only a master of evil, Darth," ripostes Ben.

Warning Luke about the spaceport of Mos Eisley, Guinness intones, "You will never find a more wretched hive of scum and villainy."

Guinness, the patient craftsman, the skilled interpreter of the screenplay's intentions, does well with his many pivotal scenes. When Luke tells Ben he's looking for Obi-Wan Kenobi, Guinness sits down in shock and says, "Obi-Wan.... Now that's a name I've not heard in a long time. A long time." When Luke suggests he might be dead, Guinness smiles. "Oh, he's not dead; not yet." "Do you know him?" "Of course I know him—he's me," Guinness confides. "I haven't gone by the name of Obi-Wan since...oh, before you were born."

Crucial to the whole middle episodes of the saga is Guinness' scene with Luke when they discuss Luke's father. Guinness tells Luke that Anakin Skywalker "was the best star pilot in the galaxy—a cunning warrior. And, he was a good friend." When Luke asks, "How did my father die?" Guinness' Obi-Wan looks down for a moment, considers, then looks up and says, "A young Jedi named Darth Vader, who was a pupil of mine until he turned to evil, helped the Empire hunt down and destroy the Jedi knights. He betrayed and murdered your father."

Lucas also allows Guinness, as Obi-Wan, to tell Luke and the audience what the Force is: "The Force is what gives a Jedi his power—it's an energy field created by all living things. It surrounds us and penetrates us; it binds the galaxy together." (Asked about the Force, Guinness said, "I'm an alleged Christian, so to that extent, yes, I do believe that something like the Force exists. But not as expressed in *Star Wars.*")

Guinness' subtle facial expressions underline his words and enhance his character's believability. After seeing Artoo's message from Princess Leia, Guinness muses and pulls at his beard. Giving Luke a sly look, he says, "You must learn the ways of the Force—if you're to come with me to Alderaan." When Luke protests that he can't go with Ben, a disappointed Guinness says, "That's your uncle talking." When Luke continues to say no, Guinness has Ben shrug dismissively and look away, saying, "You must do what you think is right, of course."

As Lucas told Dale Pollock, "Good actors really bring you something, and that is especially true with Alec Guinness, who I thought was a good actor like everyone else, but after working with him I was staggered that he was such a creative and disciplined person."

There's one scene, however, that Guinness would like to do over. When Alderaan blows up, Ben reels backward and says, "I felt a great disturbance in the Force, as if millions of voices suddenly cried out in terror and were suddenly silenced. I fear something terrible has happened." And then Guinness puts his hand to his forehead—a cliché, in his opinion. "I still go hot and cold when I think of that scene, " he confesses.

Guinness won an Academy Award nomination for best supporting actor for his work in *Star Wars*, losing out to Jason Robards' performance in *Julia*.

Combining tried-and-true elements from our common mythology, from our idea of who a hero is, and from the slam-bang action of the pulps and serials of our popular culture, *Star Wars* is an entertaining triumph. It speaks to deep needs in all of us and satisfies ancient longings Hollywood movies had all but forgotten about in the slick, cynical 1970s.

Guinness' two *Star Wars* sequels would be additional triumphs—*The Empire Strikes Back* and *Return of the Jedi*. Unfortunately, the other two theatrical films Guinness made during this period were critical and box-office failures. On television, however he triumphed as masterspy George Smiley in *Tinker Tailor Soldier Spy*.

38. *Tinker Tailor Soldier Spy* (1979)

"When you think you have him,
eel-like he eludes your grasp."
—Kenneth Tynan on Guinness

Tinker Tailor Soldier Spy (hereafter just *Tinker*) and its sequel, *Smiley's People*, are in a way the pinnacle of Guinness' acting career. Ever the master of underplaying, Sir Alec found in George Smiley, John le Carré's methodical masterspy, the perfect role for his minimalist techniques; it was the perfect fit of actor and role.

In *Newsweek*, Alexis Gelber called Guinness' performance "infinitely calibrated, stupendously low key." It is that and more. In *Tinker*, Guinness withholds so much from us that he forces us to study his every gesture, his every tic, for clues to what he's thinking. And it works. Soon, an alert viewer can decipher Guinness' bland looks, his raising of an eyebrow, his furrowing of his brow.

As Guinness told one interviewer, "If you have someone like Smiley, who's meant to be tremendously intellectual and hugely bright, obviously he's going to be silent much of the time precisely when he's listening to people and working things out. Well, you can't flick your eyes around as if to say 'I'm being bright.' It's got to be played exactly the opposite, blank, or so it seems to me, or that's how it came out," he said, adding, "I've probably gone overboard.... People may say I haven't acted it anyway. I always feel I've made a mess of it. I probably have."

Control, head of the British Secret Service (known as the Circus) sets up a top-secret incursion into Czechoslovakia called "Operation Testify." Control (Alexander Knox) tells agent Jim Prideaux (Ian Bannon) that there's a Russian agent, a "mole," among the top five men in the Circus. The traitor's Russian code name is Gerald. Control assigns each of the suspects his own code names: Percy Alleline (Michael Aldridge) is Tinker, Bill Haydon (Ian Richardson) is Tailor, Roy Bland (Terence Rigby) is Soldier, Toby Esterhase (Bernard Hepton) is Poorman, and George Smiley (Guinness) is Beggarman.

Jim Prideaux's assignment proves a trap and he is shot and captured. Six months later, we follow George Smiley as he runs into old friend Roddy

Guinness as master spy George Smiley in the six-part television dramatization of *Tinker Tailor Soldier Spy.*

Martindale. Martindale's gossipy dinner with George fills us in on the background: The blown Czech operation cost Control his job, and Percy Alleline is now head of the Circus. As Control's man, George is out, too.

At home, George finds Peter Guillam (Michael Jayston), a protégé from the Circus, waiting for him. Peter tells George that Jim Prideaux is back in England, but quarantined. Peter is to take George to see Lacon, the cabinet's head watchdog over intelligence operations.

Lacon (Anthony Bate) shows in Ricki Tarr (Hywel Bennett), a field agent gone underground. He has a story to tell: Hoping to get a Russian named Boris (Hilary Minster) to defect, Ricki finds he's a Moscow Centre–trained hood. He meets Boris' wife Irina (Susan Kodicek), who becomes his lover and tells him she knows a *big* secret, which can be told only to Alleline.

Ricki sends a flash message to London Centre, and they stall him. He finds a notebook Irina left him—just in case. There *is* a mole in the Circus, code-named Gerald, she writes, and Ricki must have been indiscreet. He tells Smiley that an unscheduled Soviet plane took off with a woman wrapped all in bandages.

George and Lacon talk. George suspected a mole six months ago, but Lacon says only that Control and George had to go. He speaks briefly of Ann Smiley and Bill Haydon's long-ago, public-knowledge affair. George takes the assignment to find the mole and is loaned Control's one-time man Mendel (George Sewell) to assist him in setting up shop. George sends Peter into the Circus to look at the logs of Ricki Tarr's information, but the duty logs for that date have been razored out.

From Connie Sachs (Beryl Reid) George learns that top Russian spymaster Karla's man in London is Polyakov (George Pravda). George suspects Polyakov is connected to Operation Witchcraft—a top-secret source of information supposedly from Moscow Centre ("Source Merlin").

George sends Peter back into the Circus, this time to steal "Testify," the file on the failed Jim Prideaux operation. While there, Peter is called into Percy Alleline's office to be grilled about seeing Ricki Tarr, presumed to have defected.

When Peter and George talk, George tells him Source Merlin works with Moscow Centre, since that's where Karla's information on Ricki Tarr must have come from—from Karla himself.

George knows that the person closest to Witchcraft could be the mole. George tells Peter of a long-ago meeting with Karla (Patrick Stewart). Karla listened to George but never said a word. A chain-smoker, he took George's cigarette lighter with him. George tells Peter that Karla is a fanatic, and that'll be his downfall.

Lacon tells George that Moscow executed a woman in March, confirming Ricki Tarr's story. Meanwhile, Prideaux is teaching at a boy's school.

George speaks to Sam (John Standing), an ex-Circus employee. Sam worked the switchboards the night of the Czech disaster and received a message from Reuters: "Western spy" shot in Czechoslovakia. Control said to deny everything. Sam says Bill Haydon arrived, took charge of everything and ran things. Bill was at Smiley's house that night—with Ann. But Bill, George muses, knew more than Sam told Ann. How?

George visits Jim Prideaux and discusses his undergraduate days with Bill Haydon, and Jim's capture. Jim says the Russians knew everything. After learning that everyone in the spy networks was shot, Jim goes to throw up while Smiley sits and smokes. Karla showed up, chain-smoking and with George's lighter. Karla spoke of Haydon and Ann Smiley.

George runs into agent/newspaper reporter Jerry Westerby (Joss Ackland). Jerry met a drunken young Czech soldier who told him they knew a spy was coming; they were all ready and waiting.

Prideaux disappears abruptly from his school post, citing family problems. George has Toby Esterhase brought in and squeezed. All the while, George senses someone following them, watching but well hidden.

In his longest speech, George tells Toby his breakdown of the Gerald-Merlin-Witchcraft-Polyakov story. The top men all meet with Polyakov. One of them is the mole, and George says it might be Toby. Toby starts to talk and explains how they meet with Polyakov.

When George and Peter leave, George tells Peter to watch his back and to look for one man alone. A figure trails Peter and George.

George later says they must alarm "Gerald" the mole sufficiently so he'll make contact with Polyakov immediately. George has Ricki Tarr go to Paris and send this message: "Have information vital to the safeguarding of the Circus. Request immediate meeting. Personal."

George and Peter bug the house where the mole will meet with Polyakov. Polyakov and the mole enter and begin talking. As the others close in, George enters the room with his pistol out and sees...Bill Haydon.

Sending for Alleline, Bland, Esterhase, and Lacon, George plays them the tape of Haydon and his Russian contact talking. Bill is taken away as a figure watches. We now see it's Jim Prideaux. George sincerely thanks Peter for all his help.

George and Bill talk and George asks him why, when, how, where? As Bill sobs, George looks on impassively, a hint of distaste on his face. Bill says western democracy has destroyed itself and that he turned eastward in the mid-1940s, giving Karla American secrets. For his efforts, Bill was granted full Soviet citizenship and awarded many medals.

After telling Lacon he's concerned about the lax security around Bill, George again questions Bill. Bill says Control was getting close to him before the Czech fiasco unseated him. George asks about Prideaux, looking sideways at Bill. "I got him home, didn't I?" snaps Bill. Bill reveals that his affair with Ann was Karla's idea; Karla always feared George and knew Ann was his weak spot. Bill sends money to a female lover, and a male one as well—underscoring his earlier relationship with Jim.

Sitting outside, Bill is approached by Jim, who asks, "Why?" Bill says the shooting wasn't a part of the plan. "But everything else was," says Jim, striking Bill's neck with a chopping blow of his hand. Bill falls to the ground, twitches, and dies. Soon, Jim is back at his school, indescribable pain and sorrow in his eyes.

Lacon wants to know who killed Bill. He asks George. George slowly lights a cigarette. He *knows* who killed Bill but he's not talking. George will "look after" the Circus for a while while the others take leave. Afterwards, some of them will be expected to resign.

Ann. She kisses George on both cheeks, but not the mouth. As they walk, they discuss Bill's betrayal. George says when he heard Bill's voice, he wanted to shoot him. He asks if she loved Bill. "No, George." He takes off his glasses, cleans them, blinking like an owl blinded by the light. "Poor George—life's such a puzzle to you, isn't it?" Ann says. George just blinks.

"John le Carré" is the pen name of David John Moore Cornwell, born in England in 1931. As suave and sophisticated in person as Peter Guillam is in his "Smiley" novels, Cornwell got into the intelligence business at age nineteen, after being drafted into the British armed services. Sent to Austria in 1952, Cornwell met real spies, the sort of hard men he'd later write about.

After his discharge, Cornwell returned to England to study German at Oxford and earned a first-class honors degree in 1956. He briefly taught at Eton but soon found the pay and the life less than he'd hoped for. After taking a Foreign Service exam, which he passed, Cornwell became a diplomat—and, perhaps, a spy.

Some former intelligence operatives—or "spies," if you like—now say Cornwell worked for both Britain's Counterespionage Service, MI 5, and the Secret Intelligence Service, MI 6. All Cornwell will say amounts to bland statements like "I have nosed around in the secret world. But it was a long, long while ago."

While assigned in West Berlin in 1961 to keep an eye on the building of the Berlin wall, Cornwell was looking for a book idea. The wall gave him one. "I thought: make the wall the beginning and the end of the story." That story became the novel *The Spy Who Came in from the Cold*, a critical and commercial success of enormous proportions. Cornwell was able to resign his post and take up writing full time.

Tinker Tailor Soldier Spy appeared after a few Cornwell miscues. Returning to secret agents, Cornwell based his story loosely on the 1963 defection of a real-life mole, Kim Philby.

The BBC hired writer Arthur Hopcraft to turn Cornwell/le Carré's finely plotted and densely written novel into a seven-part series for television. Hopcraft found it a daunting task. "It's a fascinating, deeply intriguing book," he said, "but you have to keep turning back the pages and you can't do that on the screen." Perhaps not, but Hopcraft's adaptation closely follows

John le Carré's novel, sometimes compressing things but leaving nothing out.

Although Alec Guinness had long maintained that he would never do television, he could not resist the chance to play George Smiley. Author Cornwell, adapter Hopcraft, producer Powell, and director John Irvin met with Guinness over lunch at a fashionable London restaurant. They convinced Guinness that the production would be first-rate, and he accepted the part.

Shooting the seven-part television movie took six months. Before filming began, Guinness, at Cornwell's suggestion, met the former head of MI 6, Maurice Oldfield, allegedly the model for Smiley. Smiley, as portrayed by Guinness, really doesn't resemble Oldfield and wasn't meant to. Guinness met with his "original" to pick up a feeling for the type of man he was and how he fit into his peculiar world of espionage, not to mimic him.

Alexander Knox, born in Canada in 1907, played Control. He first appeared on the British stage in 1930 and made his first film, *The Gaunt Stranger*, in 1938. Many people remember him best for playing the title role in *Wilson* (1944).

Beryl Reid, who played Connie Sachs, was born in 1918. She began her career as a "revue" comedienne, but managed to make the leap to character parts. Largely forgotten today, *The Killing of Sister George* made a stir when first released in 1968 for a few minutes of lesbian activity between Susannah York and Coral Browne. Reid was soap opera star "Sister George" in both the play and the film. (For more on the films of Knox and Reid, see notes on *Tinker* in the Appendix.)

It is hard to imagine anyone else in the role of George Smiley, so completely has Guinness made it his own. Even the character's originator, David Cornwell/John le Carré, cannot think of Smiley without visualizing Alec Guinness.

There are so many flashes of brilliance in Guinness' performance that it's difficult to single out any one moment. Guinness imbues Smiley with a precious gift: silence. Many of the other characters ask questions of George Smiley and then pause, waiting for an answer. Rarely do they get one. Guinness/Smiley says nothing, and the others, unable to stand the silence that follows, fill the gap with more talk.

When George speaks to Bill Haydon one time, Haydon asks after Ann, his ex-mistress and Smiley's wife. George shoots him a brief, piercing look. Only when he speaks of his Russian counterpart, Karla, does Guinness' Smiley reveal any emotion or speak in exclamation points: "... That's where Karla's information on Ricki Tarr must have come from!"

After Smiley's talk with Jim Prideaux, one can sense Smiley's awareness of Jim's aching for justice. Smiley several times asks Peter to watch his back, to see if a single man is following him. He frequently complains about the security around the exposed mole, around Bill Haydon. Smiley senses Jim Prideaux out there somewhere, awaiting his chance.

When Lacon refuses to increase the security around Haydon, several things become clear. Haydon is going to be killed by a vengeful Jim Prideaux... and *Smiley knows what is going to happen!* When George and Ann have their talk at the end, he tells her of wanting to shoot Bill when he, Smiley, had his pistol out and heard the mole's voice. But Smiley/Guinness, ever cautious, ever careful, leaves the matter in Jim Prideaux's trained hands.

Tinker was only Guinness' first playing of George Smiley. He would return to the role in *Smiley's People* in 1982.

39. *The Empire Strikes Back* (1980)

> "He is his own man, he is not a son anymore; he is an equal."
> — George Lucas, on Luke Skywalker after his duel
> with Darth Vader in *Empire*

"It is a dark time for the rebellion. Although the Death Star has been destroyed, Imperial troops have driven the rebel forces from their hidden base and pursued them across the galaxy.

"Evading the dreaded Imperial Starfleet, a group of freedom fighters led by Luke Skywalker has established a new secret base on the remote ice world of Hoth.

"The evil lord Darth Vader, obsessed with finding young Skywalker, has dispatched thousands of remote probes into the far reaches of space . . ."

Star Wars was good to Sir Alec Guinness. He garnered another Academy Award nomination (for best supporting actor) and his two and one-quarter percent of the net profits made him oodles of money. There was little question that he would appear in the sequel, if only because it was the "honorable" thing to do. But, for a while, Guinness' participation in *The Empire Strikes Back* (hereafter just *Empire*) was in doubt because of eye problems. Fortunately, by the time shooting at Elstree commenced, Guinness was again able to put on Ben Kenobi's monklike robes and offer advice to young Luke Skywalker.

Variety's "Har" wrote, "*The Empire Strikes Back* is a worthy sequel to *Star Wars*, equal in both technical mastery and characterization, suffering only from the familiarity with the effects generated in the original and imitated too much by others. Only boxoffice question is how many earthly trucks it will take to carry the cash to the bank. Reaching its finish, *Empire* blatantly sets up the third in the *Star Wars* trilogy, presuming the marketplace will signify its interest. It's a pretty safe assumption."

David Sterritt, in the *Christian Science Monitor*, wrote, "Sequels have been part of the *Star Wars* plan from the beginning. If all goes well, new episodes will blast off for many years to come until the saga reaches its conclusion in the ninth feature-length installment. That means a lot of happy viewing for the countless fans who made the original *Star Wars* into the biggest box-office hit of all time."

In *Films in Review*, Tom Rogers presented this glowing review: "Most sequels fail to live up to our expectations but *The Empire Strikes Back* is a wonderful exception. It is an action-packed continuation of George Lucas' *Star Wars* saga and as such, it is one of the most satisfying science fiction films ever made. All in all, *Empire* is an excellent addition to the science fiction genre."

Charles Champlin's piece for the *Los Angeles Times* began, "What can you say about *The Empire Strikes Back* that has not already been said about the Acropolis, the cotton gin, Ella Fitzgerald's voice and *Star Wars*? I wish it were a handful of minutes shorter, but this is my single caveat about another richly imaginative, engrossing and spectacular motion picture from the redoubtable George Lucas."

Richard Combs, writing for the *Monthly Film Bulletin*, argued that "...the human elements are cutely second-hand (Han Solo and Princess Leia's romantic sparring out of a Thirties comedy) and soon overplayed at the expense of comic-strip drive.... The defense that this is all good clean fantasy, closer to sword and sorcery than science fiction, is also scuttled by the imaginative shortcomings of the Yoda episode, where Muppetry meets *The Lord of the Rings*."

In his review in *New Leader*, Robert Asahina said, "There is a lot more left unexplained in this follow-up to *Star Wars*—for instance, the total lack of a conclusion." And, "No amount of lightness...can lift this movie out of the swamps of Dagobah."

Finally, David Ansen, writing in *Newsweek*, called *Empire* "Slicker and sleeker than its predecessor" but "also darker. If only for that impressive battle on the ice of Hoth, or the thrilling race through the asteroid belt, or the surprise of the final plot twist, *The Empire Strikes Back* is worth the price of admission. Even the most earthbound eyes can't deny that what they're watching is a celestial class act."

On Hoth, Luke Skywalker is attacked and knocked unconscious by an ice monster. Though Han Solo and Chewbacca are preparing to leave, they stay when they learn that Luke's not back. Han, riding a Tauntaun, goes to find Luke.

Luke escapes from the ice monster's cave, only to wander aimlessly in a blizzard. Luke collapses, looks up, and sees Ben Kenobi. "You will go to the Degobah system. There you will learn from Yoda, the Jedi master who instructed me."

Han finds and shelters Luke, and the two of them are found the next morning. Robot doctors administer to Luke's injuries. "That's *two* you owe me, Junior," says Han.

After Han and Chewie blow up an Imperial probe droid, the Empire knows where they are; an evacuation is planned. With the Imperial fleet, Darth Vader prepares for an attack on Hoth.

Luke, in his snowspeeder, joins the rebel attack on the invading Imperial

Walkers, armored tanks that walk on legs. As Vader appears on the base, Han, Leia, Chewy, and Threepio escape in the Falcon. Luke and Artoo head for the Degobah system as star destroyers and T.I.E. fighters scramble after the Falcon, unable to make light speed.

Luke crash-lands on Degobah, wondering why he came and looking for Yoda. A little creature appears and offers to take Luke and Artoo to Yoda.

Vader speaks to the emperor. Both sense a new disturbance in the Force: Luke. "The son of Skywalker must not become a Jedi," says the emperor. "If he could be turned, he would be a powerful ally," Vader argues. "He will join us or die, master."

Luke grows impatient to meet Yoda. "I cannot teach him — the boy has no patience," Yoda sighs. "He will learn patience," says Ben's disembodied voice. Yoda reluctantly agrees to train Luke.

Drawn to a cave, Luke discovers Vader waiting for him inside. Cutting off Vader's helmet, Luke discovers his own face inside. If Luke is not careful, the Dark Side could claim him, too.

Still pursued by the Imperial fleet, the Falcon hides on the hull of one of the immense Star Destroyers, floating free while they dump their garbage. Unfortunately, Boba Fett, a bounty hunter, follows the Falcon in his own ship.

Mastering the Force, Luke "sees" Han and Leia in danger in a city in the clouds. It's the future, and Han and Leia have landed at Bespin City, a mining colony run by Han's old friend and former owner of the Falcon, Lando Calrissian. Finally, Luke *must* go: His friends are in danger because of him. Ben and Yoda cannot talk him out of going. As Luke leaves, Ben says, "That boy is our last hope." "No," says Yoda, "there is another."

Lando takes Han, Leia, and Chewy to meet. . . Darth Vader, who arrived shortly before the Falcon with Imperial troops. Han is tortured but never asked any questions — Vader wants only Luke. Since Vader suggests carbon-freezing Luke to take him to the emperor, he decides to test the process on Han. When Chewy briefly goes beserk, Vader prevents Boba Fett from shooting him! Han is put into the freezing chamber; the process works, and Han is frozen alive inside a block of carbonite for the bounty hunter to take to Jabba the Hutt.

Lando sets Leia and Chewy free to try to save Han, but it's too late — Boba Fett's ship makes its escape. Luke arrives to face Vader. "Impressive. Most impressive," Vader intones when shown evidence of Luke's new powers. But it is Vader's command of the Dark Side that is impressive as he batters Luke with inanimate objects.

As Leia and the others escape in the Falcon, Luke and Vader battle above a seemingly bottomless shaft. Vader succeeds in cutting off Luke's right hand and asks Luke to join him. "Obi-Wan never told you what happened to your father," Vader says. "He told me enough, he told me you killed him," says Luke. "No, *I* am your father," Vader asserts. "Search your feelings; you know it to be true. Luke, you can destroy the emperor, he has forseen this. It is your destiny. Join me and together we can rule the galaxy as father and son. Come with me, it's the only way."

Numb, Luke lets himself fall into the shaft, tumbling outside the city itself. "Leia," he calls. Leia "hears" Luke's call and returns to pick him up. Inside the Falcon, Luke hears Vader call, "Luke." "Father," he responds, then "Ben—why didn't you tell me?"

Luke is given a new right hand, a mechanical one. Luke must become a Jedi before meeting Vader again and going back to Tatooine to rescue Han from Jabba the Hutt.

The adventures of Luke Skywalker will go on.

Lucas hired veteran Hollywood scriptwriter Leigh Brackett to write *Empire*'s script. After a long meeting with her to determine that she was indeed the right person to continue the adventures of Luke Skywalker, Lucas gave her his outline and notes for the sequel. Brackett completed her first draft in March 1978, but died just two weeks later of cancer. Lucas immediately began looking for someone to develop her first draft.

Lucas and Steven Spielberg, Lucas' friend and soon-to-be collaborator on *Raiders of the Lost Ark*, had hired Lawrence Kasdan to write the *Raiders* script on the basis of his script for *Continental Divide*. When Lucas received the *Raiders* script, he put it aside without reading it and asked Kasdan to complete Brackett's *Empire* script.

Though Lucas wrote the original story for *Empire*, he decided not to take a screenplay credit. Instead, he asked Kasdan (who kept very little of Brackett's original draft) to share screenplay credit with Brackett so her estate could benefit from the film's all-but-assured financial success. Kasdan readily agreed and began adapting Brackett's work.

Brackett had been hired for her snappy dialogue in such Howard Hawks pictures as *The Big Sleep*. Whether the bantering between Han and Leia is Brackett's or Kasdan's contribution, the late writer certainly pointed the way: "I don't know where you get your delusions, laser brain," Leia says to Han when he says she has a thing for him. In the Falcon, Leia tells Han she likes "nice men." "I'm nice men," he responds. Finally, Leia and Han kiss before he's to be put in the freezing chamber. Just before he goes in, Leia says, "I love you." "I know," Han responds.

Lucas told Kasdan that he envisioned *Empire* as having three thirty-five minute acts. Accordingly, he wanted the script to be no longer than 105 pages, "short and tight."

Kasdan chafed under Lucas' two strictly imposed guidelines—speed and clarity. Kasdan believed Lucas' glossing over of the emotional aspects of scenes (no mushy stuff for the boy wonder) in his hurry to get to the next action sequence robbed the film of deeper meanings. Lucas' response? "Well, if we have enough action, nobody will notice." As producer Gary Kurtz (whom

Lucas refused to work with again after *Empire*) once noted, Lucas is "afraid of going too slow."

Although Mark Hamill and Carrie Fisher had signed to do both proposed sequels, Harrison Ford had not. To play Han Solo again, Ford demanded that Lucas and Kasdan give the character more dimension. Actually, this was fine with Lucas; he wanted to develop a *Gone with the Wind* love triangle, and for that to work Han Solo had to become more of a handsome, dashing, Clark Gable-type character and less of a western gunslinger. "It has to be a real triangle with real emotions and at the same time, it has to end up with good-will," Lucas said of his ménage à trois.

The script builds upon dialogue and scenes from *Star Wars* and anticipates *Jedi* to a remarkable degree. For example:

— In Ben and Vader's original fight, Ben says, "You can't win, Darth. If you strike me down, I shall become more powerful than you can possibly imagine," thereby preparing us for the return of Ben as a spectral part of the Force and continuing mentor to Luke.

— When Aunt Beru says to Uncle Owen, "Luke's just not a farmer, Owen — he has too much of his father in him" and Owen responds, "That's what I'm afraid of," this dialogue (consciously or not) anticipates Vader's stunning revelation that he is Luke's father.

— When Han says, during Luke's initial attempts in *Star Wars* to use the Force, "Hokey religions and ancient weapons are no match for a good blaster at your side, kid," he's emphatically proven wrong in *Empire*'s scene where he draws and shoots Vader — who easily deflects the blasts with his gloved hand and uses the Force to snatch the blaster right out of Han's hand.

— When Boba Fett attempts to shoot Chewy at the freezing chamber, Vader knocks the bounty hunter's gun down, perhaps anticipating his moral salvation at the hands of his son in *Jedi*.

After completing *Star Wars*, Lucas decided that he was a filmmaker, not a director. He would totally oversee the production of *Empire*, but he would hand the directorial reins over to someone else, someone compatible with his ideas. Whoever he hired, Lucas decided, needed one overriding qualification: He had to respect the material.

After Lucas had looked at every "at liberty" director in and out of Hollywood, he chose Irvin Kershner, a solid craftsman who could handle the effects-laden filming while developing the characters and their relationships.

Kershner, a tall, nearly bald man, was born in Philadelphia in 1923. In high school, he played the violin and the viola while studying composition. He planned to be a great composer until, as he puts it, "I began listening to Prokofiev and Stravinsky."

During the Second World War, Kershner spent two and one-half years in England, flying missions over Germany in B-24 bombers. Later, he worked for the World Health Organization in the Middle East and for the United States Information Agency. This led, upon his return to the United States, to his directing *Confidential File*, one of the first TV documentary series. He directed his first feature film, *Stakeout on Dope Street*, in 1958.

Kershner (called "Kersh" by nearly everyone) knew he was treading on dangerous ground in trying to interpret Lucas' private fantasy world. Still, Lucas promised that the film would be Kershner's. "You know, the second part of this series is the most important one," he said, adding, "If it works, then we'll make a third and maybe a fourth. If it doesn't work, it'll be old hat and it'll destroy the real bloom on the project. So it's all up to you."

Kersh realized that *Empire*, as the middle film of the trilogy, had to be "slower and more lyrical. The themes have to be more interior, and you don't have a grand climax. *That* became the challenge."

The challenge to Lucas was making sure the original actors returned. "Having the same actors play the same roles is obviously an important aspect of the quality we're trying to achieve," Lucas said. "Sir Alec *is* Ben Kenobi. He's the real thing; I was very concerned that he come back to play the role. I just want the film to be as perfect as possible."

According to Guinness, he *did* agree to return as Ben Kenobi: "During the making of *Star Wars*, George and Gary [Kurtz] asked me if I would appear in a sequel. I told them, 'Yes, absolutely.' I was quite emphatic about it, but eight months [before shooting on *Empire* began] I developed wretched eye trouble. It threatened to blind my left eye. Specialists told me that under no circumstances must I go into bright light. So I sort of withdrew, feeling I had no option. But... it was clear the filmmakers had a problem with the scenes, and I felt that if I could help them out of a difficulty, I must do so. It was as simple as that."

Lucas, producer Kurtz, and Guinness went over the script together, trying to simplify the role to reduce any possible strain on Guinness' eyes and health.

Though Guinness had scenes with Yoda and Luke, he worked alone, in front of a velvet backing. His shimmering image would be matted into the shots with Luke and Yoda in postproduction.

A limousine brought Sir Alec for his one-day shoot, and he reminisced with Mark Hamill for several minutes before Kershner began rehearsals. Guinness found an unexpected ally in Yoda; when he demurred saying one of his philosophical speeches, he would turn to Kershner and say, "Why doesn't the little green thing do this one?" Actually, since Ben "dies" in *Star Wars*, the "little green thing" assumed much of the importance as teacher and sage that was intended for Obi-Wan. Yoda also permitted Lucas and Kasdan to work in a little more humor than Ben's almost saintly character allowed for.

Guinness made the most of his few minutes of screen time. As Kershner recalled directing him, he admired Sir Alec's unquestioned authority. "He dissected every word, each gesture in a way only great actors do. It is the timbre, the subtle movements that make the difference. It's what makes actors great."

The principal photography for *Empire* would again be shot at Elstree, but something the old studio lacked would be added: the *Star Wars* stage, a monstrous stage measuring 250 feet long, 122 feet wide, and 45 feet high. For *Empire*, the stage's main use was housing a full-scale Millennium Falcon, built by maritime engineers at Pembroke Docks in Wales. The Falcon mock-up was a steel craft measuring 65 feet in diameter and 16 feet in height and weighing 23 tons.

Filming on *Empire* got underway on March 5, 1979, with Mark Hamill and a crew of technicians braving the cold and blizzards atop a 6000-foot-high glacier in Finse, Norway, where the average temperature was 10 degrees below zero.

One very important shot in Finse—Luke's mauling by the snow creature—was intended to explain Luke Skywalker's changed appearance. Back in 1977, the day Lucas was to shoot "pick-up" scenes of Luke speeding across the sands of Tatooine in his landspeeder, Mark Hamill drove his new BMW sportscar off an incline on the Antelope Freeway and was catapulted through the windshield. "My nose was wiped right off," Hamill recalled, "and my face had to be rebuilt." Hamill got a brand-new nose, courtesy of plastic surgeons who sculptured it from ear cartilage. In *Empire*, Medical robots on Hoth repair the damage to Luke Skywalker's face, thereby explaining to the audience Luke's changed appearance.

Empire "looks pretty because Kersh took a lot of time to do it," says Lucas, not entirely fairly. "...Ultimately, it doesn't make that much difference. It was just a lot better than I wanted to make it," Lucas said. "And I was paying for it."

After seeing Kersh's rough cut, Lucas threw out half of the first 80 minutes. Kershner, editor Hersch, and producer Kurtz bluntly told Lucas *his* cut didn't work. Lucas blew up—mainly because he realized they were right. After Kershner suggested some changes, Lucas recut the film. "It came together beautifully," he says.

For all his worries, Lucas saw his $33 million investment recovered within three months. *Empire* has earned something like $165 million in worldwide box office rentals, placing it fourth on *Variety*'s All-Time Film Rental Champs list ($141,600,000 in the United States and Canada alone).

Alec Guinness would play a larger role in *The Return of the Jedi*, the concluding episode in George Lucas' middle *Star Wars* trilogy, than he had in *Empire*. In any event, the adventures of Luke Skywalker would continue.

40. *Raise the Titanic* (1980)

> "You'll have a lot more fun in your bathtub with a $2.95
> plastic model, and you won't even need byzanium."
> —David Ansen, in *Newsweek*

Raise the Titanic (hereafter just *Titanic*) was sandwiched between Guinness' appearances as Ben Kenobi in *The Empire Strikes Back* and *Return of the Jedi*. Its position puts it smack in the middle of Guinness' new golden age, but it's a throwback to his leaden turkeys of the late 1960s and early 1970s.

In his role as John Bigalow, a junior third officer in charge of cargo on the Titanic, Guinness appears on screen for all of five minutes and thirty-eight seconds—and they're the best minutes in the film. Guinness brings a much-needed touch of humanity and genuine emotion to his small part, but his few minutes are lost in a sea of espionage, Cold War superpower maneuvering, "romantic interest," and atomic-age mumbo jumbo.

Raise the Titanic, pardon the expression, sank like a rock. In *The Hollywood Hall of Shame*, a book by the Medved brothers devoted to the most expensive flops in movie history (inclusion in the book doesn't necessarily mean a film is bad, just that it was a costly box office failure), the authors point out that Lord Grade's $5 million, extraordinarily detailed, fifty-five-foot model of the Titanic was too large for the studio tank in Malta where the underwater scenes were to be shot. Grade's solution was to "build a brand-new tank with a few extra feet on all sides, at a cost of an additional $6 million."

With this sort of inspired thinking and attention to pointless detail, the film's estimated negative cost (this does not include the cost of prints, advertising, etc.) came in at $36 million. To date, *Titanic* has earned $6.8 million in domestic rentals (source: *Variety*).

To guarantee the film's success (a film must gross roughly two and one-half times its negative cost to start making money), Lord Grade signed such box office luminaries as Jason Robards, Richard Jordan, David Selby, and Anne Archer. Jordan and Selby, in particular, have little screen presence. As the James Bondish Dirk Pitt (great name, huh?) Jordan is sullen and unappealing in a role that cries out for a Steve McQueen or a Harrison Ford. As the romantic leads, Selby and Archer are mawkishly ineffectual. Archer has to mouth one of screenwriter Adam Kennedy's more memorable lines: "I can't put the wormy on the hooky." Fortunately, the Archer-Jordan-Selby triangle suddenly and without explanation disappears from the film.

Certainly, a film about the raising of the Titanic could be—should be—thrilling and moving. But we get too much plot at the film's opening and too little the rest of the way, with most of the film's eventual running time of 112 minutes (cut from 122 minutes prior to release) given over to murky underwater goings-on. What should be the film's highlight and climax, the raising of the Titanic, is treated as a throwaway: When the submersible *Deep Quest* is trapped against the Titanic's hull, the giant ship is raised in minutes. The film then goes on another twenty minutes or so, working out its dull and contrived East vs. West plot.

As you might expect, *Titanic*'s reviews were less than enthusiastic. Charles Champlin, in the *Los Angeles Times*, wrote, "*Raise the Titanic*, with loose ends hanging about, including a love triangle with Anne Archer (gravely underemployed) at its apex, fails to live up to its special effects."

John Coleman's piece in *New Statesman* began, "Elsewhere, a few more stretch-marks are added to the swollen belly of incredulity by Lord Grade's latest folly, *Raising the Titanic* [sic], which would have us believe that the famous liner sank on 14 April 1912, with a precious cargo of 'byzanium,' a 'radioactive mineral,' smuggled into its holds. Much of the action occurs underwater, which is unfortunate since little of it is visually decipherable. SOS? Save your money."

In *New York*, David Denby wrote: ". . . The footage here must be among the most tediously waterlogged sequences ever filmed. It takes forever for the little snub-nosed submersibles to find the *Titanic* on the ocean floor, and when they do there is very little thrill. *Raise the Titanic* is a folly without a dream behind it."

Finally, Archer Winston's piece in the *New York Post* seems mildly affirmative. "Eventually, despite all that splendid technical photography underwater and on top, inside submersibles and in Washington decisions of the key men, it all boils down to an elaborate melodramatic fiction, sufficiently exciting while it all happens."

Tracing supplies of a rare mineral, byzanium, to be used in a laser defense system code-named the Sicilian Project, a naval intelligence unit discovers an old mine on a Soviet-held island in the Arctic Circle. A Russian soldier is killed, and Moscow wonders what the Americans are up to.

Dirk Pitt (Richard Jordan), a civilian mining engineer, is called in by the project's leader, Admiral Sandecker (Jason Robards). Several tons of byzanium were apparently in the cargo hold of the Titanic when she sank. Pitt suggests the Titanic be found and raised.

Pitt meets the junior third officer in charge of cargo on the Titanic, an old salt named John Bigalow (Guinness). Bigalow tells Pitt of a strange man who put a gun to his head and insisted he be taken to the ship's hold—even

Guinness as Bigalow, the former crew member who survived the great liner's sinking.

though she was sinking. He looked at the cargo area and repeated over and over, "Thank God for Southby." Bigalow gives Pitt the pennant he removed from the Titanic, asking him to take it and put it back "where it belongs" if she's successfully raised.

Much opaque underwater maneuvering ensues as the navy tests its two submersibles, the *Starfish* and the *Deep Quest*. The *Starfish* goes too deep and implodes from the pressure, but the *Deep Quest* finds the Titanic at 12,700 feet.

The Russians leak word of the discovery and of byzanium's existence, forcing Sandecker to hold a news conference. He says they'll raise the ship by patching her, pumping her full of foam with 22,000 tons of lift, and attaching tanks to the ship's outer hull.

When the *Deep Quest* gets tangled up and jammed against the Titanic with Dr. Seagram (David Selby) inside, Pitt says they have no choice but to attempt raising the ship two weeks early. The attempt is successful, and Pitt raises Bigalow's pennant.

A Russian warship shows up, threatening to sink the Titanic with torpedoes if they refuse the Soviets' offer of "help." Pitt calls for his surprise": a United States atomic submarine and two jet fighters. The Soviets are foiled and watch as the Titanic is towed back to New York, reaching that port sixty-eight years after setting out from England.

The cargo boxes are found to contain gravel, but Seagram and Pitt deduce from a postcard that the byzanium is really buried in a grave in Southby ("Thank God for Southby"). For the sake of world peace, they decide to leave it there.

In Guinness' brief appearance he brings an emotional center to the film heretofore lacking. Showing Pitt his "Titanic collection," he says, "Standing as high in the water as one of your skyscrapers, longer than two rugby fields. And furnishings to match the finest mansions in England. She was one of a kind, no question about it. And God himself they said couldn't sink her. Then, in two hours, she was gone—and 1500 souls with her."

And with that, Guinness is gone from the movie, but ready to resurface as George Smiley—once again.

41. *Smiley's People* (1982)

"George, you won." "Did I? Yes, I suppose I did."
— from *Smiley's People*

Guinness' 1979 filming of *Tinker Tailor Soldier Spy* confronted him with a problem, one he also faced with the *Star Wars* sequels. As with Ben Kenobi, Guinness was strongly identified with his film characterization of George Smiley. When he was approached to play Smiley for one last time, in *Smiley's People* (hereafter just *Smiley's*), he felt he owed it to David Cornwell/John le Carré and the millions of fans of the wildly successful first series. But he made one thing clear: "There won't be a third series. Or if there is, I won't be in it."

For Guinness, returning to Smiley had the advantage of allowing him to deepen his characterization of the owlish and aging spy. Since George is "flying solo" in *Smiley's*, intent upon snaring his old adversary Karla, he is more openly human, more openly emotional, than in *Tinker*.

A Russian woman living in Paris, Madame Ostrakova (Eileen Atkins), is watched by an obvious KGB type. He introduces himself and tells her he brings word of her daughter Alexandra in Moscow, whom she has not seen for years. He tells her that Alexandra can join her in France if she'll just go to the Soviet embassy and fill out a few forms. The embassy gives her photos of her "daughter," and she realizes it is not Alexandra. She writes to "the General" in London for help.

Vladimir, the General (Curd Jurgens), receives her letter in London, reads it, and immediately calls Hamburg. Madame Ostrakova gets a letter back from the General and half a photograph. The other half is slid under her door; she admits Otto Leipzig (Vladek Sheybal). He shows her a picture — it's Oleg Kirov (Dudley Sutton), the man who approached her. She tells him the girl whose photo she saw is not her daughter. Leipzig gives her an address to write to if she needs help.

Seeing men asking about her, Ostrakova writes to the General. Soon a man on a ferry is passed a package from "the magician." The General then calls the Circus asking for his contact, "Max" — George Smiley (Guinness). He wants a "Moscow Rules" meeting. When the General arrives for the meeting

249

with the young Circus operative, he's followed. He quickly hides his cigarette pack.

Oliver Lacon (Anthony Bate) calls George and has him identify a body — the General's. Most of the face has been shot away. George looks around the murder scene, then goes to Lacon's. Saul Enderby is now in charge of the Circus; George is three years into "retirement." Most of the clandestine networks have been disbanded. Vladimir and his exiles have been mostly cut off, their money gone to other uses.

Lacon wants George to bury things *or* observe any political dangers in the situation. Meanwhile, Madame Ostrakova is pushed in front of a car. Lacon again tells George to tidy things and forget about his obsession: Karla. Later, Mostyn (Stephen Riddle) tells George that Vladimir said the meeting was about the "sandman" — Karla.

Finding one pack of cigarettes missing from a fresh carton in Vladimir's room, George guesses the proofs Vladimir had must be in the pack.

At the murder scene, George searches carefully for the missing pack before finding it high up in a tree. There's a 35mm film negative inside. George learns that Vladimir went to a certain address the day before for an hour and goes there himself. The woman doesn't want "Max" coming around again and getting her husband involved in things. Villem (William) returns and tells George he picked up a package for Vladimir yesterday.

At the headquarters of Vladimir's emigrant organization, George learns that Vladimir talked to Mikhel (Michael Gough) of "landing a big fish," of phoning Hamburg and getting street maps.

George develops the negative; it looks like a blackmail sex shot, with Kirov and Leipzig in bed with a prostitute. Kirov is Karla's man. Madame Ostrakova, recovered, is released from the hospital.

Calling himself Alan Angel, George sees the proprietor of a toney art shop — it's Toby Esterhase (Bernard Hepton), out of the service and under a new name. Toby tells George to stay retired; let things drop. When George persists, Toby tells him that Karla was looking for a legend (a cover identity) for a young girl.

On the highway, a motorcyclist pulls George over with a message from Saul Enderby: "That's it." George, however, is off to see Connie Sachs (Beryl Reid), former head of research for the Circus. When George asks her about Kirov, she says he's wearing his Karla look. She tells him Karla had a mistress whom he sent to the gulag. But Tatiana, the daughter, born in 1953, stayed with him, hating him for what she suspects he did to her mother.

George goes to Herr Kretzschmar's sex club in Hamburg, looking for Otto Leipzig. George mentions the negative and they discuss Vladimir, the General. It turns out that after being contacted by Vladimir, Otto had brought Kirov to the club to be secretly photographed and recorded in compromising situations.

George later finds Otto's bound and dead body in a houseboat. Almost

Guinness' Smiley studies a piece of evidence.

sick, George stands at a rail where he notices a fishing line in the water. He pulls up a packet with half a picture. At Kretzschmar's, George gets the rest of Otto's proofs in return for the half-picture. He tells Kretzschmar (Mario Adorf) the proof will do worse than kill the man who had Otto killed. George convinces Madame Ostrakova that he's a friend of the General. To spirit her out of her building, George calls in Peter Guillam (Michael Byrne), now married and working for the Paris embassy. He sends his proofs and a personal note to Saul Enderby. On the phone to Peter, Enderby calls George a rogue elephant.

At the Circus, George meets with Saul Enderby (Barry Foster) and staff. The proofs are sex shots on film and a transcript of Kirov's taped confession when blackmailed by Otto Leipzig. Kirov's tale is that Karla took him under his wing and had him arrange certain things, such as a legend for a twenty-six-year-old woman "agent." Karla had to use apes like Kirov for his dirty work, since his own people would be too well trained and sharp to use for personal business.

After Kirov approached Ostrakova in Paris, money began to be transferred to an account in Switzerland. After he was compromised by Leipzig, Kirov was recalled, interrogated, and executed. Karla had Vladimir and Leipzig killed and attempted the same with Madame Ostrakova. But why?

George meets his wife, Ann (Sian Phillips), and says goodbye—perhaps for good. After fearing she may have told things to Bill Haydon, George has decided not to confide in his wayward wife again.

Toby, glad to be working again, is in charge of the agents watching things in Switzerland. Grigoriev, a minor Russian official, picks up Karla's money each week and goes to a Swiss mental clinic with it. Toby's people photograph Grigoriev (Michael Lonsdale) taking the cash. Grigoriev visits a mentally unbalanced young woman at the sanitorium, who calls him Uncle Anton. Meanwhile, George gives Toby the green light: Take Grigoriev.

Confronted by blackmail photos, Grigoriev tells them about "Alexandra Ostrakova." Moscow Centre sent for him, and he was taken to see a powerful man in humble surroundings—Karla. This "priest" chain-smoked American cigarettes and told Grigoriev he would be taking money to a Swiss clinic and acting as a father figure to the schizophrenic girl he would visit there.

George goes to see "Alexandra" (Tussie Silberg), who calls him a dangerous man. She says her name is Tatiana. After seeing her, George writes a letter to Karla and tells him he knows everything. Karla cannot get help for Tatiana in Russia, and if what he's done for her leaks out, he'll be liquidated for placing love above duty. George tells him to come over and he and his daughter will be well cared for.

George is called to Berlin. Karla is coming. A lonely bridge. Someone crosses. George holds his breath, his eyes clamped tightly shut. It *is* Karla. "Oh, my dear God," George moans anxiously. Finally, Karla is across.

For one long, long moment, the two spymasters, the two champion chess players on the board of international intrigue, face each other silently, see-ing...who knows what in each other's faces. As he's led away, Karla lets fall George's cigarette lighter. Weakness has met weakness; they *are* so very similar, after all.

Peter says it's bedtime. "George, you won," he says. George responds, "Did I? Yes, I suppose I did."

After finishing a novel in which George Smiley is head of the Circus but a background figure, *The Honourable Schoolboy*, in 1977, David Cornwell (John le Carré) visited the Mideast, traveling in Lebanon, Syria, Jordan, and Israel. Cornwell hoped to gather information for another Smiley book, this one set against the tangled conflicts of the Mideast. But it was not Smiley ter-ritory; he found he could not convincingly place Smiley in this complex world. "I couldn't find the right plot for him there," he said. So Cornwell returned to England to "finish him off" with one last book—*Smiley's People*. (Cornwell would return to the Mideast in 1980, and from that experience would come a somewhat disappointing novel, *The Little Drummer Girl*.)

When it came time to dramatize *Smiley's People*, Cornwell joined with John Hopkins to write the screenplay. With John Irvin having moved on to motion pictures (*Ghost Story*) and unavailable, Simon Langton directed this second Smiley outing for the BBC.

Curd (Curt) Jurgens (1912–1982) played the General in this, his last role. He was a German leading man who entered films in 1939 and became an inter-national star after World War II. His two most famous roles were probably as Wernher von Braun in 1959's *I Aim at the Stars*, and as the sympathetic, anti-Nazi U-Boat commandant in 1957's *The Enemy Below*.

Among the other actors in *Smiley's* was Michael Gough as Mikhel, who appeared in several other Guinness films, including *The Man in the White Suit* and *The Horse's Mouth*.

If Peter Guillam looked a little different in *Smiley's* it's because another actor, Michael Byrne, and not Michael Jayston, played him this time round.

The music was written by Patrick Gowers and helped establish the mood of age and decay. For Smiley, Gowers wrote a theme based on Beethoven's later quartets, personifying the "melancholy" of old age. The Russian theme used for the opening and closing titles was also used in the story whenever Smiley unearthed a particularly significant clue.

Cornwell and fellow screenplay author John Hopkins went through several early drafts of the adaptation, struggling with the necessity to keep the flavor of the book yet streamline its complexities sufficiently for television. A few scenes were invented for the screenplay that were not in the book. As director Simon Langton observed, "Sometimes an adaptation can be very faithful to the original and you simply get an extremely prolonged version of the book. This is really no good for a script."

For the later drafts of the script, Alec Guinness joined Cornwell and went over the script page by page with him. As Langton pointed out, "Smiley is on virtually every page of the script, so it made sense to consult [Guinness] very thoroughly before going into production."

Director Langton then had four months of planning to implement the finished script and two weeks of rehearsal before shooting began. Occasionally, during the six-month shooting schedule, Langton, Guinness, and the others had time to pause and again rehearse major scenes.

Shooting took place in Switzerland, Germany, France, and Britain. (The interior of Otto Leipzig's houseboat was filmed at the old Ealing Studios, home to many of Guinness' classic films.) "The final confrontation we shot in Nottingham," Langton recalls. "We couldn't shoot it in Berlin for obvious reasons. The citizens of Nottingham let us use a road bridge [the Lady Bay Bridge] for about five days and nights."

Writing *Smiley's People* as both a novel and a screenplay left Cornwell a bit tired of his most famous creation; he was losing interest in his fictional alter ego, George Smiley. "The very success of Alec Guinness' depiction of Smiley was beginning to make him unsecret to me," Cornwell explained on a publicity tour for *The Little Drummer Girl*. "I wanted to leave myself without him as a prop, and give myself the opportunity to write about the new generation, younger people, modern problems."

Cornwell seems to have nothing for Smiley to do but die. He has finally had his revenge on Karla, using Karla's daughter against him in the same manner Karla used Ann against Smiley. George's very success has left him confronting a gigantic void in his life—and he seems to have finally put an end to his lingering attachments to Ann. One supposes that George will retreat to his books and his scholarship. After all, George won, didn't he?

As with *Tinker*, Guinness brought all his years of experience and wisdom to playing George Smiley in his last hurrah. Guinness and Cornwell make Smiley seem less a bespectacled, blinking human computer and more the emotionally motivated man he is. Waiting in Toby Esterhase's pricey art shop, Guinness' Smiley almost slides off a highly polished chair! Guinness and Beryl Reid (Connie Sachs) have a long and tricky scene together in her house as he gently gets her drunk enough to tell him what he needs.

The tension so gets to the normally calm George that, while waiting for Karla to cross the bridge in Berlin, Guinness moans, "Oh, my dear God!" Guinness so underplays George that his rare outburst of emotion is made even more affecting.

For the final scene, where George finally confronts a vanquished Karla, both men are seen in huge closeup. Guinness and Patrick Stewart (another champion underplayer) invest their exchange of fixed stares with the intensity of chess masters studying a board. For Guinness and Smiley, it is a highlight in a long and successful career. Smiley's methodical way of doing things has been rewarded; Guinness' style of acting has proven itself perfect for the role of a lifetime.

Guinness was sixty-eight when *Smiley's People* aired. But, unlike his
fictional counterpart George Smiley, Guinness had no plans for slowly fading
away.

42. *Lovesick* (1983)

"It is my professional opinion, as the person who invented
psychoanalysis, that you are now nutsy fagin."
— Sigmund Freud to Saul Benjamin in *Lovesick.*

Lovesick opened in early 1983, after *Raise the Titanic* and *Smiley's People*
and before *Return of the Jedi*. As in *Titanic*, Guinness has a small but crucial
part. In *Lovesick*, he plays the shade of Sigmund Freud, father of
psychoanalysis. His role is to pop up every once in a while and counsel
befuddled Dudley Moore, dropping snappy lines right and left.

Lovesick was writer/director Marshall Brickman's second solo film after
helping Woody Allen write many of his funniest movies. Unfortunately, on
his own, Brickman is lost. There are many scenes in *Lovesick* which recall
Allen/Brickman films like *Annie Hall*, *Manhattan* and *Sleeper*. Since Brickman obviously wrote many of the gags and lines in those very funny films, he's
hardly stealing from Woody Allen—but he *is* stealing from himself. And,
unlike Allen, he is no great shakes as a director.

Brickman's first solo effort, *Simon*, opened, played to empty theaters and
hostile audiences, and quickly closed. *Lovesick* did a little better, certainly in
the reviews, but was no more successful financially.

Lovesick takes a fantasy viewpoint of life in the Big Apple: Chloe, a young
playwright, has her first play produced by Joseph Papp and lands a major star
to act in it. Her apartment—just a simple two-level, one-bedroom with
entryway and gorgeous view—probably doesn't cost more than, oh, say
$2000–$3000 a month if not more, easily affordable by any young playwright
before her play has opened.

Guinness, as usual, comes out of *Lovesick* with his reputation and dignity
intact. And why not? He has all the film's best lines. Further, even though
we all know what a great comic actor he is, Guinness seems always to surprise
us with his droll delivery of an unexpected line.

When Guinness/Freud appears beside Saul in Chloe's bathtub, he says,
"If this were a dream, I would interpret it this way: you and I are in the womb
of this woman—the tub represents the womb—and she is giving birth to us."
When Saul naturally says, "What?" Guinness concedes, "Okay, maybe not."
And Guinness, with a perfectly straight face, later calls Saul "nutsy fagin."

In the theater, after Saul has left to eavesdrop on Chloe and Ted, Guinness/Freud stares at Chloe with widening eyes. "Attractive young woman," he says, slowly putting his cigar in his mouth.

David Ansen, in *Newsweek*, said ". . . The funny thing about Brickman's movie (assuming it doesn't hit a raw nerve) is its general inoffensiveness about a potentially touchy subject. It's as airy and charming a movie as is likely to be made about countertransference. *Lovesick* hardly stands as the definitive satire on 'the impossible profession.' But you'll get some good chuckles out of it."

In the *New Yorker*, Pauline Kael's review noted, "As he did in his first film as writer-director, the 1980 *Simon*, Brickman parodies the craziness of the highly educated and compulsively self-aware. He starts with a promising (if flimsy) situation and then wanders away from it, while the dramatic tension dribbles out. . . . The invention flags after the initial rush."

Kenneth M. Chanko, in *Films in Review*, began by noting that "writer-director Marshall Brickman almost pulls off a very special romantic comedy with *Lovesick*, but, much like his first movie, *Simon*, it's a bit too undisciplined, never achieving a sustained comedic tone. But he is getting better. *Lovesick* is often funny, but it's also all over the place. The more one considers it, the less one is impressed."

New Republic's reviewer was not at all impressed: ". . . It's so thin, so feeble, so herniatedly hip that I concluded Brickman must have some sort of grip on the money men . . . because if financiers and studio chiefs are approving Brickman's projects on the scripts' intrinsic merits, the U.S. film industry has a much darker shadow over it than I feared."

Manhattan psychiatrist Saul Benjamin (Dudley Moore) begins another routine day and endures his dreary patients: a nymphomaniac, a bored housewife, a homosexual, and Mr. Arnold, a man who never speaks.

Saul attends a birthday party for his friend Otto, a fellow shrink. Otto tells Saul that he's in lust with a patient—Chloe Allen, a twenty-year-old playwright from Minnesota. That night Saul gets a phone call from Otto's wife and learns he's died from a heart attack. Soon Chloe (Elizabeth McGovern) calls Saul and asks to be his patient.

Saul is smitten by her pale blue eyes and baby-fat face. As she tells him she has anxiety attacks, Saul begins fantasizing about her. Freud (Guinness) appears to him and asks, "Hey, what is this? What are you doing?" "Nothing," says Saul, "I'm just having a little fantasy, that's all." "That's some nothing. Have you read what I wrote on countertransference, by any chance?" "Of course." "And you're still going to treat her? You're infatuated with her. I think she likes you, too—look at the pupils: wide open, sexually receptive," Freud says.

Chloe tells him she has a play being produced by Joseph Papp, starring famous film star Ted Caruso (Ron Silver), an egomaniac who dominates

Guinness makes a convincing Sigmund Freud.

those around him, including Chloe. Chloe talks to Saul about Ted and about a sex dream she had. "*You* were watching me," she says, quickly amending the "you" to "he."

Saul's wife Katie (Anne Kerry) runs an art gallery, where Saul meets artist Jac Applezweig (Larry Rivers). While there, Saul calls Chloe but hangs up after she answers. The next day, she tells Saul of her "obscene phone call" and talks of having feelings for him.

Cancelling his sessions, Saul follows Chloe to the theater and her rehearsal. "So, how does it feel to be an obsessive-compulsive?" asks Freud from the next seat. "You're cracking. Don't you know the warning signs?" "I'm in full control," Saul says. "*Sure* you are," answers Freud. "I wrote an interesting paper about a play, *Oedipus*. Did you ever read it?"

Saul follows Chloe and Ted into the costume room, eavesdropping until his beeper goes off. He escapes in an Oedipus costume and catches a cold in the rain.

When Chloe tells Saul she keeps a diary and then forgets her purse, he takes her keys and gets into a cab to her place. Freud, in the seat with him, says, "It is my professional opinion, as the person who invented psychoanalysis, that you are now nutsy fagin." When Saul argues that Chloe left her purse and keys so he could see her journal, he asks Freud, "You never heard of a Freudian slip?" "No—what's that?" Freud asks innocently.

As Saul reads the diary, Freud says, "I see that you are flushing a brilliant career down the toilet." Saul tells Freud, "I have hands like her father." Freud, reading *Variety*, says, "Congratulations. A fetishist and an obsessive — you'll be very happy together."

Hearing Chloe and Ted arrive, Saul slips into the shower. When she turns on the shower and it stops, Chloe opens the curtain to find Saul. "Hi, it's Dr. Benjamin." He confesses reading her journal and tells her he loves her. They kiss.

Freud watches them sink onto the bed, swivels his chair, and addresses us. "It's very simple. Whenever we humans start thinking of ourselves as something better, something loftier, than the monkey, or the rabbit, or the fruit fly, then Mother Nature steps in and reminds us what we really are — animals. This is my great lesson." He shrugs. "You can take it or leave it."

Saul tells Chloe they must cool things down. She leaves, disappointed. Saul is with Mr. Arnold — who finally speaks — when Chloe calls and wants him back. Beeped from a dinner with Chloe, Saul is told by the suicidal Mr. Houseman that he needs him, but it turns out Saul has taken too many pills and *he* needs to be saved. At the gallery afterward, Saul sees Jac with Katie; both confess their affair.

Saul tells most of his patients they don't need his help and opens a clinic in a shelter. As various problems arise, Saul must face the membership committee about his unorthodox methods — returning patients' fees. Saul walks out on them, a free man.

Freud says goodbye; he's going to the mountains of Mexico. He says that psychoanalysis was an "interesting experiment. I never meant it to become an industry."

Saul and Chloe make up, and all is well.

43. Return of the Jedi (1983)

"The *Star Wars* pictures were fun to make.... A few million youngsters—who hadn't the vaguest idea who I was because they had not seen my earlier films—now have a good idea of who I am. I think I discovered a whole new audience."
—Alec Guinness.

"Luke Skywalker has returned to his home planet of Tatooine in an attempt to rescue his friend Han Solo from the clutches of the vile gangster Jabba the Hutt.

"Little does Luke know that the GALACTIC EMPIRE has secretly begun construction on a new armored space station even more powerful than the first dreaded Death Star.

"When completed, this ultimate weapon will spell certain doom for the small band of rebels struggling to restore freedom to the galaxy..."

With *Return of the Jedi* (hereafter just *Jedi*), Sir Alec Guinness completed the trilogy that began with *Star Wars* and brought him so much renewed fame and respect.

Guinness has described playing Ben Kenobi in *Jedi* as "flitting across the screen" to earn more "gold from outer space." He was somewhat reluctant to put on Ben's robes and ethereal persona again and had to be convinced by George Lucas over a lunch at his country home outside London.

Sir Alec asked for and received a modest screen credit, reflecting his limited participation in the third *Star Wars* film. "I don't mind doing it if it only takes one morning to film," he explained, "but a big credit would be unfair. I'm gone in a cough and a spit. Suppose I have a fan somewhere who has paid money to see me?"

Mark Hamill, thrilled to be working again with such a great actor, explained what Guinness' participation meant for him and for the character he plays, Luke Skywalker: "It's a joy to reach the point with Sir Alec/Ben Kenobi where I can now express my admiration for him through my actions. Not so much in trying to copy his acting style—which, of course, I never could—but in the growth in Luke's character. Now *he* is reflecting the strength I saw in Sir Alec's performance as a Jedi Knight in the original *Star Wars*, that amazing economy of both movement and gesture."

"Har," writing in *Variety*, said, "There is good news, bad news, and no news about *Return of the Jedi*. The good news is that George Lucas & Co. have perfected the technological magic to a point where almost anything and everything—no matter how bizarre—is believable. The bad news is the human dramatic dimensions have been sorely sacrificed. The no news is the picture will take in millions regardless of the pluses and minuses."

In *Cinefantastique*, Joseph Francavilla wrote, "I'm amazed at how universal the Star Wars saga is. *Return of the Jedi*, like its two predecessors, is a truly communal film. It's a universal language, a cross-cultural myth. No film, no book (not even the Bible) has ever done that. It's quite an achievement."

Time's Gerald Clarke wrote, "*Return of the Jedi* is a brilliant, imaginative piece of moviemaking. But it does not diminish the accomplishment of Lucas and his youthful team to say that there are flaws nonetheless. The most obvious, ironically, is an overemphasis on effects and a too proud display of odd-looking creatures."

Newsweek's review found that "the trilogy's two or three big pop-mystical ideas nearly expire from overuse. 'Meet your Destiny. . . Feel the power of the Dark Side. . . Give in to your anger' begin to feel like an endless tape loop."

In *Films in Review*, Gregory Solman found *Jedi* inferior to the original *Star Wars* and, especially, to the Kershner-directed *Empire*, noting that "Richard Marquand mis-directs *Return of the Jedi*. The film is often ineptly paced and structured, almost invariably lacks focus, and overuses mechanical models, with glaring deference to action scenes over acting scenes."

In the *New Yorker*, Pauline Kael found *Jedi* "an impersonal and rather junky piece of moviemaking. Even the scene that should be the emotional peak of the whole mythic trilogy—the moment when Luke removes the black visor and the helmet that have concealed Darth Vader's face—has no thrill. Luke looks into the eyes of his nightmare father, and he might be ordering a veggieburger."

Variety noted that the New York critics split on the merits of *Jedi*, with ten writing favorable reviews while seven wrote negative reviews. The negative reviews tended to call *Jedi* little more than a peg for the merchandising that would follow in its wake, or observed that the special effects overwhelmed the story and the characters.

On Tatooine, following in the footsteps of Lando Calrissian, Threepio and Artoo are admitted to the fortress of Jabba the Hutt. Artoo delivers Luke's message: a willingness to bargain for the life of Han Solo. Luke also gives the two droids to Jabba, a monstrous, ugly, sluglike creature, as a goodwill gesture.

While Lando is pretending to be a guard, a short bounty hunter appears with Chewbacca in chains and collects the reward on Chewy's head. Chewy's captor later releases Han from his frozen state and turns out to be Leia. But it's a trap, and Han is tossed in with Chewy, while Jabba makes Leia his personal slave, bound to him by chains.

Luke enters, using Jedi mind powers, but is tricked into the Rancor pit. Luke kills the monstrous Rancor, angering Jabba, who orders them all taken to the Sarlacc Pit to die.

Ready to "walk the plank," Luke is optimistic, almost cocky. Artoo, dispensing drinks on Jabba's sail barge, hurls Luke's light sabre to him and the battle is joined. Han, still unable to see, accidentally ignites Boba Fett's backpack rockets, and the bounty hunter disappears down Sarlacc's hungry maw. Leia uses her chains to choke Jabba to death before helping Luke to destroy the sail barge with a cannon blast through the deck.

In space, the reunited friends separate; Luke has unfinished business on Dagobah. A tired and enfeebled Yoda tells Luke that he will be a Jedi only when he faces and defeats Vader and admits, "Your father he is." Dying, Yoda mutters, "There is another Skywalker." The terrible knowledge of that statement shows on Luke's haunted face.

Ben appears and explains why he deceived Luke concerning Darth Vader and his father. When Luke says, "Yoda spoke of another," Ben replies, "The other that he spoke of is your twin sister. The Emperor knew as I did that if Anakin were to have any offspring, they would be a threat to him." "Leia— Leia is my sister," Luke guesses correctly.

The rebels learn that the Emperor is constructing a new Death Star near the moon of Endor, where an enemy shield generator protects it from attack. Lando will attack the Death Star while Han will assault the shield generator.

On Endor, after a frantic speeder-bike chase, Leia is separated from Han, Luke, and the others, and found by Ewoks, tiny furry creatures.

Sensing Luke on Endor, Vader promises to bring him before the Emperor. Meanwhile, Luke and the others are reunited with Leia when the Ewoks capture them. The Ewoks think Threepio is a golden god and, when Luke uses the Force to levitate him, they are impressed enough to free their captives and join their cause.

Luke tells Leia she's his sister—and Vader is their father, whom he must face alone. Luke surrenders to Vader, who acknowledges his powers but refuses to renounce the Dark Side. Vader takes Luke to the Emperor, who astounds the young Jedi by informing him that the Death Star is fully operational and that his friends on Endor are walking into a trap.

Han and Leia are captured, but freed when the Ewoks, using primitive weapons, overpower the stormtroopers. After being goaded into action by the Emperor, Luke takes up his light sabre against his father.

When Vader senses Luke's feelings for Leia, he tells his son that perhaps his sister can be turned if he cannot. Enraged, Luke battles Vader with all his fury, the music rising in intensity. Finally, Luke cuts off Vader's right hand, reversing the situation at the end of *Empire*. Luke, looking at his own hand, throws down his light sabre. Luke is a Jedi—"like my father before me."

Han and Leia blow the shield generator and Lando attacks the Death Star's core as the Emperor tortures Luke with his powers. Vader, seemingly impassive, watches as Luke cries out. Suddenly, Vader grabs the Emperor and throws him down a power shaft. Luke removes the weak and dying Vader's mask and sees. . . Anakin Skywalker, his father. "You were right, Luke," Anakin says. "Tell your sister you were right." As Anakin dies, Vader's theme is played softly and sadly. The Jedi—Anakin Skywalker—has finally returned.

As Lando destroys the Death Star, Luke takes off in a shuttle craft with his father's body. On Endor, Leia tells Han that Luke is her brother, and they kiss.

Luke burns Anakin's body, in the mask and outfit of Darth Vader, on a funeral pyre as fireworks explode overhead. Han, Leia, Chewy, Artoo, Threepio, Lando, Wedge, and finally, Luke celebrate. Luke looks offscreen and we see what he sees: the shimmering figures of Yoda, Ben, and Anakin Skywalker.

The adventures of Luke Skywalker have ended. . . for now.

Lawrence Kasdan and George Lucas shared the screenplay credit for *Jedi*, probably the last film Kasdan, a respected writer/director in his own right (*The Big Chill*) would write for someone else to direct.

It took Lucas two years to write *Star Wars*, but *Jedi*'s first draft was written in four weeks. It was Lucas' favorite script, and he flirted with the idea of directing it. Then he reconsidered: "I took one look at the amount of work and thought, 'Oh, my God, my life is complicated enough.' "

As for the teddy bear–like Ewoks and their defeat of a superior technology, it was something Lucas had wanted to put into a film since he first had the idea for *Apocalypse Now*, the project that, by default, went to his former mentor, Francis Coppola. Finally, in *Jedi*, he got to realize his dream.

Lucas chose Richard Marquand to direct *Jedi*. Born in Wales but educated in England, Marquand got into acting while studying at Cambridge. He loved rehearsals but hated performing. He joined the Royal Air Force and soon found himself doing odd jobs at a Hong Kong television station. When he returned to England he was hired by BBC-2, the government television station.

His first feature film was a horror movie, *The Legacy*, which starred Katherine Ross and Sam Elliot. *The Birth of the Beatles*, his second film, was followed by *The Eye of the Needle*, starring Donald Sutherland and Kate Nelligan. When Lucas saw *Needle*, he put Marquand's name on his list of possible directors for *Jedi*.

Asked how he picked Marquand, Lucas told *Rolling Stone*, "You want the best person for the job. You make large lists of people who could conceivably do the [film]. . . then you would go through the list and find out who is available. Then you start inquiring as to who would be interested, and that

whittles it down to a very small group. In this case, we narrowed it down to
two people. One of them was Richard."

Though Lucas stayed in the background, occasionally directing a second-
unit sequence, he hired producer Howard Kazanjian to ride herd on Marquand—something he insists Kurtz did not do with Kershner on *Empire*.

Marquand knew his role and didn't stray beyond it. "It's fair to say I'm
conducting a 120-piece orchestra and I've got the composer in the front row,"
Marquand said. I'm playing his music, and he's perfectly entitled to speak if
he wants. [Lucas] tends not to. But he's here, so I can turn to him and say,
'Look, this bar doesn't make any sense. Do you really want it?' If he says yes,
play it that way. If you feel it can go faster or slower, there's always the cadenza
where you get your chance. But it is *his* music—he wrote it." Marquand's
direction reflects both his malleability and his limited experience as a director.
He is clearly not up to the standard set by Irvin Kershner.

Since *Jedi*'s code name at Lucasfilm was *Blue Harvest*, Lucas chose that
name to be the film's production name when they shot in Arizona and in Cres-
cent City in California.

Blue Harvest, the smokescreen production, was supposed to be a horror
film, so Lucas had T-shirts printed up with the title and bearing the phrase,
"Horror Beyond Imagination." Asked if that was what *Blue Harvest* was
about, Lucas replied, "No—that's the making of the movie."

Certain pages of the *Jedi* script were specially color-coded and given to
only those cast and crew members who absolutely had to have them. Carrie
Fisher recalls that when they shot certain scenes, "they asked the crew—even
the sound man—not to listen." She learned her true identity before her scene
with Mark Hamill was shot. "I'd have laughed on camera if Mark had told me
for the first time then. It would have been like, 'Carrie, your dad isn't Eddie
Fisher. Hitler is.' "

Shooting began on January 11, 1982, with a sandstorm sequence that was
eventually cut from the film to improve the pacing. By March 10, Kazanjian
and Marquand were ready to shoot Sir Alec Guinness' scenes. But Guinness
was suffering from the flu, and director Marquand decided to shoot several
scenes with Mark Hamill first, thus allowing Guinness to work on his dialogue
and—hopefully—feel better as the day wore on. This proved to be the case.

The following day Guinness felt even better, and filming went so
smoothly that Marquand was able to move on to scenes set in the Emperor's
throne room while the second unit continued working with Guinness and
Yoda. The shot the second unit got was of Guinness and "the little green
thing" standing against a black velvet backrop for *Jedi*'s final scene.

Guinness was relieved to be working with real actors again—if you can
call Yoda a real actor. In *Empire*, all his scenes were filmed of him alone
against the backdrop. With special effects, he was given an "aura" and com-
posited into the shot with Mark Hamill. It worked out okay, but as Kazanjian
said: "...It's awfully hard to get into the scene and deliver your lines to

another actor who isn't even there." Because of a hoarseness caused by the flu, Guinness "looped," or rerecorded, his lines later.

On May 10, 1982, Harrison Ford and Mark Hamill completed their last shot together as Han Solo and Luke Skywalker. Autographing stills, Hamill wrote, "Follow the Force," and Ford signed his, "Force yourself." Ten days later, as the little people playing the Ewoks climbed out of their costumes, George Lucas watched the end of filming. There was still a year of postproduction to go. "The easy part is over," Lucas sighed.

"*Empire* and *Jedi* were what that first film was supposed to be," George Lucas says now. "[*Jedi*] is paced a little bit faster. Each movie moves a little bit faster. . . . When we started, we said, 'Okay, now we're gonna do it the way we always wanted to do. We've got the money, we've got the knowledge — this is it."

". . . . You look at the Jabba the Hutt scene [in *Jedi*] and say, 'Oh, that's what he wanted the cantina [in *Star Wars*] to be.' Or you look at the end battle, and you say, 'Oh, that's what the end battle was supposed to be in the first one.' But we couldn't have *done* this movie then. . . ."

There's an old saying: Be careful what you wish for, because you just might get it. Lucas wished for enough clout and financial backing to *really* dazzle us in *Jedi*. George Lucas and his collaborator Steven Spielberg think "*Jedi* is the best *Star Wars* movie ever made," as Spielberg puts it. I think they're wrong.

The Jabba the Hutt sequence is marvelous, mainly because of Jabba himself and because it resolves the fate of Han Solo from *Empire*. The scene in which Luke burns his father's body, dressed in his Darth Vader outfit and mask, is indescribably moving and powerful. That scene marks the end of an era — we're saying goodbye to a character of mythic dimensions. But too much of *Jedi* is. . . well, *too much*.

Lucas hurls dozens of aliens at us in the Jabba sequence, patently phony-looking aliens. The cantina scene in *Star Wars* worked precisely because it *was* a throwaway.

Lucas also cuts unmercifully back and forth between the three stories until our heads throb. In one theater, when Lucas cut from a forest scene to outer space, the audience, certain the reels were being played out of order, rioted and the showing had to be stopped!

Han and Leia's burgeoning romance, so charmingly handled and scripted in *Empire*, is all but forgotten in the relentless pace. And poor Harrison Ford, who wanted Han Solo to die in *Jedi*, seems to have inadvertently gotten his wish: Han Solo is almost absent from any meaningful participation in the film.

After *Star Wars*, a lot of cheap imitations were released. The producers of this trash thought it was the special effects that made that movie special; they were wrong. George Lucas apparently thinks the special effects make *Jedi* special; he is wrong. Apart from the film's conclusion — the return of Anakin

Skywalker, Luke's father—there is little human feeling in *Return of the Jedi*.

Many of Hollywood's *wunderkind*, those young, technically proficient directors comfortable with special effects, have looked upon classic SF films of yesteryear and said, "If someone like me, with enough money and special-effects talents behind him, remade those classics, they'd *really* be something." Well, remember the remakes of *Invasion of the Bodysnatchers*, *The Thing*, and *King Kong*, and films like *Twilight Zone — The Movie*? They weren't even close. The filmmakers left out precisely those ingredients that made the originals special: imagination, a good storyline, and characters you can care about.

Lucas and Spielberg, with unlimited budgets and access to state-of-the-art special effects, don't seem to realize that perhaps it was precisely the classics' lack of money that made their makers find ways around their limitations. (The first *Star Trek* movie went the special-effects/weak characterization route with predictable results; the sequels wisely returned to the characterizations and storylines which have kept the series on the air in syndication even today.) With Lucas overseeing the production and Spielberg directing, the first Indiana Jones film, *Raiders of the Lost Ark*, was a triumph. The second, *Indiana Jones and the Temple of Doom*, while certainly a thrilling amusement-park-ride of a movie, showed every sign of the series heading down *Jedi*'s dead-end path.

If George Lucas ever returns to his *Star Wars* saga, let's hope he rediscovers the inspiration that made *Star Wars* and *Empire* such delights. May the Force be with you, George.

44. *A Passage to India* (1984)

> "I'm usually attracted to roles I think are almost
> impossible for me to play. Don't ask me why."
> —Guinness on why he took the role of
> Professor Godbole in *A Passage to India.*

A Passage to India (hereafter just *Passage*) was Guinness' first film since *Return of the Jedi* in 1983 and was the sixth film in his ongoing collaboration with director David Lean. Lean had not made a film since the scathing reviews accorded *Ryan's Daughter* upon its release in 1970.

Before making *Lawrence of Arabia*, Lean and producer Sam Spiegel had been scouting locations in India for a film about the life of Gandhi—to be played by Alec Guinness. *Gandhi*, the 1982 Academy Award–winning film starring Ben Kingsley and directed by Richard Attenborough, showed that "serious," large-scale-but-intimate films (in other words, David Lean films) could still be made in the youth-oriented 1980s. The very success of *Gandhi*, the film Lean had wanted to make twenty years earlier, made possible Lean's version of E.M. Forster's classic 1924 novel, *A Passage to India.*

When asked by Harlan Kennedy in *Film Comment* why he likes to work with Guinness, Lean answered, "Well, Alec started his film career with me...it was a rather good working partnership."

In a Sunday *New York Times* piece on the film, Aljean Harmetz noted that "Mr. Lean's choice of Mr. Guinness is likely to be the most controversial casting in *A Passage to India.*"

Lean defended his choice of Guinness as an excellent character actor who could pull off the difficult role of Goldbole, whom he describes as "part mumbo-jumbo, part highly intelligent, cynical, part funny," with "a sort of extrasensory perception."

In Forster's novel, Godbole is described as being "elderly and wizen with a grey moustache and grey-blue eyes, and his complexion was as fair as a European's." To see Guinness as Godbole is to see Forster's description of the mystical Brahman come to living, breathing life.

Some critics and some Indian writers and intellectuals decry the point of view Lean's film takes—a British point of view, rather than an Indian. I find this a baffling criticism: What other point of view should an Anglo-American production of a classic British novel take? Indian filmmakers have the opportunity to show the British Raj (rule) from *their* unique perspective; it hardly seems fair to demand that perspective of an E.M. Forster novel or a David Lean film.

Passage's reviews were everything Lean's reviews for *Ryan's Daughter* were not. *Variety's* "Cart" wrote, "Magnificently crafted in the expected Lean manner and full of old-fashioned virtues of a sort that have largely disappeared from the modern cinema, the picture is...a return to the more intimate character pieces of [Lean's] mid-career.

"Given the context, there might be some quarrel with the casting of Alec Guinness as a lightly comic Indian sage, but his long working relationship with Lean should, by rights, obviate any serious objections."

Writing in *New York*, the usually negative David Denby says *Passage* "is built the old way, with brick, mortar, and stone. The narrative is solid, the characters pleasingly complex, the society they inhabit recognizably treacherous."

Noting Guinness' participation, Denby says, "Godbole [is] played by a rascally, flirtatious Alec Guinness, who steals scenes with his mild gaze and funny turban..." and closes by stating, "For all its pachyderms and mountains and crowds, *A Passage to India* attends to the hearts of its troubled characters, and that's something of which even the fanatically private Forster might have approved.

David Ansen's *Newsweek* review notes that "The craftsmanship of this movie is a marvel.... In this slapdash era, Lean's style appears especially seductive; there's a real passion in its gloss." About Guinness, Ansen writes, "Alec Guinness is shamelessly amusing as the transcendentally abstracted Professor Godbole," and concludes his piece by observing, "In the timing of the moonlit view of the Ganges, in the way a distant train crawls across a landscape, in the nuances that flow from one actor to another, Lean's personality is omnipresent. Relish it."

Rex Reed, in the *New York Post*, called *Passage* "The Best Movie of 1984. *A Passage to India* is genuine movie greatness. It is David Lean's masterpiece."

The Gannett News Service's William Wolf called it "A rich and memorable movie of the highest order, from master director David Lean. The acting is extraordinary."

Vincent Canby of the *New York Times* called *Passage* "David Lean's best work since *The Bridge on the River Kwai* and *Lawrence of Arabia*...intimate, funny and moving."

Arriving in India, Adela Quested (Judy Davis) and Mrs. Moore (Peggy Ashcroft), travel to Chandrapore to meet Ronny Heaslop (Nigel Havers), who is Mrs. Moore's son and Miss Quested's likely future husband. Both women are distressed by the condescending way the British treat the Indians and saddened to see that Ronny, the city magistrate, is well on his way to becoming a "proper sahib."

Mrs. Moore meets a handsome young Indian, Doctor Aziz (Victor Banerjee), at a moonlit mosque, and the moslem Aziz is impressed by Mrs. Moore's respect for both the mosque and himself.

Since Mrs. Moore and Adela wish to meet Indians socially, Turton, the "Collector" (Richard Wilson), arranges a "bridge" party — a social gathering to bridge East and West. Adela and Mrs. Moore are again mortified by the traditions of the British Raj, which reduce the Indians to second-class citizens in their own country. Adela meets Richard Fielding (James Fox) and arranges to meet Professor Godbole and Doctor Aziz at Fielding's residence.

When Mrs. Moore meets the Brahman Professor Godbole (Guinness), she is troubled by his knowing and penetrating gaze and immediately drops her eyes. She and Fielding go off, leaving Adela with Aziz and Godbole, who explains that Mrs. Moore is a reincarnation of an earlier existence. Aziz impetuously invites the two women on a picnic at the Marabar caves.

An angry Ronny breaks up the gathering and drives Adela and his mother home. At a polo match, Adela tells Ronny she thinks their marriage would be a mistake.

Bicycling into the countryside, Adela comes upon an ancient abandoned temple with massive erotic carvings. The blatantly sexual images disturb her, and she is frightened away by a band of screeching monkeys. Adela now says she *will* marry Ronny.

Fielding and Godbole miss the train to the caves when the professor's prayers make them arrive too late at the station. At the first cave, Mrs. Moore feels claustrophobic and is unsettled by a strange echo. She drops out of the expedition, leaving Aziz and Adela to go on alone with the guide.

Aziz leaves Adela alone for a moment after she asks about his dead wife. Adela enters a cave alone. Returning, Aziz cannot find her. Suddenly, Adela is in full flight down the mountain. She is picked up by Mrs. Callendar (Anne Firbank), leaving a bewildered Aziz behind.

Back at Chandrapore, Aziz is arrested as Fielding promises to find out why and to help him. Hysterical, wounded by brambles and thorns, Adela has accused Dr. Aziz of attacking her. Aziz languishes in jail while his personal things are violated and his name besmirched. Fielding's loyalty to Aziz prompts him to renounce his membership in the Chandrapore Club.

Mrs. Moore leaves Chandrapore by train. Sensing a presence outside, she looks out the window to see Professor Godbole pressing his palms together and holding his arms above his head in a silent gesture of communion and farewell.

After the trial begins, Mrs. Moore, aboard a ship at sea, hears the threatening echo from the cave and collapses and dies. At the trial, Adela, led back to her eventful experiences at the caves by prosecutor McBryde (Michael Culver), suddenly confesses that she's no longer sure she was attacked, and Aziz is freed. Mrs. Moore is buried at sea.

Because Adela is an outcast from her own people, Fielding reluctantly sees her safely to his college quarters. Adela notes that, after confessing to her "hallucination," the echo in her head is gone. Aziz, having seen Fielding with his "enemy," feels their friendship cannot last. At last Aziz is an Indian.

Aziz begins again in a town near the Himalayas, where Godbole is the minister of education. Godbole tells Aziz that Fielding has tracked him down and is coming to see him, bringing along his wife—whom Aziz supposes must be Adela Quested.

But Fielding introduces Aziz to Stella (Sandra Hotz [Lady Lean]), his wife and the daughter of Mrs. Moore. Feeling restored, Aziz writes to Adela back in England. She reads his letter and stares out a rain-streaked window— what is in her heart we cannot guess.

David Lean wanted to return to picture making with what he hoped would be the best and most complete account of the H.M.S. *Bounty* saga, with particular attention paid to restoring Captain Bligh's reputation. As Lean has said, "Captain Bligh is a much maligned man. I think he was a terrific chap, though he had no sense of humor. Christian was a young man who just got swept away by the South Seas."

Lean and his favorite collaborator, Robert Bolt (*Lawrence of Arabia*, *Doctor Zhivago*) wrote the interconnected scripts for two separate films. The first would end with what Lean calls "the fantastic voyage of Captain Bligh in the open boat across the Pacific to Australia." The second would focus on "the search by a terrible man called Captain Edwards for Christian and his men."

Although Lean called the scripts "the best I've ever had," neither film was made. The productions got as far as the building of a full-scale Bounty in Tahiti, but after Bolt had been incapacitated by a stroke, producer Dino De Laurentiis showed up to tell Lean that the film was off because he could not come up with financing to produce one film, let alone two.

(*The Bounty* was finally made by Dino De Laurentiis and released in 1984. Directed by Roger Donaldson and starring Anthony Hopkins as Captain Bligh and Mel Gibson as Christian, the film was more critically than financially successful. Leonard Maltin's *TV Movies* called it "interesting all the way, but emotionally aloof.")

In 1958, after seeing the play that Santha Rama Rau had fashioned from Forster's novel, Lean wanted very much to make a film version of the book. Many people believed the book to be unfilmable—including Forster himself. Forster didn't like the cinema and was afraid that a film would not do justice to his finely wrought characterizations.

Forster died in 1970, and the rights to his novel became the property of King's College, Cambridge. Eventually, John Brabourne, who'd tried unsuccessfully for twenty-five years to purchase the film rights, was able to secure them from King's College. Brabourne and coproducer Richard Goodwin called Lean to suggest he direct the picture. Lean's first comment was "What *did* happen in the caves?"

For the first ten years of his life, Richard Goodwin had lived in India, and he returned in 1958 to make *Harry Black and the Tiger* with John Brabourne. Before *Passage*, the team of Brabourne and Goodwin was best known for producing several Agatha Christie mysteries, beginning with *Murder on the Orient Express* in 1974. Brabourne also produced Guinness' 1962 film *H.M.S. Defiant*.

Goodwin has said getting the rights to the movie was easier than getting the money to produce it: "One studio said they would give us the money if we had an explicit rape scene in the caves. Another said it was a waste having a central character played by Peggy Ashcroft because young people are bored by old people." Lean called the studio executives "money-obsessed," and observed that one studio head would back the film only if Adela rather than the aged Mrs. Moore could encounter Aziz in the moonlight at the mosque.

Surviving at the Bel-Aire Hotel by living on their American Express cards and ignoring bills, the two producers were constantly turned down. "Everybody said, 'This will be a good art house film' when they turned us down," Lean told reporter Aljean Harmetz.

As the production date grew nearer, it was necessary for Lean to dip into his own funds to finance the trip to India to find suitable locations. As Lean told Harmetz, "I went out on a limb and hoped for the best."

Finally Brabourne and Goodwin put together the money for the production, including a "pre-buy" for pay-TV by Home Box Office. Because of HBO's up-front money, *Passage* was filmed with a screen aspect ratio of 1.85:1. Cinematographer Ernest Day "marked the ground glass of the Panaflex Gold with two vertical side lines to indicate TV cutoff." Obviously, *Passage* will lose much on TV, but it was filmed with its eventual sale to that medium in mind.

Since Robert Bolt was unable to work with Lean on the script, Maggie Unsworth, Lean's script supervisor since 1942, suggested that Lean "have a go" at the script himself.

It wasn't easy. While Lean credited Forster's novel for its "wonderful interplay of characters," he found Forster's "storytelling" abilities to be limited. Lean also discovered that he could not convincingly show the novel's famous ending and, hence, has been castigated by the "it's-not-exactly-like-the-book" crowd for changing the original:

> "Why can't we be friends now?" said [Fielding], holding [Aziz] affectionately. "It's what I want. It's what you want."
> But the horses didn't want it—they swerved apart; the earth didn't want it, sending up rocks through which riders must pass single file; the temples, the tank, the jail, the palace, the birds, the carrion, the Guest House, that came into view as they issued from the gap and saw Mau beneath: they didn't want it, they said in their hundred voices, "No, not yet," and the sky said, "No, not there."

When interviewer Harlan Kennedy noted that Lean had to compress incidents in the novel and invent others, he asked Lean about the scene where Adela encounters the erotic temple carvings and is menaced by the monkeys. "That's totally mine, yes," Lean said. He noted that he added the "temple" scene to vividly depict Adela's slowly awakening sexual desires, making her charges against Dr. Aziz seem more plausible. "I meant it to be sort of sexually frightening," Lean explained, "you know, her feelings, the roaring, and, my God, the monkeys going after her."

Lean retained Ronny's snide remark about Aziz's collar climbing up his neck—showing his supposed fundamentally Indian "slackness that reveals the race."

Lean can allow us to hear the echo of the Marabar caves directly and literally on his Dolby stereo soundtrack, but Forster rendered the same sound, unforgettably, this way: " 'Boum' is the sound as far as the human alphabet can express it, or 'bou-oum,' or 'ou-boum' ...."

To Mrs. Moore, in the novel, the echo, touching deep within her soul, seems to murmur, "Pathos, piety, courage—they exist, but are identical, and so is filth. Everything exists, nothing has value." Lean's script does not (cannot?) make clear the spiritual bonding the echo induces between Mrs. Moore and Professor Godbole, or the futility it inspires, causing her to retreat from India and leave Aziz to his fate.

The novel also leaves open the possibility that if anything *did* happen at the caves, the guide could have done it. Lean, probably sensibly, does not further complicate an already complicated situation by allowing that speculation to enter the film.

Passage began principal photography on November 14, 1983, in Bangalore, India. The Maharajah's palace in Bangalore was a ten-minute drive from the film company's main hotel, and its extensive grounds provided Lean with a convenient "back lot" on which to build his sets depicting the fictitious Chandrapore.

Covering almost six acres, the sets—including bungalows and a complete street bazaar—were so convincing that old India hands were fooled into thinking them the real thing.

The Marabar caves are at the heart of the novel, and the film and Lean selected Ramanagaram and Savandurga for the crucial scenes set there. While the spectacular and multicolored granite cliffs were photographically perfect—the sun fell on them all day—they had no natural caves. The company's technicians simply blasted openings into the face of the cliffs, and the cave interiors were sets constructed in England.

Other Shepperton studio sets, in addition to the cave interiors, included the train interiors, the courtroom interior, and the exterior of the ocean liner (which was also partly a matte painting).

An arduous journey by car from Bangalore, on a 7,000-foot-high plateau, is the town of Ootacamund (called "Ooty" by the British soldiers in the days of the Empire). The rack railway that winds its way up from the plains was used—steam engine, wooden railway cars, and all—for the scenes showing Dr. Aziz and the two Englishwomen on their way to the Marabar caves. Victor Banerjee ("I'm Douglas Fairbanks!") did his own stunt work, hanging onto the side of the train as it crossed over a gorge.

The film's final scenes were shot in Kashmir, where Dr. Aziz's office was constructed to overlook the wooden bridge of Fateh Kadel which spans the Jhelum River at Srinagar.

Guinness went to India in January, 1984, "to see what I could absorb" and to study the movements of Brahmans to perfect the fatalistic Professor Godbole's walk. As Guinness noted, "Until I decide how a character walks, nothing happens."

Guinness worked hard to learn an intricate temple dance, which was to end the film, but Lean decided to cut it—something Sir Alec did not appreciate: "I have a great fondness for David, but the atmosphere on the *Passage* set was overly tense. And we did have a dust-up concerning the small dancing scene I had. The dancing was nothing great, but I had rehearsed quite a bit for it, and then David didn't even come round the day I did it. He said he never liked Indian dancing anyway."

There is a more crucial moment from the novel which Lean did not include in his screenplay. When Ronny arrives at Fielding's place and sees Adela mingling too familiarly with Aziz and Godbole ("I don't like to see an English girl left smoking with two Indians"), there is a moment of great tension. It is precisely at this instant that Professor Godbole, earlier asked to sing, begins to do so—dissolving the tension. I think Lean's omission is a great loss for both the film and for Guinness' performance.

As Godbole, Guinness is, as always, subtle, perceptive, and insinuatingly authentic. His Godbole speaks and acts much the same as the Godbole of Forster's novel, yet Guinness brings him to life in a way Forster's prose cannot. Maddeningly obscure and fatalistic, Guinness' Godbole is a welcome breath of humor. Where some see Lean's condescension, others (including this author) see a character who indeed represents the "inscrutability" of the East.

The important central role of Dr. Aziz went to Indian actor Victor Banerjee. Lean interviewed Banerjee at great length. Finally, after six hours of discussion, Banerjee blurted out, "David, am I playing Dr. Aziz?" "Of course you are," Lean told him.

At the start of filming, Lean and Banerjee clashed over the latter's accent: the Indian actor did not wish to play "an obedient English sheepdog." Banerjee won out, and he gives a performance of astonishing range and subtlety.

Judy Davis, an Australian actress born in 1956, is best known for the Australian-made *My Brilliant Career* (1979), for which she won a British Film Academy award. Round-faced and serious looking, she nonetheless is almost too pretty to portray the unattractive Adela Quested. Davis' performance is top-notch and complements Banerjee's perfectly.

Dame Peggy Ashcroft was born in 1907 and made her first film in 1933. She came to more prominence with a role in Hitchcock's classic 1935 film *The Thirty-Nine Steps*, and first appeared on Broadway in Robert Morley's *Edward, My Son*. After spending most of 1982 in India filming Paul Scott's *The Jewel in the Crown* for British television, Dame Peggy had no desire to spend 1984 there filming *Passage*. But Lean prevailed upon her to play the part of Mrs. Moore, and she grudgingly accepted.

As Mrs. Moore, Dame Peggy is warm, open, human, and vulnerable. Her disgust at the British Raj is communicated directly and simply to the audience, and her death leaves the viewer saddened and compelled to ponder the meaning of life.

James Fox, born in 1939, has the role of Fielding, the good-hearted schoolteacher who befriends both Dr. Aziz and Adela. Apart from Mrs. Moore, he is the only admirable Briton on view in the film.

Despite their dust-ups, Guinness and Lean remain friends. Guinness, however, has confessed to losing some of the old fire: "I owe him an enormous debt. He's very authoritative, a very strong personality...something of a perfectionist. Like me? Maybe when I was young I was—but I think I've chucked that aside. I like things to be neatly and cleanly done...but I don't mind now if they're a bit wrong."

Even in India, Guinness and Lean are known and revered for their considerable joint accomplishments: When the two men entered a restaurant together, the orchestra began to play the "Colonel Bogey March" from *The Bridge on the River Kwai*.

Lean has admitted having "thoughts that *Passage* might be my last movie." Certainly, at seventy-six, Lean cannot hope to withstand the rigors of film direction much longer, no matter how fit and healthy he remains today. If *Passage* does turn out to be his last film, he could not ask for a better capstone to a long and distinguished career.

After *Passage*, Guinness signed to portray Cervantes' addled knight in a new version of *Don Quixote*, to be filmed in Spain in 1985, and co-starring Leo McKern as his faithful servant, Sancho Panza.

For Guinness, the work continues.

Filmography:
Cast and Crew Credits

1. *Great Expectations*

Great Britain. Cineguild-Rank. Released by Universal-International Pictures. 1946. 118 min. (10,620 feet). B/W.

Producer: Ronald Neame. Director: David Lean. Executive producer: Anthony Havelock-Allan. Screenplay: David Lean, Ronald Neame, and Anthony Havelock-Allan with Kay Walsh and Cecil McGivern, based on the novel by Charles Dickens. Director of photography: Guy Green. Camera operator: Nigel Huke. Sound: Stanley Lambourne, Desmond Dew, and Gordon K. McCallum. Music: Walter Goehr, Kenneth Pakeman, G. Linley. Art direction: Wilfred Shingeton. Production designer: John Bryan. Conductor: Walter Goehr with the National Symphony Orchestra. Editor: Jack Harris. Production manager: Norman Spencer. Costumes: Sophie Harris of Motley; Margaret Furse, assistant. Continuity: Margaret Sibley. Choreography: Suria Magito.

With

John Mills (Pip), Anthony Wager (Pip as a Boy), Valerie Hobson (Estella), Jean Simmons (Estella as a Girl), Bernard Miles (Joe Gargery), Francis L. Sullivan (Jaggers), Finlay Currie (Magwitch), Alec Guinness (Herbert Pocket), John Forrest (Herbert as a Boy), Marita Hunt (Miss Havisham), Ivor Bernard (Wemmick), Freda Jackson (Mrs. Joe), Torin Thatcher (Bentley Drummle), Eileen Erskine (Biddy), Hay Petrie (Uncle Pumblechock), George Hayes (Compeyson, the Scar-Faced Convict), Richard George (Sergeant), Everly Gregg (Sarah Pocket), John Burch (Mr. Wopsie), O.B. Clarance (the Aged Parent), Anne Holland (a Relation).

2. *Oliver Twist*

A GFD/Cineguild Production. Distributed by Eagle-Lion and United Artists. 1948/1951. 116 min. U.S. 104 min. (9360 feet). B/W.

Producer: Ronald Neame. Director: David Lean. Screenplay: David Lean and Stanley Haynes. Based on the novel *Oliver Twist* by Charles Dickens. Photography: Guy Green. Camera operator: Oswald Morris. Sound: Stanley Lambourne and G.K. McCallum. Music: Sir Arnold Bax. Conductor: Muir Matheson. Orchestra: Philharmonic Orchestra of London; Harriet Cohen, solo pianoforte. Art direction: John Bryan. Editor: Jack Harris. Production manager: Norman Spencer. Assistant director: George Pollock. Costumes: Margaret Furse. Makeup: Stuart Freeborn. Continuity: Margaret Sibley.

With

Alec Guinness (Fagin), Robert Newton (Bill Sikes), Kay Walsh (Nancy), John Howard Davies (Oliver), Francis L. Sullivan (Mr. Bumble, the Beadle), Henry Stevenson (Mr. Brownlow), Mary Clare (the Matron), Anthony Newley (the Artful Dodger), Josephine Stuart (Oliver's Mother), Ralph Truman (Monks), Gibb McLaughlin (Mr. Sowerberry), Amy Veness (Mrs. Bedwin), Frederick Lloyd (Mrs. Grimwig), Henry Edwards (Police Official), Ivor Barnard (Chairman of the Board), Maurice Denham (Chief of Police), Michael Dear (Noah Claypole), Michael Ripper (Barney), Peter Bull (Landlord of the Three Cripples Inn), Deirdre Doyle (Mrs. Thingummy), Diana Dors (Charlotte), Kenneth Downy (Workhouse Master), W.G. Fay (Bookseller), Edie Martin (Annie), Gravely Edwards (Mr. Fang), John Potter (Charley Bates), Maurice Jones (Workhouse Doctor), and Hattie Jacques and Betty Paul.

3. Kind Hearts and Coronets

Great Britain. Ealing Studios. 1949. 106 min. (9540 feet). B/W.

Producer: Michael Balcon. Director: Robert Hamer. Screenplay: Robert Hamer and John Dighton, from the novel *Israel Rank* by Roy Horniman (1910). Director of photography: Douglas Slocombe. Production supervisor: Hal Mason. Assistant director: Norman Higgans. Sound supervisor: Stephen Dolby. Sound recordist: John Mitchell. Art direction: William Kellner. Editor: Peter Tanner. Continuity: Phyllis Crocker. Music: Mozart.

With

Dennis Price (Louis Mazzini/His Father), Joan Greenwood (Sibella), Valerie Hobson (Edith), Alec Guinness (Young Ascoyne D'Ascoyne/Ascoyne D'Ascoyne/Henry D'Ascoyne/Reverend Lord Henry D'Ascoyne/Lady Agatha D'Ascoyne/Admiral Lord Horatio D'Ascoyne/General Lord Rufus D'Ascoyne/Ethelred D'Ascoyne, Eighth Duke of Chalfont), Audrey Fildes (Mrs. Mazzini), John Penrose (Lionel), John Salew (Mrs. Perkins), Anne Valery (Girl in Punt), Barbara Leake (Schoolmistress), Peggy Ann Clifford (Maud), Cecil Ramage (Counsel), Hugh Griffith (Lord High Steward), Clive Morton (Governor), Miles Malleson (Hangman), Arthur Lowe (Reporter).

4. A Run for Your Money

Great Britain. A GFD release of an Ealing Studios–Michael Balcon Production. 1949. 85 min. (7650 feet). B/W.

Producer: Michael Balcon. Director: Charles Frend. Associate producer: Leslie Norman. Screenplay: Charles Frend, Leslie Norman, and Richard Hughes. Story: Clifford Evans. Additional dialogue: Diana Morgan. Director of photography: Douglas Slocombe. Art director: William Kellner. Editor: Michael Truman. Music: Ernest Irving.

With

Donald Houston (Dai), Meredith Edwards (Twm), Moira Lister (Jo), Alec Guinness (Whimple), Hugh Griffith (Huw), Julie Milton (Bronwen), Clive

Morton (Editor), Joyce Grenfell (Mrs. Pargeter), Dorothy Bramhall (Jane), Edward Rigby (Beefeater), Gabrielle Brune (Crooner), Patric Doonan (Conductor), Leslie Perrins (Barney), Peter Edwards (Davies), Desmond Walter-Ellis (Photographer), Andrew Leigh (Pawnbroker).

5. Last Holiday

Great Britain. An ABPC-Watergate Production. Released by Associated British–Pathé. 1950. 83 min. (7470 feet). B/W.

Producers: Stephen Mitchell, A.D. Peters, and J.B. Priestly. Director: Henry Cass. Screenplay: J.B. Priestly. Photography: Ray Elton. Editor: Monica Kimick. Music: Francis Chagrin.

With

Alec Guinness (George Bird), Beatrice Campbell (Sheila Rockingham), Kay Walsh (Mrs. Poole), Coco Aslan (Gambini), Jean Colin (Daisy Clarence), Muriel George (Lady Oswington), Brian Worth (Derek Rockingham), Esme Cannon (Miss Fox), Bernard Lee (Inspector Wilton), Sidney James (Joe Clarence), Campbell Cotts (Belinghurst), Moultries Kelsall (Sir Robert Kyle), Madame E. Kirkwood-Hackett (Miss Hatfield), Wilfred Hyde-White (Chalfont), Erick Maturin (Wrexham), Helen Cherry (Miss Mellows), Ernest Thesiger (Sir Trevor Lampington), Heather White (Maggie, the Maid).

6. The Mudlark

United States. A Darryl F. Zanuck Presentation. Twentieth Century–Fox Productions Limited. (Filmed at London Film Studio. Shepperton, England.) 1950. 99 min. (8910 feet). B/W.

Producer: Nunnally Johnson. Director: Jean Negulesco. Screenplay: Nunnally Johnson. Based on the novel of the same name by Theodore Bonnet. Director of photography: Georges Perinal. Art director: L.P. Norman. Special effects: W. Percy Day. Film editor: Thelma Myers. Sound recordist: Buster Ambler. Music: William Alwyn. Played by the Royal Philharmonic Orchestra. Conducted by: Muir Mathieson.

With

Irene Dunne (Queen Victoria), Alec Guinness (Benjamin Disraeli), Andrew Ray (Wheeler, the Mudlark), Finlay Currie (John Brown), Beatrice Campbell (Lady Emily Prior), Anthony Steel (Lieutenant Charles McHatten), Raymond Lovell (Sergeant Footman Naseby), Majorie Fielding (Lady Margaret Prior), Ronan O'Casey (Slattery), Edward Rigby (the Watchman), Robin Stevens (Herbert), William Strange (Sparrow), Constance Smith (Kate Noonan), Kynasion Reeves (General Sir Ponsonby), Wilfred Hyde-White (Tucker), Earnest Clark (Hammond).

7. The Lavender Hill Mob

An Ealing Studios Production. 1951. General Film Distributors, Ltd. 78 min. (7020 feet). B/W.

Producer: Michael Balcon. Director: Charles Crichton. Original screenplay: T.E.B. Clarke. Production supervisor: Hal Mason. Director of photography: Douglas Slocombe. Editor: Seth Holt. Unit production manager: Slim Hand. Art director: William Kellner. Sound supervisor: Stephan Dalby. Camera operator: Jeff Seaholme. Assistant director: Norman Higgans. Recordist: Leslie Hammond. Continuity: Phyllis Crocker, Costume designer: Anthony Pendleson. Special effects: Sydney Pearson. Makeup: Earnest Taylor and H. Wilton. Additional photography: Geoffrey Faithful. Special processes: Geoffrey Dickinson. Associate producer: Michael Truman. Music: Georges Auric. Played by the Philharmonia Orchestra conducted by Ernest Irving.

With

Alec Guinness (Holland), Stanley Holloway (Pendlebury), Sidney James (Lackery), Alfie Bass (Shorty), Majorie Fielding (Mrs. Chalk), Edie Martin (Miss Evesham), Ronald Adam (Bank Official), Clive Morton (Police Sergeant), John Gregson (Farrow), Sidney Tafler (Stallholder), Patrick Barr (Inspector), Meredith Edwards (P.C. Edwards), Robert Shaw (Police Scientist), Michael Trubshawe (British Ambassador), Audrey Hepburn (Chiquita), and Jacques Branius, Paul Demel, Eugene Deckers, and Andrea Malandrinos.

8. The Man in the White Suit

An Ealing Studios Release (released in the United States by the Rank Organization and Universal–International). 1951. 85 min. (7650 ft.) B/W.

Producer: Michael Balcon. Director: Alexander Mackendrick. Screenplay: Roger MacDougall, John Dighton, and Alexander Mackendrick. Cinematographer: Douglas Slocombe. Art director: Jim Moraban. Editor: Bernard Gribble. Special effects: Sidney Pearson. Special processes: Geoffrey Dickinson. Associate producer: Sidney Cole. Sound editor: Mary Hubberfield. Additional photography: Lionel Banes. Costume design: Anthony Mendleson. Makeup: Ernest Taylor and Harry Frampton. Scientific advisor: Geoffrey Myers. Music: Benjamin Frankel. Played by: The Philharmonia Orchestra. Conducted by: Ernest Irving. Production supervisor: Hal Mason.

With

Alec Guinness (Sidney Stratton), Joan Greenwood (Daphne Birnley), Cecil Parker (Alan Birnley), Michael Gough (Michael Corland), Ernest Thesiger (Sir John Kierlaw), Howard Marion Crawford (Cranford), Vida Hope (Bertha), John Rudling (Wilson), Patric Doonan (Frank), Duncan Lamont (Harry),

Henry Mollison (Hoskins), Harold Goodwin (Wilkins), Colin Gordon (Hill), Joan Harben (Miss Johnson), Arthur Howard (Roberts), Roddy Hughes (Green), Stuart Latham (Harrison), Miles Malleson (the Tailor), Edie Martin (Mrs. Watson), Mandy Miller (Gladdie/the Little Girl), Charlotte Mitchel (Hill Girl), Olaf Olson (Knusen), Ewan Roberts (Fotheringay), Charles Saynor (Pete), Russell Waters (Davidson), Brian Worth (King), George Benson (the Lodger), Frank Atkinson (the Baker), Charles Cullum (First Company Director), F.B.J. Sharp (Second Company Director), Scott Harold (Express Reporter), Jack Howarth (Receptionist), Jack McNaughton (Taxi Driver), Judith Furse (Nurse), Billy Russell (Night Watchman).

9. The Card/The Promoter

A J. Arthur Rank/British Film Makers Production. Released in the United States by Universal–International. 1952. 91 min. (8190 feet). Color.

Producer: John Bryan. Director: Ronald Neame. Screenplay: Eric Ambler. Based on the novel The Card by Arnold Bennett. Director of photography: Oswald Morris (B.S.C.). Editor: Clive Donner. Associate producer: Bob McNaught. Production controller: Arthur Alcott. Art director: T. Hopewell Ash. Exterior photography: Ernest Steward. Sound recordists: C.C. Stevens and Gordon K. McCallum. Sound editor: Harry Miller. Costumes: "Motley." Assistant director: Max Varnel. Makeup: W. Partleton. Hairdressing: Biddy Chrystal. Special effects: W. Warrington. Dance arranger: Suria Magito. Music: William Alwyn. Conducted by Muir Mathieson.

With

Alec Guinness (Edward Henry "Denry" Machin), Glynis Johns (Ruth Earp), Valerie Hobson (the Countess of Chell), Petula Clark (Nellie Cotterill), Edward Chapman (Mr. Duncalf), Veronica Turleigh (Mrs. Machin), George Devine (Mr. Calvert), Gibb McLaughlin (Emery), Frank Pettingell (Police Superintendent), Joan Hickson (Mrs. Codleyn), Michael Hordern (Bank Manager), Alison Leggatt (Mrs. Cotterill), Peter Copley (Shillitoe), Deirdre Doyle (Widow Hullins), and Joey the Mule.

10. Malta Story

Great Britain. A J. Arthur Rank Organization Presentation. A Theta Film Production. Released by United Artists. 1953. 103 min. (9270 feet). B/W.

Producer: Peter de Sarigny. Director: Brian Desmond Hurst. Screenplay: William Fairchild and Nigel Balchin. Story: William Fairchild. Based on an idea by Thorold Dickinson and Peter de Sarigny. Director of photography: Robert Krasker. Film editor, second unit director: Michael Gordon. Production manager: H.R.R. Attwooll. Assistant director: George Pollock. Music:

William Alwyn. Conducted by: Muir Mathieson. Art director: John Howell.
Second unit cameraman: E. Steward. Camera operator: H.A.R. Thomson.
Sound editor: Eric Wood. Sound recordists: John W. Mitchell and Gordon
K. McCallum. Special effects: Bill Warrington and Albert Whitlock. Effects
cameraman: Bert Marshall. Makeup: W.T. Partleton. Continuity: Tilly Day.
Production controller for Pinewood Studios: Arthur Alcott.

With

Alec Guinness (Flight Lieutenant Peter Ross), Jack Hawkins (Air Officer Com-
manding), Anthony Steel (Bartlett), Muriel Pavlow (Maria), Flora Robson
(Melita), Rence Asherson (Joan), Ralph Truman (Admiral Banks), Reginald
Tate (Payne), Hugh Burden (Eden), Ronald Adam (Control Operator), Nigel
Stock (Guiseppe), Harold Siddons (Matthews), Colin Loudan (O'Conner),
Edward Chaffers (Stripey), Stuart Burge (Paolo), Noel Willman (Hobley),
Rosalie Crutchley (Carmella), Jerry Desmonde (General), Ivor Barnard (Old
Man), Michael Medwin (Ramsey), Peter Bull (Flying Officer).

11. *The Captain's Paradise*

Great Britain. London Films. 1953. 93 min. (8370 feet). B/W.

Producer: Anthony Kimmins. Director: Anthony Kimmins. Screenplay: Alec
Coppel and Nicholas Phipps, from an original story by Alec Coppel. Director
of photography: Ted Scaife. Music: Malcom Arnold.

With

Alec Guinness (Captain Henry St. James), Celia Johnson (Maud), Yvonne De
Carlo (Nita), Charles Goldner (Chief Officer Ricco), Miles Malleson (Lawrence
St. James), Bill Fraser (Absalom), Tutte Lemkow (Principal Dancer), Nicholas
Phipps (the Major), Walter Grisham (Bob), and Ferdy Mayne, George
Benson, Alejandro Martinez, Andreas Melandrines, Armando Guinle, Paul
Armstrong, Roy Purcell, Raymond Hoole, Henry Longhurst, Bernard Rebel,
Ambrosine Philpotts, Catherine Ferrez, Roger Delgado, Walter Crisham,
Joyce Barbour, Peter Bull, Claudia Grey, Ann Heffernan, Arthur Gomez, Joss
Ambler, Victor Fairly, Michael Balfour, Robert Adair, Sebastion Cabot, and
Jacinta Dicks.

12. *Father Brown / The Detective*

Great Britain. A Facet Production. Released by Columbia Pictures. (Made at
Riverside Studios, London, England). 1954. 91 min. (8190 feet). B/W.

Producer: Paul F. Moss. Director: Robert Hamer. Associate producer: Vivian
A. Cox. Based on the "Father Brown" stories by G.K. Chesterton. Adapted
by Thelma Schnee. Screenplay by Thelma Schnee and Robert Hamer. Music:
Georges Auric. Played by: the Royal Philharmonic Orchestra. Conducted by:

Muir Mathieson. Director of photography: Harry Waxman. Production manager: Leigh Aman. Editor: Gordon Hales. Art director: John Hawksworth. Camera operator: Jimmy Bawden. Assistant director: Max Varnel. Continuity: Phyllis Crocker. Costume designer: Julia Squire. Makeup: Bob Lawrence. Hair stylist: Pauline Trent. Sound recordists: George Burgess and L.B. Bulkeley.

With

Alec Guinness (Father Brown), Peter Finch (Flambeau), Cecil Parker (the Bishop), Joan Greenwood (Lady Warren), Bernard Lee (Inspector Valentine), Sidney James (Bert Parkinson), Gerard Oury (Inspector Dubois), Ernest Thesiger (the Viscomte), Ernest Clark (Bishop's Secretary), Aubrey Woods (Charlie), John Salew (Station Sergeant), Sam Kydd (Scotland Yard Sergeant), John Horsely (Inspector Wilkins), Jack McNaughton (Railway Guard), Hugh Dempster (Man in Bowler Hat), Eugene Deckers (French Cavalry Officer), Betty Bascomb (French Widow), Diana Van Proosdy (Waitress), Diono Galvani (Italian Professor), Lance Maraschal (Texan Millionaire), Noel Howlett (Auctioneer), Marne Maitland (Maharajah), Austin Trevor (the Herald), Hugo Schuster (Optician), Guido Lorraine (Cafe Patron), Jim Gerald (French Station Master), Daniel Clerice (Garagiste), Everly Gregg (Governess), and the Singers and Dancers of the Matisconia de Macon.

13. *To Paris with Love*

Great Britain. GFD/Two Cities. 1955. 78 min. (7020 feet). Technicolor.

Producer: Antony Darnborough. Director: Robert Hamer. Screenplay: Robert Buckner. From a story by Sterling Noel. (Additional material— uncredited—by Robert Hamer and Antony Darnborough). Music: Edwin Astley. Conducted by Muir Mathieson. Art director: Maurice Carter. Production controller: Arthur Alcott. Editor: Anne V. Coates. Camera operator: Dudley Lovell. Recordists: Gordon K. McCallum, C.K. Stevens. Makeup: W.T. Partleton. Assistant director: Stanley Hosgood. Technicolor consultant: Joan Bridges. Sound editor: Roger Cherril.

With

Alec Guinness (Col. Sir Edgar Fraser), Odile Versois (Lisette Marconnet), Vernon Gray (Jon Fraser), Jacques Francois (Victor de Colville), Elina Labourdette (Sylvia Gilbert), Austin Trevor (Leon de Colville), Claude Romain (Georges Duprez), Maureen Davis (Suzanne de Colville), Jacques Brunius (Aristide Marconnet), Pamela Sterling (Mme. Marconnet), Molly Hartley Milburn (Mme. Alvarez), Michael Anthony (Pierre), Andre Mikhelson (Head Porter), Jacques Cey (Night Porter), Nicholas Bruce (Night Clerk), Toni Frost (Vendeuse).

14. The Prisoner

Great Britain. B & D Film Corporation. Released by Columbia Pictures. 1955. 94 min. (8460 feet). U.S. 91 min. B/W.

Producer: Vivian A. Cox. Director: Peter Glenville. Screenplay and story: Bridget Boland. Director of photography: Reg Wyer. Editor: Freddie Wilson. Music: Benjamin Frankel.

With

Alec Guinness (the Cardinal), Jack Hawkins (the Interrogator), Wilfred Lawson (the Jailer/Cell Warden), Kenneth Griffin (the Secretary), Ronald Lewis (the Warder/Guard), Jeanette Sterks (the Girl), Raymond Huntley (the General), Mark Dignam (the Governor), Gerard Heinz (the Doctor), and Michael Golden, Denis Shaw, Percy Herbert, Violet Farebrother, and Carl Duering.

15. The Ladykillers

Great Britain. A Michael Balcon Production for Ealing Studios. Presented by the J. Arthur Rank Organization. Released by Continental Distributing, Inc. 1955. 97 min. (8730 feet). Technicolor.

Producer: Michael Balcon. Director: Alexander Mackendrick. Screenplay: William Rose, from his story. Director of photography: Otto Heller. Associate producer: Seth Holt. Editor: Jack Harris. Music: Tristram Cary. Art direction: Jim Morahan.

With

Alec Guinness (Professor Marcus), Katie Johnson (Mrs. Wilberforce), Cecil Parker (Major Courtney), Herbert Lom (Louis Harvey), Peter Sellers (Harry Robinson), Danny Green (One Round Lawson), Jack Warner (Police Superintendent), Philip Stainton (Police Sergeant), Ewan Roberts (Constable), Frankie Howerd/Howard (Barrow Boy), Kenneth Conner (Taxi Driver), Fred Griffiths (Junkman), Harold Goodwin (Clerk), Stratford Johns (Security Guard), Edie Martin (Lettice), Helen Burls (Hypatia), Evelyn Kerry (Amelia), Phoebe Hodgson (Fourth Guest), Leonard Sharp (Pavement Artist), and Sam Kydd, Neil Wilson, Michael Corcoran, Robert Moore, Madge Brindley, and Peter Williams.

16. The Swan

A Dore Schary Production. MGM. 1956. 108 min. (9720 feet). Cinemascope. Eastman Color.

Producer: Dore Schary. Director: Charles Vidor. Screenplay: John Dighton.

From the play *The Swan* by Ferenc Molnar. Directors of photography: Joseph Ruttenberg and Robert Surtees. Music: Bronislau Kaper. Art directors: Cedric Gibbons and Randall Duell. Set decorators: Edwin B. Willis and Henry Grace. Color consultant: Charles K. Hagedon. Women's costumes: Helen Rose. Film editor: John Dunning. Recording supervisor: Dr. Wesly C. Miller. Assistant director: Ridgeway Callow. Hairstyles: Sidney Guilleroff. Makeup: William Tuttle.

With

Grace Kelly (Princess Alexandra), Alec Guinness (Prince Albert), Louis Jourdan (Dr. Nicholas Agi, the Professor), Jessie Royce Landis (Princess Beatrix), Agnes Moorehead (Queen Maria Dominika), Brian Aherne (Father Hyacinth), Leo G. Carroll (Caesar), Estelle Winwood (Symphorosa), Van Dyke Parks (George), Christopher Cook (Arsene), Robert Coote (Captain Wunderlich), Doris Lloyd (Countess Sibenstoyn), Edith Barrett (Beatrix's Maid).

17. *Barnacle Bill / All at Sea*

Great Britain. Ealing Studios. A Michael Balcon Production. Distributed by MGM. 1957. 87 min. (6030 feet). B/W.

Producer: Michael Balcon. Director: Charles Frend. Associate producer: Dennis Van Thal. Story and screenplay: T.E.B. Clarke. Director of photography: Douglas Slocombe. Art director: Alan Withy. Production supervisor: Hal Mason. Editor: Jack Harris. Unit production manager: Alfred Marcus. Sound supervisor: Stephen Dalby. Camera operator: Chic Waterson. Assistant director: Tom Pevsner. Recordist: Cyril Swern. Continuity: Jean Graham. Sound editor: Alistair MacIntyre. Makeup: Harry Frampton. Hairdresser: Elsie Alder. Dress designer: Sophie Devane. Radar photography: John Stewart. Music: John Addison. Played by: the Sinfonia of London. Conducted by: Dock Mathieson.

With

Alec Guinness (William Horatio Ambrose/Six Ancestors). Irene Browne (Arabella Barrington), Maurice Denham (Mayor), Victor Maddern (Figg), Percy Herbert (Tommy), George Rose (Bullen), Lionel Jeffries (Garrod), Harold Goodwin (Duckworth), Warren Mitchell (Obnoxious Entertainer), Miles Malleson (Old Angler), Frederick Piper (Harry), Richard Wattis (Registrar of Shipping), Eric Pohlmann (Liberama Consul), Jackie Collins (June), Donald Churchill (Teddy Boy), Donald Pleasance (Bank Teller), Allan Cuthbertson (Councillor).

18. *The Bridge on the River Kwai*

United States. A Horizon Pictures/Columbia Pictures Release. 1957. 161 min. (14,490 feet). Color.

Producer: Sam Spiegel. Director: David Lean. Screenplay: Pierre Boulle, Carl Foreman, Calder Willingham, and Michael Wilson. From the novel of the same name by Pierre Boulle. Director of photography: Jack Hilyard. Camera operator: Peter Newbrook. Sound: John Cox and John Mitchell. Music: Malcolm Arnold. *Colonel Bogey March* by Kenneth J. Alford. Music performed by: the Royal Philharmonic Orchestra. Art direction: Donald M. Ashton and Geoffrey Drake. Editor: Peter Taylor. Production manager: Cecil F. Ford. Production executive: William N. Graf. Assistant directors: Gus Agosti and Ted Sturgis. Construction manager: Peter Dukelow. Technical advisor: Major-General L.E.M. Perowne. Consulting engineers: Husband and Company, Sheffield, England. Bridge constructed by Equipment and Construction Company, Ceylon. Wardrobe: John Apperson. Continuity: Angela Martelli.

With

William Holden (Shears), Jack Hawkins (Major Warden), Alec Guinness (Colonel Nicholson), Sessue Hayakawa (Colonel Saito), James Donald (Doctor Clipton), Geoffrey Horne (Lieutenant Joyce), Andre Morrell (Colonel Green), Peter Williams (Captain Reeves), John Boxer (Major Hughes), Percy Herbert (Grogan), Harold Goodwin (Baker), Ann Sears (Nurse), Henry Okawa (Captain Kanematsu), K. Katsumoto (Lieutenant Miura), M.R.B. Chakrabanhu (Yai), Viliaiwan Seeboonreaung, Ngamta Suphaphongs, Javanart Punychoti, Kannikar Dowklee (Siamese Girls).

19. The Horse's Mouth

Great Britain. A Knightsbridge Production. Released by Lopert Films, distributed by United Artists. 1958. 96 min. (8640 feet). Color.

Producer: John Bryan. Director: Ronald Neame. Screenplay: Alec Guinness, based on the novel by Joyce Cary. Executive producer: Albert Fennell. Assistant director: Colin Brewer. Photography: Arthur Ibbetson. Camera operator: John Harris. Music: "Lt. Kije" by Sergei Prokofieff. Arranged by: Kenneth V. Jones. Conducted by: Muir Mathieson. Continuity: Yvonne Axworthy. Art direction: Bill Andrews. Editor: Anne V. Coates. Sound supervisor: John Cox. Makeup: Harold Fletcher. Miss Turleigh's gowns by: Julia Squires. Hairstyles: Pearl Tipaldi. Production manager: R.I.M. Davidson. Gulley Jimson's paintings by: John Bratby. Other paintings loaned by: the O'Hana Gallery, Wildenstein and Company, the Beaux Arts Gallery, and the Marborough Galleries.

With

Alec Guinness (Gulley Jimson), Kay Walsh (Coker), Renée Houston (Sara), Mike Morgan (Nosey), Robert Coote (Sir William Beeder), Veronica Turleigh (Lady Beeder), Arthur Macrae (Alabaster), Michael Gough (Abel, the Sculptor), Reginald Beckwith (Captain Jones), Ernest Thesiger (Hickson),

Gillian Vaughan (Lolle, Abel's Model), Richard Caldicott (Robert, Hickson's Butler), Richard Leech (Hodges, Lift Operator), John Kidd (Pawnbroker), Elton Ollivierre (Black Model), May Hallett (Maid), Rose Howlett (Cook), and Jeremy Judge (Dickie).

20. *The Scapegoat*

Great Britain. A Du Maurier–Guinness Production. MGM. 1959. 92 min. (8280 feet). B/W.

Producer: Michael Balcon. Director: Robert Hamer. Based on the novel of the same name by Daphne Du Maurier. Adaptation: Gore Vidal. Screenplay: Robert Hamer. Director of photography: Paul Beeson. Production designer: Elliot Scott. Production supervisor: Hal Mason. Editor: Jack Harris. Production manager: L.C. Rudkin. Sound supervisor: Stephen Dalby. Sound recordist: Norman King. Special photographic effects: Tom Howard. Assistant director: Tom Peysner. Camera operator: Herbert Smith. Continuity: Beryl Booth. Sound editor: Lionel Selwyn. Makeup: Harry Frampton. Hairdresser: Elsie Alder. Dress designer: Olga Lehmann. Art director: Alan Withy. Music: Bronislau Kaper. Associate producer: Dennis Van Thal.

With

Alec Guinness (John Barratt and Jacques De Gue), Bette Davis (the Countess), Nicole Maurey (Bela), Irene Worth (Francoise), Pamela Brown (Blanche), Annabel Bartlett (Marie-Noel), Geoffrey Keen (Gaston, the Chauffeur), Noel Howlett (Dr. Aloin), Peter Bull (Aristide), Leslie French (Inspector), Maria Britneva (Maid), Eddie Byrne (Barman), Alexander Archdale (Gamekeeper), and Peter Sallis (Customs Official).

21. *Our Man in Havana*

Great Britain. A Columbia Release of a Carol Reed Production. 1960. 111 min. (9990 feet). B/W.

Producer/director: (Sir) Carol Reed. Screenplay: Graham Greene, from his own novel. Associate producer: Raymond Anzarut. Art director: John Box. Editor: Bert Bates. Cinemascope photography: Oswald Morris. Assistant director: Gerry O'Hara. Camera operator: Denys N. Coop. Continuity: Margaret Shipway. Assistant art director: Syd Cain. Sound supervisor: John Cox. Sound recordists: John W. Mitchell and Red Law. Sound editor: Ted Mason. Makeup: Harry Frampton. Hair dresser: Gordon Bond. Costume designer: Phyllis Dalton. Wardrobe: Arthur Newman and Betty Adamson. Music played by: Frank and Laurence Deniz.

With

Alec Guinness (Jim Wormold), Burl Ives (Dr. Hasselbacher), Maureen O'Hara

(Beatrice), Ernie Kovacs (Captain Segura), Noel Coward (Hawthorne), Ralph Richardson ("C"), Jo Morrow (Milly), Paul Rogers (Carter), Gregoire Aslan (Cifentes), Jose Prieto (Lopez), Timothy Bateson (Rudy), Duncan Macrae (MacDougal), Maurice Denham (Naval Officer), Raymond Huntley (Army Officer), Hugh Manning (RAF Officer), Maxine Audley (Teresa), Yvonne Buckingham (Stripteaser), Ferdy Mayne (Professor Sanchez), Karel Stepanek (Dr. Braun), Gerik Schjelderup (Svenson), and Elisabeth Welsh (Beautiful Woman).

22. Tunes of Glory

Great Britain. A United Artists release of a Colin Lesslie Production. 1960. 107 min. (9630 feet). Technicolor.

Producer: Colin Lesslie. Director: Ronald Neame. Screenplay: James Kennaway, based on his novel. Director of photography: Arthur Ibbetson. Production designer: Wilfred Shingleton. Editor: Anne V. Coates. Music composed and conducted by: Malcom Arnold. Executive producer: Albert Fennell. Assistant director: Colin Brewer. Production manager: Patrick Marsden. Camera operator: Austin Dempster. Continuity: Rita Davison. Sound supervisor: John Cox. Recordists: Bert Ross and Red Law. Dubbing editor: Leslie Hodgson. Assistant art director: Martin Atkinson. Makeup: Henry Frampton. Hairdressing: Barbara Ritchie. Wardrobe: Charles Guerin.

With

Alec Guinness (Lieut. Col. Jock Sinclair), John Mills (Lieut. Col. Basil Barrow), Dennis Price (Maj. Charlie Scott), John Fraser (Cpl. Piper Fraser), Susannah York (Morag Sinclair), Kay Walsh (Mary), Duncan Macrae (Pipe Major MacLean), Gordon Jackson (Capt. Jimmy Cairns), Alan Cuthbertson (Capt. Eric Simpson), Percy Herbert (R.S.M. Riddick), Keith Faulkner (Piper Adam), Richard Leech (Capt. Alec Rattray), Peter McEnery (Lieut. David MacKinnon), Paul Whitsun Jones (Maj. Dusty Miller), William Marlowe (Lieut. Rory), and Gerald Harper (Maj. Hugo MacMillan).

23. A Majority of One

A Mervyn Le Roy Production. Warner Bros. Pictures. 1961. 156 min. (14,040 feet). Technicolor.

Producer/Director: Mervyn Le Roy. Screenplay: Leonard Spigelgass, based on his play. Director of photography: Harry Stradling, Sr. Art director: John Beckman. Set decorator: Ralph S. Hurst. Film editor: Philip W. Anderson. Music: Max Steiner. Orchestrations: Murray Cutter. Sound: Stanley Jones. Assistant director: Gil Kissel. Costumes: Orry-Kelly. Makeup: Jean Burt Reilly. Hairstyles: Jane Shugrue. Technical advisor: Takemo K. Sinohara.

With
Rosalind Russell (Mrs. Jacoby), Alec Guinness (Koichi Asano), Ray Danton (Jerome Black), Madlyn Rhue (Alice Black), Mae Questel (Mrs. Rubin), Marc Marno (Eddie), Gary Vinson (Mr. McMillan), Sharon Hugueny (Bride), Frank Wilcox (Noah Putnam), Francis De Sales (American Embassy Representative), Yuki Shimoda (Mr. Asano's Secretary), Harriet MacGibbon (Mrs. Putnam), Alan Mowbray (Captain Norcross), Tsuruko Koibayashi (Mr. Asano's Daughter-in-Law).

24. *H.M.S. Defiant/Damn the Defiant!*

Great Britain. A G.W. Film. A John Brabourne Production. Distributed by Columbia Pictures. 1962. CinemaScope. 101 min. (9090 feet). Technicolor. (U.S.: Eastman Color by Pathé.)

Producer: John Brabourne. Director: Lewis Gilbert. Screenplay: Nigel Kneale and Edmund H. North. Based on the novel *Mutiny* by Frank Tilsley. Director of photography: Christopher Challis. Camera operator: Austin Dempster. Focus: John Jordan, Roy Ford. Camera grip: Jack Roche. Art director: Arthur Lawson. Assistant art director: Don Picton. Set dresser: Terence Morgan II. Scenic artist: Ted Barnes. Draughtsmen: Ted Tester, Bill Bennison. Film editor: Peter Hunt. Assistant editor: Norman Wanstall and Gerry Arbeid. Music composed by: Clifton Parker. Music conducted by Muir Mathieson. Sound recording: H.L. Bird and Red Law. Boom operator: Ken Ritchie. Dubbing editor: Winston Ryder. First and second assistant directors: Jack Causey, Claude Watson, and Jim Brennan. Production manager: Richard Goodwin. Location manager: Richard Porter. Continuity: Shirley Barnes. Production secretary: Marguerite Green. Wardrobe supervisor: Jean Fairlie. Makeup: Freddie Williamson and Michael Morris. Hairdresser: Gordon Bond. Special effects supervisor: Howard Lydecker. Special effects technician: Ernie Sullivan. Special effects properties: J. Ryan. Technical advisor: Comdr. D.H. Angel. Fight arranger: William Hobbs. Still photographer: Bert Cann. Construction manager: W. Mclaren. Properties: Tom Frewer. Chargehand electrician: Jackie Sullivan. Casting advice: John Bird.

With
Alec Guinness (Captain Crawford), Dirk Bogarde (Lieutenant Scott-Padget), Maurice Denham (Surgeon Goss), Nigel Stock (Senior Midshipman Kilpatrick), Richard Carpenter (Lieut. Ponsonby), Peter Gill (Lieut. D'Arblay), David Robinson (Harvey Crawford), Robin Stewart (Pardoe), Ray Brooks (Hayes), Peter Greenspan (Johnson), Anthony Quayle (Vizard), Tom Bell (Evans), Murray Melvin (Wagstaffe), Victor Maddern (Dawlish), Brian Pringle (Sergeant Kneebone), Johnny Briggs (Wheatley), Brian Phelan (Grimshaw), Toke Townley ("Silly Billy" Whiting), Declan Mulhololand (Morrison), Walter Fitzgerald (Admiral Jackson), Joy Shelton

(Mrs. Crawford), Anthony Oliver (Tavern Leader), Russel Napier (Flag Captain), Michael Coles (Flag Lieutenant), Andre Maranne (Colonel Giraud), and Ann Lynn (Young Wife).

25. *Lawrence of Arabia*

A Horizon Pictures Production. Released by Columbia Pictures through BL-C. 1962. 222 min. (19,980 feet). Super Panavision 70. Technicolor.

Producer: Sam Spiegel. Director: David Lean. Screenplay: Robert Bolt. Director of photography: F.A. Young. Music: Maurice Jarre. Editor: Anne V. Coates. Second-unit directors: Andre Smagghe and Noel Howard. Second-unit photography: Skeets Kelly, Nicholas Roeg and Peter Newbrook. Musical arrangements: Gerard Schurmann. Music coordinated by: Morris Stoloff. Played by: the London Philharmonic Orchestra. Conducted by: Sir Adrian Boult. Production designer: John Box. Art direction: John Stoll. Set decorations: Dario Simoni. Sound: John Cox, Winston Ryder and Paddy Cunningham. Costumes: Phyllis Dalton. Makeup: Charles Parker. Hairstyles: A.G. Scott. Production manager: John Palmer. Location manager: Douglas Twiddy. Assistant director: Roy Stevens.

With

Peter O'Toole (Lawrence), Alec Guinness (Prince Faisal), Anthony Quinn (Auda Abu Tayi), Jack Hawkins (General Allenby), Jose Ferre (Turkish Bey), Anthony Quayle (Colonel Brighton), Claude Rains (Mr. Dryden), Arthur Kennedy (Jackson Bentley), Donald Wolfit (General Murray), Omar Sharif (Sherif Ali Ibn el Kharish), I.S. Johar (Gasim), Gamil Ratib (Majid), Michel Ray (Farraj), Zia Mohyeddin (Tafas), John Dimech (Daud), Howard Marion Crawford (Medical Officer), Jack Gwillim (Club Secretary), and Hugh Miller (R.A.M.C. Colonel).

26. *The Fall of the Roman Empire*

United States. A Bronston–Roma Production. Released by Paramount Pictures. 1964. 188 min. (16,920 feet). Also 180 and 153 min. versions. Ultra-Panavision 70. Technicolor.

Producer: Samuel Bronston. Director: Anthony Mann. Executive associate producer: Michael Waszynski. Associate producer: Jaime Prades. Original screenplay: Ben Barzman, Basilio Franchina, and Phil Yordan. Second-unit director: Yakima Canutt. Director second-unit operations: Andrew Marton. Photography: Robert Krasker. Second-unit photography: Cecilio Paniagua. Set design: Veniero Colasanti. Production designer: John Moore. Film editor: Robert Lawrence. Assistant film editor: Magdalena Paradell. Music: Dimitri Tiomkin. Sound: David Hilyard. Sound recordist: Gordon K. McCallum.

Sound effects editor: Milton Burrow. First and second unit assistant directors: Jose Lopez Rodero and Jose Maria Ochoa. Executive production manager: C.O. Erickson. Continuity: Elaine Schreyeck. Costumes: Venerio Colasanti and John Moore. Wardrobe: Gloria Mussetta. Makeup: Mario Van Riel. Hairdressing: Grazia De Rossi. Special effects: Alex Weldon. Assistants: Jose Lopez Rodero and Jose Maria Ochoa. Historical consultant: Will Durant. Dialogue coach: George Tyne. Supervising technician: Carl Gibson. Supervising electrician: Buno Pasqualini. Prop master: Stanly Detlie. Casting: Maude Spector. Frescoes: Maciek Piotrowski.

With

Sophia Loren (Lucilla), Stephen Boyd (Livius), Alec Guinness (Marcus Aurelius), James Mason (Timonides), Christopher Plummer (Commodus), Anthony Quayle (Verulus), John Ireland (Ballomar), Mel Ferrer (Cleander), Omar Sharif (Sohamus), Eric Porter (Julianus), Douglas Wilmer (Niger), Peter Damon (Claudius), Andrew Keir (Polybius), George Murcell (Victorinus), Lena von Martens (Helva), Gabriella Licudi (Tauna), Rafael Luis Calvo (Lentuluss), Norman Wooland (Virgilianus), Virgilio Teixeira (Marcellus), Michael Gwynn (Cornelius), Guy Rolfe (Mariuss), Finlay Currie (Caecina).

27. Situation Hopeless But Not Serious

United States/Germany. Castle Productions. Distributed by Paramount Pictures. 1965. 97 min. (8730 feet). B/W.

Producer/Director: Gottfried Reinhardt. Assistant producer: Jose de Villaverde. Production executive: Kurt Hartmann. Second unit director: Walter Boos. Screenplay: Silvia Reinhardt. Adaptation: Jan Lustig. Based on the novel *The Hiding Place* by Robert Shaw. Director of cinematography: Kurt Hasse. Art director: Rolf Zehebauer. Film editor: Walter Boos. Music: Harold Byrns. Sound: Walter Ruhland. Assistant director: Henri Sokal. Production manager: Michael Bittins. Costumes: Ilse Dubois. Makeup artists: Arthur Schramm and Albert Nagel.

With

Alec Guinness (Herr Frick), Michael Conners (Lucky Finder), Robert Redford (Hank Wilson), Anita Hoefer (Edeltraud), Mady Rahl (Lissie), Paul Dahlke (Herr Neusel), Frank Wolff (Quartermaster Sergeant), John Briley (Sergeant), Elisabeth Von Molo (Wanda), Carola Regnier (Senta).

28. Doctor Zhivago

United States. A Carlo Ponti Production. Distributed by MGM. 1965. 197 min., cut to 180 min. (16,200 feet). Panavision. Metrocolor.

Producer: Carlo Ponti. Director: David Lean. Executive producer: Arvid L. Griffin. Screenplay: Robert Bolt, based on the novel by Boris Pasternak. Photography: Freddie Young. Second-unit photography: Manuel Berenguer. Camera operator: Ernest Day. Art director: Terence Marsh. Assistant art directors: Ernest Archer, Bill Hutchinson, and Roy Walker. Associate art director: Gil Parrondo. Set decorator: Dario Simoni. Production designer: John Box. Film editor: Norman Savage. Original music composed and conducted by: Maurice Jarre. Sound recordist: Paddy Cunningham. Sound editor: Winston Ryder. Rerecording: Franklin Milton and William Steinkamp. Assistant directors: Roy Stevens, Pedro Vidal, and Jose Maria Ochoa. Production supervisor: John Palmer. Production managers: Agustin Pastor and Douglas Twiddy. Continuity: Barbara Cole. Costume designer: Phyllis Dalton. Makeup: Mario Van Riel. Hairstyles: Grazia De Rossi and Anna Cristofani. Special effects: Eddie Fowlie. Chief electrician: Miguel Sancho Ruiz. Construction: Gus Walker and Fred Bennett. Dialogue coach: Hugh Miller.

With

Omar Sharif (Yuri Zhivago), Julie Christie (Lara), Geraldine Chaplin (Tonya Gromeko), Tom Courtenay (Pasha Antipov [Strelnikov]), Alec Guinness (Yevgraf Zhivago), Rod Steiger (Komarovsky), Ralph Richardson (Alexander Gromeko), Siobhan McKenna (Anna Gromeko), Rita Tushingham (the Girl), Adrienne Corri (Amelia), Geoffrey Keen (Professor Kurt), Jeffrey Rockland (Sasha), Lucy Westmore (Katya), Noel Willman (Razin), Gerard Tichy (Liberius), Klaus Kinski (Kostoyed), Jack MacGowran (Petra), Maria Martin (Gentlewoman), Tarek Sharif (Yuri, age 8), Mercedes Ruiz (Tonya, age 7), Roger Maxwell (Beef-Faced Soldier), Inigo Jackson (Major), Virgilio Teixeira (Captain), Bernard Kay (Bolshevik), Erik Chitty (Old Soldier), Jose Nieto (Priest), Mark Eden (Young Engineer), Emilio Carrer (Mr. Sventytski), Gerhard Jersch (David), Wolf Frees (Comrade Yelkin), Gwen Nelson (Comrade Kaprugina), Jose Maria Caffarel (Militiaman), Brigitte Trace (Streetwalker), Luana Alcaniz (Mrs. Sventytski), Lili Murati (Train Jumper), Peter Madden (Political Officer), Katherine Ellison (Raped Woman), Maria Vico (Demented Woman), Dodo Assad Bahador (Dragoon Colonel).

29. *Hotel Paradiso*

United States. MGM/Trianon Productions. Distributed by MGM. 1966. 100 min. (9000 feet). Panavision. Metrocolor.

Producer/Director: Peter Glenville. Associate producer: Pierre Jourdan. Screenplay: Peter Glenville and Jean-Claude Carriere. Director of photography: Henri Decae and Gilbert Chain. Color consultant: Jacques Dupont. Set decorator: Robert Christides. Production designer: Francois de Lamothe. Film editor: Anne V. Coates. Music and musical director: Lawrence Rosenthal. Sound recordist: Cyril Swern. Sound editor: Jonathan Bates.

Dubbing mixer: J.B. Smith. Assistant director: Georges Pellegrin. Production manager: Georges Gillet. Unit manager: Philippe Modave. Continuity: Alice Ziller. Costume designer: Jacques Dupont. Chief makeup artists: Louis Bonnemaison and Odette Berroyer. Chief hairdresser: Alex Archambault.

With

Alec Guinness (Benedict Boniface), Gina Lollobrigida (Marcell Cot), Robert Morley (Henri Cot), Peggy Mount (Angelique Boniface), Douglas Byng (Mr. Martin), Robertson Hare (the Duke), David Battley (George, the Bellboy), Ann Beach (Victoire), Dario Moreno (Turk), Derek Fowldes (Maxime), Leonard Rossiter (Inspector), Akim Tamiroff (Anniello, the Innkeeper), Marie Bell (La Grande Antoinette), Eddra Gale (Hotel Guest), Candy Le Beau, Helen Mathison, Denise Powell, and Melody Kaye (Mrs. Martin's Daughters), and Peter Glenville (Georges Feydeau).

30. The Quiller Memorandum

United States/Great Britain. Rank Organization–Ivan Foxwell Productions–Carthay Films. Distributed by Twentieth Century–Fox Film Corporation. National General Productions. 1966. 105 min. (9450 feet). Panavision. Color by De Luxe.

Producer: Ivan Foxwell. Director: Michael Anderson. Screenplay: Harold Pinter. Based on the novel *The Berlin Memorandum* by Adam Hall. Director of photography: Erwin Hillier. Camera operator: John Winbolt. Second-unit cameraman: H.A.R. Thomson. Art director: Maurice Carter. Associate art director: Jack Maxsted. Set dresser: Arthur Taksen. Film editor: Frederick Wilson. Music composed and conducted by: John Barry. Song: "Wednesday's Child" by: John Barry (music) and Mack David (lyrics). Sung by: Matt Monro. Sound editor: Archie Ludski. Sound recordists: C.C. Stevens and John Aldred. Assistant director: Clive Reed. Production supervisor: Sydney Streeter. Unit manager: Bernard Williams. Continuity: Joan Kirk. Wardrobe: Carl Tom. Makeup: W.T. Partleton. Hairstyles: Stella Rivers. Special effects: Lee Bowie and Arthur Beavis.

With

George Segal (Quiller), Alec Guinness (Pol), Max von Sydow (Oktober), Senta Berger (Inge), George Sanders (Gibbs), Robert Helpmann (Weng), Robert Flemyng (Gibbs' Associate), Peter Carsten (Hengel), Edith Schneider (Headmistress), Gunter Meisner (Hassler), Robert Stass (Jones), Ernst Walder (Gruber), Philip Madoc and John Rees (Oktober's Men).

31. The Comedians

United States/Bermuda/France. A Peter Glenville Production. MGM–Maximillian Productions–Trianon Productions. Distributed by MGM. (Filmed on location in Dahomey, Nice, and Paris). 1967. 160 min. (14,400 feet). Panavision. Metrocolor.

Producer/Director: Peter Glenville. Screenplay: Graham Greene, from his novel of the same name. Director of photography: Henri Decae. Camera operator: Ernest Day. Art director: Francois de Lamothe. Set dresser: Robert Christides. Film editor: Francoise Javet. Music composed and conducted by: Laurence Rosenthal. Sound recordist: Cyril Swern. Sound editor: Jonathan Bates. Dubbing mixer: Jacques Carrere. Assistant director: Jean-Michel Lacor. Production supervisor: Louis Wipf. Assistant to the producer: Judith Coxhead. Unit manager: Lucien Lippens. Continuity: Alice Ziller. Miss Taylor's gowns: Tiziani of Rome. Miss Taylor's hairstyles: Alexandre of Paris.

With

Richard Burton (Brown), Elizabeth Taylor (Martha Pineda), Alec Guinness (Major Jones), Peter Ustinov (Ambassador Pineda), Paul Ford (Smith), Lillian Gish (Mrs. Smith), Raymond St. Jacques (Captain Concasseur), Zacks Mokac (Michel), Roscoe Lee Browne (Petit Pierre), Douta Seck (Joseph), Albia Peters (Cesar), Gloria Foster (Madame Philipot), Robin Langford (Angelito), Georg Stanford Brown (Henri Philipot), James Earl Jones (Dr. Magiot), Cicely Tyson (Marie Therese).

32. Cromwell

Great Britain. An Irving Allen Production. Distributed by Columbia Pictures. 1970. 139 min. (12,510 feet). Panavision. Technicolor.

Producer: Irving Allen. Director: Ken Hughes. Associate producer: Andrew Donally. Script: Ken Hughes. Script consultant: Ronald Harwood. Photography: Geoffrey Unsworth. Editor: Bill Lenny. Second-unit director: Harold Kress. Production designer: John Stoll. Music composed and conducted by: Frank Cordell. Second-unit photography: Wilkie Cooper. Camera operator: Peter MacDonald. Art director: Herbert Westbrook. Assistant art director: Bill Bennison. Set dresser: Arthur Taksen. Sound editor: Alfred Cox. Sound recordists: Leslie Hammond and Bob Jones. Assistant director: Ted Sturgis. Production supervisor: Frank Bevis. Continuity: Margaret Unsworth. Costume designer: Vittorio Novarese. Wardrobe supervisor: John Wilson-Apperson. Makeup: Neville Smallwood. Hairdressing: Bobbie Smith. Special effects: Bill Warrington. Stunt supervisor: Gerry Crampton. Casting: Maude Spector. Spanish army liaison: Antonio San Ridruejo.

With

Richard Harris (Oliver Cromwell), Alec Guinness (King Charles I), Robert Morley (Earl of Manchester), Dorothy Tutin (Queen Henrietta Maria), Frank Finley (John Carter), Timothy Dalton (Prince Rupert), Patrick Wymark (Earl of Stafford), Patrick Magee (Hugh Peters), Nigel Stock (Sir Edward Hyde), Charles Gray (Lord Essex), Michael Jayston (Henry Ireton), Richard Cornish (Oliver Cromwell II), Anna Cropper (Ruth Carter), Michael Goodliffe (Solictor General), Jack Gwillim (General Byron), Basil Henson (Hacker),

Patrick Holt (Captain Lundsford), Stratford Johns (President Bradshaw), Geoffrey Keen (John Pym), Anthony May (Richard Cromwell), Ian McCulloch (John Hampden), Patrick O'Connell (John Lilburne), John Paul (General Digby), Llewellyn Rees (The Speaker), Robin Stewart (Prince of Wales), Andre Van Gyseghem (Archbishop Rinuccini), Zena Walker (Mrs. Cromwell), John Welsh (Bishop Juxon), Douglas Wilmer (Thomas Fairfax), Anthony Kemp (Henry Cromwell), Stacy Dorning (Mary Cromwell), Melinda Churcher (Bridget Cromwell), George Merritt (Old Man/William), Gerald Rowland (Drummer Boy), Josephine Gillick (Elizabeth Cromwell).

33. Scrooge

Great Britain. Waterbury Films. Distributed by National General Pictures. 1970. 115 min. (2350 feet). Panavision. Technicolor.

Producer: Robert H. Solo. Director: Ronald Neame. Executive Producer: Leslie Bricusse. Associate Producer: David Orton. Screenplay: Leslie Bricusse. Based on the novella *A Christmas Carol* by: Charles Dickens. Director of photography: Oswald Morris. Camera operator: Jim Turrell. Associate music supervisor: Herbert W. Spencer. Production design: Terry Marsh. Costume design: Margaret Furse. Film editor: Peter Weatherley. Special effects: Wally Veevers. Titles designed by Ronald Searle. Executed by Trickfilm. Assistant director: Ted Sturgis. Art director: Bob Cartwright. Chief makeup artist: George Frost. Chief hair stylist: Bobbie Smith. Production manager: Ed Harper. Continuity: Elaine Schreyeck. Set dresser: Pamela Cornell. Special effects cameraman: Jack Mills. Sound supervisor: Jack Cox. Sound mixer: Jock May. Dubbing editor: James Shields. Dubbing mixer: Bob Jones. Music editor: Ken Runyon. Music recorded at CTS, London. Colour by Humpries London. Musical sequences staged by: Paddy Stone. Music conducted and supervised by: Ian Fraser. (Songs: "A Christmas Carol," "Christmas Children," "I Hate People," "Father Christmas," "See the Phantoms," "December the Twenty Fifth," "Happiness," "You...You," "I Like Life," "The Beautiful Day," "Thank You Very Much," "I'll Begin Again.")

With

Albert Finney (Scrooge), Alec Guinness (Marley's ghost), Edith Evans (Ghost of Christmas Past), Kenneth More (Ghost of Christmas Present), Laurence Naismith (Fezziwig), Michael Medwin (Nephew), David Collings (Bob Cratchit), Anton Rodgers (Tom Jenkins), Suzanne Neve (Isabel), Frances Cuka (Mrs. Cratchit), Derek Francis, Roy Kinnear (Portly Gentlemen), Mary Peach (Nephew's Wife), Paddy Stone (Ghost of Christmas Yet to Come), Kay Walsh (Mrs. Fezziwig), Gordon Jackson (Nephew's Friend), Richard Beaumont (Tiny Tim), Geoffrey Bayldon (Toyshop Owner), Molly Weir, Helena Gloag (Women Debtors), Reg Lever (Punch and Judy Man), Keith Marsh (Well Wisher), Marianne Stone (Party Guest), Philip Da Costa,

Raymond Hoskins, Gaynor Hodgson, Nicholas Locise, Peter Lock, Joy Leigh, Sara Gibson, Clive Moss, John O'Brien, David Peacock, Michael Reardon, Karel Scargill, Terry Winter, Stephen Garlick (the Children).

34. Brother Sun, Sister Moon

Great Britain/Italy. Vic Film (Productions) Ltd., London and Euro International Films s.p.a., Rome. Distributed by Paramount Pictures. (Filmed on location in Italy and at Centro Dear, Rome.) 121 min. (10,890 feet). Panavision. Technicolor.

Producer: Luciano Perugia. Director: Franco Zeffirelli. Original story and screenplay: Suso Cecchi D'Amico, Lina Wertmuller, and Franco Zeffirelli. English dialogue: Kenneth Ross. Words and music composed and sung by: Donovan. Music coordinated, arranged, and conducted by: Ken Thorne. Photography: Ennio Guarnieri. Production designer: Corenzo Mongiardino. Costume designer: Danilo Donati. Supervising editor: Reginald Mills. Associate to the producer: Dyson Lovell. Production manager: Mario di Base. Production assistants: Paolo de Andreis and Sergio Galiano. Assistant directors: Carlo Cotti and Rinaldi Ricci. Art director: Gianni Quaranta. Architect: Giorgio Giovanni. Set dresser: Carmelo Patrono. Camera operator: Bernard Waterson. Focus puller: John Vidgeon. Continuity: Yvonne Axworthy. Editor: John Rushton. Sound editor: Leslie Hodgson. Sound: Delta Sound, Ltd. Makeup: Otello Sisi. Hairdressing: Luciano Vito. Costumes: Farani-Rome, Cerratelli-Florence, and Veste-Rome. Musical research: Alfredo Bianchini. Musical publishers: Famous Music Corporation. Titles designed by: Sergio Salaroli. Publicity: Marika Aba.
With
Graham Faulkner (Francesco [St. Francis of Assisi]), Judi Bowker (Clare), Alec Guinness (Pope Innocent III), Leigh Lawson (Bernardo), Kenneth Cranham (Paolo), Michael Feast (Silvestro), Nicholas Willatt (Giocondo), Valentina Cortese (Pica), Lee Montague (Pietro di Bernadone), John Sharp (Bishop Guido), Adolfo Celi (Regional Governor), Francesco Guerrieri (Deodato).

35. Hitler: The Last Ten Days

A Wolfgang Reinhardt (London) and West Film (Rome) Production. A Paramount Pictures–Tomorrow Entertainment Release. (Made at Shepperton Studios, England.) 1973. 106 min. (9540 feet). Panavision. Color.

Producer: Wolfgang Reinhardt. Director: Ennio de Concini. Screenplay: Ennio de Concini, Maria Pia Fusco, and Wolfgang Reinhardt. English screenplay adaptation: Ivan Moffet. Based on *The Last Days of the Chancellery* by Gerhard Boldt. Production supervisor: Norman Priggen. Photography: Ennio Guarnieri. Music: Mischa Spoliansky. Editor: Kevin Conner. Technical advisor: Gerhardt Boldt. Assistant director: Richard Dalton.

With

Alec Guinness (Adolf Hitler), Simon Ward (Hauptmann Hoffman), Adolfo Celi (General Krebs), Diane Cilento (Hanna Reitsch), Gabriele Ferzetti (Fieldmarshal Reitel), Eric Porter (General Von Greim), Doris Kunstmann (Eva Braun), Joss Ackland (General Burgdorf), John Barron (Dr. Stumpfegger), John Bennett (Josef Goebbels), Sheila Gish (Frau Christian), Julian Glover (Fegelein), John Hallam (Guensche), Barbara Jefford (Magda Goebbels), Mark Kingston (Martin Bormann), Ann Lynn (Fraulein Junge), Angela Pleasence (Trude), Philip Stone (General Jodl), Timothy West (Professor Gebhardt), William Abney (Voss), Kenneth Colley (Gerhardt Boldt), James Cossins (German Officer).

36. Murder by Death

United States. A Columbia Pictures Release. A Rastar Production. 1976. 94 min. (8460 feet). Panavision. Color.

Producer: Ray Stark. Director: Robert Moore. Screenplay: Neil Simon. Associate producer: Roger M. Rothstein. Director of photography: David M. Walsh. Supervising film editor: Margaret Booth. Production designer: Stephen Grimes. Music: Dave Grusin. Film editor: John F. Burnete. Costumes: Ann Roth. Casting: Jennifer Shull. Title design: Wayne Fitzgerald. Title drawings: Charles Addams. Assistant director: Fred T. Gallo. Second assistant director: David O. Sosna. Script continuity: Julia Tucker. Special effects: Augie Lohman. Camera operator: Roger Shearman, Jr. Sound mixer: Jerry Jose. Sound effects editor: Frank Warner. Rerecording: Ted Rudloff. Music editor: George Probert. Assistant film editor: Michael A. Stevenson. Apprentice film editor: John Brice. Art director: Harry Kemm. Set decorator: Marvin March. Makeup supervision: Charles Schram. Makeup: Joseph Di Bella. Hairstylist: Vivienne Walker. Men's costumer: Tony Faso. Women's costumer: Agnes G. Henry. Assistant to the producer: Frank Bueno. Assistant to the production manager: Shari Leibowitz. Dialogue coach: George Rondo. Key grip: Richard Moran. Gaffer: Norman Harris. Property master: Terry E. Lewis. Stills: Mel Traxel. Boom operator: Joseph Kite. Assistant cameraman: Robert Edesa. Auditor: Vince Martinez.

With

Eileen Brennan (Tess Skeffington), Truman Capote (Lionel Twain), James Coco (Milo Perrier), Peter Falk (Sam Diamond), Alec Guinness (Bensonmum), Elsa Lanchester (Jessica Marbles), David Niven (Dick Charleston), Peter Sellers (Sidney Wang), Maggie Smith (Dora Charleston), Nancy Walker (Yetta), Estelle Winwood (Nurse Withers), James Cromwell (Marcel, the Chauffeur), Richard Narita (Willie Wang) and Myron the Dog as Himself.

37. Star Wars

A Lucasfilm Ltd. Production. Released by Twentieth Century–Fox. (Photographed in Tunisia, Tikal National Park, Guatemala, Death Valley National Monument, California, and EMI Elstree Studios, Borehamwood, England.) 1977. 121 min. (10,890 feet). Panavision. Technicolor.

Producer: Gary Kurtz. Director/Screenplay: George Lucas. Production designer: John Barry. Director of photography: Gilbert Taylor. Music: John Williams. Performed by: the London Symphony Orchestra. Special photographic effects supervisor: John Dykstra. Special production and mechanical effects supervisor: John Stears. Film editors: Paul Hirsch, Marcia Lucas, and Richard Chew. Production supervisor: Robert Watts. Production illustration: Ralph McQuarrie. Costume designer: John Mollo. Art directors: Norman Reynolds and Leslie Dilley. Makeup supervisor: Stuart Freeborn. Production sound: Derek Ball. Casting: Irene Lamb, Diane Crittenden, and Vic Ramos. Supervising sound editor: Sam Shaw. Special dialogue and sound effects: Ben Burtt. Supervising music editor: Kenneth Wannberg. Rerecording mixers: Don MacDougall, Bob Minkler, Ray West, Mike Minkler, Lester Fresholtz, and Richard Portman.
Miniature and Optical Effects Unit
First cameraman: Richard Edlund. Second cameraman: Dennis Muren. Composite optical photography: Robert Blalack (Praxis). Production supervisor: George E. Mather. Matte artist: P.S. Ellenshaw. Effects illustration and design: Joseph Johnston. Chief model maker: Grant McCune. Animation and rotoscope design: Adam Beckett. Computer animation and graphic displays: Dan O'Bannon, Larry Cuba, John Wash, Jay Teitzell, Image West. Film control coordinator: Mary M. Lind.
With
Mark Hamill (Luke Skywalker), Harrison Ford (Han Solo), Carrie Fisher (Princess Leia Organa), Peter Cushing (Grand Moff Tarkin), Alec Guinness (Ben [Obi-Wan] Kenobi), Anthony Daniels (C3PO), Kenny Baker (R2D2), Peter Mayhew (Chewbacca), David Prowse (Lord Darth Vader), Phil Brown (Uncle Owen Lars), Shelagh Fraser (Aunt Beru Lars), Jack Purvis (Chief Jawa), Alex McGrindle (General Dodonna), Eddie Byrne (General Willard), Drewe Henley (Red Leader), Dennis Lawson (Red Two [Wedge]), Garrick Hagon (Red Three [Biggs]), Jack Klaff (Red Four [John "D"]), William Hootkins (Red Six [Porkins]), Angus McInnis (Gold Leader), Jeremy Sinden (Gold Two), Graham Ashley (Gold Five), Don Henderson (General Taggi), Richard Le Parmentier (General Motti), Leslie Schofield (Commander #1).

38. Tinker Tailor Soldier Spy

Great Britain. A BBC Production, in Association with Paramount Pictures. 1979. Approx. 300 min. (27,000 feet). Color.

Producer: Jonathan Powell. Director: John Irvin. Script: Arthur Hopcraft. Photography: Tony Pierce-Roberts. Designer: Austin Spriggs. Script editor: Betty Willingale. Dubbing editor: Paul Ashton. Film editor: Chris Wimble. Dubbing mixer: Stanley Morcom. Film recordist: Malcom Webberley. Makeup artist: Elizabeth Rowell. Costume designer: Joyce Mortlock. Graphic designer: Douglas Burd. Assistant floor managers: Christabel Albery and Jeremy Silberston. Director's assistant: Frances Alcock. Production unit manager: Marcia Wheeler. Production assistants: Peter Grimwade and Tony Virgo. Music composed and conducted by: Geoffrey Burgon.

With

Alec Guinness (George Smiley), Bernard Hepton (Toby Esterhase), Terence Rigby (Roy Bland), Michael Aldridge (Percy Alleline), Ian Richardson (Bill Haydon), Alexander Knox (Control), George Sewell (Mendel), Ian Bannon (Jim Prideaux), Michael Jayston (Peter Guillam), Nigel Stock (Roddy Martindale), Anthony Bate (Oliver Lacon), Hywel Bennett (Ricki Tarr), Milos Kirek (Barak), Eugene Lipinski (Czech Guard), Alec Sabin (Fawn), Brian Hawksley (Bookseller), Beryl Reid (Connie Sachs), Warren Clarke (Alwyn), Jean Rimmer (Senior Secretary), Patrick Stewart (Karla), John Standing (Sam Collins), Majorie Hogan (Alisa Brimley), Joe Prami (Paul Skordeno), Daniel Beecher (Spikely), Duncan Jones (Roach), Mandy Cuthbert (Molly Purcell), Joss Ackland (Jerry Westerby), John Wells (Headmaster), Betty Hardy (Headmaster's Mother), Jo Apted (Linda), Thorley Walters (Tufty Thessinger), Hilary Minster (Boris), Susan Kodicek (Irina), Frank Moorey (Lauda Strickland), Frank Compton (Bryant), Stephen Earle (Norman), Pauline Letts (Mrs. Pope Graham), Guy Standeven (Fleming-Smith), George Pravda (Polyakov), and Sian Phillips (Ann Smiley).

39. The Empire Strikes Back

A Lucasfilm Ltd. Production. Released by Twentieth Century–Fox. (Photographed on the Hardangerjokulen Glacier, Finse, Norway and at EMI Elstree Studios, Borehamwood, England.) 1980. 124 min. (11,160 feet). Panavision. Color by Rank Film Laboratories. Prints by Deluxe.

Producer: Gary Kurtz. Director: Irvin Kershner. Screenplay: Leigh Brackett and Lawrence Kasdan. Story: George Lucas. Executive producer: George Lucas. Production designer: Norman Reynolds. Director of photography: Peter Suschitzky. Editor: Paul Hirsch. Special visual effects: Brian Johnson and Richard Edlund. Associate producers: Robert Watts and James Bloom. Music: John Williams. Performed by: the London Symphony Orchestra. Design consultant and conceptual artist: Ralph McQuarrie. Art directors: Leslie Dilley, Harry Lange, and Alan Tomkins. Set decorator: Michael Ford. Production supervisor: Bruce Sharman. Operating cameraman: Kelvin Pike and David Garfath. Makeup and special creature design: Stuart Freeborn.

Costume designer: John Mollo. Property master: Frank Bruton. Sound design and supervising sound effects editor: Ben Burtt. First assistant director: David Tomblin. Matte photography consultant: Stanley Sayer. Gaffer: Laurie Snane. Lighting equipment and crew from Lee Electric. Chief makeup artist: Graham Freeborn. Wardrobe supervisor: Tiny Nicholls. Property supervisor: Charles Torbett. Construction manager: Bill Welch. Sound editors: Richard Burrow, Teresa Eckton, and Bonnie Koehler. Production sound: Peter Sutton. Rerecording: Bill Varney, Steve Maslow, and Gregg Landacker. Music recording: Eric Tomlinson. Orchestrations: Herbert W. Spencer. Assistant production manager: Patricia Carr. Second assistant directors: Steve Lanning and Roy Button. Location manager: Philip Kohler. Continuity: Kay Rawlings and Pamela Mann. Casting: Irene Lamb, Terry Liebling, and Bob Edmiston. Stunt coordinator: Peter Diamond. Production accountant: Ron Phipps. Unit publicist: Alan Arnold. Second unit directors: Harley Cokliss, Peter Mac-Donald, and John Barry. Second unit cameramen: Chris Menges and Geoff Glover. Second unit assistant directors: Dominic Fulford, Bill Westley, and Ola Solum.

Production and Mechanical Effects Unit
Mechanical effects supervision: Nick Allder. Location unit supervisor: Allan Bryce. Senior effects technicians: Neil Swan and Dave Watkins. Robot fabrication and supervision: Andrew Kelly and Ron Hone.

Miniature and Optical Effects Unit
Effects director of photography: Dennis Muren. Effects cameramen: Ken Ralson and Jim Veilleux. Optical photography supervisor: Bruce Nicholson. Optical printer operators: David Berry, Kenneth Smith, and Donald Clark. Art director—visual effects: Joe Johnston. Stop motion animation: John Berg and Phil Tippett. Matte painting supervisor: Harrison Ellenshaw. Matte artists: Ralph McQuarrie and Michael Pangrazio. Modelshop foreman: Steve Gawley. Chief model maker: Lorne Peterson. Animation and rotoscope supervisor: Peter Kuran. Visual effects editorial supervisor: Conrad Buff. Production administrator: Dick Gallegly. Production accountant: Ray Scalice. Electronics systems designer: Jerry Jeffress. Special project coordinator: Stuart Ziff. Equipment engineering supervisor: Gene Whiteman. Design engineer: Mike Bolles. Supervising stage technician: T.E. Moehnke. Miniature pyrotechnics: Joseph Viskocil, Dave Pier, and Thaine Morris.

With
Mark Hamill (Luke Skywalker), Harrison Ford (Han Solo), Carrie Fisher (Princess Leia), Billy Dee Williams (Lando Calrissian), Anthony Daniels (C3PO), Frank Oz (Performing Yoda), David Prowse (Darth Vader), Peter Mayhew (Chewbacca), Kenny Baker (R2D2), Alec Guinness (Ben [Obi-Wan] Kenobi), Jeremy Bullock (Boba Fett), John Hollis (Lando's Aide), Jack Purvis (Chief Ugnaught), Des Webb (Snow Creature), Kathryn Mullen (Performing Assistant for Yoda), Clive Revill (Voice of Emperor), Kenneth Colley (Admiral Piett), Julian Glover (General Veers), Michael Sheard (Admiral

Ozzel), Michael Culver (Captain Needa), John Dicks, Milton Johns, Mark Jones, Oliver Maguire, and Robin Scobey (other Imperial Officers), Bruce Boa (General Rieekan), Christopher Malcom (Zev [Rogue 2]), Dennis Lawson (Wedge [Rogue 3]), Richard Oldfield (Hobbie [Rogue 4]), John Morton (Dak [Luke's Gunner]), Ian Liston (Janson [Wedge's Gunner]), John Ratzenberger (Major Derlin), Jack McKenzie (Deck Lieutenant), Jerry Harte (Head Controller), and Norman Chancer, Norwich Duff, Ray Hassett, Brigitte Kahn, and Burnell Tucker (Other Rebel Officers).

40. Raise the Titanic

United States/Great Britain. Lord Grade Presents a Marble Arch Production. Released by AFD. (Filmed in the United States, Greece, England, and Malta.) 1980. 112 min. (10,080 feet). Color.

Producer: William Frye. Director: Jerry Jameson. Screenplay: Adam Kennedy. Adaptation: Eric Hughes. Based on the novel by Clive Cussler. Executive producer: Martin Starger. Director of photography: Matthew F. Leonetti. Production designer: John F. Decuir. Film editors: J. Terry Williams, Robert F. Shugrue. Music: John Barry. Casting: Mike Fenton and Jane Feinberg. Production manager: Robin Clark. First assistant director: Jim Westman. Art director: John DeCuir, Jr. Camera operator: Bill Johnson. First assistant cameraman: Dennis Matsuda. Production sound mixer: Dean Gilmore. Boom man: Glen Lambert. Set decorator: Mickey S. Michaels. Set decorator/Washington, D.C.: Raphael Breton. Property masters: Larry Bird, Ken Zimmerman. Script supervisor: Ray Quiros. Makeup: Bob Dawn. Hairstylist: Cherie. Wardrobe supervisor: John Anderson. Wardrobe: Diane Oohoon. Key gaffer: John Baron. Technical coordinator: Don Nobles. Special effects supervisor: Alex Weldon. Production coordinator: Nancy Meyer. Boat master: Manny Louis. Still photographer: Ralph Nelson. Technical advisors: Don Keach, Don Walsh. Navy technical advisor: Captain Bill Greaves. Sound effect editors: William H. Wistrom, Ross Taylor. Music editor: Ken Hall. Model and mechanical effects supervisor: John Richardson. Director model unit (Malta): Ricou Browning. Matte effects supervisor: Wally Veevers.

With

Jason Robards (Admiral James Sandecker), Richard Jordan (Dirk Pitt), David Selby (Dr. Gene Seagram), Anne Archer (Dana Archibald), Alec Guinness (John Bigalow), J.D. Cannon (Captain Joe Burke), Bo Brundin (Captain Andre Prevlov), M. Emmet Walsh (MCPO Vinnie Giordino), Norman Bartold (Kemper), Elya Baskin (Marganin), Dirk Blocker (Merker), Robert Broyles (Willis), Paul Carr (Nicholson), Michael C. Gwynne (Bohannon), Harvey Lewis (Kiel), Charles MacCaulay (Busby), Stewart Moss (Koplin), Michael Pataki (Munk), Marvin Silbersher (Antonov), Mark L. Taylor (Spence), Maurice Kowalewski (Dr. Silverstein), Nancy Nevinson (Sarah),

Trent Dolan (Isbell), Paul Tuerpe (Klink), Sander Vanocur (TV Commentator), Ken Place (Drummer), Michael Ensign (Northacker), Craig Shreeve (Gunther), Brendan Burns (Carter), Jonathan Moore (Captain Parotkin), George Whiteman (Beck), Hilly Hicks (Woodson), Alexander Firsow (Stoynik), Roy Evans (Gravedigger #1), and Tom Curnow (Gravedigger #2).

41. Smiley's People

Great Britain. A BBC Production in Association with Paramount Pictures. 1982. Approx. 300 min. (27,000 feet). Color.

Producer: Jonathan Powell. Director: Simon Langton. Screenplay: John le Carré and John Hopkins. Photography: Kenneth Macmillan. Designer: Austin Spriggs. Film editors: Clare Douglas and Chris Wimble. Dubbing mixer: Ken Hains. Dubbing editors: John Strickland and Michael Parker. Film recordist: Malcom Webberley. Makeup artist: Elizabeth Rowell. Chief grip: Roy Russell. Visual effects designer: Steward Brisdon. Costume designer: Sheila Beers. Properties buyer: David Privett. Graphic designer: Stewart Austin. Assistant floor managers: Riitta Lynn and Gordon I. Ronald. Production assistants: Jenny Doe and Diana Brookes. Production associate: Marcia Wheeler. Swiss location managers: Renato Egger and Sandor Von Orosz. Production managers: Marion McDougall, Jeremy Silberston, and Richard Cox. Music composed and conducted by: Patrick Gowers.

With

Alec Guinness (George Smiley), Curd Jurgens (Vladimir, the General), Bernard Hepton (Toby Esterhase), Dudley Sutton (Oleg Kirov), Michael Gough (Mikhel), Vladek Sheybal (Otto Leipzig, the Magician), Bill Paterson (Luader Strickland), Michael Elphick (Detective Chief Superintendent), Mario Adorf (Klaus Kretzschmar), Michael Byrne (Peter Guillam), Barry Foster (Saul Enderby), Michael Lonsdale (Grigoriev), Sian Phillips (Ann Smiley), Patrick Stewart (Karla), Maureen Lipman (Stella Craven), Ingrid Pitt (Elvira), Paul Herzberg (Villem Craven), Harry Walker (Murgotroyd), Stephen Riddle (Nigel Mostyn), Trevor Cooper (Sergeant Pike), Renny Krupinski (Attaché Kuznetsov), Germaine Delbat (Madame la Pierre), Jacques Maury (Sergi), Alex Jennings (P.C. Hall), Vincent Grass (Paris Bus Driver), Yves Peneau (Dmitri), Catherine Ohotnikoff and Francois Clavier (People in Warehouse), Andre Penvern (Cafe Waiter), Okon Jones (Mr. Lamb), Gita Denise (Russian Embassy Official), Margit Rauthe (Leipzig's Girlfriend), Louba Geitchinoff (Woman on Metro), Andrew Bradford (Ferguson), Alan Rickman (Mr. Brownlow), Jan Carey (Paris Hospital Sister), Anna Wing (Woman at Westbourne Terrace), Ken Sickler (Taxi Driver), Peter Guinness (Hari Krishna Monk), Tanya Rees (Beckie Craven), Vass Anderson (Mr. Carson), William Wilde (Blue Diamond Waiter), Nina Zuckerman (Art Gallery Receptionist), Robin Langford (Blue Diamond

Receptionist), Jeffrey Kime (Paris Ambulance Driver), Alexander Koupan, Alain Serres, and Vladimir Tihomiroff (Russian Agents), Alex Buchanan, Venetia Day, Cindy Shelley, and Susie Silvey (Cabaret Performers), Tessy Kuhls (Frau Kretzschmar), Lucy Fleming (Molly Meakin), Carl Duering (Walther), Jonathan Burn (Edmonds), Guy Standeven (British Embassy Official), Elisabeth Goebel (Woman at Water Camp), Christiane Carstens and Maithias Ditner (Young Couple), Caroline Sihol (Marie-Claire Guillam), Michael Feldman (Stango), Frank Crompton (Circus Janitor), Jean Champion (Monsieur la Pierre), Marie-Helene Daste (Madame Delbarre), Georges Hubert (Monsieur Delbarre), Serge Berry (Paris Policeman), Rosalie Crutchley (Mother Felicity), Julia McCarthy (Millie McCraig), Richard Leech (Uncle Harry), Inioo Gallo (Franz), Margaret Henry (Mrs. Tremera), Lucinda Curtis (Sister Beatrice), Victoria Elliott (Grigorieva), Hans Peter Blumer (Tun Cafe Proprietor), Marion Garai (Litzi Menertzhagen), Margrit Knecht (Dolly Meinertzhagen), Lucinda Curtis (Sister Beatitude), Joe Praml (Skordeno), Eugene Lipinski (De Silsky), Roswita Dost (Sanitorium Nurse).

42. *Lovesick*

A Ladd Company Production. Released by Warner Bros. 1983. 96 min. (8640 feet). Technicolor.

Producer: Charles Okun. Director/Writer: Marshall Brickman. Director of photography: Gerry Fisher. Production designer: Philip Rosenberg. Costume designer: Kristi Zea. Editor: Nina Feinberg. Music: Philippe Sarde. Casting: Juliet Taylor. Music arranged and conducted by: Peter Knight. Solo flute: Julius Baker. Production manager: Charles Okun. First assistant director: Thomas Reilly. Second assistant director: Lewis Gould. Location manager: Roger Paradiso. Script supervisor: B.J. Bjorkman. Set decorator: Gary Bronk. Camera operator: Dick Mingalone. Production sound mixer: Stephen Scanlon. Makeup: Fern Buchner.

With

Dudley Moore (Dr. Saul Benjamin), Elizabeth McGovern (Chloe Allen), Alec Guinness (Sigmund Freud), Wallace Shawn (Otto), Gene Saks (Frantic Patient [Mr. Houseman]), Ron Silver (Ted Caruso), John Huston (Larry Geller, M.D.), Alan King (Lionel Gross, M.D.), Selma Diamond (Harriet Singer, M.D.), Renee Taylor (Mrs. Mondragon), Christine Baranski (Nymphomaniac Patient), Kent Broadhurst (Gay Patient), Lester Rawlins (Mr. Arnold, the Silent Patient), Anne Kerry (Katie Benjamin), Susanne Barrie (Otto's Wife), Larry Rivers (Jac Applezweig), Richard B. Shull (Psychiatrist at Party), David Strathain (Marvin Zuckerman), Anne DeSalvo (Case Interviewer), Kaylan Pickford (Anna Geller), Anne Gillespie (Actress), John Tillinger (Play Director), Jeff Natter (Stage Manager), Peggy LeRoy Johnson (Second Actress).

43. Return of the Jedi

A Lucasfilm Ltd. Production. Released by Twentieth Century–Fox. (Photographed in Buttercup Valley, Death Valley, and Smith River, California and EMI–Elstree Studios, Borehamwood, England.) 1983. 133 min. (11,970 feet). Panavision. Color by Rank Film Laboratories. Prints by Deluxe.

Producer: Howard Kazanjian. Director: Richard Marquand. Screenplay: Lawrence Kasdan and George Lucas. Executive producer: George Lucas. Coproducers: Robert Watts and Jim Bloom. Production designer: Norman Reynolds. Director of photography: Alan Hume. Editors: Sean Barton, Marcia Lucas, and Duwayne Dunham. Visual effects: Richard Edlund, Dennis Muren, and Ken Ralston. Costume designers: Aggie Guerard Rodgers and Nilo Rodis-Jamero. Mechanical effects supervision: Kit West. Makeup and creature design: Phil Tippett and Stuart Freeborn. Sound design: Ben Burtt. Music by: John Williams. First assistant director/second unit director: David Tomblin. Casting: Mary Selway Buckley. Location director of photography: Jim Glennon. Additional photography: Jack Lowin. Production sound: Tony Dawe and Randy Thom. Supervising music editor: Kenneth Wannberg. Music recording: Eric Tomlinson. Orchestrations: Herbert W. Spencer. Chief articulation engineer: Stuart Ziff. Production supervisor: Douglas Twiddy. Production executive: Robert Latham Brown. Unit production manager: Miki Herman. Assistant production manager: Patricia Carr. Associate to producer: Louis G. Friedman. Conceptual artist: Ralph McQuarrie. Art directors: Fred Hole and James Schoppe. Set decorators: Michael Ford and Harry Lange. Property master: Peter Hancock. Chief hairdresser: Patricia McDermott. Stunt coordinator: Glenn Randall. Stunt arranger: Peter Diamond. Production controller: Arthur Carroll. Production accountant: Margaret Mitchell. Script supervisor: Pamela Mann Francis. Location script supervisor: Bob Forest. Location casting: Dave Eman and Bill Lytle. Assistant to Mr. Kazanjian: Kathleen Hartney Ross. Assistant to Mr. Bloom: John Syrjamaki. Assistant to Mr. Lucas: Jane Bay. Assistant art directors: Michael Lamont, John Fenner, and Richard Dawking. Set dresser: Doug Von Koss. Construction manager: Bill Welch. Assistant construction manager: Alan Booth. Operating cameramen: Leo Napolitano and Bob La Bonge. Aerial photography: Ron Goodman and Margaret Herron. Matte photography consultant: Stanley Sayer. Chief makeup artists: Tom Smith and Graham Freeborn. Hairdressers: Mike Lockey and Paul Le Blanc. Sculptural designers: Chuck Wiley and James Howard. Chief moldmaker: Wesley Seeds. Creature consultants: Jon Berg and Chris Walas. Production/creature coordinator: Patty Blau. Assistant sound editors: Chris Weir, Bill Mann, Gloria Borders, Suzanne Fox, Kathy Ryan, and Nancy Jencks. Rerecording engineer: Tomlinson Holman. English lyrics: Joseph Williams. Huttese lyrics: Annie Arbogast. Ewokese lyrics: Ben Burtt. Special effects supervisor: Roy Arbogast. Special effects foreman: William David Lee.

Wire specialist: Bob Harman. Location special effects: Kevin Pike and Mike Wood. Choreographer: Gillian Gregory. Location choreographer: Wendy Rogers.

Miniature and Optical Effects Unit — Industrial Light and Magic
Art director/visual effects: Joe Johnston. Optical photography supervisor: Bruce Nicholson. Supervising visual effects editor: Arthur Repola. Production coordinators: Warren Franklin and Laurie Vermont. Production illustrator: George Jenson. Matte painting artists: Chris Evans and Frank Ordaz. Matte photography: Neil Krepela and Craig Barron. Stop motion animator: Tom St. Amand. Head effects animators: Garry Waller and Kimerly Knowlton. Visual effects editors: Howard Stein, Peter Amundson, and Bill Kimberlin.

With

Mark Hamill (Luke Skywalker), Harrison Ford (Han Solo), Carrie Fisher (Princess Leia), Billy Dee Williams (Lando Calrissian), Anthony Daniels (C3PO), Peter Mayhew (Chewbacca), Sebastian Shaw (Anakin Skywalker), Ian McDiarmid (the Emperor), Frank Oz (Performing Yoda), James Earl Jones (as the Voice of Darth Vader), David Prowse (Darth Vader), and Alec Guinness (Ben [Obi-Wan] Kenobi), Kenny Baker (R2D2/Paploo), Michael Pennington (Moff Jerjerrod), Kenneth Colley (Admiral Piett), Michael Carter (Bib Fortuna), Dennis Lawson (Wedge), Tim Rose (Admiral Ackbar), Dermot Crowley (General Madine), Caroline Blakiston (Mon Mothma), Warwick Davis (Wicket), Jeremy Bulloch (Boba Fett), Femi Taylor (Oola), Annie Arbogast (Sy Snootles), Claire Davenport (Fat Dancer), Jack Purvis (Teebo), Mike Edmonds (Logray), Jane Busby (Chief Chirpa), Malcom Dixon (Ewok Warrior), Mike Cottrell (Ewok Warrior), Nicki Reade (Nicki), Adam Bareham (Star Destroyer Controller #1), Jonathan Oliver (Star Destroyer Controller #2), Pip Miller (Star Destroyer Captain #1), Tom Mannion (Star Destroyer Captain #2), Jabba Puppeteers: Toby Philpott, Mike Edmonds, and David Barclay. Other Puppeteers: Michael McCormick, Deep Roy, Simon Williamson, Hugh Spirit, Swim Lee, Michael Quinn, and Richard Robinson.

44. *A Passage to India*

Great Britain/United States. A John Brabourne/Richard Goodwin Production in Association with John Heyman and Edward Sands and Home Box Office. Distributed by Columbia Pictures. (Filmed on location in India and at Shepperton Studios.) 1985. 163 min. (14,670 feet). Panavision. Technicolor Processing/Metrocolor Prints.

Producers: John Brabourne and Richard Goodwin. Director: David Lean. Screenplay: David Lean. Based on the novel of the same name by E.M. Forster and the play of the same name by Santha Rama Rau. Director of photography: Ernest Day. Editor: David Lean. Music: Maurice Jarre. Production designer: John Box. Art directors: Leslie Tomkins, Clifford Robinson, Rak Yedekar, and

Herbert Westbrook. Set decorator: Hugh Scaife. Costume designer: Judy Moorcroft. Dolby sound: John Mitchell. Assistant directors: Patrick Cadell, Christopher Figg, Nick Laws, Arundhati Rao, and Ajit Kumar. Camera operator: Roy Ford. First assistant camera operator: Frank Elliot. Second-unit cameraman and effects: Robin Browne. Casting: Priscilla John.

With

Judy Davis (Adela Quested), Victor Banerjee (Doctor Aziz), Peggy Ashcroft (Mrs. Moore), James Fox (Richard Fielding), Alec Guinness (Professor Godbole), Nigel Havers (Ronny Heaslop), Richard Wilson (Turton), Antonia Pemberton (Mrs. Turton), Michael Culver (McBryde), Art Malik (Mahmoud Ali), Saeed Jaffrey (Hamidullah), Clive Swift (Major Callendar), Anne Firbank (Mrs. Callendar), Roshan Seth (Amritrao), Sanda Hotz (Stella).

Appendix:
Information on Actors and Awards

Great Expectations

Awards and honors:

The Academy Awards for 1947
Cimematography (Black-and-White) — Guy Green
Nominee for Best Picture
Nominee for Best Director
Nominee for Best Screenplay — Lean, Havelock-Allen, and Neame
Best Art Direction/Set Direction (Black-and-White) — John Bryan;
    Wilfred Shingleton
The New York Times Ten Best List for 1947
Time Magazine's Ten Best List for 1947
National Board of Review Annual Awards
One of the ten best films of 1946

Oliver Twist

Newton is best known for playing Long John Silver in Walt Disney's 1950 version of *Treasure Island* and in a 1954 British television series called *Long John Silver*. His other films include *Reunion* (his 1932 debut); *Fairwell Again* (1937), *Jamaica Inn* (1939), *Major Barbara* (1940), *Hatter's Castle* (1941), *This Happy Breed* (1944), *Odd Man Out* (1946), *Blackbeard the Pirate* (1952), *Androcles and the Lion* (1953), *The Beachcomber* (1954), and *Around the World in Eighty Days* (1956).

Anthony Newley's first film appearance was *Oliver Twist*. Born in 1931, he went on to become a composer, singer, and light comedian.

Awards and honors:
The New York Times Ten Best List for 1951
Time Magazine's Ten Best List for 1951

Venice Film Festival Prizes for 1948
Best Sceneography (Design)—John Bryan

Kind Hearts and Coronets

Apparently many of the interior scenes in *Kind Hearts* were shot at Pinewood Studios because *Passport to Pimlico* overran its shooting schedule by several weeks and the sound stages at Ealing were not available. Some film historians have charged that this getting away from the watchful eyes of the Ealing in-group was the main reason *Kind Hearts* differed so greatly from the typical Ealing production. As I've noted in the *Kind Hearts* chapter, I believe the film's unique qualitites were the result of the genius of Robert Hamer and Alec Guinness and *not* of its being shot on "alien" soundstages.

Robert Hamer's other films: *San Demetrio London* (as writer only—though there is evidence he directed several sequences, 1943), *Dead of Night* (writer/director "mirror sequence," 1945), *Pink String and Sealing Wax* (1945), *It Always Rains on Sunday* (w/d, 1947), *The Spider and the Fly* (1949), *His Excellency* (w/d, 1952), *The Long Memory* (w/d, 1952), *Father Brown** (1954), *To Paris with Love** (1954), *The Scapegoat** (1959), *School for Scoundrels* (1960), *A Jolly Bad Fellow* (writer only, 1963).

Dennis Price's other films: *A Canterbury Tale* (1944), *A Place of One's Own* (1944), *The Magic Bow* (1946), *Hungry Hill* (1946), *Dear Murderer* (1947), *Jassy* (1947), *Holiday Camp* (1947), *Master of Bankdam* (1947), *The White Unicorn* (1947), *Good Time Girl* (1948), *The Bad Lord Byron* (1948), *The Dancing Years* (1949), *The Adventurers* (1950), *Lady Godiva Rides Again* (1951), *The House in the Square* (1952), *Song of Paris* (1952), *The Intruder* (1952), *That Lady* (1954), *Oh Rosalinda* (1955), *Private's Progress* (1955), *Charley Moon* (1956), *The Naked Truth* (1958), *I'm All Right, Jack* (1959), *Tunes of Glory** (1960), *Victim* (1961), *Play it Cool* (1962), *Tamahine* (1963), *A High Wind in Jamaica* (1965), *Ten Little Indians* (1965), *Horror of Frankenstein* (1970), *Twins of Evil* (1971), *Alice's Adventures in Wonderland* (1972), *Theatre of Blood* (1972), etc.

Awards and honors:
Venice Film Festival Awards for 1949
Best Screenography—William Kellner
National Board of Review Awards for 1950
Best Actor—Alec Guinness
Time Magazine's Ten Best list for 1950

A Run for Your Money

The films of Charles Frend: *The Big Blockade* (1942), *The Foreman Went to France* (1942), *San Demetrio, London* (1943), *Return of the Vikings* (1944),

---

* denotes an Alec Guinness film

Johnny Frenchman (1945), *The Loves of Joanna Godden* (1947) *Scott of the Antarctic* (1948), *A Run for Your Money** (1949), *The Magnet* (1950), *The Cruel Sea* (1952), *Lease of Life* (1954), *The Long Arm* (1956), *Barnacle Bill** (1957), *Cone of Silence* (1960), *Torpedo Bay* (1962), *Ryan's Daughter* (2nd unit, 1970), and others.

Last Holiday

Among the films of Henry Cass: *Lancashire Luck* (1937), *29 Acacia Avenue* (1945), *The Glass Mountain* (1948), *No Place for Jennifer* (1949), *Young Wives' Tale* (1951), *Castle in the Air* (1952), *Father's Doing Fine* (1952), *Windfall* (1955), *The Reluctant Bride* (1955), *No Smoking* (1955), *Bond of Fear* (1956), *Breakaway* (1956), *The High Terrace* (1956), *The Crooked Sky* (1957), *Booby Trap* (1957), *Professor Tim* (1957), *Blood of the Vampire* (1958), *The Hand* (1960), *Give a Dog a Bone* (1966), others.

The Mudlark

Among the films of Irene Dunne: *Leathernecking* (1930), *Cimarron* (1931), *Back Street* (1932), *Symphony of Six Million* (1932), *Ann Vickers* (1933), *Stingaree* (1934), *Roberta* (1935), *Magnificent Obsession* (1935), *Show Boat* (1936), *Theodora Goes Wild* (1936), *The Awful Truth* (1937), *Love Affair* (1939), *My Favorite Wife* (1940), *A Guy Named Joe* (1943), *Anna and the King of Siam* (1946), *Life with Father* (1947), *I Remember Mama* (1948), and *Never a Dull Moment* (1950). Dunn made only one film after *The Mudlark*, the 1952 comedy *It Grows on Trees*.

Among the films of Nunnally Johnson: *The House of Rothschild* (writer, 1934), *Cardinal Richelieu* (w, 1934), *Jesse James* (w, 1939), *Tobacco Road* (w, 1941), *The Moon Is Down* (w,p, 1943), *The Keys of the Kingdom* (w, 1944), *The Dark Mirror* (w, 1946), *Rommel, Desert Fox* (w,p, 1951), *How to Marry a Millionaire* (w,p, 1953), *The Man in the Grey Flannel Suit* (w,d, 1956), *The Man Who Understood Women* (w,p,d, 1959), *The World of Henry Orient* (p, 1964), and many others.

Among the films of Finlay Currie: *Sleeping Car to Trieste* (1948), *The History of Mr. Polly* (1949), *Trio* (1950), *Treasure Island* (1950), *Quo Vadis* (1951), *People Will Talk* (1952), *Ivanhoe* (1952), *Rob Roy* (1953), *The End of the Road* (1954), *Ben Hur* (1959), *Who Was Maddox?* (1964), and many others.

The Lavender Hill Mob

Among T.E.B. Clarke's other films: *Johnny Frenchman* (1945), *Against the Wind* (1947), *Hue and Cry* (1946), *Passport to Pimlico* (1948), *The Blue Lamp* (1950), *The Titfield Thunderbolt* (1953), *Barnacle Bill** (1957), *Law and*

Disorder (1958), *Gideon's Day* (1958), *Sons and Lovers* (1960), *The Horse Without a Head* (1963), *A Man Could Get Killed* (1966), others.

Among Charles Crichton's other films: *For Those in Peril* (1944), *Dead of Night* (segment, 1945), *Painted Boats* (1945), *Hue and Cry* (1946), *Against the Wind* (1947), *Another Shore* (1948), *Train of Events* (1949), *Dance Hall* (1950), *Hunted* (1952), *The Titfield Thunderbolt* (1953), *The Love Lottery* (1954), *The Divided Heart* (1954), *The Man in the Sky* (1956), *Law and Disorder* (1957), *Floods of Fear* (1958, also writer), *The Battle of the Sexes* (1959), *The Boy Who Stole a Million* (1960), *The Third Secret* (1963), *He Who Rides a Tiger* (1965), others.

Among the films of Stanley Holloway: *The Rotters* (1921), *Road House* (1934), *Squibs* (1935), *The Vicar of Bray* (1936), *Major Barbara* (1941), *Salute John Citizen* (1942), *The Way Ahead* (1944), *Champagne Charlie* (1944), *This Happy Breed* (1944), *The Way to the Stars* (1945), *Brief Encounter* (1945), *Nicholas Nickleby* (1947), *Hamlet* (1948), *The Magic Box* (1951), *The Beggar's Opera* (1953), *Meet Mr. Lucifer* (1953), *No Love for Johnnie* (1961), *My Fair Lady* (1964), *The Flight of the Doves* (1971) and many others.

Awards and honors:
> *The Academy Awards for 1951*
> Nominee for Best Actor — Alec Guinness
> Best Writing (story and screenplay) — T.E.B. Clarke
> *The National Board of Review Awards for 1951*
> Best Script — T.E.B. Clarke
> *The British Film Academy Awards for 1951*
> Best British Film
> *The Directors Guild of America Awards: 1952 (Quarterly Awards)*
> Charles Crichton
> *The Venice Film Festival Prizes for 1951*
> Best Scenario — T.E.B. Clarke
> *Time Magazine's Ten Best List for 1951*

The Man in the White Suit

Among the films of Joan Greenwood: *The Gentle Sex* (1942), *A Girl in a Million* (1945), *The October Man* (1947), *Saraband for Dead Lovers* (1948), *Whiskey Galore* (1949), *Kind Hearts and Coronets** (1949), *The Importance of Being Earnest* (1952), *Father Brown** (1954), *Moonfleet* (1955), *Mysterious Island* (1962), *Tom Jones* (1963), *The Moon Spinners* (1964), others.

Among the films of Cecil Parker: *The Silver Spoon* (1933), *The Lady Vanishes* (1938), *Caesar and Cleopatra* (1945), *Captain Boycott* (1947), *Quartet* (1948), *The Chiltern Hundreds* (1949), *Father Brown** (1954), *The Ladykillers** (1955), *The Court Jester* (1955), *Indiscreet* (1958), *A Tale of Two Cities* (1958), *Moll Flanders* (1965), *Oh What a Lovely War* (1969), others.

Awards and honors:
  The Academy Awards for 1952
    Nominee for Best Screenplay
  The National Board of Review Awards for 1952
    One of the five best foreign films of 1952
  Time Magazine's Ten Best List for 1952

The Card/The Promoter

Among the films of Glynis Johns: *South Riding* (1936), *49th Parallel* (1941), *Perfect Strangers* (1945), *Miranda* (1947), *State Secret* (1950), *The Sword and the Rose* (1953), *Rob Roy* (1953), *The Court Jester* (1956), *The Sundowners* (1960), *The Chapman Report* (1962), *Mary Poppins* (1964), *Don't Just Stand There* (1968), *Vault of Horror* (1973), others.

Miss John's father is Mervyn Johns, the Welsh character actor who appeared in Ealing Studios' famous horror anthology *Dead of Night* as the man whose nightmare held the stories together.

Malta Story

Among the films of Brian Desmond Hurst: *The Tell-Tale Heart* (1934), *Riders to the Sea* (1935), *Ourselves Alone* (1936), *The Tenth Man* (1936), *Sensation* (1936), *Glamorous Night* (1937), *Prison Without Bars* (1938), *On the Night of the Fire* (1939), *The Lion Has Wings* (co-director, 1939), *Dangerous Moonlight* (1941), *Alibi* (1942), *The Hundred Pound Window* (1943), *Theirs is the Glory* (1946), *Hungry Hill* (1946), *The Mark of Cain* (1947), *Trottie True* (1949), *Scrooge* (in U.S. — *A Christmas Carol*, 1951), *Simba* (1954), *The Black Tent* (1956), *Dangerous Exile* (1957), *Behind the Mask* (1958), *His and Hers* (1960), *The Playboy of the Western World* (1962), others.

The Captain's Paradise

Among the films of Anthony Kimmins: *Keep Fit* (1937), *Mine Own Executioner* (1947), *Flesh and Blood* (1950), *Who Goes There?* (1952), *Aunt Clara* (1954), *The Amorous Prawn* (1962).

Among the films of Alec Coppel (1910–1972): *Over the Moon* (1939), *Mr. Denning Drives North* (1951), *The Gazebo* (1959), *Moment to Moment* (1966), *The Bliss of Mrs. Blossom* (1969).

Awards and honors:
  The Academy Awards for 1953
    Nominee for Best Motion Picture Story — Alec Coppel
  Time Magazine's Ten Best List for 1953

Father Brown / The Detective

Among the films of Peter Finch: *Dad and Dave Come to Town* (1937), *Rats of Tobruk* (1944), *The Power and the Glory* (1945), *The Miniver Story* (1950), *Elephant Walk* (1954), *The Dark Avenger* (1955), *Simon and Laura* (1955), *The Battle of the River Plate* (1956), *A Town Like Alice* (British Film Academy award, 1956), *Kidnapped* (1959), *The Nun's Story* (1959), *The Sins of Rachel Cade* (1960), *The Trials of Oscar Wilde* (1960), *No Love for Johnnie* (BFA, 1961), *The Pumpkin Eater* (1964), *The Flight of the Phoenix* (1965), *Far from the Madding Crowd* (1967), *The Legend of Lylah Clare* (1968), *The Red Tent* (1969), *Sunday Bloody Sunday* (BFA, 1971), *Lost Horizon* (1973), and *Network* (AA, 1976).

Awards and honors:
  National Board of Review Awards
  Among the Ten Best Foreign Films of 1954

The Prisoner

Among Bridget Boland's screenplays: *Gaslight* (1939), *Spies of the Air* (1940), *The Lost People* (1948), *War and Peace* (1956).
  Among Peter Glenville's films: *Me and the Colonel* (1958), *Summer and Smoke* (1960), *Term of Trial* (1961), *Becket* (1964), *Hotel Paradiso** (1966), and *The Comedians** (1967).

Awards and honors:
  The New York Times Ten Best List for 1955
  The National Board of Review Awards for 1955
  Best Foreign Picture.

The Ladykillers

Among the films of Peter Sellers: *Penny Points to Paradise* (1951), *The Smallest Show on Earth* (1957), *The Naked Truth* (1958), *I'm All Right, Jack* (1959), *Lolita* (1962), *The Wrong Arm of the Law, The Pink Panther, Dr. Strangelove* (all 1963), *The Wrong Box* (1966), *I Love You Alice B. Toklas* (1968), *The Magic Christian* (1969), *The Return of the Pink Panther* (1975), *Murder By Death** (1976), *Being There* (1979), and many others.

Awards and honors:
  The Academy Awards for 1956
  Best Original Screenplay — William Rose
  The British Academy Awards for 1956
  Best British Actress — Katie Johnson
  Best Screenplay (British Film) — William Rose

The Swan

Among the films of Charles Vidor: *The Mask of Fu Manchu* (1933), *Double Door* (1934), *Sensation Hunters* (1934), *Strangers All* (1935), *The Arizonian* (1935), *She's No Lady* (1937), *My Son, My Son* (1940), *Ladies in Retirement* (1941), *The Tuttles of Tahiti* (1942), *Cover Girl* (1943), *A Song to Remember* (1945), *Gilda* (1946), *It's a Big Country* (1951), *Hans Christian Andersen* (1952), *Love Me or Leave Me* (1955), *The Joker is Wild* (1958), *A Farewell to Arms* (1958), *Song Without End* (1959), others.

The Bridge on the River Kwai

Among the films of William Holden (1918–1981, born William Beedle): *Golden Boy* (1939), *Invisible Stripes* (1940), *Our Town* (1940), *Those Were the Days* (1940), *Arizona* (1940), *I Wanted Wings* (1941), *Texas* (1941), *The Fleet's In* (1942), *The Remarkable Andrew* (1942), *Meet the Stewarts* (1942), *Young and Willing* (1943), *Blaze of Noon* (1947), *Dear Ruth* (1947), *Variety Girl* (1947), *Rachel and the Stranger* (1948), *Apartment for Peggy* (1948), *The Man from Colorado* (1948), *The Dark Past* (1949), *The Streets of Larado* (1949), *Miss Grant Takes Richmond* (1949), *Dear Wife* (1949), *Father Is a Bachelor* (1950), *Sunset Boulevard* (1950), *Union Station* (1950), *Born Yesterday* (1950), *Force of Arms* (1951), *Submarine Command* (1951), *Boots Malone* (1952), *The Turning Point* (1952), *Stalag 17* (AA, 1953), *The Moon Is Blue* (1953), *Forever Female* (1953), *Escape from Fort Bravo* (1953), *Executive Suite* (1954), *Sabrina* (1954), *The Country Girl* (1954), *The Bridges at Toko-Ri* (1954), *Love Is a Many-Splendored Thing* (1955), *Picnic* (1955), *The Proud and the Profane* (1956), *Toward the Unknown* (1956), *The Key* (1958), *The Horse Soldiers* (1959), *The World of Suzie Wong* (1960), *Satan Never Sleeps* (1962), *The Counterfeit Traitor* (1962), *The Lion* (1962), *Paris When It Sizzles* (1964), *The Seventh Dawn* (1968), *The Christmas Tree* (1969), *The Wild Bunch* (1969), *Wild Rovers* (1971), *The Revengers* (1972), *The Blue Knight* (TV, 1972), *Breezy* (1973), *Open Season* (1974), *Network* (1976), others.

Among the films of Jack Hawkins (1910–1973): *The Lodger* (1932), *The Fallen Idol* (1948), *State Secret* (1950), *Angels One Five* (1952), *The Cruel Sea* (1952), *The Malta Story** (1953), *The Prisoner** (1955), *The Two Headed Spy* (1958), *The League of Gentlemen* (1959), *Ben Hur* (1959), *Lawrence of Arabia** (1962), *Rampage* (1963), *Zulu* (1963), *Guns at Batasi* (1964), *Lord Jim* (1965), *Waterloo* (1970), *Nicholas and Alexandra* (1971), *Tales That Witness Madness* (1973), others.

Awards and honors:
  The Academy Awards for 1957
    Best Picture
    Best Director
    Best Actor

Best Screenplay Based on Material from Another Medium
Best Cinematography—Jack Hildyard
Best Score—Malcom Arnold
Best Film Editing—Peter Taylor
Nominee for Best Supporting Actor—Sessue Hayakawa
The New York Film Critics Awards for 1957
Best Motion Picture
Best Actor
Best Direction
The National Board of Review Awards for 1957
Best American Picture
Best Director
Best Actor
Best Supporting Actor—Sessue Hayakawa
One of the Ten Best American Films of 1957
The British Film Academy Awards for 1957
Best Film
Best British Film
Best British Actor
Best Screenplay (British Film)
The Directors Guild of America Awards for 1957
Most Outstanding Directorial Achievement
The Golden Globe Awards for 1957
Best Motion Picture—Drama
Best Director
Best Actor—Drama
The New York Times Ten Best List for 1957
Time Magazine's Ten Best List for 1957
Fifty Most Significant American Films
Performing Arts Council of the University of Southern California/
panel of film producers and critics: *Kwai* is number 30.
Total Film Rentals for Kwai *as of January 14, 1981 (Source:* Variety*):*
$17,195,000.

The Horse's Mouth

Among the films of Kay Walsh (1914–): *Get Your Man* (1934), *In Which We Serve* (1942), *This Happy Breed* (1944), *The October Man* (1947), *Oliver Twist** (1948), *Encore* (1950), *Last Holiday** (1950), *Tunes of Glory** (1960), *The Witches* (1966), *Scrooge** (1970), *The Ruling Class* (1971), others.

If the music sounds familiar ("Lt. Kije" by Sergei Prokofieff), that's because Woody Allen used it for *Love and Death*.

Awards and honors:
The Academy Awards for 1958

Nominee for Best Screenplay Based on Material from Another
Medium — Alec Guinness
National Board of Review Awards for 1958
Best Supporting Actress — Kay Walsh
Among the five best foreign films of the year
The New York Times Ten Best List for 1958
Time Magazine's Ten Best List for 1958

The Scapegoat

Among the films of Bette Davis: *Bad Sister* (1931), *The Man Who Played God* (1932), *Cabin in the Cotton* (1932), *Twenty Thousand Years in Sing Sing* (1932), *Of Human Bondage* (1934), *Front Page Woman* (1935), *Dangerous* (AA, 1935), *The Petrified Forest* (1936), *Satan Met a Lady* (1936), *Jezabel* (AA, 1938), *Dark Victory* (1939), *Juarez* (1939), *The Private Lives of Elizabeth and Essex* (1939), *The Letter* (1940), *The Great Lie* (1941), *The Bride Came COD* (1941), *The Little Foxes* (1941), *The Man Who Came to Dinner* (1941), *Now Voyager* (1942), *Watch on the Rhine* (1943), *Mr. Skeffington* (1943), *The Corn Is Green* (1945), *June Bride* (1948), *All About Eve* (1950), *Phone Call from a Stranger* (1952), *The Virgin Queen* (1955), *A Pocketful of Miracles* (1961), *Whatever Happened to Baby Jane?* (1962), *Hush Hush Sweet Charlotte* (1964), *The Nanny* (1965), *Bunny O'Hare* (1971), *Burnt Offerings* (1976), and many others.

Our Man in Havana

Burl Ives, born Burl Icle Ivanhoe in 1909, is known for his folk-singing career ("A Little Bitty Tear") and for his many films. A capable villain or robust hero, Ives is best known in films for his role as "Big Daddy" in 1957's *Cat on a Hot Tin Roof*. His films include: *Smoky* (1946), *East of Eden* (1954), *The Big Country* (Academy Award for Best Supporting Actor, 1958), *The Brass Bottle* (1964), *Rocket to the Moon* (1967), *The McMasters* (1970), and *The Only Way Out Is Dead* (1970).

Ives also appeared in two television series: *O.K. Crackerby* (1965), and *The Bold Ones* (1969).

Ernie Kovacs (1919–1962) is best known for his zany television show, which pioneered many of the video "tricks" common today and dealt in surrealistic video sight gags. His films include: *Bell, Book and Candle* (1958), *It Happened to Jane* (1958), *Wake Me When It's Over* (1960), *Strangers When We Meet* (1960), *North to Alaska* (1960), *Pepe* (1960), *Five Golden Hours* (1961), and *Sail a Crooked Ship* (1962).

Sir Noel Coward (1899–1973) was a man of many talents. He was an actor / writer / composer / director who seemingly excelled in any branch of show business he put his hand to. Among his many films: *Hearts of the World* (1918), *The Scoundrel* (1935), *In Which We Serve* (1941, in which Coward was the producer/director/star/writer), *The Astonished Heart* (1949), *Around the World in 80 Days* (1956), *Surprise Package* (1960), *Paris When It Sizzles* (1964), *Bunny Lake Is Missing* (1965), *Boom* (1966) and *The Italian Job* 1969).

Tunes of Glory

John Mills, born in 1908, performed in musical comedies before making his first film, *The Midshipmaid*, in 1932. His career began to bloom in the mid 1940s with roles in such popular films as the Coward/Lean paean to British seamen, *In Which We Serve* (1942). He became a major international star with the release of *Great Expectations* in 1946. His daughters Hayley and Juliet followed him into films and into successful careers of their own.

Among the films of John Mills: *Goodbye Mr. Chips* (1939), *This Happy Breed* (1944), *The Way to the Stars* (1945), *Great Expectations** (1946), *Scott of the Antarctic* (1948), *The History of Mr. Polly* (also producer, 1949), *The Rocking Horse Winner* (1950), *Hobson's Choice* (1953), *Above Us the Waves* (1955), *Around the World in 80 Days* (1956), *Tiger Bay* (1959), *The Chalk Garden* (1963), *The Wrong Box* (1966), *The Family Way* (1966), *Oh What a Lovely War* (1969), *Run Wild Run Free* (1969), *Ryan's Daughter* (AA for Best Supporting Actor, 1971), *Young Winston* (1972), *The Devil's Advocate* (1979), and many others.

John Mills and his wife Mary became quite close to Guinness during the filming of *Tunes*. As Mills relates in his autobiography, *Up in the Clouds, Gentlemen Please*, he and Mary were almost convinced to convert to Roman Catholism after Guinness spent many long hours talking about his conversion. However, when Mary was seventeen and on a cruise in the Red Sea, a young Jesuit priest who'd just spent ten years in the Gobi Desert had flung himself at her and bit her lip! Were it not for that rather unsettling experience, the Mills' might have embraced Guinness' newfound faith.

Duncan Macrae (Pipe Maj. MacLean) was born in 1905 and died in 1967. His film appearances were few but impressive: *The Brothers* (1947), *The Kidnappers* (1953), *Our Man in Havana** (1959), *Casino Royale* (1967), and others.

Gordon Jackson (Capt. Jimmy Cairns) was born in 1923. His film roles include: *Whiskey Galore* (1948), *The Great Escape* (1962), *The Ipcress File* (1965), *The Prime of Miss Jean Brodie* (1969), *Run Wild Run Free* (1969) and others.

Awards and honors:
Venice Film Festival Prizes—1960
    Best Actor—John Mills
The New York Times Ten Best List for 1960
The Academy Awards for 1960
    Nominee for Best Screenplay Based on Material from Another Medium—James Kennaway

A Majority of One

Among the films of Rosalind Russell (1908–1976): *Evelyn Prentice* (1934), *The President Vanishes* (1934), *Reckless* (1935), *Rendezvous* (1935), *It Had to Happen* (1936), *Under Two Flags* (1936), *Night Must Fall* (1937), *The Citadel* (1938), *The Women* (1939), *His Girl Friday* (1940), *No Time for Comedy* (1940), *Hired Wife* (1940), *Design for Scandal* (1941), *My Sister Eileen* (1942), *Sister Kenny* (1946), *Mourning Becomes Electra* (1948), *A Woman of Distinction* (1950), *Picnic* (1956), *Auntie Mame* (1958), *Gypsy* (1962), *Five Finger Exercise* (1962), *The Trouble with Angels* (1966), *Oh Dad, Poor Dad* (1967), *Where Angels Go Trouble Follows* (1968), *Rosie* (1968), *The Unexpected Mrs. Pollifax* (1970), others.

Among the products mentioned by name in the dialogue in this most *commercial* motion picture: Smith Brothers Cough Drops, Lifesavers, Old Dutch Cleanser, Dr. Pepper, and Coca-Cola.

Awards and honors:
> *The Academy Awards for 1961*
> Nominee for Best Cinematography (Color)—Harry Stradling
> *The Golden Globe Awards for 1961*
> Best Motion Picture—Comedy
> Best Actress—Musical/Comedy—Rosalind Russell
> Best Film Promoting International Understanding

H.M.S. Defiant/Damn the Defiant!

Among the films of Dirk Bogarde: *Esther Waters* (1947), *Quartet* 1948), *Boys in Brown* (1949), *The Blue Lamp* (1959), *Doctor in the House* (1953), *Desperate Moment* (1953), *Simba* (1954), *The Sea Shall Not Have Them* (1954), *The Sleeping Tiger* (1954), *Doctor at Sea* (1955), *Cast a Dark Shadow* (1955), *Doctor at Large* (1956), *The Spanish Gardner* (1956), *A Tale of Two Cities* (1958), *The Doctor's Dilemma* (1959), *The Singer Not the Song* (1960), *Victim* (1961), *The Mind Benders* (1963), *The Servant* (British Film Award, 1963), *Doctor in Distress* (1964), *King and Country* (1964), *Darling* (BFA, 1965), *Modesty Blaise* (1966), *Sebastian* (1967), *The Damned* (1969), *Death in Venice* (1970), *The Serpent* (1972), *The Night Porter* (1974), and many others.

Lawrence of Arabia

Among the films of Peter O'Toole: *Kidnapped* (1959), *Savage Innocents* (1959), *The Day They Robbed the Bank of England* (1960), *Becket* (1964), *Lord Jim* (1965), *What's New Pussycat?* (1965), *How to Steal a Million* (1966), *The Night of the Generals* (1966), *The Bible* (1966), *Great Catherine* (1967), *The Lion in Winter* (1968), *Goodbye Mr. Chips* (1969), *Country Dance*

(1970), *Murphy's War* (1970), *Under Milk Wood* (1971), *The Ruling Class* (1971), *Man of la Mancha* (1972), *Rosebud* (1975), *Man Friday* (1975), *Foxtrot* (1975), others.

Awards and honors:
> *The Academy Awards for 1962*
> > Best Picture
> > Best Director
> > Best Cinematography—F.A. Young
> > Best Art Direction/Set Direction (Color)—John Box, John Stroll; Dario Simoni
> > Sound—Shepperton Studio Sound Department and John Cox
> > Film Editing—Anne V. Coates
> > Best Music Score—Substantially Original—Maurice Jarre
> > Nominee for Best Actor—Peter O'Toole
> > Nominee for Best Supporting Actor—Omar Sharif
> > Nominee for Best Screenplay Based on Material from Another Medium—Robert Bolt
>
> *The British Academy Awards for 1962*
> > Best Film
> > Best British Film
> > Best British Actor—Peter O'Toole
> > Best Screenplay (British film)—Robert Bolt
>
> *National Board of Review Awards for 1962*
> > Best Director—David Lean
> > Among the Best English Language Films
>
> *The Director's Guild of America Awards for 1962*
> > Director award for 1962—David Lean
>
> *Golden Globe Awards for 1962*
> > Best Motion Picture—Drama
> > Best Director—David Lean
> > Best Supporting Actor—Omar Sharif
> > Best Cinematography (Color)—F.A. Young
>
> *Readers' Favorite Ten Films of All Time, Los Angeles Times* (1967)
> > Number 10
>
> *Top Fifty American Film Institute Films*
> > Number 29
>
> *Top 200 Moneymaking Films (Variety)*
> > ($16,700,000 in rentals) Number 165
>
> *Fourth Moneymaker of 1963 (Variety)*
> > $9,000,000 in rentals

The Fall of the Roman Empire

Among the films of Sophia Loren: *Woman of the River* (1955), *Scandal in Sorrento* (1955), *The Pride and the Passion* (1957), *Boy on a Dolphin* (1957), *Legend of the Lost* (1957), *The Key* (1958), *Houseboat* (1958), *The Millionairess* (1961), *El Cid* (1961), *Five Miles to Midnight* (1962), *Marriage Italian Style* (1964), *Arabesque* (1966), *A Countess from Hong Kong* (1966), *Man of La Mancha* (1972), *The Cassandra Crossing* (1977), others.

Among the films of Stephen Boyd: *An Alligator Named Daisy* (1955), *The Man Who Never Was* (1956), *Island in the Sun* (1957), *The Bravados* (1958), *Jumbo* (1962), *Genghis Khan* (1964), *The Oscar* (1966), *The Bible* (1966), *Shalako* (1968), *Carter's Army* (TV, 1971), *The Squeeze* (1977), and others.

Among the films of James Mason: *Late Extra* (1935), *Fire Over England* (1936), *The Return of the Scarlet Pimpernel* (1938), *I Met a Murderer* (1939), *Hatter's Castle* (1942), *The Night Has Eyes* (1942), *The Seventh Veil* (1945), *The Wicked Lady* (1946), *Odd Man Out* (1946), *Madame Bovary* (1949), *The Desert Fox* (as Rommel, 1951), *Five Fingers* (1952), *The Desert Rats* (1953), *Julius Caesar* (as Brutus, 1953), *20,000 Leagues Under the Sea* (as Capt. Nemo, 1954), *A Star Is Born* (1954), *North by Northwest* (1959), *Journey to the Center of the Earth* (1959), *Lolita* (1962), *Georgy Girl* (1966), *The Last of Sheila* (1973), *Cross of Iron* (1977), and many others.

Among the films of Christopher Plummer: *Wind Across the Everglades* (1958), *The Sound of Music* (as Baron von Trapp, 1965), *Inside Daisy Clover* (1965), *Oedipus the King* (1967), *The Royal Hunt of the Sun* (1969), *Waterloo* (as the Duke of Wellington, 1970), *The Spiral Staircase* (1975), *The Man Who Would Be King* (1975), *Jesus of Nazareth* (TV, 1977), others.

Awards and Honors:
    The Golden Globe Awards for 1965
      Best Original Score—Dimitri Tiomkin

Situation Hopeless But Not Serious

Among the films of Robert Redford: *Inside Daisy Clover* (1965), *The Chase* (1966), *This Property Is Condemned* (1966), *Barefoot in the Park* (1967), *Tell Them Willie Boy Is Here* (1969), *Downhill Racer* (1969), *Little Fauss and Big Halsy* (1970), *The Candidate* (1972), *The Way We Were* (1973), *The Sting* (1973), *All the President's Men* (1976), and *The Natural* (1984).

Among the films of Michael Conners (born Kreher Ohanian in 1925), *Sudden Fear* (1952), *The Ten Commandments* (1956), *Good Neighbor Sam* (1964), *Stagecoach* (1966), *Kiss the Girls and Make Them Die* (1967).

Doctor Zhivago

Among the films of Omar Sharif: *Lawrence of Arabia** (1962), *The Fall of the Roman Empire** (1964), *The Yellow Rolls-Royce* (1964), *Genghis Khan*

(1965), *Funny Girl* (1968; caused an uproar in Egypt when he kissed Jewish Barbra Streisand), *Mackenna's Gold* (1968), *Che!* (1969), *The Last Valley* (1970), *The Tamarind Seed (1974), Funny Lady* (1975), *Crime and Passion* (1975), and others.

Among the films of Julie Christie: *Crooks Anonymous* (1962), *Billy Liar* (1963), *Young Cassidy* (1964), *Darling* (Academy Award, 1965), *Fahrenheit 451* (1966), *Far from the Madding Crowd* (1967), *Petulia* (1968), *The Go-Between* (1971), *McCabe and Mrs. Miller* (1971), *Don't Look Now* (1974), *Shampoo* (1975), *Demon Seed* (1977).

Among the films of Tom Courtenay: *Billy Liar* (1963), *The Loneliness of the Long Distance Runner* (1963), *King and Country* (1964), *King Rat* (1965), *The Day the Fish Came Out* (1967), *A Dandy in Aspic* (1968), *Otley* (1969), *One Day in the Life of Ivan Denisovich* (1971), others.

Among the films of Rod Steiger: *Teresa* (1951), *On the Waterfront* (1954), *Oklahoma* (1955), *The Court Martial of Billy Mitchell* (1955), *Jubal* (1956), *The Harder They Fall* (1956), *Run of the Arrow* (1957), *Al Capone* (1958), *The Mark* (1961), *The Pawnbroker* (BFA, 1965), *The Loved One* (1965), *In the Heat of the Night* (AA, BFA, 1967), *The Illustrated Man* (1969), *Waterloo* (as Napoleon, 1971), *A Fistful of Dynamite* (1971), *W.C. Fields and Me* (1976), and many others.

Awards and honor:
   The Academy Awards for 1965
      Best Screenplay Based on Material from Another Medium — Robert Bolt
      Best Cinematography — Freddie Young
      Best Musical Scoring / Substantially Original — Maurice Jarre
      Best Art Direction / Set Direction — Color — John Box and Terry Marsh; Dario Simoni
      Nominee for Best Picture
      Nominee for Best Director
      Nominee for Best Supporting Actor — Tom Courtenay
   The National Board of Review Awards for 1965
      Best Actress — Julie Christie
      Among the Best English-Language Films
   The Golden Globe Awards for 1965
      Best Motion Picture — Drama
      Best Director — David Lean
      Best Actor — Omar Sharif
      Best Screenplay — Robert Bolt
      Best Original Score — Maurice Jarre
   Top MGM Moneymakers List
      Number 2

Los Angeles Times' "Best of the '60s Survey"
Number 7—Readers' choice
Best Dramatic Direction, number 2—Readers' choice
Best Adapted Screenplay, number 2 (readers), number 1 (industry)
Best Dramatic Producer, number 2 (Carlo Ponti)—Readers' choice

Hotel Paradiso

Among the films of Gina Lollobrigida: *Belles de Nuit* (1952), *Bread, Love, and Dreams* (1953), *Beat the Devil* (1954, also starring Robert Morley), *Trapeze* (1956), *Solomon and Sheba* (1959), *Come September* (1961), *Woman of Straw* (1964), *Strange Bedfellows* (1965), *Buona Sera, Mrs. Campbell* (1968), and others.

Among the films of Robert Morley: *The African Queen* (1951), *Beat the Devil* (1954), *Around the World in Eighty Days* (1956), *Oscar Wilde* (1960), *The Alphabet Murders* (1965), *Theatre of Blood* (1973), and many others.

The Quiller Memorandum

Among the films of George Segal: *The Young Doctors* (1961), *The Longest Day* (1962), *Act One* (1962), *The New Interns* (1964), *Ship of Fools* (1965), *King Rat* (1965), *Who's Afraid of Virginia Woolf?* (1966), *The St. Valentine's Day Massacre* (1967), *Bye Bye Braverman* (1968), *No Way to Treat a Lady* (1968), *The Southern Star* (1969), *The Bridge at Remagen* (1969), *Loving* (1970), *The Owl and the Pussycat* (1970), *Where's Poppa?* (1970), *The Hot Rock* (1972), *Blume in Love* (1973), *A Touch of Class* (1973), *The Black Bird* (1975), *Russian Roulette* (1976), *The Duchess and the Dirtwater Fox* (1976), *Rollercoaster* (1977), and many others.

Among the films of Harold Pinter: *The Servant* (1963), *The Caretaker* (1964), *The Pumpkin Eater* (British Film Award, 1964), *Accident* (1967), *The Birthday Party* (1969), *The Go Between* (1971), *The Homecoming* (1973), *Butley* (director, 1973), *The Last Tycoon* (1976).

Among the films of Michael Anderson: *Waterfront* (1950), *Hell Is Sold Out* (1951), *House of the Arrow* (1954), *The Dam Busters* (1955), *1984* (1955), *Around the World in Eighty Days* (1956), *Chase a Crooked Shadow* (1957), *Shake Hands with the Devil* (1959), *The Wreck of the Mary Deare* (1959), *The Naked Edge* (1961), *Flight From Ashiya* (1962), *Operation Crossbow* (1965), *The Shoes of the Fisherman* (1968), *Doc Savage* (1975), *Conduct Unbecoming* (1975), *Logan's Run* (1976), others.

The Comedians

Among the films of Richard Burton: *The Last Days of Dowlyn* (1948), *Now Barabbas Was a Robber* (1949), *Waterfront* (1950), *The Woman With*

No Name (1950), *Green Grow the Rushes* (1951), *My Cousin Rachel* (1952), *The Robe* (1953), *The Desert Rats* (1953), *Prince of Players* (1954), *The Rains of Ranchipur* (1955), *Alexander the Great* (1956), *Sea Wife* (1957), *Bitter Victory* (1958), *Look Back in Anger* (1959), *The Bramble Bush* (1959), *Ice Palace* (1960), *The Longest Day* (1962), *Cleopatra* (1962), *The VIPs* (1963), *Becket* (1964), *The Night of the Iguana* (1964), *The Sandpiper* (1965), *The Spy Who Came In from the Cold* (1965), *Who's Afraid of Virginia Woolf?* (1966), *The Taming of the Shrew* (1967), Dr. *Faustus* (1967), *The Comedians* (1967), *Boom* (1968), *Where Eagles Dare* (1968), *Staircase* (1969), *Anne of the Thousand Days* (1970), *Raid on Rommel* (1971), *Villain* (1971), *The Assassination of Trotsky* (1972), *Hammersmith Is Out* (1972), *Massacre in Rome* (1974), *The Klansman* (1974), *The Voyage* (1975), *Exorcist II: The Heretic* (1977), *Equus* (1977), *The Medusa Touch* (1978), *The Wild Geese* (1978), *Absolution* (1981), *Tristan and Isolt* (1981), *Circle of Two* (1981), *Wagner* (1983).

At the time of his death, Burton was preparing to make *The Wild Geese II*, a sequel to his 1978 hit.

Among the films of Elizabeth Taylor: *There's One Born Every Minute* (1942), *Lassie Come Home* (1943), *Jane Eyre* (1943), *National Velvet* (1944), *Courage of Lassie* (1945), *Life with Father* (1947), *A Date with Judy* (1948), *Little Women* (1949), *Father of the Bride* (1950), *Father's Little Dividend* (1951), *Quo Vadis* (1951), *A Place in the Sun* (1951), *Ivanhoe* (1952), *Elephant Walk* (1954), *Beau Brummell* (1954), *The Last Time I Saw Paris* (1955), *Giant* (1956), *Raintree County* (1957), *Cat on a Hot Tin Roof* (1958), *Suddenly Last Summer* (1959), *Butterfield 8* (Academy Award, 1960), *The VIPs* (1963), *Who's Afraid of Virginia Woolf?* (AA, 1966), *Reflections in a Golden Eye* (1967), *The Only Game in Town* (1969), *Night Watch* (1973), *Ash Wednesday* (1973), *The Blue Bird* (1976), etc.

Films made from Graham Greene's works include: *This Gun for Hire* (1942), *The Ministry of Fear* (1943), *Confidential Agent* (1945), *The Man Within* (1946), *Brighton Rock* (1947), *The Fugitive* (1948), *The Fallen Idol* (1948), *The Third Man* (1949), *The Heart of the Matter* (1953), *The Stranger's Hand* (1954), *The End of the Affair* (1955), *The Quiet American* (1958), *Our Man in Havana* (1959), *Travels with My Aunt* (1973), and others.

Awards and honors:
   The National Board of Review Awards for 1967
   Best Supporting Actor—Paul Ford
   Among the Best English-Language Films of the Year

Cromwell

Among the films of Richard Harris: *Alive and Kicking* (1958), *Shake Hands with the Devil* (1959), *The Wreck of the Mary Deare* (1959), *The Long the Short and the Tall* (1961), *The Guns of Navarone* (1961), *Mutiny on the Bounty* (1962), *This Sporting Life* (1963), *The Red Desert* (1964), *Major*

Dundee (1965), *The Heroes of Telemark* (1965), *The Bible* (1966), *Hawaii* (1966), *Caprice* (1966), *The Molly Maguires* (1969), *A Man Called Horse* (1969), *The Snow Goose* (TV, 1971), *The Deadly Trackers* (1973), *Juggernaut* (1975), *Robin and Marian* (1975), *The Return of a Man Called Horse* (1976), and others.

Among the films of Ken Hughes: *Wide Boy* (1952), *Black 13* (1953), *Little Red Monkey* (also writer, 1953), *Confession* (and writer, 1953), *Timeslip* (and writer, 1953), *The House Across the Lake* (and writer, 1954), *Joe Macbeth* (and writer, 1955), *The Long Haul* (1957), *Jazzboat* (1960), *The Trials of Oscar Wilde* (and writer, 1960), *The Small World of Sammy Lee* (and writer, 1963), *Of Human Bondage* (1964), *Casino Royale* (co-director, 1967), *The Internecine Project* (1974), *Alfie Darling* (1974), *Sextette* (1978), and others.

Awards and honors:
   The Academy Awards for 1970
   Best Costume Design — Nino Novarese

Scrooge

Among the films of Albert Finney: *The Entertainer* (1959), *Saturday Night and Sunday Morning* (1960), *Tom Jones* (1963), *Night Must Fall* (1963), *Two for the Road* (1967), *Charlie Bubbles* (1968), *Gumshoe* (1971), *Murder on the Orient Express* (1974), *Wolfen* (1981), *Looker* (1981), *Annie* (1982), etc.

Awards and honors:
   The Golden Globe Awards
   Best Actor — Musical / Comedy — Albert Finney

Brother Sun, Sister Moon

Among the films of Valentina Cortesa: *The Glass Mountain* (1948), *Thieves Highway* (1949), *Malaya* (1950), *The House on Telegraph Hill* (1951), *Les Miserables* (1952), *The Barefoot Contessa* (1954), *Magic Fire* (1956), *Barabbas* (1962), *The Visit* (1964), *Juliet of the Spirits* (1965), *The Legend of Lylah Clare* (1968), *Day for Night* (1973), and others.

Hitler: The Last Ten Days

Among the films of Adolfo Celi: *Escape into Dreams* (1950), *That Man from Rio* (1964), *Von Ryan's Express* (1965), *El Grecco* (1966), *Grand Prix* (1967), *The Honey Pot* (1967), *Murders in the Rue Morgue* (1971), *And Then There Were None* (1975), and others.

Among the films of Diane Cilento: *Wings of Danger* (1952), *Passage Home* (1955), *The Admirable Crichton* (1957), *Jet Storm* (1959), *The Naked*

Edge (1961), *Rattle of a Simple Man* (1964), *Hombre* (1967), *The Wicker Man* (1973), others.

Among the films of Eric Porter: *The Heroes of Telemark* (1965), *The Lost Continent* (1968), *Hands of the Ripper* (1971), *Nicholas and Alexandra* (1971), *Callan* (1974), and many others.

Murder by Death

Among the *many* films of David Niven: *Barbary Coast* (1935), *Thank You Jeeves* (1936), *Dodsworth* (1936), *The Prisoner of Zenda* (1937), *The Dawn Patrol* (1938), *Wuthering Heights* (1939), *Bachelor Mother* (1939), *Raffles* (1940), *A Matter of Life and Death* (*Stairway to Heaven*) (1946), *Soldiers Three* (1951), *The Moon Is Blue* (1953), *Around the World in Eighty Days* (1956), *My Man Godfrey* (1957), *Separate Tables* (Academy Award, 1958), *The Guns of Navarone* (1961), *55 Days at Peking* (1963), *Casino Royale* (as Sir James Bond, 1967), others.

Among the films of Peter Falk: *Wind Across the Everglades* (1958), *Pretty Boy Floyd* (1959), *The Great Race* (1965), *Anzio* (1968), *Castle Keep* (1969), *Husbands* (1970), *A Woman Under the Influence* (1976), and many others.

Star Wars

Awards and honors:
  The American Film Institute Survey
    Number Eight on the Top Ten List
  Take One Survey — Best of the Decade, 1968–1977:
    One of the Best American Films of the Decade
  The New York Times Ten Best List for 1977
  Time Magazine's Ten Best List for 1977
  Los Angeles Times' Readers' Top Ten in 1977
  The Academy Awards for 1977:
    Best Art Direction/Set Direction—Norman Reynolds and Leslie Dilley; Roger Christian.
    Best Original Score—John Williams
    Best Sound—Don MacDougall, Ray West, Bob Minkler, and Derek Ball.
    Best Film Editing—Paul Hirsch, Marcia Lucas, and Richard Chew.
    Best Costume Design—John Mollo.
    Best Visual Effects—John Stears, John Dykstra, Richard Edlund, Grant McCune, and Robert Blalack.
    Special Achievement Award for Sound Effects—Benjamin Burtt, Jr.
    Scientific or Technical Awards, Class II—John C. Dykstra for the development of the Dykstraflex Camera and Alvah J. Miller and Jerry Jeffress for the engineering of the Electronic Motion Control

System used in concert for multiple exposure visual effects motion picture photography.

Nominee for Best Picture

Nominee for Best Director

Nominee for Best Supporting Actor—Alec Guinness

Nominee for Best Original Screenplay—George Lucas

National Board of Review Awards for 1977:

Among the Best English-Language films

The Golden Globe Awards for 1977:

Best Original Score—John Williams

The British Academy Awards for 1978:

Best Soundtrack—Don MacDougall, Ray West, Bob Minkler, and Derek Ball.

Anthony Asquith Award (Original Film Music)—John Williams

Los Angeles Film Critics Association:

Best Picture of 1977

Best Music Score—John Williams

Tinker Tailor Soldier Spy

Among the films of Alexander Knox: *The Sea Wolf* (1940), *Sister Kenny* (1946), *The Judge Steps Out* (1947), *Paula* (1952), *The Sleeping Tiger* (1953), *Reach for the Sky* (1956), *The Wreck of the Mary Deare* (1959), *Crack in the World* (1965), *Accident* (1966), *Skullduggery* (1969), *Nicholas and Alexandra* (1971), and many others.

Among the films of Beryl Reid: *The Belles of St. Trinian's* (1954), *Star!* (1968), *Inspector Clouseau* (1968), *The Assassination Bureau* (1962), *Dr. Phibes Rises Again* (1972), *Psychomania* (1972), *No Sex Please We're British* (1973), *Joseph Andrews* (1976), others.

The Empire Strikes Back

Among the films of Irvin Kershner: *The Young Captives* (1959), *The Hoodlum Priest* (1961), *Face in the Rain* (1963), *The Luck of Ginger Coffey* (1964), *A Fine Madness* (1966), *The Flim Flam Man* (1967), *Loving* (1970), *Up The Sandbox* (1972), *S.P.Y.S.* (1974), *The Return of a Man Called Horse* (1976), *Eyes of Laura Mars* (1978), *Never Say Never Again* (1983), and others.

Awards and honors:

Time Magazine's Ten Best List for 1980

The Academy Awards for 1980:

Best Sound—Bill Varney, Steve Maslow, Gregg Landaker, and Peter Sutton.

Special Achievement Award—Visual Effects

The British Academy Awards for 1980:

Anthony Asquith Award (Original Film Music)—John Williams

Smiley's People

Among the films of Curd Jurgens: *The Devil's General* (1954), *An Eye for an Eye* (1956), *And Woman Was Created* (1957), *Me and the Colonel* (1957), *The Blue Angel* (1958), *Tamango* (1960), *Lord Jim* (1964), *The Assassination Bureau* (1968), *Nicholas and Alexandra* (1971), *The Spy Who Loved Me* (1977), and many others.

Return of the Jedi

For more information, especially concerning special effects on *Jedi* and the other *Star Wars* films, see the following sources:

Volume 6, Issue 4/Volume 7, Issue 1 (double issue, 1978) of *Cinefantastique* is chock-full of information, interviews, still photographs, and behind-the-scenes shots of the cast, crew, and effects people in action.

Once Upon A Galaxy: A Journal of the Making of The Empire Strikes Back by Alan Arnold (Del Rey, 1980) is a good source of information not only about *Empire*, but *Star Wars* as well.

Cinefex numbers two and three (August 1980 and December 1980) offer quite detailed and technical information concerning *Empire*'s special effects. Many revealing photographs. *Cinefex* number 13 (July 1983) does the same for *Jedi*.

Skywalking, the Life and Films of George Lucas by Dale Pollock (Harmony, 1983) has a wealth of information on Lucas and the three *Star Wars* episodes. Highly recommended.

The Making of Return of the Jedi, edited by John Phillip Peecher (Del Rey, 1983), offers many behind-the-scenes stills and anecdotes about the filming of the last *Star Wars* episode, *Jedi*.

For really interested readers, various issues of *American Cinematographer*, a magazine aimed at professional cinematographers, offer more technical information concerning all three *Star Wars* films.

American Film, Film Comment, Starlog, Famous Monsters, and other film publications have run *Star Wars* articles and photos.

A Passage to India

Awards and honors:
   National Board of Review Awards for 1984
      Best Picture
      Best Director
      Best Actor—Victor Banerjee
      Best Actress—Peggy Ashcroft
   New York Film Critics Circle
      Best Picture

Best Director
Best Actress—Peggy Ashcroft
Golden Globe Awards for 1984
Best Foreign Film
Best Supporting Actress—Peggy Ashcroft
Best Film Score—Maurice Jarre
The Academy Awards for 1984
Best Supporting Actress—Peggy Ashcroft
Best Original Score—Maurice Jarre
Nominee for Best Picture
Nominee for Best Director
Nominee for Best Actress—Judy Davis
Nominee for Best Art Direction—John Box (Art director) and Hugh
  Scaife (Set director)
Nominee for Best Cinematography—Ernest Day
Nominee for Best Costume Design—Judy Moorcroft
Nominee for Best Editing—David Lean
Nominee for Best Sound—Graham V. Hartstone, Nicholas Le
  Messurier, Michael A. Carter, and John Mitchell
Nominee for Best Screenplay—Based on Material from Another
  Medium: David Lean
Director's Guild of America
Nominee for Best Director
"At the Movies" Ten Best List
Number 7 (Gene Siskel)
Time Magazine's Ten Best List for 1984

Notes

Introduction

Guinness' comments about not being related to the Guinness Brewing family, his recalling Ernest Milten's Hamlet as the greatest performance he ever saw, his quote about not remembering the miseries of the war, and his recollection of his Sicily landing are from John Reese's article, "He Always Steals the Show," in *The Saturday Evening Post*, January 25, 1958.

The "you'll-never-make-an-actor" quote, the Gielgud-meeting-Guinness and first-acting-job quotes, and Guinness' recollections of his 4" x 4" misadventure at the advertising agency can be found in a number of the sources I'm listing here, including *Time* (April 21, 1958), *The Saturday Evening Post* (January 25, 1958), and the *New York Times Magazine* (April 6, 1952).

Both "Guinness Is What Guinness Acts," in the April 6, 1952, *New York Times Magazine*, and "Least Likely to Succeed," *Time*'s cover story for April 21, 1958, offer versions of Guinness' memorable first stage appearance in his school production of *Macbeth*.

The Guinness/Redford conversation is from Thomas Meehan's "Between Actors — A Conversation," in the December 1964 *Show*.

The anonymous quote concerning Guinness' acting school audition is from the *New York Times Magazine*, April 6, 1952, as is Guinness' quote concerning his twelve shillings and Equity.

Guinness' fond recollection of Gielgud's stage disaster is from "Catching Up With the Evasive Sir Alec," *Life*, June 19, 1964.

The Hebrews quote and Guinness' complaint about never wearing trousers come from *Time*, April 21, 1958.

Guinness' story about the small boy who mistook him for a real priest is from *Alec Guinness — A Celebration*, by John Russell Taylor (Boston: Little, Brown, 1984).

Oliver Twist

Breen's handwritten objection and other material concerning censorship problems with the film came from Henry Hart's article, "The Miracle and Oliver Twist," in *Films in Review*, May, 1951.

Kind Hearts and Coronets

The quotes by Hamer concerning his script (producing one "not noticeably similar" to anything else; and dialogue "at the time of Caligari") are from "Interview with Hamer," by Freda Bruce Lockhart, in the October–December 1951 issue of *Sight and Sound*, a British film publication.

The Guinness quote concerning the difficulties of playing eight characters is from "Guinness—Man of Many Faces," by Joseph Newman, in *Colliers*, July 26, 1952.

The Lavender Hill Mob

Guinness use of the word "fubsy" and his characterization of the film as "a romp," are from Kenneth Tynan's book *Alec Guinness* (London: Rockliff, 1953).

The Card / The Promoter

Guinness' quote about "ruts" and his quote about allowing his son Matthew to appear in the film are both from Newman's "Guinness—Man of Many Faces."

The Captain's Paradise

Guinness' and De Carlo's comments concerning their Mambo prowess are from "One Man's Mambo," in *Colliers*, June 13, 1953.

The Malta Story

The "almost juvenile" quote by Guinness is from Taylor, *Alec Guinness—A Celebration*.

Father Brown

Guinness' quote about Robert Hamer's "concentrated ear" is from Guinness' article "Life with a Pinch of Salt" in *Films and Filming*, November, 1965.

Derek Hill's article quoted in this chapter was titled, "Man of Many Faces," and appeared in *Films and Filming*, February, 1955.

The Prisoner

Glenville's comments about doing the material as both play and film are from his article "Reflections of Becket," *Films and Filming*, April 1964.

Lawrence of Arabia

Guinness' quote about working with the same directors over and over and his comments on David Lean, are from his amusing article, "Life With a Pinch of Salt."

Lean's comments on writer Bolt's script are from "Out of the Wilderness," by David Lean, *Films and Filming*, January, 1963.

The Scapegoat

The two Bette Davis quotes concerning her dissatisfaction with Guinness are from Allan Hunter's *Alec Guinness on Screen* (Glasgow: Polygon, 1982).

The Horse's Mouth

Guinness' quotes about not being able to finish the novel but wanting to make a film from it, and about the voice he finally settled on for Gulley Jimson, are both from Gene Phillips' article "Talent Has Many Faces" in *Focus On Film*, Autumn 1972.

Our Man in Havana

Guinness' quote about Greene "being there first," and the Reed/Guinness disagreement over the playing of Wormwold are both from Phillips' "Talent Has Many Faces."

Tunes of Glory

Guinness' comment on Neame's direction and his quote concerning the challenges of acting are both from his "Life With a Pinch of Salt."

The Fall of the Roman Empire

Mann's comment about no "rose petal" scenes is from a preview of the film in the August–September 1963 *Cinema*, a British film publication.

Situation Hopeless but Not Serious

Guinness' quote concerning his accepting the role is from his "Life with a Pinch of Salt."

The Redford/Guinness conversation is from Meehan's "Between Actors — A Conversation."

Doctor Zhivago

Writer Robert Bolt's discussion of the novel vs. the script is quoted from Alain Silver and James Ursini, *David Lean and His Films* (London: Leslie Frewin, 1974).

Hitler: The Last Ten Days

Guinness' recollections of being insured to play Hitler and of how few people reacted to him in uniform and makeup are from "Closed Set! No Entry Non Entrare," by Iain McAsh, in the British film magazine *Films Illustrated*, November, 1972.

Star Wars

The Guinness quote concerning *Star Wars*' popularity and his "My God, it's science fiction!" quote after he'd gotten the script, are from *Once Upon a Galaxy: A Journal of the Making of The Empire Strikes Back*, by Alan Arnold (New York: Del Rey, 1980).

The Lucas McGovern quote concerning the origin of the word "Wookiee" is from Paul Scanlon's August 25, 1977, *Rolling Stone* interview, "The Force Behind George Lucas."

Harrison Ford's quote about the reaction of the English crew to Lucas and the actors is from Dale Pollock's *Skywalking: The Life and Films of George Lucas* (New York: Harmony, 1983).

Guinness' quotes about the Force and his being a Christian, and about feeling "hot and cold" about his acting in one scene, are from *Time*, January 2, 1978.

John Williams' quotes about writing the music are from the *Star Wars* original soundtrack album liner notes.

Tinker, Tailor

Guinness' quote concerning his playing of the role of Smiley is from Taylor's *Alec Guinness — A Celebration*.

The quotes and information concerning Cornwell's being a spy are from *Newsweek*, March 7, 1983.

The Empire Strikes Back

The Lucas/Kurtz quotes about the film's pacing, Lucas' "it's your film" comment to Kershner, and Guinness' willingness to let the "little green thing" take dialogue are all from Pollock's *Skywalking*.

Kershner's comments about working with Sir Alec are from Arnold's *Once Upon a Galaxy*.

Smiley's People

The Guinness quote concerning his not appearing in any more Smiley productions is from Taylor's *Alec Guinness — A Celebration*.

The quotes from director Langton are from "The Making of Smiley's People," by David Jon Wiener, *American Cinematographer*, November 1983.

Return of the Jedi

The opening quote by Guinness is from the October 30, 1983, edition of *Family Weekly*.

The quote by Guinness concerning his reluctance to take a "big credit" on the film, Mark Hamill's quote about working with Guinness again, and Marquand's comments on directing and on working for Lucas are from John Phillip Peecher, ed., *The Making of Return of the Jedi* (Del Rey, 1983).

Lucas' quote about not directing *Jedi* is from Pollock's *Skywalking*.

Lucas' quote concerning all three films is from Paul Scanlon's article, "George Lucas Wants to Play Guitar," *Rolling Stone*, July 21/August 4, 1983.

A Passage to India

David Lean's quote ("What *did* happen in the caves?") is from Aljean Harmetz's article, "David Lean Films a Famous Novel," the *New York Times*, December 1984.

A number of Lean quotes on the script and the filming of the novel are from Harlan Kennedy's interview in the February 1985 issue of *Film Comment*.

Victor Banerjee's quote ("David, am I playing Dr. Aziz?") is from Jay Cocks' December 31, 1981, *Time* article. Also from that same article is Guinness' quote about the tense atmosphere on Lean's set.

Guinness' quotes about perfecting the way his characters walk and the information about the Indian orchestra playing the "Colonel Bogey" march are from John Culhane's article, "Alec Guinness: Prince Among Players," *Reader's Digest*, February, 1985.

Guinness' quotes concerning his "debt" to David Lean, and his attraction to "impossible roles," are from "The Many Faces of Guinness," by Linda Winer in *USA Today*, January 2, 1985.

Bibliography

Armes, Roy. *A Critical History of British Cinema*. London: Martin Secker & Warburg, 1978.

Arnold, Alan. *Once Upon a Galaxy: A Journal of the Making of the Empire Strikes Back*. New York: Del Rey, 1980.

Barr, Charles. *Ealing Studios*. Woodstock, NY: The Overlook Press, 1980.

Basinger, Jeanine. *Anthony Mann*. Boston: Twayne, 1979.

Cary, Joyce. *The Horse's Mouth*. New York: Harper & Row, 1957.

Denby, David, ed. *Film 70/71*. New York: Simon and Schuster, 1971.

Durgnat, Raymond. *A Mirror for England*. New York: Praeger, 1971.

Evans, Peter. *Peter Sellers: The Mask Behind the Mask*. New York: Signet/N.A.L., 1980.

Fitzgerald, Michael G. *Universal Pictures*. New Rochelle, NY: Arlington House, 1977.

Gifford, Denis. *British Cinema*. New York: Barnes, 1968.

Guinness, Sir Alec. *Blessings in Disguise*. New York: Alfred A. Knopf, 1986.

Halliwell, Leslie. *The Filmgoer's Companion*. 6th ed. New York: Avon, 1978.

_____. *Halliwell's Film Guide*. 4th ed. New York: Charles Scribner's Sons, 1983.

Hunter, Allan. *Alec Guinness on Screen*. Glasgow: Polygon, 1982.

Magill, Frank N., ed. *Magill's Survey of Cinema*. Englewood Cliffs, NJ: Salem Press; 1st series: 1980, 2nd series: 1981.

Maltin, Leonard, ed. *TV Movies*. New York: Signet/N.A.L., 1982.

Manvel, Roger. *New Cinema in Britain*. New York: Dutton, 1969.

McClelland, Doug. *The Unkindest Cuts*. Cranbury, NJ: Barnes, 1972.

Medved, Harry, and Medved, Michael. *The Hollywood Hall of Shame*. New York: Perigee, 1984.

Mills, John. *Up in the Clouds, Gentlemen Please*. New Haven, CT, and New York: Ticknor & Fields, 1981.

Peecher, John Phillip, ed. *The Making of Return of the Jedi*. New York: Del Rey, 1983.

Perry, George. *Forever Ealing*. London: Pavilion, 1981.

Pollock, Dale. *Skywalking: The Life and Films of George Lucas*. New York: Harmony, 1983.

Roud, Richard, ed. *Cinema: A Critical Dictionary*. New York: Viking, 1980.

Sarris, Andrew. *The American Cinema*. New York: Dutton, 1968.

Schumach, Murray. *The Face on the Cutting Room Floor*. New York: Morrow, 1964.

Silver, Alain, and Ursini, James. *David Lean and His Films*. London: Leslie Frewin, 1974.

Steinberg, Cobbett. *Reel Facts*. New York: Vintage, 1978.

Taylor, John Russell. *Alec Guinness: A Celebration*. Boston: Little, Brown, 1984.

Thomas, Tony. *Music for the Movies*. Cranbury, NJ: Barnes, 1973.

Tynan, Kenneth. *Alec Guinness*. London: Rockliff, 1953.

Vermilye, Jerry. *The Great British Films*. Secaucus, NJ: Citadel, 1978.

Willis, John. *Screen World Annual*. New York: Crown.

Index

Bold numbers indicate a photograph on that page.
A **bold** title indicates an Alec Guinness film.

T